D0532445

'Larry Dossey has been at the forefr[...] medicine for over 20 years. In this [...] his unique blend of considered rese[...] personal insights to bear on a wide range of medical and indeed human issues. It is a rich feast that significantly advances the case for the basic nonlocal nature of consciousness which science and medicine will one day embrace.'

DAVID LORIMER, Project Director of the
Scientific and Medical Network

'A magnificent collection of essays which demonstrate Dossey's true humanity, gentleness and spiritual development and which should be on the mandatory reading list of anyone in the healing or ministering profession.'

PETER FENWICK, FRCPsych

'The essays in *Healing beyond the Body* are wide-ranging and exciting – from dreams to creativity to prayer to immortality – but they all explore the nature of consciousness and its role in healing. Larry Dossey reminds us that ultimately healing is about self-discovery, self-discovery is about spirit, and spirit is about consciousness.'

KEN WILBER, author of *A Theory of Everything:
An Integral Vision for Business, Politics,
Science, and Spirituality*

'Larry Dossey is a wise, great-hearted, and good-humored guide on our journey toward healing ourselves and our planet. Reading his graceful essays on humor and love, physicians and food, physics and faith, we are informed, delighted, and transformed.'

JAMES S. GORDON, M.D., author of
Manifesto for a New Medicine

'Dr Larry Dossey's insights will long be remembered for changing the way we think about the world. Delightful, human, funny, poignant, and surpassingly wise, his essays are a national treasure. Readers will cherish this book to savor again and again.'

JOAN BORYSENKO, author of *Minding the Body, Mending
the Mind*, and *A Woman's Journey to God*

Also by Larry Dossey

Reinventing Medicine
Be Careful What You Pray For . . . You Just Might Get it
Prayer Is Good Medicine
Healing Words: The Power of Prayer and the Practice of Medicine
Meaning & Medicine
Recovering the Soul
Beyond Illness
Space, Time & Medicine

HEALING
beyond
the BODY

MEDICINE AND
THE INFINITE REACH
OF THE MIND

LARRY DOSSEY, M.D.

PIATKUS

PIATKUS

First published in Great Britain in 2002 by Time Warner Paperbacks
This edition published 2009 by Piatkus Books

Copyright © 2001 by Larry Dossey

The moral right of the author has been asserted

All rights reserved
No part of this publication may be reproduced, stored in a retrieval
system, or transmitted in any form or by any means, without the prior
permission in writing of the publisher, nor be otherwise circulated in any
form of binding or cover other than that in which it is published and
without a similar condition including this condition being imposed on the
subsequent purchaser

A CIP catalogue record for this book
is available from the British Library

ISBN 978-0-7499-2994-7

Typeset by Palimpsest Book Production Ltd,
Grangemouth, Stirlingshire
Printed and bound in Great Britain by Clays Ltd, St Ives plc

Papers used by Piatkus Books are natural, renewable and recyclable
products made from wood grown in sustainable forests and certified
in accordance with the rules of the Forest Stewardship Council

Mixed Sources
Product group from well-managed
forests and other controlled sources
www.fsc.org Cert no. SGS-COC-004081
© 1996 Forest Stewardship Council

Piatkus Books
An imprint of
Little, Brown Book Group
100 Victoria Embankment
London EC4Y 0DY

An Hachette Livre UK Company
www.hachettelivre.co.uk

www.piatkus.co.uk

*For the physicians, nurses, and other
health-care professionals who are reclaiming
the title of 'healer,' and for the researchers
who are exploring how healing operates
beyond the body.*

The subtlety of nature is vastly superior to that of argument.

— SIR FRANCIS BACON —

ACKNOWLEDGMENTS

THESE ESSAYS APPEARED ORIGINALLY in the peer-reviewed journal *Alternative Therapies in Health and Medicine*. I am grateful to Bonnie Horrigan, the journal's publisher, for permission to print them here, and to Michael Muscat, my editor at *Alternative Therapies* I recommend checking out their web site at *www.alternative-therapies.com*.

Deepest thanks also to Arielle Eckstut and Kitty Farmer, my literary agents, and to the team at Shambhala Publications – Sam Bercholz, Jonathan Green, and Peter Turner, for giving this book a home; Joel Segel, my insightful editor; DeAnna Satre, for copy-editing; and Peter Bermudes, for getting the word out.

And most of all to Barbara, my wife, for her unconditional love and support.

CONTENTS

HEALING BEYOND THE BODY

INTRODUCTION

I'LL NEVER FORGET A WOMAN who came to me trembling, in tears, and nearly speechless with rage. She had just returned from my hospital's intensive care unit, where her mother, my patient, was dying. Her mother was unconscious and on several life-support systems, and nothing was working. The daughter had just been chased from the bedside because visiting hours were over; further visitation, she was told, was 'against policy' and would 'interfere.'

Her mother died in the night, alone.

Being separated from her dying mother seemed to this woman to be the ultimate indignity. She was prepared to damn the whole of modern medicine, not only for its ineffectiveness, but for its callousness as well. She remained embittered toward a system that, as far as she was concerned, neither worked nor cared.

This experience captures so many of the reasons people currently object to modern health care – as inhumane, remote, cold, uncaring, too mechanical and technical, too expensive, too heroic, and often too late. When medicine fails and patients and family members are overwhelmed with disappointment and grief, it does not comfort them to be reminded of medicine's successes. For them, only the immediate moment is real.

When will medicine change? The question is not when or whether, but in what direction and to what degree. Medicine has always changed; historically it is one of the most dynamic forces in human culture, and today is no different.

Currently, medical science sizzles with new developments. The decoding of the human genome is essentially complete, which will lay bare the book of our DNA and make possible undreamed-of therapies. Gene manipulation and the transfer of DNA from one individual to another are in the wind, and researchers are predicting the elimination of many genetically based diseases. New surgical procedures are continually surfacing, as are new drugs. Advances in organ transplantation are proceeding apace. The list of new developments seems to grow day by day.

But for all this heady talk, when people actually encounter 'the system,' disappointment often follows, as it did for the daughter of my dying patient. The main reason is not that people get sick or even that they die. The primary problem is the realization that something vital has been left out of modern medicine – the human mind and its role in healing. This missing element has left a gaping hole, which the most dazzling technical break-throughs will never fill.

Haven't we already come to terms with the mind in healing? Today, everyone knows that consciousness is a factor in health. An army of psychologists and psychiatrists stands ready to teach us how to mold our mind in healthier ways, and stress management has become a growth industry. Even so, we have not yet given the mind its due.

In the essays that follow, we will go beyond the ordinary ways of viewing the mind. We will examine how our thoughts and emotions affect not only our own bodies but the bodies of others, at a distance, outside their awareness.

Some readers may consider this idea outrageous. To retard this reaction, I suggest keeping in mind the following points: In current science,

1. no one knows what the mind is and where it comes from;
2. no one knows how the mind interacts with the brain;
3. there is no evidence whatever that the brain produces the mind;
4. no one knows what happens to the mind prior to birth or following death.

This means, quite simply, that the level of ignorance within science about the origin, function, and destiny of human consciousness is appalling. In view of this, we are justified in boldly exploring new territory that might shed light on the nature of the human mind and its role in health.

We are slowly moving toward a vision of consciousness that frees the mind from its identity with the physical brain and body. The reasons for the emerging view are based in scientific fact. The implications for medicine are immense, including the possibility that healing forces may extend, and be applied from, beyond the physical reaches of the body. And if our minds genuinely extend beyond the body, this presents the possibility that our consciousness may survive bodily death – that our minds are both immortal and eternal.

Some of the phenomena we'll be examining here are widespread and well documented; others are more isolated, perhaps more easily dismissable – to those who wish to do so – as mere conjecture. Some of the data are very strongly suggestive, some merely interesting. My point here is less to suggest answers than to open us up to new possibilities, new ways of thinking 'outside the box.'

When will medicine change? It is changing now, and it is shaping our lives. Let's explore how.

Part One

MEANING

Introduction

W<small>E PHYSICIANS ARE SIMPLE CREATURES.</small> We like to see the world in black-and-white terms – illness is bad, health is good, and disease means nothing more than the physical breakdown of the body. To speak of the meaning or deeper significance of an illness, or how such meaning might affect our health, seems beyond the scope of our mission, something for philosophers or psychologists to mull over. But as we examine our own experience and listen to the stories our patients tell us, we gradually put together a different picture.

When I was a battalion surgeon in Vietnam, I learned a lot about the connections between meaning and health. I was an idealistic young physician fresh out of my internship, eager to stamp out any disease I encountered. A major threat to the young soldiers in my battalion was malaria, which was endemic throughout Southeast Asia. One of my responsibilities was to make sure they took their antimalarial pills to prevent their getting sick. I preached the horrors of malaria to the young troops, trying to impress on them how our combat readiness and their survival depended on avoiding this lethal illness. I quickly discovered that many of the soldiers did not share my concerns. Some of them actually wanted to contract malaria, because a debilitating illness was their ticket home. They preferred the risk of malaria to a sniper's bullet or an ambush. Consequently, they would fake taking their medication. One young man whom I evacuated with shaking chills and fever gave me a high five as he was being loaded onto the medevac helicopter. 'I'm outa here, Doc! Malaria is my best friend!' he said with a laugh.

I realized that meaning and malaria were bound up together, and that I could not do a good job as a combat doc without taking this into account. To me, malaria meant a deadly condition that should be prevented if possible or eliminated by any means at hand. To my battalion commander, malaria meant a drain on personnel and a threat to combat preparedness. To many of the young soldiers, malaria was desirable and should actually be courted as a way of escaping the perils of Vietnam. To me, then, malaria was an opportunity to do my job effectively. The battalion commander, on the other hand, saw it as an unwelcome threat to his ability to carry out his mission. It presented that same threat to the soldiers – but they saw that threat as a lifesaver. One disease, three meanings, all different.

The conflict in meanings I encountered in Vietnam occurs every day in clinics and hospitals. For instance, in a five-year study, researchers found that only one-third of women with breast cancer who used alternative medicine in addition to conventional treatment told their personal physicians they had done so. The women's three main reasons were a belief that their doctors weren't interested, would respond negatively and criticize them, or had inadequate training in alternative medicine or were biased against it. In other words, the women experienced profound conflicts with their doctors about the meaning of conventional medicine. To the doctors, conventional medicine was almost a religion, something they'd staked their careers and their patients' lives on – and would no doubt stake their own lives on when the time came. To many women, on the other hand, it was a potentially helpful system, but also a potentially uncaring, intimidating, biased, and close-minded one. Conflicts such as these can lead to serious problems because, although some alternative therapies are beneficial, others are harmful or may interact negatively with conventional medications.

As we will see, sometimes it isn't the actual life event that is crucial but the meaning we attach to it. The same set of circumstances can affect health differently, depending on how we interpret it. Consider job stress. Men who hate their job have a higher incidence of heart attacks, which are more likely to occur on Monday morning, around nine o'clock, than at any other time. Women, in contrast, do not seem to be affected by job stress to the same degree. In one study, job stress had little effect on the course of women who were already diagnosed with heart problems. Of far greater importance for their future health was the level of stress in their marriage. In our culture, jobs generally mean different things to men and women. Men's personal identity and self-esteem are more tightly connected with their job than is the case for women, for whom familial and marital relationships may be more meaningful – thus the gender differences in how jobs affect health.

In the essays that follow, we will see that meaning and health are related in two main ways. First, health *means* something – it mirrors, represents, and symbolizes what is taking place in our life. Conversely, the *meanings* we find in life – the meaning of a relationship, a job, a particular therapy – can affect our mind and body and thus our health.

In part 1 we will see how this double movement of meaning is a vital factor in our life, and how meaning can make the difference in life and death.

1

What Does Illness Mean?

Everything in this world has a hidden meaning.
Men, animals, trees, stars, they are all
hieroglyphics. . . . When you see them, you
do not understand them. You think they are
really men, animals, trees, stars.
It is only later that you understand.
— NIKOS KAZANTZAKIS —
Zorba the Greek

'CANCER IS THE BEST THING that ever happened to me!' This comment, which was not uncommon, never failed to irritate me as a young physician. Although the illness varied, the message was always the same: The disease led to an increase in wisdom and understanding, and held lessons that paradoxically made life better. The illness, it seemed, meant something.

I was not impressed. Humans will stop at nothing, I told myself, to rationalize their plight. When we face problems we can't control, we try to put the best face on them in order to preserve our self-esteem, dignity, and sense of self-worth. My patients were trying to make the best out of a terrible situation. The possibility that cancer could contain positive value seemed absurd.

In the no-nonsense world of internal medicine I inhabited, the concept of meaning seemed a philosophical nicety that could safely be ignored. Meaning might have a place in the dreary libraries of philosophers but not in coronary care units and oncology wards. Meanings belonged to the mind only; they floated safely above the clavicles and did not influence the rest of the body. If negative, they might cause anxiety or tension, but at most they were a nuisance with no bottom-line consequence. But what of the reports from patients indicating that disease could send people back to the drawing boards of reality and transform their lives?

The meaning of illness is only one sense in which the question of meaning arises in medicine. There is also the issue of whether perceived meanings, once present, can influence health and illness. Are perceived meanings causal? Do positive meanings increase health, and are negative ones harmful? Again, the patients' stories were unambiguous. They were convinced that their perceived meanings, manifesting as thoughts, attitudes, and beliefs, figured heavily in their health.

Meaning and Science

It has been difficult to ask these questions in contemporary medicine. Health and illness, we're told, are a function of what the atoms and molecules in our bodies happen to be doing at any given time. They follow the so-called blind laws of nature, which are inherently meaningless. This implies that meaning is something we read into nature, not something that can legitimately be read out of it. The molecular biologist Jacques Monod expressed this point of view in his book *Chance and Necessity*, which powerfully influenced a generation of scientists. 'The cornerstone of scientific method,' he confidently proclaimed, is 'the *systematic* denial that "true" knowledge can be got at by interpreting phenomena in terms of final causes – that is to say, of "purpose."' For Monod, purpose and the related concept of meaning do not belong in science because they do not exist in the natural world that science studies. To believe otherwise, Monod implied, is scientific heresy.

I, like most physicians, accepted this point of view. In fact, I liked it very much. It was clean, unadorned, and it was courageous as well. It demonstrated the principle of parsimony, one of the cornerstones of modern science. It excluded anthropomorphism by refusing to project human qualities and feelings onto the natural world.

But after entering clinical practice, I discovered that it is much easier to hold this view if one is dealing with mitochondria in test tubes than if one is treating sick human beings. Mitochondria don't talk back. What would Monod have concluded, I have since wondered, if he had spent time in an intensive care unit instead of at a laboratory bench? What if he had heard a dozen patients a day tell their stories? Would meaning still have seemed silly? This is not a rhetorical question. Many of the scientists who have interpreted nature as meaningless and purposeless – particle physicists, molecular biologists, geneticists, even mathematicians and theorists – have approached nature at the remotest levels. They have never seen a patient; they have not heard 'meaning stories' day after day. Shielded from this data, how can they confidently exclude a role for meaning and purpose at the human level?

'I Do It with Meaning'

I once admitted a patient to the coronary care unit with excruciating chest pain that I believed was caused by a heart attack. After his pain had subsided and he was all wired up, Frank, to relieve his boredom, positioned his bedside table in such a way that he could view the cardiac monitor behind him in the flip-up mirror. By the time I went by to see him on evening rounds, he had a trick up his sleeve. 'Doc,' he said, 'keep your eye on the monitor. I want to show you something.' Frank closed his eyes. The oscilloscope registered a steady rate of about eighty per minute. Then it fell gradually, settling in the sixties. 'Now watch this,' Frank said, his eyes still shut. The heart rate climbed slowly into the nineties. Frank beamed. He knew I didn't know what was going on. I checked to see whether he was holding his breath, clenching his fists, or maneuvering in some way to affect his heart rate, but he seemed perfectly placid and relaxed. In the next twenty-four hours I went to visit him several times. He became increasingly adroit at changing his heart rate, and he seemed delighted that I was perplexed. I knew that individuals could learn to control their heart rate in biofeedback laboratories, but I knew also that this usually requires a skilled instructor, several sessions, and a relaxed environment. Frank didn't fit this picture. He had learned his skill, without instruction, in one of the most stressful situations imaginable – being hospitalized for a possible heart attack.

Frank's tests were normal; he had not sustained a myocardial infarction. When I went by to discharge him, I said, 'I give up. How do you do it?' This was the question he had been waiting for. 'I do it with meaning,' he said. 'If I want my heart rate to fall, I close my eyes and focus on the chest pain. I let it *mean* to me that it's only indigestion or perhaps muscle pain. I know it's nothing; I'll be back to work tomorrow. If I want to increase the heart rate, I switch the meaning. I think the worst: I've had a real heart attack, I'll never get back to work, I'm just waiting around for the big one.'

I was impressed. Frank had turned the cardiac monitor into a meaning meter, which was giving a direct readout of the impact of perceived meaning on a crucial indicator of cardiovascular function. He helped me understand that meanings are not ethereal entities confined to the mind. They are translated into the body, and as I was later to discover, they can make the difference in life and death.

What Do You Think about Your Health?

'Is your health excellent, good, fair, or poor?' According to several studies done over the past few years, the answer people give to this simple question is a better predictor of who will live or die over the next decade than in-depth physical examinations and extensive laboratory tests. This question is a way of asking what our health means to us – what it represents or symbolizes in our thoughts and imagination.

A remarkable study on health perceptions and survival by sociologist Ellen L. Idler of Rutgers University and Stanislav Kasl of the Department of Epidemiology and Public Health at Yale Medical School was published in 1991. Results of the study involving more than twenty-eight hundred men and women aged sixty-five and older were consistent with the results of five other large studies taking in more than twenty-three thousand people aged nineteen to ninety-four. All these studies lead to the same conclusion: Our own opinion about the state of our health is a better predictor than physical symptoms and objective factors such as extensive exams and laboratory tests, or behaviors such as cigarette smoking. For instance, people who smoked were twice as likely to die over the next twelve years as people who did not, whereas those who said their health was 'poor' were seven times more likely to die than those who said their health was 'excellent.'

These studies do not mean that physical symptoms and harmful behaviors should be ignored or that physical examinations and laboratory tests should be abandoned. They remain vitally important. The larger lesson is that they are not, of themselves, sufficient; our medical attention must also be trained on the issues of meaning, no matter how slippery we may consider them to be.

'Is It the Fourth?'

History is replete with stories of how perceived meanings have made life-and-death differences in health. George L. Engel of the University of Rochester School of Medicine investigated 170 cases of 'emotional sudden death,' a condition that has been reported from ancient times to the present. Engel found that the emotions immediately preceding collapse and death were heavily tinged with perceived meanings. The three major categories were 'personal danger or threat of injury, whether real or symbolic' (27 percent); 'the collapse or death of a close person' (21 percent); and 'during the period of acute grief (within 16 days)' (20 percent).

Similar instances involve two founding fathers and presidents of the United States: John Adams and Thomas Jefferson. Both died on July 4, 1826, the fiftieth anniversary of the signing of the Declaration of Independence. As recorded by his doctor, Jefferson's last words were, 'Is it the Fourth?' Jefferson's and Adams's deaths seem to mean something; they reach beyond the purely physical; they symbolize something greater than the blind play of atoms.

Skeptics are generally unmoved. Why shouldn't Jefferson and Adams die on July 4? They have 1 in 365 chances of doing so. Nothing remarkable here!

Meaning is Inevitable

It's no use, in my opinion, to argue that disease means nothing. One can insist that the illness should mean nothing, as Susan Sontag has eloquently done in her influential book *Illness as Metaphor*, but this is a hopeless ideal. Anyone who is seriously ill will find or create meaning to explain what is happening. It is simply our nature to do so, and I have never seen an exception to this generalization. Even if we claim that our illness means nothing, as did Sontag in her experience with cancer, we are nonetheless creating and inserting meaning into the event. Here the meaning takes the form of denial of any underlying signifi-cance, purpose, or pattern, which is meaning of a negative kind. But *negative* meaning is not the same as *no* meaning. We may tell ourselves that our illness is nothing more than an accidental, purposeless, random event, that it is simply a matter of our atoms and molecules just being themselves. But this denial of meaning is meaning in disguise. It can assure us, for example, right or wrong, that the illness is not our fault, that we were not responsible for it, that it 'just happened,' which can be a great consolation. Thus, negative meaning can be extremely meaning*ful*.

Meaning and Science: Another View

One gets the impression that the debate within science about meaning and purpose is final or is nearing completion and that all good scientists know that nature is blind, meaningless, and purpose-less. However, first-rate scientists, many of Nobel caliber, who have inquired deeply into the place of meaning in nature have disagreed with the point of view expressed by Monod and others.

Sir Arthur Eddington (1882–1944), the English astronomer and astrophysicist, was such a person. He was one of the first theo-rists to fully grasp relativity theory, of which he became a leading exponent. He made important contributions to the theoretical physics of motion, evolution, and the internal constitution of stellar systems. For his outstanding contributions he was knighted in 1930. Eddington was not only an exemplary scientist but an eloquent writer and accomplished philosopher as well, and he possessed a penetrating wit. He pointed to the practical impossibility and the absurdity of attempting to live one's life as if it were devoid of any meaning higher than the purely physical.

> The materialist who is convinced that all phenomena arise from electrons and quanta and the like controlled by mathematical formulae, must presumably hold the belief that his wife is a rather elaborate differential equation, but he is probably tactful enough not to obtrude this opinion in domestic life. If this kind of scientific dissection is felt to be inadequate and irrelevant in ordinary personal relationships, it is surely out of place in the most personal relationship of all – that of the human soul to a divine spirit.

The preference of scientists for a tidy, aseptic world without meaning and purpose is itself a meaning, one smuggled into science in the name of objectivity. This point of view is a preferred aesthetic, but it is not science.

In fact, it is a misconception to say that science has disproved meaning in nature. Nothing could be further from the truth. *The failure to prove meaning in nature is not the same thing as disproving it.* It is more accurate to say that science has nothing to say about meaning and purpose, to acknowledge that these issues are a blank spot on the scientific map. Science can tell us that electrons and protons attract each other but not what this phenomenon means, whether there is a purpose behind it, or whether it is a good thing. That is why the proper response of the physical sciences to questions of meaning is, I believe, silence. And that is why science, properly understood, is more a friend than an enemy to questions of meaning.

This point of view is eloquently expressed by transpersonal psychologist Ken Wilber in his book *Quantum Questions*. Although speaking of the relationship of physics and religion, his observations apply equally to the relationship of science and meaning:

> Whereas classical physics was theoretically *hostile* to religion, modern physics is simply *indifferent* to it – it leaves so many

theoretical holes in the universe that you may (or may not) fill them with religious substance, but if you do, it must be on philosophic or religious grounds. Physics cannot help you in the least, but it no longer objects to your efforts. Physics does not support mysticism, but it no longer denies it . . . Many people are . . . disappointed or let down by the apparently thin or weak nature of [this development], whereas, in fact, this view . . . is probably the strongest and most revolutionary conclusion vis à vis religion that has ever been 'officially' advanced by theoretical science itself. It is a monumental and epochal turning point in science's stance towards religion; it seems highly unlikely that it will ever be reversed, since it is logical and not empirical in nature . . . therefore, it, in all likelihood, marks final closure on that most nagging aspect of the age-old debate between the physical sciences and religion . . . What more could one possibly want?

A Release from Pathology's Curse

'Cancer is the best thing that ever happened to me.' Now I believe, many years later, that this comment often represents great wisdom and insight and can be a healing force. In psychologist C. G. Jung's *Letters* it is evident that he knew how the discovery of meaning could ease the burden of disease. He wrote about the domain of the numinous, that transcendent place where life's richest meanings are found: 'The approach to the numinous is the real therapy and inasmuch as you attain to the numinous experiences you are released from the curse of pathology. Even the very disease takes on a numinous character.'

One of the most numinous meanings encountered by patients during severe illness is a belief in an afterlife. To the skeptical clinician these interpretations may seem jejune, desperate gropings in the face of impending death. But even though therapists may not share the beliefs of their patients that 'something more' follows death, the most humane and compassionate response might be one of loving support. The most shameful behavior is to engage in a contest of meanings with a patient, denigrating or ridiculing what one does not agree with. Jung emphasized the extraordinarily sensitive nature of meaning and the need for tolerance:

> If . . . from the needs of his own heart, or in accordance with the ancient lessons of human wisdom . . . anyone should [believe in] . . . what is inadequately and symbolically described as 'eternity' – then critical reason could counter no other argument than the *non liquet* of science. Furthermore, he would have the inestimable advantage of conforming to a bias of the human psyche which has existed from time immemorial and is universal. Anyone who does not draw this conclusion . . . has the indubitable certainty of coming into conflict with the truths of his own blood . . . This means the same thing as the conscious denial of the instincts – uprootedness, disorientation, meaninglessness . . . Deviation from the truths of the blood begets neurotic meaninglessness, and the lack of meaning is a soul-sickness whose full extent and full import our age has not as yet begun to comprehend.

Is it ethically and morally wrong to indulge a patient in his or her meanings if we are convinced they are erroneous or misplaced? If the patient's belief is destructive to health, we must intervene. But we must not be self-indulgent and must not burden the patient with our views. This is easy to do; patients may be vulnerable to anything said by someone in a white coat. If we disagree with the spiritual meanings our patients find during illness, perhaps we can find justification for remaining silent in science, recalling that on questions of meaning and purpose, science itself is mute.

Meaning and Alternative Medicine

Meaning is often disregarded in modern life. Not only are we told (erroneously) that science has proved there is no meaning in nature, we are also assured that God is dead. As a result, we find ourselves a society that is spiritually malnourished and hungry for meaning. This understood, it becomes easier to see why alternative therapies are enjoying a renaissance. Although I know of no data to support this observation, I believe generally that alternative therapy practitioners are much more cordial to questions of meaning in illness than physicians, psychiatrists, and psychologists. They are more willing to entertain the symbolic side of illness and to suppose that health and illness may reflect more than the blind play of atoms. Patients respond warmly to this point of view because it feels good to have one's quest for meaning acknowledged or to have one's meanings affirmed. The immense popularity of alternative therapies and therapists may be due in large measure to the fact that they help people find meaning in their lives when they need it most.

The Shadow Side

Making a place for meaning in medicine may cause problems. These have to do with extremism. 'The pendulum of the mind oscillates between sense and nonsense, not between right and wrong,' Jung wrote. 'The *numinosum* is dangerous because it lures men to extremes.'

If the pendulum was once completely in the physical corner of the atoms and molecules, it can also swing wildly to the side of meaning. Then we may regard illness as having no physical component whatever and believe that it is caused only by negative perceptions, thoughts, attitudes, and beliefs. The idea that illness is totally a function of the various expressions of consciousness, including perceived meanings, is common in the New Age. Convinced that the mind is everything, people easily succumb to New Age guilt – a sense of failure, shame, and inadequacy – if they get sick. Meaning can then supplant the physical altogether. The belief that mental factors, including perceived meanings, are the only cause of illness can lead to disastrous consequences such as the refusal to employ physical methods (for example, drugs and surgical procedures) when they might be lifesaving.

These excesses make it all too easy to criticize the search for meaning in illness. Because the search so often goes astray, many physicians want nothing to do with it. If the pendulum must swing, they say, better it swing toward the physical. This attitude is common. Even Eddington experienced a longing for the comforts of the physical view when he was painstakingly elucidating the connections between science and mysticism. He acknowledged 'a homesickness for the paths of physical science where there are more or less discernible handrails to keep us from the worst morasses of foolishness.' But in spite of the intellectual queasiness he experienced, Eddington persevered in his search for meaning. And so, I believe, must we.

Meaning Therapy

The reason we must persevere in the search for meaning has largely to do with science. Many 'meaning studies' are beginning to elucidate the considerable role of meaning in health – for example, the already-mentioned study by Idler and Kasl showing the potent effect of perceived meanings on longevity. Studies also show that the meaning of the relationship with one's spouse is a major factor in the clinical expression of heart disease; that the meaning of a job and one's level of job dissatisfaction can be major predictors of heart attack; that attention to the meanings surrounding heart disease, when combined with dietary discretion, exercise, and stress management, can improve cardiac performance and reverse coronary artery obstructions; that the bereavement and mourning following a spouse's death are associated with severe immune dysfunction; that negative perceptions of one's daily job can increase the risk for heart attack; and that for certain cancer patients, group therapy in which questions of meaning are addressed can double survival time following diagnosis.

These studies represent the pendulum at midpoint. They show that attention to states of consciousness need not replace physical interventions but can be used effectively in conjunction with them.

These findings are about meaning therapy, in which therapists deliberately attempt to reshape negative meanings into positive ones. If we choose to call these attempts 'psychology,' 'behavioral therapy,' or some other psychologically oriented term, we should be careful that we do not assign them second-class status in the process. Meaning therapy is no stepchild of allopathic medicine.

Its effects are as real as those of drugs and surgical procedures. The studies referred to above show that reforming meaning can elicit significant clinical responses and can even make the difference in life and death.

The Challenge of Meaning

Contemporary physicians – I say this as someone who has been in the trenches of internal medicine for two decades – hear that modern medicine is too technical, remote, and cold; that we don't take enough time with our patients; that we focus on their bodies and avoid questions of meaning, leaving such questions to psychologists, ministers, and priests. Yet most physicians continue to rely on the physically based methods we know best, justifying this approach with evidence that they do work. But if orthodox methods are so effective – and they are sometimes fabulously successful – why is the public not more grateful? Why the concerted attempt to dismantle the profession and 'manage' it differently?

Much of society's disillusionment with modern medicine lies in the failure of medical practitioners to acknowledge the importance of meaning in their patients' lives and illnesses. If physicians continue to minimize or ignore the role of meaning in health, we will continue to lose influence. The contest between conventional and alternative therapies is not just about economics, efficacy, safety, and availability; it is about meaning as well. We are discovering a painful fact: no matter how technologically effective modern medicine may be, if it does not honor the place of meaning in illness, it may lose the allegiance of those it serves.

In the future, when historians dissect our age, they may be shocked that we in science chose to place such a high value on the 'systematic denial' of purpose and meaning. They may wonder why we chose to ignore the visions of such thinkers as physicist David Bohm, who said, 'Meaning is being,' and C. G. Jung, who saw the importance of meaning and had the courage to speak about it: 'Meaning makes a great many things endurable – perhaps everything . . . Through the creation of meaning . . . a new cosmos arises.' 'Meaninglessness . . . is . . . equivalent to illness.'

If practitioners of alternative therapies are to fulfill their promise, they will have to continue to honor the place of meaning in health and illness. We must resist the temptation to treat meaning as the 'new penicillin' or the latest surgical technique, which can be applied in a purely utilitarian way. In the rush to gain respectability, practitioners of alternative medicine will feel immense pressure to minimize or denigrate expressions of consciousness such as meaning. This temptation must be resisted, or alternative therapies will deserve little more than a footnote in history. We already have therapies aplenty that deny meaning. We do not need more.

As a result of the numerous studies affirming the crucial role of meaning in medicine, making a space for meaning has never been more justifiable. Are we up to the challenge?

2

Whatever Happened to Healers?

Medicine men aren't horses.
You don't breed them.
— LAME DEER —
Sioux medicine man

W<small>HEN</small> I <small>BEGAN TO EXPLORE</small> the world of alternative medicine nearly three decades ago, I discovered that I would have to expand my vocabulary considerably if I wanted to communicate with therapists. For example, they often used the word *healer*, which was not part of the lexicon of medical school. In fact, I do not recall the term's ever being used in my medical training. I had no feel for this expression and thought it quaint. If my medical colleagues and I had been called healers, we would not have known whether we were being praised or damned. We were training to become surgeons, internists, and pathologists, not healers.

I realized also that alternative therapists used *healing* differently than we did in medical school. We'd learned that healing was something that occurred automatically in wounds and incisions, whereas my alternative therapy friends believed that healing had something to do with consciousness. They furthermore differentiated healing from curing, and they mysteriously maintained that 'a healing' could occur even in the event of death.

Not much has changed since my encounter with these ideas. The concept of the healer remains virtually absent in medical training, including nursing, dental, and even alternative therapy schools, and *healing* continues to be used in a narrow physiologic sense.

Whatever happened to healers? Have we simply run out of them? Surely not; all cultures seem to have produced them in abundance. They continue to abound – those passionate, idealistic young persons whose desire to be involved in healing is mysterious, powerful, and often inexplicable. They simply 'know' they must become healers, and they will do almost anything to fulfill their calling. Hearkening to a deep and primal drive, they often migrate to medical schools, the healing path that currently enjoys the most emphatic social sanction. Yet this can be a painful, suffocating experience for many of them because most medical schools have a completely different view of the nature of healers and healing than that of the natural-born healers themselves. Thus we encounter a paradox: our medical schools, which of all our institutions should be most attuned to nourishing and developing the natural healing talents of gifted young people, seem adept at extinguishing them.

The Letter

I know this because the young healers tell me so. For years I've received missives from medical students all over the country, which I've come to refer to as The Letter. The Letter always bears the stamp of an individual student's pain and disillusionment, usually beginning in the first year of medical school. The students say that their impulse to be a healer is being snuffed out. Many want advice about medical schools that will nurture their healing instincts, which, they say, is 'the reason I went to medical school.' Some indicate that they will do anything to transfer to such a school, if only they can identify one. The following letter, written in June 1995, is an example from a student, whose name is withheld.

Dear Dr Dossey:

Soon I'll be a second-year medical student. After last semester I began to glimpse some of the terrible realities in medicine today, and I started to question my resolve to be a doctor. I even seriously considered leaving medical school.

Lecture after lecture, I heard dry professors and doctors speak at breakneck speed about ways to crush the human person into the spiritless formula of science. At the same time, I saw some second-year friends turn sour and cold with stress, and I began to wonder whether I would end up the same way. I wasn't sure I could nourish my soul in such an environment.

I was chosen by my anatomy professor as a candidate for the summer Anatomy Teaching Fellowship. I struggled with this offer, but eventually listened to my whispering conscience. I refused the fellowship, because I needed my summer to refuel spiritually and to discover new things. This decision . . . threw me into a tumultuous questioning as my soul rose to assert itself.

Recently I attended an ecumenical prayer retreat. I felt a deep peace pervade my soul. By the end of the retreat, I felt more at ease with my role as a medical student. I felt that I, as a person, was in the place where I belonged.

Since then, my eyes have been opened. I am slowly emerging from a period of darkness, brooding, uncertainty, and fear which has hung over me for the past month or so. I realize that, rather than being changed for the worse, I can in fact heal in small ways and change things for the better. I know that the trick lies in humbly nurturing in oneself a perspective of simplicity and beauty.

Tough-minded observers who view medical school as a rite of passage have little patience with the sort of complaints contained in The Letter. They often say these comments originate from a few weak-willed, disgruntled complainers who shouldn't be in medical school in the first place. Medical school is difficult and ought to be; those who can't take it need not apply. Others, including many physicians who have endured the process of medical training, sense there is something terribly wrong with the way we train physicians. For example, San Diego psychiatrist Dennis Gersten wrote to me:

My medical school class had a 6% mortality rate, not to mention a high morbidity rate. One fellow, who had been free of melanoma for five years, quickly flared up with a recurrence during the first year of medical school and died. One woman killed herself. The week before graduation there was a series of freak accidents. One fellow was fishing in Alaska; his boat capsized and he drowned. Another guy was fishing in a foot-deep stream. He waded across the river, slipped on a stone, hit his head, became unconscious, and was washed downstream and drowned. During gross anatomy the morbidity rate was unbelievable. Students got sick, got in more auto wrecks.

Institutionalized Abuse?

Medical students also encounter frequent psychological and physical abuse. The problem goes beyond overwork and sleep deprivation. It involves verbal, physical, psychological, sexual, and racial abuse; various forms of intimidation; and being placed at unnecessary medical risk. At one major medical school, 80 percent of seniors reported being abused during their training, and more than two-thirds stated that at least one of the episodes was of 'major importance and very upsetting.' Sixteen percent of the students surveyed said the abuse would 'always affect them.' In another survey of third-year medical students, the perception of mistreatment (particularly verbal abuse and 'unfair tactics') was pervasive. Three-fourths of the students reported having become more cynical about academic life and the medical profession as a result of these episodes. Two-thirds felt that they were worse off than their peers in other professions. More than one-third con-sidered dropping out of medical school, and one-fourth would have chosen a different profession had they known in advance about the extent of the mistreatment they would experience. Another study of medical student abuse indicates that the effects of mistreatment are not trivial but are associated with measurable psychopathological consequences.

These problems are not restricted to the United States. The 1998 BBC television series *Doctors at Large*, for example, revealed the abuse of British medical students by their teachers. Because of such stresses, an estimated 18 percent to 25 percent of newly qualified

British physicians never enter medical practice, or leave medicine shortly after qualifying.

How can we expect medical students to emerge as compassionate physicians when they are treated so uncompassionately in their training? If one wanted to snuff out the healing instinct and the idealism that students often bring to medical school, one could hardly imagine a more efficient method.

The long-term consequences of the medical school experience may involve not just psychological but physical health as well. For almost thirty years, Dr Caroline B. Thomas of the Johns Hopkins Medical School performed psychological tests on every incoming medical student. She followed the students over time, and at the end of the study, examined the test scores for correlations between the psychological profiles and the diseases the students developed. The findings were disturbing. Students whose psychological tests showed that they could not externalize their feelings – those who kept things bottled up inside – developed fatal cancer of all types later in life at an increased incidence. The implications are chilling. Medical schools in general foster the internalization of feelings – the 'I can take it' attitude in which one never complains, no matter how difficult the situation – that correlated in Thomas's study with the eventual development of cancer.

Physicians for the Twenty-first Century

As the practice of medicine is being reshaped, we are being afforded the opportunity to take a fresh look at many hallowed concepts and customs, such as how the impulse in medical students to be a healer can be identified and fostered, and how medical education can be made healthier. One of the most admirable examinations of how medical students are selected and trained is the report 'Physicians for the Twenty-first Century,' commissioned by the Association of American Medical Colleges. Published in 1984, it remains current. Following are some excerpts from the report:

- [We do] not wish to invoke the hysterical hyperbole of crisis, nor do we wish to impugn the high quality of much [reform] that is being done. However, we perceive a continuing erosion of general education for physicians, an erosion that has not been arrested but is instead accelerating. We see continuing pressures to which we must accommodate with vigor and deliberate determination lest critical and irreversible damage is done.

- Every student should be caring, compassionate, and dedicated to patients . . . Ethical sensitivity and moral integrity, combined with equanimity, humility, and self-knowledge, are quintessential qualities of all physicians.
- Students are led to think that their education depends upon memorizing as much information as possible. Consequently, they lack a clear idea of the skills, values, and attitudes that are important . . . Medical faculties must limit the amount of factual information that students are expected to memorize.
- The priority most medical faculty members accord to research, patient care, and training of residents and graduate students has militated against the education of medical students.
- The traditional objectives of college education – to sharpen one's critical and analytical skills and to investigate the varieties of human experience through balanced studies in the natural and social sciences and in the humanities – are . . . displaced by students' preoccupation with whatever they think they need to do to get into medical school. A premedical syndrome . . . is often described. Students who exhibit this syndrome take course after course in the sciences but avoid advanced studies in the humanities and in other nonscience fields . . . By the time their college studies are completed, these students often have forfeited the intellectual challenges and rewards that study in the humanities could have afforded.

In a revealing passage, the authors cite a 1932 report issued by the Association of American Medical Colleges Commission on Medical Education that acknowledges something intangible about the training of a healer, something that cannot be brought about by tinkering with the curriculum and reshuffling the same old worn cards:

The medical course cannot produce a physician. It can only provide the opportunities for a student to secure an elementary knowledge of the medical sciences and their application to health problems, a training in the methods and spirit of scientific inquiry, and the inspiration and point of view which come from association with those who are devoting themselves to education, research, and practice. Medicine must be learned by the student, for only a fraction of it can be taught by the faculty. The latter makes the essential contributions of guidance, inspiration, and leadership in learning. The student and the teacher, not the curriculum, are the crucial elements in the educational program.

Becoming a Healer: Transformation

Our profession's discomfort with healers, healing, and healing power is a historical aberration. For fifty thousand years shamans and native healers of every variety have believed they possess the power to heal and that they were meant to be healers – convictions shared by their cultures. This same inchoate drive lies latent in many medical students, and it beckons them toward medicine. Learning how to actually use this power was never considered just an exercise of the intellect, as it is now regarded. Becoming a healer exercised every aspect of one's being – a process that is vividly captured in the words of an Iglulik Eskimo shaman:

> I endeavored to become a shaman by the help of others; but in this I did not succeed. I visited many famous shamans, and gave them great gifts ... I sought solitude, and here I soon became very melancholy. I would sometimes fall to weeping, and feel unhappy without knowing why. Then, for no reason, all would suddenly be changed, and I felt a great, inexplicable joy, a joy so powerful that I could not restrain it, but had to break into song, a mighty song, with only room for the one word: joy, joy! And I had to use the full strength of my voice. And then in the midst of such a fit of mysterious and over-whelming delight I became a shaman, not knowing myself how it came about. But I was a shaman. I could see and hear in a

totally different way. I had gained my *qaumanEq*, my enlightenment, the shaman-light of brain and body, and this in such a
manner that it was not only I who could see through the
darkness of life, but the same light also shone out of me, imper-
ceptible to human beings, but visible to all the spirits of earth
and sky and sea, and these now came to me and became my
helping spirits.

If a single word could describe the process of becoming a shaman,
it might be *transformation*. The transformative experiences described
by the Iglulik shaman would cause a modern psychiatrist to
shudder. Most faculty members entrusted with the education of
medical students would consider such experiences bizarre and
pathological. If a student were to report such a transformation, he
or she would almost certainly be scheduled for an appointment in
the department of psychiatry.

Healers or Frankensteins?

In modern medical education 'transformation' has been supplanted
by 'information.' The result is the production of counterfeits –
physicians who cannot heal and who regard 'healing power' as a
quaint anachronism.

Hyperbole? Consider the following observations in a provocative essay, 'American Medical Education: Has It Created a
Frankenstein?' in the *American Journal of Medicine:*

> The present group of recently trained physicians are, in general,
> insensitive, have poor patient rapport, are deficient in general
> medical knowledge and examination skills, and have little
> concern for medicine's impact on society . . . Further, few young
> people in medicine appear to be either emotionally or intellec-
> tually satisfied with their profession . . . The current time-
> consuming training process often takes bright, creative young
> adults with a love for helping people, and turns them into cold,
> distant persons who have lost many of their original ideals
> regarding the practice of medicine . . . [thereby] producing a

physician with qualities 180 degrees opposite those it states it believes in.

Occasionally there is a spasm of awareness that something is seriously wrong, and recommendations are made for physicians to do things differently. These suggestions are sometimes surprising, such as a proposal in *Lancet* that physicians and medical students take acting lessons. This would enable them to appear to care and be empathic with patients, whether they were or not. There is also an occasional glimmer that clinical outcomes are connected with something more than algorithms and objectivity. Consider, for example, a controlled study dealing with homeless people in an inner-city emergency room. Those patients who were deliberately given compassionate, empathic care – qualities endorsed by all genuine healers – demonstrated fewer repeat visits and greater satisfaction with treatment.

Information Is Not Transformation

Sensing that something is awry in the way physicians are trained, a common response of medical schools has been to provide students with more information, or with information with a slightly different focus – courses (often optional) in medical ethics, medical humanities, or medical history. But this strategy often makes no real difference, because information is being confused with trans-formation. The young protohealers are not hungry for more facts but for experiences that can help them connect with those deep psychological and spiritual urges that have manifested throughout history as a commitment to the healing arts.

The informational approach to solving problems in medical education is immensely seductive. It can also be deadly. As Neil Postman, chair of the Department of Culture and Communications at New York University, puts it, we have created

a new problem never experienced before: information glut, information incoherence, information meaninglessness . . . We have transformed information into a form of garbage, and ourselves into garbage collectors. Like the sorcerer's apprentice, we are awash in information without even a broom to help us get rid of it. Information comes . . . at high speeds, severed from import and meaning. And there is no loom to weave it all into fabric. No transcendent narratives to provide us with moral guidance, social purpose, intellectual economy. No stories to tell us what we need to know, and what we do not need to know.

If our medical schools are once again to produce healers, they will have to foster transformation of the inner life of the students who entrust themselves to the educational process. Postman suggests: 'We will need to consult our poets, playwrights, artists, humorists, theologians, and philosophers, who alone are capable of creating or restoring those metaphors and stories that give point to our labors, give meaning to our history, elucidate the present, and give direction to our future.'

'Transformation' is a robust project, and we should not underestimate the magnitude of this task. 'We're asking a young physician to become a wise old person, and to do it in 4 years of medical school. That's a lot,' observed the late molecular biologist and cancer researcher Helene Smith, who believed an infusion of shamanic knowledge into modern medicine would be a good thing. But becoming a wise healer has always been a difficult and lengthy undertaking, even for the shamans. In fact, it was by no means certain that the shaman would survive; the process of transformation sometimes ended in death.

I do not mean to suggest that our medical schools fail completely in their mission. Authentic healers do emerge from them, though not as commonly as they should, and often in spite of the educational process and not because of it. Neither do I wish to imply that the inadequacies we have been addressing are the sole fault of the schools themselves. Medical schools reflect the values of the society in which they exist. If something is amiss in them, the problem can usually be identified in the society as a whole as well. At the root of the problem lies the fact that we, as a culture, have turned our collective back on healing. We should not kid ourselves: we are all in this together, jointly entranced by a physicalistic approach to health and illness and dazzled by the promises of technology to right every conceivable misfire of the body. Against this backdrop, healers and healing have been shoved aside and very nearly forgotten, and we are paying the price. Ignoring the role of consciousness, soul, spirit, and meaning – stock items in the arsenal of authentic healers – we have birthed a malaise that permeates not just the healing profession but our entire society. The casualties have been not just healers and healing but the soul and spirit of a culture.

'For the Hope of Wisdom'

These sorts of observation are often dismissed as unduly pessimistic. Those who continue to have unbridled faith in science and technology say we need more physical science, not less. Perhaps. But even insiders are worried. Typical is the following passage from *The Medusa and the Snail* by the late physician-author Lewis Thomas, who was once called the most listened-to physician in America. Here Thomas hints at what we have lost and what we need to recover, not just in medicine but in our society at large.

> These ought to be the best of times for the human mind, but it is not so. All sorts of things seem to be turning out wrong, and the century seems to be slipping through our fingers here at the end, with almost all promises unfulfilled. I cannot begin to guess at all the causes of our cultural sadness, not even the most important ones, but I can think of one thing that is wrong with us and eats away at us. We do not know enough about ourselves. We are ignorant about how we work, about where we fit in, and most of all about the enormous, imponderable system of life in which we are embedded as working parts. We do not really understand nature, at all. We have come a long way indeed, but just enough to become conscious of our ignorance. It is not so bad a thing to be totally ignorant; the hard thing is to be partway along toward real knowledge, far enough to be aware of being ignorant. It is embarrassing and depressing, and it is one of our troubles today.

It is a new experience for all of us. Only two centuries ago we could explain everything about everything, out of pure reason, and now most of that elaborate and harmonious structure has come apart before our eyes. We are dumb.

This is, in a certain sense, a health problem after all. For as long as we are bewildered by the mystery of ourselves, and confused by the strangeness of our uncomfortable connection to all the rest of life, and dumbfounded by the inscrutability of our own minds, we cannot be said to be healthy animals in today's world.

We need to know more. To come to realize this is what this seemingly inconclusive century has been all about. We have discovered how to ask important questions, and now we really do need, as an urgent matter, for the sake of our civilization, to obtain some answers. We now know that we cannot do this any longer by searching our minds, for there is not enough there to search, nor can we find the truth by guessing at it or by making up stories for ourselves. We cannot stop where we are, stuck with today's level of understanding, nor can we go back. I do not see that we have a real choice in this, for I can see only the one way ahead. We need science, more and better science, not for its technology, not for leisure, not even for health or longevity, but for the hope of wisdom which our kind of culture must acquire for its survival.

Which Way Out?

Young healers who follow their calling to medical school and who become disenchanted are often deeply affected by the malaise Thomas describes. They are like the canaries in the mine, a distant early warning system alerting the rest of us to the poisonous effects of not just our view of health but our view of reality itself. Without saying so, they are crying out for nothing less than a different worldview, an alternative to the picture of reality served up in medical school.

What might such a worldview look like? As essayist Thomas Kelting put it,

The most satisfying and successful model . . . would be one which jointly satisfies our three broadest categories of need: practical, theoretical, and spiritual. Practical needs include our desire to predict and shape our world . . . Our theoretical need is to make reality appear intelligible to our kind of intellect; we prefer descriptions of reality in which the universe is seen to be a coherent, cognitively penetrable realm of phenomena, to descriptions in which it appears otherwise. Our spiritual need goes well beyond the requirement of the intellect for coherence and intellectual precision, to our need to find a meaningful connectedness between ourselves and the rest of being. We hunger for a sense of purpose, destiny and value, grounded not only in ourselves, but in the larger nature of things. We also seek comfort and love, not just for, and from, one another, but for, and from, this greater realm of being.

The worldview affirmed in medical education tends to be 'lopsided and spotty,' Kelting says. 'We ignore our spiritual require-ments, and pursue [exclusively] models of reality that allow us to succeed in manipulating nature.' Outside the scholarly environ-ment, we often drift to the other extreme:

We pursue spirituality in a vacuum, as if there were no place for the prosaic physical universe, with its discoverable regular-ities, in a spiritual worldview. But spirituality should not be fueled by a desire to escape the lessons of the discursive intellect – that there are constraints we must live by. And, the preoccupation with physical reality and its exploitation, to which the discur-sive intellect seems so well suited, must not be allowed to escalate into the obsessive and spiritually astringent materialism that is suffocating Western society.

We should be grateful to the young healers who are so painfully at odds with the medical school environment. They are illumi-nating the schizophrenic situation we have slipped into as a society, with its divisions between the practical, theoretical, and spiritual aspects of our worldview, and they are challenging us to heal these splits.

Today there are signs that medical education is at long last shifting in a more humanistic direction. Consider, for example, the changes taking place around issues of spirituality. The evidence that spiritual factors – a sense of meaning, purpose, values, as well as religious practice – are important in health and illness is abundant and is increasing. Epidemiologist Jeffrey S. Levin, author of *God, Faith, and Health*, who originated the phrase *epidemiology of religion*, wrote to me that 'this body of work [the religion-and-health studies], I can state confidently, shows a strong, overwhelmingly consistent protective effect for religion; and my own empirical work confirms this finding.' Levin is only one of a number of researchers investigating the health effects of, broadly speaking, a spiritual approach to life. A decade ago, this information was almost totally ignored by the nation's 125 medical schools. Today, however, about eighty medical schools have developed courses or lecture series emphasizing the connections of spirituality and health.

Wounded Healers

Chiron, the centaur in Greek mythology who taught the art of healing, was wounded by a poisoned arrow. Although he extracted the arrow, he could not remove the poison, which he carried forever in his body. Chiron is immortal and cannot die, but neither can he be entirely healthy. He is the exemplar of the wounded healer, one who paradoxically heals and is in need of healing.

We are collectively wounded – healers, medical schools, and the culture that spawns them. Can we extract the arrow? Can we rid ourselves of at least some of the poison?

Ecologist Paul Ehrlich observes, 'The first rule of intelligent tinkering is to save all the parts.' Our medical schools have tinkered with young healers for generations. I believe they have saved the parts – vision, soul, and spirit in medicine have never really died – and can summon the courage required to put them back together in a pattern resembling a healer.

Researcher Helene Smith offers a hopeful view of medicine's ability to meet these challenges. 'The medical establishment actually is much better at changing than many other institutions,' she says.

'If you think about some other institutions, like education or religion, how fast do [they] change? Doctors, for all their getting a bum rap of being conservative, are actually on the forefront of changing quickly.'

If our medical schools are to produce healers, they must first stop destroying them. This will require reducing or eliminating the many ways the medical school experience has become dehumanizing. An exemplary step in this direction is the Health Awareness Workshop for first-year medical students, which has been available at the University of Louisville Medical School since 1981. The course was developed by Joel Elkes, M.D., professor emeritus of psychiatry, and Leah J. Dickstein, M.D., professor in the Department of Psychiatry and Behavioral Sciences and associate dean for faculty and student advocacy.

The Health Awareness Workshop, Dickstein and Elkes reported, rests on the recognition that 'the medical student is a person at risk,' that 'some of these risks are avoidable,' and that 'other-care is best begun with self-care.' This four-day course is offered to entering medical students prior to enrollment and commencement of studies. Although it is voluntary, more than 90 percent of freshmen elect to participate. Topics include mode of life as a factor in illness and disability; the psychobiology of human adaptation, stress, and the stress response; the physiology of nutrition, exercise, and relaxation; the psychology of time management and study skills; listening and the give-and-take of relationships; substance abuse and the impaired physician; gender issues in medicine; and introductions to the ethics of medical practice and the place of belief in healing. In addition to the didactic presentation of scientific data, an experiential, participatory, 'fun' approach to learning is included in the workshop through involvement in music, art, acting, film, singing, and chanting; a 'nutritional picnic' and pizza supper; aerobic exercise, softball, and a 'fun run'; and a river cruise on the *Belle of Louisville*. The students learn of the history of the city of Louisville and the University of Louisville School of Medicine.

Second-year students volunteer to be 'health tutors' to groups of sixteen freshmen. They share their anxieties, coping styles, and lessons learned, and even serve as chefs in preparing healthy foods for the incoming students. Faculty members, usually selected by the sophomore students, play a similar role. Workshop sessions are also held for the spouses, children, and significant others of the incoming students. As a result of these interactions, a social network forms between student and student and between student and faculty. The resulting message delivered by the medical school to the incoming students is clear and unmistakable: We care about you – your physical, psychological, and spiritual well-being – and we will go to great lengths to help you become a skilled physician and a fulfilled human being.

But in our enthusiasm for change, let us not deceive ourselves. It would be a mistake to suppose that there is a formula for generating healers. There never has been. Becoming a healer remains largely a mysterious process not amenable to manipulation and control, as the experience of the Iglulik shaman illustrates, and as Lame Deer, the Sioux medicine man, warns in the epigraph at the beginning of this chapter. We note again the 1932 report by the Commission on Medical Education: 'The medical course cannot produce a physician.' Neither can it produce a healer.

Malcolm Muggeridge once distinguished between first- and second-rate pursuits in life. 'It is possible only to succeed at second-rate pursuits – like becoming a millionaire or a prime minister, winning a war, seducing beautiful women, flying through the stratosphere, or landing on the moon,' he said. But first-rate pursuits, 'involving, as they must, trying to understand what life is about and trying to convey that understanding,' are much more difficult. Becoming a healer is a first-rate pursuit that is exceedingly arduous. So let us not saddle our medical schools with a responsibility they cannot meet, such as producing healers on demand. Let us expect them instead to prepare the soil in which healing can flourish and from which healers can flower.

The Letter Revisited

I occasionally imagine receiving The Letter from a future medical student. What might it look like? Here's my fantasy, and also my hope:

Dear Dr Dossey:

In a couple of months I will complete my residency program. May I tell you what the past few years have been like?

From earliest memory I have wanted to be a healer. This is inexplicable; no one in my family has ever been involved with medicine. I followed my vision through college, but not until I entered medical school were my deepest intuitions affirmed. I began medical school expecting to be overwhelmed with information and drudgery; instead I encountered wisdom and inspiration. For the first time in my life I discovered genuine healers – professors who in course after course seemed to be a combination of physician, scientist, mentor, and shaman. They understood that healing is a special calling, and they honored the tug I had always felt. Because of their unfailing support, my vision has never been stronger.

Medical school was a difficult undertaking; I expected and wanted it to be that way. It has also been transformative. I know I have awakened to something immensely worthwhile and that this awareness will continue to flower for the rest of my life.

One day I surprised my favorite professor by calling him a Wise Guide. He smiled knowingly and told me that my task henceforth is to pass my knowledge on, healer to healer, as it has been conveyed to me. I was thrilled by his response! He was acknowledging me as a colleague and welcoming me into that invisible college of healers that stretches from antiquity to the present.

I feel blessed to have experienced medical school. It's been a spiritual experience. I wanted you to know.

3

Suffering on the Job

SURFING THE INTERNET IS POPULAR these days, but I confess that I often prefer a simpler pleasure – surfing my tattered red dictionary, flipping pages, scanning the etymologies of words. On a recent excursion through *Webster's New World Dictionary*, the back-to-back words *job* and *Job* caught my eye. Were they related, I wondered? The origin of *job*, I found, is obscure. One meaning of the term is 'anything one has to do; task; chore; duty.' This implies that a job is unpleasant; we do it against our will, or a job contains an element of suffering. And the biblical name Job, I discovered, is of Greek and Hebrew origin and is defined as 'a man who endured much suffering.'

Is this an accidental correlation of language – a job as a type of suffering and Job as a sufferer? In any case, millions of workers are like Job – patient sufferers trapped in jobs they do not like, from which they cannot escape. Many stick them out because they *expect* work to be unpleasant. They agree with Mark Twain, who wrote in *The Adventures of Tom Sawyer*, 'Work consists of whatever a body is obliged to do . . . Play consists of whatever a body is not obliged to do.'

Work and Suffering

Not long ago, the connections between work and suffering were taken for granted. Injury and death were a common consequence of work. Consider mining. In certain counties in the Pennsylvania anthracite country, in the period just following the Civil War, between 1.5 and 3 percent of all miners were seriously injured or died each year. In the age of steam, explosions and burns were expected hazards of the workplace. Belts, pulleys, gears, and levers regularly crippled or killed workers. When they did, nobody was surprised.

Job suffering and the epidemic of work-related tragedies did not dim our national enthusiasm for progress in the late nineteenth and early twentieth centuries. As historian Edward Tenner writes in his excellent book *Why Things Bite Back: Technology and the Revenge of Unintended Consequences*, 'Americans from 1880 to 1929 were probably more optimistic about the electrical, mechanical, and chemical transformation of society than any other people have ever been. Neither the sinking of the *Titanic* in 1912 nor the devastation of the First World War could destroy their confidence.'

The Birth of the Bug

The work-related problems our forebears faced were, in a sense, simple. Exploding boilers, sinking ships, and collapsing mine shafts were highly visible, large-scale catastrophes, and people could usually determine what went wrong – with effort and planning, similar problems could be prevented. But in the waning years of the nineteenth century, a new type of workplace problem began to be glimpsed. The new source of suffering for the worker was invisible, unpredictable, and therefore sinister – the bug.

The concept of the bug – 'that perverse and elusive malfunctioning of hardware and later of software,' as Tenner put it – was an accepted item of shop slang by the 1870s. Thomas Alva Edison, the American inventor, mentions it in an 1878 description of his method of creativity and invention: 'The first step is an intuition and it comes with a burst, then difficulties arise – this thing gives out and then that – "Bugs" – as such little faults and difficulties are called – show themselves, and months of intense watching, study and labor are requisite before commercial success – or failure – is certainly reached.' According to Tenner, the term *bug* seems to have originated with telegraphers. By the time Edison mentioned the word, Western Union had more than twelve thousand stations; their frequently filthy condition may have inspired the term. Instances are known in which the bug metaphor seemed literally to spring to life – as in 1945, when a moth in a relay caused the crash of the Mark II electrochemical calculator that the navy was running at Harvard.

Resistentialism

Bugs are considered by most people to be accidental or random imperfections. From time to time, however, a different picture has been suggested – the idea that the 'things' of the workplace, such as machines, computers, and software, may not be as inanimate as we think and that they may object to being dominated and subjected to our service. The English essayist Paul Jennings (1918–1989) called this 'resistentialism,' which, he said, 'is concerned with what Things think about men.' Sometimes, Things fight back. As Jennings put it, 'Man's increase in [an] illusory domination over Things has been matched . . . by the increasing hostility (and greater force) of the Things arrayed against him.'

If resistentialism is real, workers may be like conquerors occupying a foreign country. They must always be on their toes because they never know when the subjugated and enslaved machines will rebel. Are computer bugs actually guerrilla tactics, the electronic equivalent of booby traps and trip wires?

It is legitimate to ask, Who is dominating whom on the work site? Who are the slaves and who are the masters? Do we control work, or is work controlling us? More and more workers are working longer hours, sometimes at more than one job, to make ends meet. Might this be the ultimate revenge of the Things we use – smothering us with work while creating the belief that we are running the show? Could this be the reason behind Parkinson's Law, 'Work expands so as to fill the time available for its completion'?

Regardless of their origins, bugs are an unquestionable source of suffering for the modern worker. Protecting against them requires constant vigilance, which is a price paid by any conqueror. Workers in modern, automated environments must continually back up files, guard against software viruses, and store information off-site. These new sources of suffering affect not just office workers but anyone who depends on computers. I have several friends who are professional writers, some of whom have suffered considerably from their dependence on computers. One has a recurrent night-mare in which she cannot locate the manuscript of her next book on her computer's menu. Like a lost wanderer, she becomes desperate, panics, and awakens in a sweat – a kind of 'resistential crisis.' Another saw her first novel evaporate after a power surge during an electrical storm; she had neglected to make a backup. The other individual lost years of work when a fire destroyed her home, including her computer, disks, and hard copy backup. When I heard of these events, I put myself in my friends' places. A computer-addicted writer myself, I felt the suffering they were experiencing, and I mourned for them.

Isolation in the Workplace

Many of the distresses described by modern workers are almost certainly related to the increasing isolation they feel in automated workplaces. 'In the last thirty years, the office may have grown more quiet but it has also become more tense and lonely,' says Tenner. Paradoxically, workers feel cut off and estranged by the very tools that link them electronically to others.

In her book *In the Age of the Smart Machine*, social psychologist Shoshana Zuboff describes the price employees pay for becoming estranged from each other in the workplace:

> Automation meant that jobs which had once allowed them to use their bodily presence in the service of interpersonal exchange and collaboration now required their bodily presence in the service of routine interaction with a machine. Jobs that had once required their voices now insisted they be mute . . . They had been disinherited from the management process and driven into the confines of their individual body space. As a result, the employees in each office became increasingly engulfed in the immediate sensations of physical discomfort.

For one of Zuboff's interviewees, work is a combination of disease and slavery: 'No talking, no looking, no walking. I have a cork in my mouth, blinders for my eyes, chains on my arms. With the radiation [from my computer] I have lost my hair. The only way you can make your production goals is give up your freedom.'

This is reminiscent of an observation Einstein made in 1950: 'If A is success in life, then A equals x plus y plus z. Work is x; y is play; and z is keeping your mouth shut.'

As corporate downsizing has become standard, isolation on the job has taken another form – what's been called 'survivor guilt.' This is a feeling of self-blame for being the employee who *isn't* fired. Guilty survivors have trouble delighting in their own good fortune; they are preoccupied by the problems of their fired colleagues. Not only do they feel isolated because there are fewer employees to relate to but their sense of guilt also builds a wall of estrangement between them and their laid-off colleagues and former friends. When guilty survivors add to this the lingering worry that they may be next to get the ax, their sense of defensiveness and aloneness can become oppressive.

An Omni-Collar Problem

Isolation on the job is part of the more general problem of job stress, which is not limited to specific occupations. Both white- and blue-collar workers are involved. When British researchers at the University of Manchester rated job stress according to the factors of pay, control of job activities, physical work environment, and stress-related disorders, they found that miners, police officers, prison officers, and construction workers occupied the most stressful jobs. Completing the list, in decreasing order of job stress, were airline pilots, journalists, advertising executives, dentists, actors, nurses, firefighters, teachers, social workers, bus drivers, and postal workers.

The problem of job suffering is also universal. The UN's International Labor Organization (ILO) says job stress is increasing to the point of a worldwide epidemic. 'Waitresses in Sweden, teachers in Japan, postal workers in America, bus drivers in Europe, and assembly line workers everywhere are all showing signs of job stress,' a 1993 ILO report noted.

The Japanese are especially fearful. They have even coined a term for death by overwork – *karoshi*. According to one survey, 40 percent of all Japanese workers fear they will literally work themselves to death. They have good reason for concern: they produce 10 percent of the world's exports with just 2 percent of the world's population. Lawyers representing the families of *karoshi* victims estimate that between ten thousand and thirty thousand Japanese workers die from overwork each year. The families of survivors are campaigning for legal recognition of the condition, and *karoshi* hotlines have been set up in most of Japan's main cities to help accomplish this goal.

The Sisyphus Syndrome

One of the worst forms of isolation on a job comes from being locked into a stressful, repetitive task that creates separation not just from other workers but also from freedom for decision making. Researchers have suggested the term *Sisyphus reaction* for this situation. The description of this problem goes back more than sixty years. The pattern is that of a driven, effort-oriented person who strives against great odds but with very little sense of accomplishment or satisfaction. (In Greek mythology, Sisyphus, king of Corinth, was banished to Hades and condemned to push an enormous stone up the side of a hill – only to have it roll down again, requiring him to repeat the labor endlessly without success.) The Sisyphus syndrome differs from the type A behavior pattern mainly because of the lack of emotional fulfillment.

Clinical evidence for the Sisyphus syndrome abounds. For several years, various researchers have been developing the concept of 'job strain,' defined as high psychological demands and low decision latitude on the job. The concept of job strain captures the 'joyless striving' of the Sisyphus myth. Cornell researchers Peter L. Schnall and Robert Karasek and their colleagues have demonstrated that job strain is not just psychological. It is associated with increased diastolic blood pressure while at work, as well as an increase in the mass of the heart's main pumping chamber, the left ventricle.

Not surprisingly, therefore, people who work in jobs with a great deal of job strain have a higher incidence of myocardial infarction. These jobs, again, are positions that are typified by high psychological demands and low decision latitude. Examples include waiters, office computer operators, gas station attendants, firemen, mail workers, freight handlers, and certain assembly line workers.

However, in a recent study at Duke University Medical Center of mostly white-collar workers undergoing coronary angiography, job strain was not correlated with the prevalence of coronary artery disease. The reasons for this discrepancy with previous studies are unclear. Would the outcome of the study have been different if more blue-collar workers were included? Are Americans getting better at coping with job strain?

John Henryism

Sherman A. James, an epidemiologist at the University of Michigan-Ann Arbor, has described *John Henryism* – a personality pattern that is particularly susceptible to the effects of high job strain. John Henry is the hero of an American folk song who tried to out-perform a steam-powered drill tunneling through a mountain, using only a hammer and a hand-held tool. His heroic effort proved fatal – he fell dead upon completion of his task.

According to James, John Henryism means taking the difficult way out when faced with tough challenges. The John Henrys among us say things like, 'When things don't go the way I want them to, it just makes me work even harder' or 'Once I make up my mind to do something, I stay with it until the job is completely done.' People who respond this way are said to have an internal locus of control. They think they can control any situation if they work hard enough.

This response appeals to people who believe that effort is always rewarded and that one can always pull oneself up by one's boot-straps. This is a valuable strategy if you live in a segment of society in which effort is rewarded. 'But in the world inhabited by people born into poverty, with limited educational or occupational opportunities, where prejudice and racism reign, it can be a disaster to be a John Henry – to decide that those insurmountable odds could have been surmounted if only you had worked even harder.' Sometimes the mountain cannot be moved, no matter how hard one tries.

John Henryism often involves an intense sense of isolation and alienation that has been experienced by millions of workers – being cut off from the future and the rest of society by advances in technology. John Henry could not adapt. He held on to hand tools and muscle, and was trampled in the process.

The John Henrys among us, like the Sisyphuses, pay with their hearts. Could this be one reason that high blood pressure is a major problem in African-Americans? Stress researcher Robert M. Sapolsky says, 'The cardiovascular risks of John Henryism are most severe among the people who most resemble the mythical John Henry himself, working-class African-Americans.'

The Paradox of Privacy

Workers are discovering they must cope with the growing practice of having their performance 'electronically monitored' by supervisors – a polite term that to many employees means spying and snooping. Managers are learning that employees require trust and confidence to do their best and that these qualities can be seriously eroded by policing workers with invisible, silent technology.

We can have too little isolation as well as too much. Paradoxically, then, the modern workplace reveals the need for privacy as well as for social interaction. Isolation is not an altogether dirty word.

Disembodiment

One of the most pernicious forms of isolation in the modern workplace comes from being cut off from one's own body.

Before the age of automation, when many tasks were performed by hand, workers often wore their tools as extensions of their bodies. Tenner tells us that 'a scythe, for example, was custom-proportioned to the cultivator's body as a suit of clothes might be.'

Any manual tool, if properly designed and contoured, can be a joy to use. This is probably one reason why gardening remains one of the most popular hobbies in our culture. Fine gardening tools that fit the body are still available, from pruning shears to spades. I suspect this is why many gardeners have a sacred reverence for their tools and treat them as if they were alive.

Any skilled surgeon knows what it's like to *be* a tool. A neurosurgeon once told me that during surgery he *is* the tip of his scalpel. Anyone who really knows how to use a stethoscope knows what it's like to become the heart or lungs one is auscultating. I have known musicians who feel as if they become the strings and keys of the instruments they play. But most workers do not seem to relate to their tools in this way. How does one wear a computer? A calculator? A magnetoencephalograph?

Museum curator James R. Blackaby has pointed out that we have ceased to be tool *users* and have become tool *managers* by directing and controlling processes that take place rather than shaping them. I recently rediscovered the difference in using and managing tools when, in going through storage boxes I had not opened in years, I came across the slide rule I had used in college math courses. It is a dinosaur, having been exterminated in its head-on collision with the electronic calculator. My old slide rule beckoned and I picked it up, slid it back and forth, and multiplied two times two just for the fun of it. When the answer turned out to be four, I was actually surprised and elated. I felt I had genuinely participated in producing this result and that the outcome somehow depended on me. Not only was it fulfilling to get the right answer, but feeling the gorgeous instrument's perfect friction as I slid it back and forth was sensual as well. The whole experience felt magical. Although I am grateful for the blessings of electronic calculators, I realized, holding the slide rule, how we have become disembodied from our work, and for a brief moment I glimpsed what we have lost.

The Decline of 'Sneakernet'

How are bodies ignored in workplaces? In many automated work sites, as we've seen, walking and talking – the body's participation in work – is frowned on. The workstation has become an island of self-sufficiency, cutting off its inhabitants from contact with others. Taking time out to walk to a colleague's area and consult with him or her can be seen as goofing off at worst and as a lack of ingenuity at best; one should be able to handle all the duties through interacting with one's computer, not by chatting with coworkers.

The networked office of the 1990s has reduced the need for what has been called 'sneakernet' – trips to supply rooms, filing cabinets, printout racks, printers, fax machines, and other computers. Just as word processing eliminates the breaks that conventional typing requires, networked communications, especially document imaging, eliminates the walking from working. Each single instance of time or task saving may improve productivity in itself, yet taken together they can promote dangerous semi-immobility.

The situation has become Faustian. On one hand, office communications researchers are studying ways of reducing the necessity of walking to face-to-face meetings. On the other, ergonomists are trying to find ways to offset the problems of reduced motion.

The 'Barbarian Bed'

It is not just computers that isolate us in the modern office; office chairs do the same. They tether us to a single spot, like hobbles or a chain. It is not the chairs' fault, of course; they can isolate us or bring us together, depending on how we use them. Thoreau, describing his cabin at Walden Pond, said 'I had three chairs in my house: one for solitude, two for friendship, three for society.'

Chairs not only isolate us; they can injure us as well by causing chronic back pain or sciatica through poor design. Modern designers of office furniture seem to agree with the original Chinese term for the chair: barbarian bed.

The psychological effects of chairs can be immense and are not often considered. Chairs can be potent symbols of power in the office and boardroom. Tenner notes that from a mechanical standpoint, the high-backed, heavily upholstered 'executive' chairs, 'long on status but short on support for the lower back, still pass in some circles as badges of corporate eminence.'

The Body Fights Back

As modern work has become increasingly cerebral, the body has become increasingly isolated. We are discovering, however, that bodies do not tolerate being ignored. They are screaming to be noticed, as if they wanted once again to be given greater participation in work. They are being heard. As Tenner notes, 'Bodies were never noticed much in computing until they started to take revenge in the form of lost time, lawsuits, and workers' compensation claims.'

A great deal of attention is being paid to so-called cumulative trauma disorders involving the upper extremities, such as carpal tunnel syndrome, which are believed to be caused by repetitive motions required by modern computers. Almost always these are experienced by workers seated in chairs, which many experts believe play a key role. But repetitive strain injuries don't compare in frequency to back pain. There are forty times more back-pain cases among office workers than cumulative trauma disorders. Office workers have higher rates of back injury than longshoremen and truckers.

It is difficult to avoid the conclusion that the psyche is involved. In a study of low back pain in 31,200 employees at the Boeing Company in the Seattle-Tacoma area, there was no difference in incidence of low back pain and disability in white- and blue-collar workers. It did not matter whether the employee stood on an assembly line or sat at a desk. The best explanatory factor was job satisfaction, which had been assessed by supervisors using job ratings within the six months prior to the back problem.

The Nature of Work

When we participate in work we know is not worthwhile, we experience the most destructive form of isolation possible. Doing worthless work implies that *we* are worthless; and unless we have a sense of self-worth we feel like an outcast, cut off from the world of the living.

On his ninetieth birthday, W.E.B. Du Bois, the African-American historian and educator, wrote to his newborn great-grandson: 'The return from your work must be the satisfaction which that work brings you and the world's need of that work. With this, life is heaven, or as near heaven as you can get. Without this – with work which you despise, which bores you, and which the world does not need – this life is hell.'

How many workers doubt the value of the work they do? How many long for a job that contributes a sense of meaning, value, and purpose to their life, that affirms their worth as a person? How many suffer from the nagging concern that their work promotes mindless consumption or is environmentally destructive but do not know how to find work that is more fulfilling?

We *are* our work – for better or worse. 'Every man's work, whether it be literature or music or pictures or architecture or anything else, is always a portrait of himself,' Samuel Butler said. And if we cannot say that we actually love our work, something is wrong, and we will pay a price for the isolation resulting from the psychological and spiritual estrangement from our tasks. 'Work is love made possible,' the poet Kahlil Gibran said. 'And if you cannot work with love but only with distaste, it is better that you should leave your work and sit at the gate of the temple and take alms of those who work with joy.'

Isolation and Medicine

Why should work-related isolation concern health-care professionals? It has health consequences such as those resulting from the Sisyphus syndrome and John Henryism, as we've seen. Evidence increasingly suggests that communing with others is good for one's health. The richer one's social networks, the lower the incidence of illness and death from a variety of diseases. Even animals like to be touched, talked to, and fussed over. In one controlled study, which will be discussed later, rabbits who were held, touched, and petted were largely spared the development of atherosclerosis of their coronary arteries and aorta, even though they ate a diet high in fat.

These issues are also personally relevant to health-care professionals. One might think that the practice of medicine is immune from the effects of isolation and disembodiment because physicians perform interviews and do physical examinations, which require them to interact with and touch people. But physicians are caught up in the trend toward disembodiment, like modern workers in general. Taking a history is becoming increasingly automated. Some physicians have predicted that the physical exam may become a lost art, replaced by body scans and probes of various sorts. Even psychiatry, one of the last bastions of talking in medicine, is becoming transformed, as interpersonal counseling is being increasingly set aside in favor of drug management.

Where We Went Wrong

An increasing number of businesses and organizations are taking measures to counteract the isolation and lack of control experienced by the modern worker. These include the following:

- making work teams responsible for a variety of tasks
- introducing job sharing and flextime
- worker retraining
- adopting a less confrontational style of management
- giving workers more decision-making latitude

We can be grateful for these developments. But why did we create the problems in the first place? Some of them, after all, seem so obvious in retrospect. Why didn't we see them coming? As Tenner indicates, it is difficult to avoid the conclusion that we were taken in by our fantasies:

> The shift to automated monitoring, administration, and distribution in the modern office once seemed to promise a new age of more healthful and satisfying work. Within the workplace, the prophets of automation foresaw a golden age of human creativity – once electrical and electronic devices had successfully replaced drudgery. IBM's ... Thomas J. Watson's mantra [was] 'Machines should work. People should think.' ... In the 1950s, American notables [predicted that] ... by ... 1980 ... making a living would no longer be an issue.

Believing these prophecies required us to sell ourselves short. Experts in many fields assured us that human beings were nothing more than complex versions of the computers and gadgets that were expected to transform our lives. If isolation and disembodiment were not problems for mainframes and display terminals, neither were they concerns of ours. If computers didn't experience job strain, neither would we.

The Humanity of Humans, the Rattiness of Rats

Defining ourselves as entities who needed only to *think* in the workplace, as IBM's Watson urged, seemed so *modern*. But even as these predictions were being made, it was becoming apparent that something had been left out. For example, as psychologist Lawrence LeShan describes in *The Dilemma of Psychology*, on the eve of the electronic revolution, surveys were made of the prestigious *Journal of Comparative and Physiological Psychology* and its predecessors back to 1911. The surveyors concluded that psychology, as represented in this journal, 'had become the science of rat learning . . . The rat, representing less than .001 percent of all living creatures, was used in 58 percent of reported studies. The rest of the studies used primates (11 percent), cats (5.1 percent), humans (9 percent), and birds (5 percent). Other species reports were less than 1 percent each.'

With the decline of behaviorism, rats and nonsentient creatures began to lose their allure as models for understanding human behavior. Computers became increasingly attractive as replacements. They seemed to offer unlimited potential for understanding ourselves – the anatomy and physiology of the brain serving as the hardware, and 'consciousness' (whatever that was) as the software. Yet the computer-based models of human behavior shared a major feature with animal-based models – the certainty that feelings could be ignored.

LeShan questions the value of both animals and computers in understanding ourselves:

The academic psychologists, by and large, seem determined to have as little to do with real life as [they] possibly can. If they cannot substitute white rats for people, they will make a determined effort to substitute computers. One can legitimately ask what the rat and the computer are doing in the psychology laboratory – what either one has to do with the joys and pains of being human. As Arthur Koestler put it about two of the more prominent academic psychologists: 'Both [Watson and Skinner] are engaged in question-begging on an heroic scale, apparently driven by an almost fanatical urge to deny at all costs the humanity of the man and the rattiness of the rat.'

Although the computer is still cherished by many as the best model for understanding human mental function, particularly by researchers in the field of artificial intelligence, not everyone is convinced of its value. 'The computer is probably no better and no worse as a metaphor for the brain than earlier mechanical metaphors,' philosopher John Searle notes. 'We learn as much about the brain by saying it's a computer as we do by saying it's a telephone switchboard, a telegraph system, a water pump, or a steam engine.'

Workplaces Inner and Outer

Efficiency experts, ergonomic consultants, and time-motion gurus will never solve all the isolation-related problems we experience in the workplace. Their insights will always need to be supplemented by those of visionaries who have thought deeply about the nature of work, its role in human life, and our connections with each other.

In 'We Are Transmitters,' D. H. Lawrence offered one of the loveliest descriptions of work that I know of – work as life, flow, and giving.

> As we live, we are transmitters of life.
> And when we fail to transmit life, life fails to flow
>   through us.
>
> And if, as we work, we can transmit life into our work,
> life, still more life, rushes into us to compensate, to
> be ready and we ripple with life through the days.

Give, and it shall be given unto you
is still the truth about life . . .
It means kindling the life-quality where it was not,
even if it's only in the whiteness of a washed
   pocket-handkerchief.

In facing the problems posed by isolation, we should always recall that our primary workplace is not the job we go to for eight hours a day but our inner self, our psyche. This is where we craft our life, including the meanings and values that guide us. Too many of us project onto the outer work site the turmoil of our inner workplace. Even if all the failings of the modern work site were somehow remedied, our discomforts on the job will never be solved unless we lay to rest the isolation and estrangement we feel from the inside. Fulfillment on the job requires serenity within.

Joseph Campbell, the great mythologist, once spoke of the unpleasantness he experienced when going on vacation. The problem, he said, was that his work *was* his play. Setting aside his work on a vacation *prevented* pleasure instead of increasing it.

Anyone familiar with Campbell's work is aware of its sacred dimension. Can we imagine the possibility of restoring a sense of sacredness to our work? If so, we might understand why the Benedictine order chose as their ancient motto, '*Orare est laborare, laborare est orare*' – 'To pray is to work, to work is to pray.'

Is our age too cynical to take seriously the possibility of the transformation of labor? The hope remains, I believe, that if we can be healed from the inside, work can be transformed on the outside – but only then. Robert Frost spoke of this possibility in 'Two Tramps in Mud Time':

But yield who will to their separation.
My object in living is to unite
My avocation with my vocation
As my two eyes make one in sight.

4

The Eating-Papers

IN 1992 I WAS INVITED to give a lecture at a magnificent health resort in Baja California, along with my wife, Barbara; Dr Jeanne Achterberg, senior editor of *Alternative Therapies*; and Dr Frank Lawlis of the *Alternative Therapies* advisory board. The setting was majestic: mountains, high desert, and turquoise skies. One night, while I was presenting my lecture, I began to feel sick. Feverish and faint, I had to struggle during the final moments of my talk to remain on my feet. Even though I felt horrible, I recall being amused by the irony that I, the visiting physican-expert, had become ill while lecturing on health. Was this a cosmic lesson in humility? With Barbie's help I managed to walk to my room and collapse. Within minutes I was shaken by the severest chills I have ever experienced, and I had a high fever. I knew I might be septic and that I should consider emergency medical treatment. But for reasons I will explain later, I chose to remain where I was.

My wife is one of the most gifted holistic nurses I have ever known, so I felt in good hands. She also alerted Jeanne and Frank of my illness, and my friends made a house call. I could not have had better attendants. I know that Jeanne and Frank are healers, because every time I'm in their presence I come away feeling better, which is the best criterion I know. Frank, moreover, is a born shaman who is as much at home with a drum and rattle as in a consulting office. In fact, his Santa Fe office resembles a shaman's lair, with masks and rattles, feathers and fur, totems and fetishes – and a few unidentifiable items – everywhere.

Shivering with bone-shaking chills, I asked Frank to assist me by writing some words on a small piece of paper that might aid in my healing – whatever he considered appropriate. My only stipulation was that he not tell me what he wrote. Frank beamed – a shaman up to a challenge. When he finished, I asked him to fold the paper as compactly as possible so I could not read it. Then I asked Barbie for a glass of water and swallowed the paper, which was the size of a large capsule. Now, as confident as if I were hospitalized in the world's finest intensive care unit, I lay back, closed my eyes, and drifted into unconsciousness.

For three days and nights I felt as if I might die – semidelirious, febrile, in and out of consciousness, too weak to talk. Barbie discovered the next day that several people had come down with a similar illness. Some were so sick they required evacuation back to the United States for emergency medical care. Stubbornly, I chose to remain where I was with no treatment except for forcing fluids – and the paper I had eaten. Then I gradually began to recover, although I was not back to normal for weeks following our return home.

Frank stayed in close contact. At first he was disappointed in the paper he had prepared for me. But I suggested that, because I didn't die, the therapy may have been lifesaving. In fact, if the paper had been a drug, we might be singing its praises for snatching me from the jaws of death.

In choosing to ingest words scribbled on paper, I had not dreamed up a new therapy. I was invoking an ancient healing custom I'd learned about from Jeanne in a book she had previously loaned me: *The Diary of a Napoleonic Footsoldier*, by Jakob Walter, of whom more below.

Eating-Papers: Historical Examples

Napoleon Bonaparte invaded Russia on June 22, 1812, after conquering all of Europe between Paris, Hamburg, and Rome. As Louis Leo Snyder recounts in *Great Turning Points in History*, Napoleon's strategy was simple: achieve control of the East, thereby forcing the capitulation of the English. But for various reasons – disease, the deadly Russian winter, incompetence and nepotism in the chain of command, insubordination and failure of morale, problems of supply, and the stubborn Russian resistance – Napoleon was routed. By December 18 he was back in Paris, cursing 'the Russian colossus' and denouncing Russia as the enemy of all Europe as he rode through the Arc de Triomphe in humiliation.

Jakob Walter was a foot soldier in Napoleon's Grande Armée, which had once made Europe tremble. But as 1812 ended, the army was in such disarray that in a military sense it had ceased to exist. Most of Walter's six hundred thousand fellow soldiers were frozen corpses strewn across the Russian steppes. One of the greatest catastrophes took place as the retreating French army attempted to cross the Berezina River. As the Russians closed in for the kill, the French soldiers hastily tried to construct bridges. The crossing was made in panic and thousands were drowned in the icy waters or were trampled underfoot. In *War and Peace*, Tolstoy compared the plight of Napoleon's remnant to that of a wounded beast 'that feels its death at hand, and knows not what it is doing. Very often the wounded creature, hearing a stir, rushes to meet the hunter's shot, runs forward and back again, and itself hastens its own end.'

Wairy Louis Constant, Napoleon's valet, wrote in his memoirs that after the Berezina crossing the weather became so cold that birds were found on the ground frozen stiff. Soldiers seated themselves with their heads in their hands and their bodies bent forward to try to relieve the pain of hunger, and were often found dead in that position by morning. The vapor of the breath froze on eyebrows, and icicles grew on beards and mustaches. Frozen soldiers who could not feel pain burned themselves at bivouac fires trying to melt the ice on their bodies and clothes. Artillerymen, seeking warmth, held their hands to the noses of horses.

Toward the end of this headlong flight, Jakob Walter became seriously ill with chills and fever, which 'shook me frightfully,' he later wrote. He was so weak he could not carry his weapons and left them behind. Better than any other measure, this reveals how desperately ill Walter was. Becoming separated from one's weapons is one of the most dreaded fates that can befall a soldier, and all warriors will do anything to prevent such a thing from happening.

Unable to continue, Walter and two of his comrades, who also had the fever 'at its worst stage,' took refuge in a tavern. Walter gave this account of their recovery:

> The next day a citizen of the town came to the inn . . . and asked what ailed us three . . . We answered him that each of us had the fever. 'The fever?' said he. 'I can help you get rid of that.' This he really did, sitting down, writing three notes, and saying that each of us should now eat one of them. I, at least, had little faith that such a thing could help. Nevertheless, I ate mine, too; and when the time came for me to be shaken frightfully again, I waited longer and longer, and actually the fever left not only me but also my other two comrades at the same time. This seemed miraculous and delightful to all of us, and we thanked this good man, without whom certainly none of us would have escaped death.

The Dead Man's March

A related event involved one of the most barren areas in the American Southwest: the Jornada del Muerto, or the Dead Man's March, a roughly one hundred-mile stretch of desert in the Socorro and Sierra counties of central New Mexico. This area is so remote and forbidding that the United States government chose it for the location of Trinity Site, where the first atomic bomb was detonated. Here the mountains force the Rio Grande to turn west and land travelers to go east. Crossings of this waterless stretch have always been extremely hazardous.

Historian and novelist Paul Horgan, in his Pulitzer Prize-winning book *Great River: The Rio Grande in North American History*, describes how the custom of eating words on paper – Jakob Walter's cure – was responsible for how this region got its name.

In the 1600s the Spanish struggled to maintain a colonial presence amid the native Pueblo tribes whose beliefs they did not understand. Their bastion was Santa Fe, founded in 1610 along a creek that flows into the Rio Grande a few miles away. For many years Santa Fe was a mere collection of clay houses surrounding a small plaza – the only Spanish town in this immense area other than the tiny outpost at El Paso.

Although their Catholic beliefs compelled them to adopt an official horror toward the superstitions of the Pueblo tribes, the Spanish settlers were fascinated by them as well. As a result, Horgan states, 'In Santa Fe private sorceries ate away at the edges of society, and scared people, and made them gossip and doubt.' For example, when Indians worked as house servants, they brought their occult beliefs along with them. Spanish women would implore the Indians to provide love potions and herbs to ensure success, the recovery of lost articles, and magical protection.

On one occasion a young Spaniard was admitted to a native kiva, an underground ceremonial chamber. There the young man deliberately pricked himself with an awl, without any bleeding or pain. This marvelous feat was observed by a young boy who accompanied him and who reported it to a Spanish official. Again, on another occasion, in the presence of the boy and two women, the young man stabbed himself with a dagger and a knife without creating wounds. The Catholic settlers were horrified by these events and believed they indicated that demons or witches were in their midst. An explanation was demanded. The young man explained how, at mass one day, a German trader from Sonora who had come up with the supply trains had joined him in the choir loft and had written something on some slips of paper. The German explained that if the young man ate them they would make him invulnerable for twenty-four hours. He swallowed one of them at once and found that he then could not injure himself with a blade. The young man revealed that the papers he ingested read '+A.B.V.A. + A.D.A.V.+.'

The terrified Spanish official alerted the Catholic prelate at nearby Santo Domingo pueblo. The prelate denounced the German, who was arrested, tried, and imprisoned. Months later he escaped with the aid of an Indian and fled south on the road that ran alongside the Rio Grande. Five soldiers were sent to capture him and his accomplice. Near the spring of El Perillo in the long desert passage that veered east of the river and the mountains, the soldiers found a pair of blue trousers and a blue doublet lined with otter fur. Nearby they found human hair and bones gnawed by animals, all of which the soldiers identified as those of the 'German witch,' who they supposed was killed by the Indian traveling with him. So they named the desert passage after the ill-fated German: Jornada del Muerto, the Dead Man's March.

Eating Your Words: Esszettel

The experiences of Jakob Walter and the German trader in colonial New Mexico reflect a custom whose origins are lost in history – the eating of prayers, Bible verses, or magic formulas written on different media, such as slips of paper, fruit, bread, or the consecrated wafer of the Eucharist. In German the slips of paper are called *Esszettel* ('eating-papers') or *Essbilder* ('eating-pictures' or 'eating-images'). Sometimes the letters so inscribed were washed and the water drunk, which was said to accomplish the same purpose: the conveying of the power of the letters or words. This was not merely a pagan custom but often a blending of folk and Christian beliefs, as when a cross was cut in the surface of a loaf of bread before it was baked and eaten. These practices were widespread, appearing in France, Italy, Germany, and Russia.

According to a belief from Holstein, people sick with fever would write the following inscription on a slip of paper and eat it: 'Fever stay away. [The individual's name] is not at home.' A report dating to 1452 describes how people would write on apples, lead, or other substances and give them to others to eat or wear around their neck. Sometimes prescriptions would be written on buttered bread with a quill that had been dipped upside down in ink. The bread would then be given to the sick person on three consecutive Fridays after sunrise and before sunset. In Saxony the buttered bread was given within twenty-four hours to anyone bitten by a mad dog. A treatment for epilepsy required writing a magic formula on paper with a needle with which one had sewn something for a dead person, then warming the paper over milk steam and giving it to the epileptic child on buttered bread to eat. A treatment for fever involved eating three almonds inscribed with certain characters. Another therapy involved cutting a gingerbread into three-inch-square pieces, inscribing each piece appropriately, and feeding them to the sick person.

Eating-papers were not limited to humans. Papers with magic

formulas were also fed to mad dogs (getting a rabid animal to eat paper without the dog's biting the feeder must have been challenging) and to other animals to prevent infertility. They were also fed to animals to prevent rabies, which must have been one of the earliest forms of immunization.

Before dismissing these beliefs as superstitions we've outgrown in our steady march to enlightenment, we should look deeper. When we permit our children to eat animal crackers or cookies baked in the form of beasts, are we yielding to similar urges that have receded into our unconscious mind? When we bake gingerbread men, inscribe and decorate them, and then consume them limb by limb, are we hearkening to the old drives?

Also, the medications we 'eat' resemble the eating-papers of old. Pharmaceutical companies inscribe their tablets and capsules with numbers, names, and elaborate symbols. They may not regard these as magical formulas, but the inscriptions nevertheless make a difference in potency. Aspirin tablets made by Bayer, scored with the famous 'Bayer cross,' have a more powerful effect than plain generic aspirin tablets of the same strength.

Color matters, too. In one study, medical students were given either blue or pink placebo capsules, with the suggestion in both cases that they were either sedatives or stimulants. Students who ingested the blue placebos were twice as likely to experience drowsiness, compared with those who received the pink ones, even though both were 'dummy' pills with no known effect.

The timeworn explanation for the effects of the eating-papers is the placebo response – the power of positive thinking, suggestion, and expectation. However, before attributing all the effects of the eating-papers to the mind, we should ponder other reasons for their being therapeutic. One can imagine several materialistic hypotheses. The carbon in the ink may have acted as an adsorbent to bind noxious substances in the gastrointestinal tract, similar to the action of charcoal, which today is prescribed for this purpose. The paper or bread on which words were written could have been moldy with microbes having antibacterial activity. Who knows what substances with medicinal value may have been carried into the body of someone eating papers in ancient times?

Or – and here is the possibility that fascinates me – the eating papers might have served as a vehicle or intermediary device for the empathic intentions, thoughts, wishes, or prayers of the person administering them – what has traditionally been called psychic or spiritual healing.

Intermediary Objects and Healing

It's easy to dismiss our ancestors' beliefs in the power of words on paper to bring about healing, but the truth is that modern physicians also write words on paper. These are called prescriptions, and many are for worthless or even harmful medications. Like eating-papers bearing magical symbols, prescriptions have their own special inscription: 'Rx,' an old Latin symbol for 'recipe.'

Do our modern *Esszettel* have something in common with the magic formulas scribbled on paper in medieval Europe? I propose that both of them may function as a legitimizing factor for the intentions of the person administering them, whether the prescriber is a medieval folk healer, a shaman, or a modern, white-coated physician, and whether the intention is called a thought, a wish, or a prayer. Whether an eating-paper or a modern prescription, the object may serve as a go-between that makes healing possible.

Almost all healers use some sort of intermediary agent to symbolize and access their power. We physicians are drowning in them. They range from white coats, stethoscopes, a mystifying vocabulary, and computed tomographic (CT) scanners to thousands of pills and surgical procedures. We generally deny that symbolic objects possess any real power of their own. Yet I wonder . . .

Consider the experience of a teenage patient of mine I'll call David. Ten years ago he was involved in an automobile accident that resulted in a fracture of his neck with injury to his spinal cord. The fracture was between the second and third cervical vertebrae, high up in the neck, a site that is usually fatal. The neurologist caring for him was so convinced David would die that he withdrew orders for an MRI. He placed him in tongs – a device inserted into each side of his skull, with which traction could be applied in an attempt to prevent further damage to his spinal cord – put him on a respirator, inserted a feeding tube, and sent him to the intensive care unit so his family could have one final visit before he died.

The family was told that David would probably not survive the night. He could not swallow, could not breathe on his own, and had no feeling or movement from the neck down. The physician explained that David had only a slim thread of spinal cord tissue not completely severed and that he should not even have survived the trip to the hospital and the emergency treatment. The doctor asked the family to pray for a miracle but quickly added that he'd never seen one.

David did not die as predicted, so a tracheostomy was done. Although there was no improvement, he remained alert and tried to talk. David's family tried to read his lips, but he became angry when he was unable to get his words across. He hated the ventilator, and his primary wish was to get off it.

David's family belonged to a Christian religious group that believed strongly in healing. According to their beliefs, healing could be transferred to the person in need by anointing a physical object with healing power, then placing it in contact with the needy individual. This was often done by a group of believers passing around a piece of cloth, each person holding it in his or her hands and saying a prayer for healing, then placing the cloth on the individual's body where healing was needed. David's church congregation anointed a prayer cloth for him, and his dad brought it to the hospital and tied it around his upper left arm.

David would not allow the hospital personnel to remove the cloth. Even when it became soiled he refused to let it be washed, fearing the healing power would be neutralized.

In addition, David requested special prayers for his breathing. His family had another cloth anointed by the church group, and it was pinned over David's chest.

David slowly improved. Ten years following his accident he breathes without a respirator and eats a normal diet. He can transfer from his electric chair without help and can take a few steps with a cane and some assistance with his balance. He has learned to operate a specially equipped van and attends college alone.

Although David's neurologist continues not to believe in miracles, he has no explanation for David's survival and improvement.

Another case involving an intermediary object is that of eighteen-year-old Tim, who was hospitalized with severe chest injuries following an auto accident. His pulmonary status deteriorated and he developed acute respiratory distress syndrome. Tim was eventually intubated and placed on a respirator. Unable to talk, he wrote the name 'Willie' for his mother. She knew immediately this meant Willie Nelson, Tim's favorite country-and-western singer. His mom immediately brought his Willie Nelson tape collection and a cassette player to his bedside, along with two red bandanas, Willie Nelson's trademark. Tim had his mom tie one bandana around his head and another across the palm of his right hand. He was deeply attached to the objects and would not allow them to be removed, even when his clinical condition began to worsen. Just before he died he raised his hand with the red bandana and gave his dad a 'high five,' a gesture that had special meaning between them. His parents realized that this was Tim's signal that everything was okay and that they should let him go.

These cases are not rare. Anyone working in ICUs knows that families are always bringing objects to the bedside that have special significance for patients – stuffed animals, photos, crucifixes, and so on. The examples above illustrate different ways of employing such objects: deliberately attempting to infuse the object with special power, as in the case of the prayer cloth, and allowing the object to function symbolically, as with the red bandanas.

Experiments with Intermediary Objects

Some of the most ingenious experiments exploring the role of intermediary objects in healing have been undertaken by Bernard Grad at McGill University in Montreal.

In one experiment Grad investigated whether mental depression might produce a negative effect on the growth of plants. This idea fits with the common belief that some people have green thumbs and that one's thoughts and emotional states may play a role in how vigorously plants respond. Grad theorized that if plants were watered with water that had been held by depressed people, they would grow more slowly than if watered with water held by people in an upbeat mood. A controlled experiment was devised using a man known to have a green thumb and two patients in a psychiatric hospital – a woman with a depressive neurosis and a man with a psychotic depression.

Each person held a sealed bottle between his or her hands for thirty minutes. Then the solution was used to water barley seeds. The green-thumbed man was in a confident, positive mood at the time he held his solution, and his seeds grew faster than did those of the others or the controls. Unexpectedly, the normally depressed, neurotic woman responded to the experiment with a brighter mood, asking relevant questions and showing great interest. She cradled her bottle of water in her lap as a mother might hold a child. Her seeds also grew faster than did those of the controls. The man with the psychotic depression was agitated and depressed at the time he held his solution; his seeds grew slower than did those of the controls. Grad's study suggests that emotions may influence healing both positively and negatively and that physical objects may mediate these influences.

Grad performed a similar experiment, this time with a healer. Barley seeds were damaged by watering them with a one percent saline solution. First the healer held in his hands the beaker of saline with which the seeds in the experimental group were to be watered, in an attempt to mitigate the retardant effect of the saline. He did not similarly 'treat' the saline used to water the control seeds. The experiment was repeated three times with similar results: seeds watered with the 'treated' saline germinated and grew better than did those watered with untreated saline. This study strongly suggests that healing intention may somehow be mediated through a secondary vehicle or agent.

In another experiment, Grad studied mice in whom goiters had been produced by withholding iodine from their diet and giving them thiouracil. The rate of thyroid growth was measured by weighing the thyroids of the mice after they had been sacrificed. Seventy mice were divided into three groups: (1) a baseline-control group, which received no treatment; (2) a healer-treated group, which was held in special boxes by a healer for fifteen minutes twice daily for five days a week and once on Saturdays; and (3) a heat-control group, which was kept in cages heated to the same temperature and for the same length of time as the 'held' group. The thyroids of the healer-treated group of mice grew significantly more slowly than did those of both the controls.

In a variation of this experiment, Grad divided thirty-seven mice on a goiter-producing diet into treatment and control groups. This time the healing was given via an intermediary object: wool and cotton held in the hands of the healer for fifteen minutes, once the first day and twice for the next twenty-four days of the study. Ten grams of 'treated' cotton and wool were placed in each cage of the treatment group, containing four or five mice each, for one hour, morning and evening, six days a week, while control mice were exposed in their cages to cotton and wool not treated by the healer. Mice in contact with the healer-held intermediate substance developed goiters significantly more slowly than did control mice.

The Grad studies are well-designed experiments worthy of the attention of anyone interested in the role of mental intentionality, prayer, and intermediate objects in healing. They do not stand alone. Approximately 150 studies in 'healing,' in which an individual attempts to deliver a healing influence to a distant biological system, have appeared to date. In roughly half to two-thirds of these experiments, a statistically positive result has been seen. These outcomes are not explainable by known physical mechanisms and therefore pose great challenges (and great opportunities) to our understanding of the role of consciousness in the world, as will be discussed later in the chapter 'The Return of Prayer.' In Grad's words:

> Although little can be said about the nature of the force that is producing the biological effects . . . or the mechanism whereby it acts, the experiments on wound healing [not described here] and plant growth have demonstrated that the so-called 'laying on of hands,' at least when done by certain individuals, has objective demonstrable effects which, because it was done on animals and on saline poured over plants, can hardly be explained as being due to the power of suggestion . . . Moreover, the fact that the phenomenon was observed in animals as high in the evolutionary scale as mice and in organisms as low in the scale as barley seeds points to the fundamental nature of whatever it is that is producing the effect . . . [These] phenomena as revealed in these experiments throw new light on the basic unity of man, animal, and plant.

Although they may believe in prayer, many people would never use a physical carrier or vehicle for their prayers such as a prayer cloth or holy water, because they consider these customs quaint and archaic. But a vehicle is present whether they realize it or not, as a consequence of the nature of intercessory prayer. *Intercessory* comes from words meaning to 'go between.' When people pray for others, *they themselves* are the intermediary object – the go-between – linking the object of their prayer with what they consider to be the benevolent power of a Supreme Being.

'As Regards Hospitals'

Returning to my own experience with an intermediary object during my illness – an eating-paper – I pondered for a long time afterward why I elected not to go to a modern hospital. It is a decision I do not advocate. In fact, if a patient of mine were suffering a similar problem, I would have hospitalized her in a heartbeat. At the time, however, I did not doubt my decision for a moment.

In her research on the life of Florence Nightingale, my wife recently unearthed a fascinating paper of Nightingale's called 'Note on the Aboriginal Races of Australia,' which was read in England in 1864 to the annual meeting of the National Association for the Promotion of Social Sciences. The paper perfectly described my attitude during my illness. Nightingale quotes Dr Hale, the Bishop of Perth, as follows:

> As regards hospitals, I am sorry to say that it is so impossible to keep the poor natives . . . under any kind of restraint when they are sick – they so completely set at defiance all rules and regulations – that anything like regular hospital treatment is quite out of the question in their case . . . Their unmanage-ableness in illness arises from a deeper feeling than that of mere restlessness . . . They are constantly haunted by the idea that they would be better almost anywhere else than where they are.

Nightingale observed that Australian natives would often escape from hospitals, 'yet that dying native,' Bishop Salvado of Port Victoria reported to her, 'a few weeks afterward, when every one that knew him believed him to be dead and buried, is as strong and healthy as ever, having travelled perhaps fifty or more miles on foot.'

I wasn't actually fleeing from a hospital during my illness, but like the natives in Nightingale's report, I didn't want to be confined to one. This was not a frivolous decision; as an internist I realized the gravity of my situation and was willing to put my life on the line in support of my choice.

This experience brought me face-to-face with the ambivalence I feel toward my own profession. I'm not alone; thousands of physicians in America currently feel likewise. An example is Judith J. Petry, M.D., F.A.C.S., who abandoned her career as a surgeon and is now medical director of the Vermont Healing Tools Project in Brattleboro, Vermont, as well as a consultant in complementary and alternative medicine in Westminster, Vermont. 'I am often asked why I left the practice of surgery,' she noted in a presentation during the third annual *Alternative Therapies* symposium, in 1998.

My answer has always been that my practice no longer harmonized with my beliefs. I felt that I was unable to function on all levels of my being. Surprisingly, the only people who didn't seem to understand this were surgeons. My medical colleagues, friends, and even strangers shook their heads knowingly and understood immediately how impossible it must have been to remain healthy while practicing surgery. Many offered examples of their own or shared a family's experiences with surgery, and most of these stories ranged from disturbing to horrific.

Dr Petry eloquently summarizes the attitude of an increasing number of physicians, evoking feelings that help to explain why millions of people are drawn to alternative medicine. In 'Why Patients Use Alternative Medicine: Results of a National Study,' in the *Journal of the American Medical Association*, Stanford University School of Medicine researcher John A. Astin points to the *spiritual* reasons behind the choices people make in medical care:

Users of alternative health care are more likely to report having had a transformational experience that changed the way they saw the world[, lending] partial support to the hypothesis that involvement with alternative medicine may be reflective of shifting cultural paradigms regarding beliefs about the nature of life, spirituality, and the world in general . . . A subset of individuals may be attracted to these nontraditional therapies because they find in them an acknowledgment of the importance of treating illness within a larger context of spirituality and life meaning . . .

Results from the present study lend support to the notion that for many individuals, the use of alternative health care is part of a broader value orientation and set of cultural beliefs, one that embraces a holistic, spiritual orientation to life.

My choice to rely solely on an unorthodox approach to getting well is not typical of the way most people use alternative medicine. 'The vast majority of individuals appear to use alternative therapies in conjunction with, rather than instead of, more conventional treatment,' Astin emphasizes. I might have, too, if they had been available; a complementary approach is the one I advocate and almost always employ in my own life.

Food as a Vehicle for the Divine and Demonic

Eating-papers are a way for *good* influences to be introduced into the body. This is hardly a radical idea when compared to one of the most prevalent customs within Christianity: the Eucharist, or Holy Communion, in which consecrated food is believed to be actually transformed into Jesus' body as it is eaten.

Can *evil* also enter the body via the things we ingest? Biblical teachings suggest that the answer is yes. After Jesus told his twelve disciples that one of them would betray him, he gave a piece of bread to Judas. When Judas ate it, Satan entered into him and he immediately went out and arranged for Jesus' betrayal. The practice of blessing food prior to eating it may be related to the fear that food can be a vehicle for introducing demons into the body.

The possibility that a spirit can enter the body via food or drink was taken seriously in medieval Europe and influenced the use of love charms. Here is an example, related by Harvard theologian Morton Smith in *Jesus the Magician*: 'Spell said to the cup. Say seven [times], "you are wine; you are not wine but the head of Athena. You are wine; you are not wine but the entrails of Osiris, the entrails of Iao Pakerbeth, Eternal sun . . . As soon as you go down in to the entrails of [named person] let her love me for the whole time of her life."'

Eating and Attitude

It is always difficult to distinguish the effects of ingested substances from those of the imagination. This was dramatically illustrated in a workshop on shamanism conducted by anthropologist Michael Harner, Ph.D., in which my wife and I were enrolled. Dr Harner and all the participants were seated in a circle. Without a word of explanation, Dr Harner produced a brown paper sack from which he took a gnarled, dried root, yanked off a piece, and chewed and swallowed it. Then, with great ceremony he said, 'You do not have to participate!' and passed the substance around the circle. No one declined, of course. 'Now go outside,' Dr Harner instructed. 'Pay particular attention to leaves on trees, blades of grass, and clouds. We'll meet back in an hour and share our experiences.' By the time the group reconvened, everyone was in an altered state of consciousness. Some people were having glorious visions. Eventually someone asked, 'Dr Harner, what *was* that stuff?' 'You've probably got some in your kitchen at home,' he replied. 'It's ginger-root – a great spice, but not a hallucinogen.'

With a simple demonstration, Dr Harner had driven home his point: it's often the eater, not what's eaten, that matters most.

Nutritional Anomalies

The lore surrounding intermediary objects, as well as Grad's controlled experiments with them, suggests that our thoughts can modify the effects of physical substances, which can then act on the body. Does this include the action of the foods we eat?

Today nutrition scientists largely consider the human body to be a 'black box' we stuff with certain items. These items are then acted on by chemical processes that are the same for everyone, before being excreted. This approach embodies the maxim of Leonardo da Vinci: 'Man and the animals are merely a passage and channel for food.' The trick is to discover what should be put in the box.

Modern nutrition has largely become the search for a formula that can be generalized to the greatest number of people possible. This approach was firmly in place by the mid-twentieth century, the heyday of minimum daily requirements, which people came to believe were handed down from God. According to thinking, all human beings have essentially the same nutritional require-ments for a given age group and sex.

But everywhere we look we see suggestions that an ideal nutri-tional formula does not exist. Consider, for example, Thomas Alva Edison, one of the most wildly creative geniuses our society ever produced. Edison's diet was wretched. For many years his only foods were milk and an occasional glass of orange juice. He did not believe in exercise, chewed tobacco continuously, and smoked several cigars a day. Yet despite ulcers, diabetes, and Bright's disease, Edison's achievements continued to the end of his life. It is possible to argue, of course, that if Edison had eaten properly he would have been healthier and even more creative. But if what we eat is as critical to mental function as we are often led to believe, Edison's miserable dietary habits should have doomed him to the life of a dullard.

René Dubos (1901–1982), the microbiologist, ecologist, and philosopher, was one of the best-known scientists of the twentieth century. Dubos was fascinated by a profound nutritional anomaly – the huge variation of nutrients on which humans can subsist and thrive. He promoted the idea of nutritional individuality – that one's nutritional requirements were woven into the web of one's life, making wholesale formulas risky. 'Voltaire was a midget compared with Washington,' he noted,

but outlived him by seventeen years and was at least as influ-ential on the course of history. The small prewar Japanese could not play basketball with Americans; nevertheless, they were excellent soldiers and proved immensely successful in the tech-nological and economic world of the postwar period. The new generation of richly fed Japanese is much taller than the preceding one but we do not know that its members will live longer or be happier. A good, abundant nutritional regimen will keep us alive, make us grow to a certain size, and protect us from deficiency diseases, but beyond that, we really do not know much about its effects on our bodies, our society, and the future of civilization.

Dubos did not deny that gross nutritional generalizations could be made, but he insisted also that human individuality must always be taken into account. To illustrate, he described two famous physicians he knew during his early career at the Rockefeller Institute for Medical Research. One was Henry William Welch, one of the greatest architects of medical and public health sciences in the United States in the twentieth century. The other was Oswald T. Avery, famous for his research in infectious diseases and for having first proved that DNA is the carrier of hereditary characteristics. Welch and Avery were the same height, had been educated similarly in college and medical school, spent most of their lives in academic medicine, remained bachelors, smoked a lot, almost never exercised, and were tireless talkers. But in nutritional behavior they were miles apart.

Welch enjoyed rich food and had a gargantuan appetite. He preferred sumptuous, well-seasoned foods, was inordinately fond of sweets, and was prone to end his meal with several helpings of ice cream (which meant real cream in those days). He adored wine and hard liquor. He was proud that his most violent form of exercise was taking off his shoes at night and putting them on in the morning. He became obese early in life, was fun-loving, and remained intellectually active right up to the end of his life. He died of cancer at the age of eighty-five.

Avery, by contrast, ate sparingly. His ideal meal was two slices of toast, a few leaves of lettuce, and several cups of coffee. 'We used to say that he could be in nutritional balance only by fixing atmospheric nitrogen,' Dubos writes. During the thirty years Dubos knew him, Avery's weight never exceeded ninety pounds, yet he was constantly active in laboratory work and scientific debates. He suffered from mild hyperthyroidism, which took a more active form during a period of disappointment in his research program. Following surgery and a few months of rest, he returned to the lab and resumed his work. He died of cancer in his seventy-ninth year. Dubos notes:

> As far as I know, no nutritional studies were carried out on Welch or Avery. One can take it for granted that genetic differences played a role in their contrasting attitudes toward food intake and responses to it, but one can also assume that their nutritional habits and their metabolism were profoundly affected by other aspects of their life, and probably by their early experiences. It takes more than a knowledge of foodstuffs to create a science of human nutrition.

In a study of a large group of beggars in India, all of them were found to pursue a diet that had long been deficient in calories, iron, calcium, phosphorous, vitamins A, B, C, and D, and animal protein. To their astonishment, the researchers discovered that only 4 percent of the beggars showed obvious signs of nutritional deficiency, and radiographic studies showed most of them having a normally calcified skeleton. Among the female beggars, the diet had no markedly deleterious effect on either pregnancy or lactation, and the growth rate of children in the group was only slightly lower than normal.

How can humans tolerate such miserable dietary patterns? Dubos believed that chronic food shortage triggers processes in the body that enable an individual to adapt to poor nutritional intake. During the 1940s he participated in research in Guatemala. Although the nutritional status of Guatemalan villagers was rather miserable, and many children and young adults died of infection in childhood, Dubos writes that

> those who survived to adulthood, although of short stature and seemingly frail, were capable of far greater physical efforts than those expected of vigorous Europeans and North Americans, such as carrying heavy burdens on their backs over long distances up and down mountains. Physiological studies showed that they could maintain themselves on a diet that would have

meant starvation for most Europeans and especially for North Americans. Furthermore, these skinny people, grossly under-nourished according to our standards, commonly lived to a good old age.

I focus on these anomalies not to denounce nutritional science but to suggest that a physically based, formulaic approach that leaves no room for our emotional and spiritual life has no hope, in principle, of succeeding.

Lessons from Rabbits

The capacity for emotions to influence nutritional status appears deeply rooted in the animal world. A group of investigators from the Ohio State University School of Medicine were studying the effects of a diet high in fat and cholesterol in rabbits. At the end of a certain period the rabbits were killed and certain arteries in their bodies were examined for evidence of atherosclerosis. This process of cholesterol deposition forms obstructions and ulcera-tions in arteries, and in humans results in vascular diseases such as heart attacks and strokes.

The results of the study should have been rather predictable because it was known at the time from previous studies that this sort of diet would regularly cause flagrant atherosclerotic changes in the arterial system of rabbits. But when a certain group of the test rabbits demonstrated atherosclerotic changes that were 60 percent less than those of the overall group, the investigators were astonished.

No obvious explanation for this unexpected result was found. Finally, however, an unplanned and unexpected variable was discovered: the rabbits who were affected less severely were those fed and cared for by one particular investigator who, during the course of the experiment, regularly took the rabbits from their cages and petted, stroked, and talked to them.

Was this mere coincidence? Many bioscientists would have considered laughable the possibility that such rabbit-human inter-changes could play a role in atherosclerotic vascular disease and would have passed over this possibility. After all, atherosclerotic vascular disease is an *objective* affair rooted in molecular processes, and the war against it should be fought on the battleground of the cell, not the psyche – so molecular thinking goes.

To test this 'coincidence,' a controlled study was designed in which two groups of rabbits were again fed the same diet and were treated identically, except that one group was removed from their cages several times a day for petting and attention, each time by the same person. The results: the petted group once again demonstrated a 60 percent lower incidence of atherosclerosis.

Seeking to further reduce the possibility of coincidence, the Ohio State investigators repeated the study. The results were the same in all three experiments. Touching, petting, handling, and gentle talking emerged as a crucial determinant in the disease process that kills more Americans than any other.

Food as an Intermediary Object

The Ohio State rabbit study suggests that the effects of food can be modified by emotions. If we are in a relaxed, positive emotional state when we eat, do we, like the rabbits, respond to our food in a healthier fashion? Or if we are anxious about our food, is it more likely to harm us?

It is customary to say that our body, not the food we put in it, is in the driver's seat. But I wish to suggest an alternative possibility – that food may function as an intermediary object such as an eating-paper or prayer cloth that is imbued with power related to human wishes, prayers, intentions, and thoughts.

The belief that the nonhuman, physical world is sentient to some degree is ancient. (Sentience in the physical world will be discussed further in the chapter 'Reenchanting the World.') This concept is making a comeback as a result of the work of scholars such as David Ray Griffin, professor of philosophy and religion at the School of Theology at Claremont and Claremont Graduate School in California. In his book *Parapsychology, Philosophy, and Spirituality*, Griffin advocates panentheism (as opposed to pantheism), the idea that there is a gradation or spectrum of the divine element throughout the entire natural world. Nothing, Griffin suggests, is as 'dead' as we have supposed. Lyall Watson takes a similar stand in *The Nature of Things: The Secret Life of Inanimate Objects*: 'I am a biologist and as such was trained to distinguish the living from the non-living, to identify the parameters of life and to confine my attention to organic systems of a certain complexity . . . But . . . life, it seems, is not so easily defined. And "things," even those that are totally inorganic and undeniably inanimate, sometimes behave as though they are alive, on occasion even sentient.'

Watson believes that physical objects may take on our 'emotional fingerprints' and 'become charged by long and intimate contact with a living system . . . Just by giving them value, we may alter them and the way they interact with the rest of the world, in some subtle yet important ways.'

Does this include the food we eat?

Spiritual Anorexia

We no longer enjoy an intimate, friendly relationship with food. '[Our entire culture] has an eating disorder. We are more detached from our food than at any time in history,' says Joan Gussow, Ed.D., professor emeritus of nutrition and education at Teacher's College, Columbia University.

Our mistrust of food has become so profound that instead of blessing it before eating it we probably ought to de-hex it. Writing in *Psychology Today*, Paul Roberts states: 'The fact is, Americans worry about food – not whether we can get enough, but whether we are eating too much. Or whether what we eat is safe. Or whether it causes diseases, promotes brain longevity, has antioxidants, or too much fat, or not enough of the right fat. Or contributes to some environmental injustice. Or is a breeding ground for lethal microbes.'

Affluence is part of the problem. It has freed us to agonize over food and to obsess and negotiate with ourselves about what we can and can't have. 'We've managed to turn our feelings about making and eating food – one of our most basic, important, and meaningful pleasures – into ambivalence,' says Paul Rozin, professor of psychology at the University of Pennsylvania and a pioneer in the study of why we eat what we eat. Food has become so abundant, says Roberts, that 'we've become free to write our own culinary agendas – to eat for health, fashion, politics, or many other objectives – in effect, to use our food in ways that often have nothing to do with physiology or nutrition . . . [and to carry on] in ways that would have flabbergasted our ancestors. It's the gastronomic equivalent of too much time on our hands.'

Nutritional information also adds to our confusion and anxiety. For example, beginning in 1981, scientists touted the cholesterol-lowering effects of soluble fiber, especially oat bran. The mania over this particular food invaded my medical practice at Dallas Diagnostic Association. One of my dietary-conscious colleagues, who also liked to cook, began to bring oat bran muffins to our office so that we culinary heathens could be exposed to these nutritional blessings. Although we dutifully ate them, the gratitude he reaped was not uniform; one of my cynical colleagues dubbed them 'thud muffins,' a moniker that stuck.

But by 1990, after Americans had begun a love affair with oat bran, a Boston research team cast a cloud of doubt on its alleged benefits. Frank M. Sacks and his colleagues at the Harvard University School of Medicine and Brigham and Women's Hospital gave specially prepared 'supplements' in the form of muffins and entrées to twenty hospital employees. For six weeks, half the group received high-fiber supplements containing oat bran and the rest received similar foods in which low-fiber Cream of Wheat and white flour replaced the oat bran. After a two-week break, the groups' supplements were switched.

Neither diet affected blood pressure, and both diets lowered the mean serum cholesterol of the volunteers by 7 percent to 7.5 percent. No significant difference was found between the two diets in terms of cholesterol-lowering ability. Based on this limited study, the researchers concluded that 'oat bran has little inherent cholesterol-lowering action' in those with normal cholesterol levels, or apparently in those with elevated values. They suggested that people concerned about high cholesterol would be better served by increasing their intake of complex carbohydrates, 'whatever the fiber content.'

What is the effect of imbroglios like this on how we relate to our plate? What sort of 'emotional fingerprint' might our foods be absorbing from us as a result of the ambivalence they trigger?

Food Politics

Remember the good old days when we thought our choices about nutrition affected only ourselves? Now we are beginning to realize that our food choices affect not just our bodies but the earth itself. That's the message from a session called 'National Impacts of Recommended Dietary Changes' at an annual meeting of the American Association for the Advancement of Science. The participants reviewed not just the health consequences of a 'good' diet but also the beneficial effects on everything from land, water, fuel, and mineral use to the cost of living, employment rates, and the balance of international trade. Around 90 percent of our grains and legumes and 50 percent of our fish catch is fed to livestock. J. B. Penn of the United States Department of Agriculture described how a dietary shift from animal products to vegetables, grains, and fruits would involve some relocation and retraining of agricultural workers. The associated reduction in food costs would shift personal spending into other sectors of the economy. Meats, for example, are five to six times more expensive than foods containing an equal amount of vegetable protein, and eating animal foods adds about four thousand dollars a year to the average family's budget, including the costs of increased medical care.

The benefits from shifting away from animal products ripple endlessly. The lower demand for foreign oil, minerals, and farm machinery and the greater availability of legumes and grains for export would reduce our trade deficit, minimize our dependence on foreign energy suppliers, and strengthen the value of the dollar abroad. So, to our *fear* of food we can now add *guilt* – guilt about harming not just ourselves by our food choices but also our planet. No one knows how fear and guilt affect how we metabolize our food, but we can probably take for granted that they don't help.

Guilt has played a role in nutrition for a very long time. For generations the mantra of moms, when they wanted us to clean our plates, was, 'Think of all the starving Chinese children!' Yet the guilt our mothers engendered was minor compared with the guilt some people feel when they contemplate the global reper-cussions of their food choices. Who doesn't feel a little remorseful that thousands of acres of Amazon rain forest were being cleared to grow cattle to produce the beef in our hamburgers? That the smoke that choked Texas during the summer of 1998 was wafted northward from fires in southern Mexico, many of which were deliberately set to clear grazing land for cattle for the United States ground beef industry? That about a billion people go to bed hungry every night around the globe, a figure that could be reduced by switching to veggie burgers?

Social pressures have long shaped the eating habits of Americans. British anthropologist Mary Douglas states that by the turn of the twentieth century the American diet had settled into a classic format she dubs '1A-plus-2B': one serving of meat plus two smaller servings of vegetables or starches. When immigrants came to this country they felt enormous pressures to conform. To be good American citizens they had to eat like Americans. Roberts describes how Italian families were constantly lectured by Americanizers against mixing their foods. In the early 1900s, a social worker paid a visit to an Italian family recently settled in Boston. They were making progress in settling into their new home, language, and culture, but there was a troubling sign: 'Still eating spaghetti,' the social worker reported. 'Not yet assimilated.'

Harvey Levenstein, Ph.D., author of *Revolution at the Table*, reported similar obstacles faced by Polish immigrants. 'Not only did [Poles] eat the same dish for one meal, they also at it from the same bowl. They therefore had to be taught to serve food on separate plates, as well as to separate the ingredients.'

Nutritional correctness can be difficult to distinguish from polit-ical correctness. When talk show host Oprah Winfrey was sued in 1997 by the Texas beef industry because of her remarks about the potential health risks of 'mad cow disease,' the battle was largely portrayed in the media as a liberal-versus-conservative ideological struggle. Winfrey represented left-wing, progressive, vegetarian thought, whereas the Texas cattlemen stood for big money, corporate ranching, right-wing conservatism, and cholesterol. The cattlemen lost.

My favorite local bakery calls one of its best-selling desserts Triple Bypass Chocolate Cake, implying that eating a slice is flirting with suicide and that anyone who partakes of it must be morally degenerate. In contrast, eating something that tastes like cardboard is widely considered a courageous exercise in self-denial. We attach moral values to what we eat without realizing it, as when we refer to eating something yummy as 'sinful.'

Food morality is also a factor in how we judge others. In a study by Arizona State University psychologists Richard Stein and Carol Nemeroff, fictitious students who were described as eating a good diet – fruit, homemade wheat bread, chicken, and potatoes – were rated by test subjects as more moral, likable, attractive, and in shape than identical students who ate a 'bad' diet of steak, hamburgers, fries, doughnuts, and double-fudge sundaes.

In the 1920s American consumers had only a few hundred food products to choose from, only a small portion of which bore a name brand. By 1965 some 800 new products were being introduced every year. Thirteen hundred new products appeared in 1975; in 1985 there were 5,617; and 16,863 new items hit the market in 1995. Today we are drowning in food choices. Faced with this situation, many people throw up their hands in a 'what's the use' attitude and persist in eating things they feel comfortable with, whether they are good for them or not. Or they vacillate in 'dietary schizophrenia – trying to balance their indulgences with bouts of healthy eating, as in eating 3 slices of chocolate cake one day and only fiber the next,' as the Roberts article in *Psychology Today* put it.

A Solution?

I do not know a remedy for our tortured attitudes toward food. But I am concerned that we may be engaging unconsciously in a colossal experiment, creating innumerable intermediary objects in the form of food, which we are imbuing with negative attitudes that have the potential to harm us.

All is not lost; islands of food sanity still exist. For example, contrast our attitudes with those in France: 'The French have no ambivalence about food: it's almost purely a source of pleasure,' reports Rozin.

It is encouraging, too, that a few experts have begun to write wisely about the connections between nutrition and spirituality. These books depart from the one-size-fits-all, formulaic approaches to eating. Among my favorite works that emphasize this perspective are Marc David's *Nourishing Wisdom*, Deborah Kesten's *Feeding the Body, Nourishing the Soul*; and cardiologist Dean Ornish's many books.

I propose also that it might be a good idea to bring back an ancient custom – fasting – as a way of restoring a sense of reverence and gratitude for the foods we eat. I can think of no better way of neutralizing our ambivalence toward food than going without it for a while. I'm not talking about pseudofasts – 'juice fasts' or 'fruit fasts,' which are not really fasts at all – but about cutting ourselves off from food altogether and winging it with water for a spell. Anyone interested in this time-honored practice has a lot of information to choose from; my search has turned up sixty-two books on the subject. Before embarking on a genuine fast, however, make sure it's safe by consulting a health-care professional. Also examine your reasons for fasting. Do you want merely to lose weight, or are you seeking to explore your relationship with food or to clarify your spiritual vision? Medically oriented books such as *Fasting and Eating for Health* by Joel Fuhrman, M.D., can also help, as can spiritually based books such as John Piper's *A Hunger for God*.

Fasting might help us realize that 'eating for health' is only one approach to nutrition – and a limited one at that. Our soul needs nourishment as much as our body. As the French aesthete Anthelme Brillat-Savarin said in the early 1800s: 'The truth is that at the end of a well-savored meal both soul and body enjoy a special well-being . . . [and] the spirit grows more perceptive.'

5

War: A Vietnam Memoir

'THE GOAL OF THE MILITARY is simple,' says a friend of mine who has worked at the Pentagon, 'killing people and breaking things.' In addition to being killed, people are among the 'things' in war that get broken. War not only shatters limbs; it can deprive us of our very sense of meaning, distort the mental framework with which we make sense of the world, blur our notions of right and wrong, sickness and health, selfishness and heroism. Vietnam was like most wars, from this point of view, yet few of us stopped to consider these things as we were being swept up in it. I was no exception.

I volunteered to serve in Vietnam in 1969, fresh out of my internship. There was nothing noble in my decision. All young physicians were being drafted at the time, and I figured I had a better shot at a decent assignment if I joined up. My strategy didn't work.

In the six-week period of officer training prior to leaving for Vietnam, my cynical attitude toward the military hardened as I was exposed to a series of career officers assigned to indoctrinate us in our new roles as army physicians. I was appalled by their cheerful enthusiasm. I considered myself wiser than they, because I could see the insanity of war and they could not. I made a solemn vow that I would never, under any circumstance, take undue risks should I find myself in a hazardous situation in Vietnam. I considered the possibility of danger unlikely, however, because my chances of being assigned to a medical facility in a safe zone, I thought, were quite good.

Again my calculations failed. I was assigned as a battalion surgeon – an inflated title – to a mechanized infantry battalion attached to an airborne brigade of paratroopers. I was shocked to discover that positions like this actually existed for physicians. I was issued an M-16 rifle, a .45 pistol, a bandolier for extra ammunition clips, a combat knife, and a flak jacket, which was a Kevlar vest that repelled bullets and shrapnel – all of which, in addition to a small medical aid bag I put together, would become my constant companions for the following year.

Again the unexpected happened. After only a few days on the front lines I began renouncing all my previous resolutions and started to actually court danger. I began volunteering for combat patrols and assault missions, and signed up for paratrooper 'jump' school. As I increasingly identified with my new role, I seriously considered asking for reassignment to the army's Officer Candidate School back in the States, so I could return to Vietnam with my own infantry company to command. When, after six months of hazardous duty, it came time for me to rotate to a safe assignment at a rear hospital, I declined the opportunity and elected to stay in the field with the casualties and carnage for an additional six months – in spite of the fact that by then I knew the war was insane. But, in a way, so was I.

Vietnam, II Corp, Landing Zone English, 1969. I reach the remote outpost in time to see the crew of the disabled armored personnel carrier walking away from it. They are sullen and splattered with blood. I notice that the tanklike vehicle has a hole in its side, made by a rocket-propelled grenade. Where did all the blood come from? I climb atop the APC, drop down through the open hatch into the claustrophobic chamber, and find myself sitting next to a young soldier. He has no head. I peer into the base of his skull – an empty, bone-white bowl that previously contained a brain. Looking around, I see the man's missing brain tissue stuck on every wall of the APC. His head suffered a direct hit from the rocket, and they both exploded.

His insignia tells me he is a sergeant. His hands are folded limply in his lap, as if he is meditating. I notice a bulge in the breast pocket of his uniform. I unbutton it and remove his wallet, which is stuffed with photographs of his pretty wife and two beaming children. The oldest child is a little girl in pigtails and braces. In the picture she towers over her brother and holds his hand.

I respectfully replace the sergeant's wallet. Then I lean against my headless comrade, shoulder to shoulder, and begin to cry. It's been almost a year since I arrived in Vietnam, and I am tired of the carnage – physically, emotionally, spiritually. The count-less, blood-soaked soldiers I have patched up and resuscitated before sending them back to the MASH-type hospitals; the days spent in Vietnamese hamlets treating malaria, tuberculosis, and exotic diseases I could only guess at; the lucky misses during mortar bombardments; 200+ hours spent in helicopters, and the near-crashes – the surreal chaos replays itself as tears flow.

'Doc! What the hell is taking you so long?' One of my medics is concerned about what is going on inside the APC. I am needed elsewhere. I stifle my emotions and stuff them into some part of my mind I've learned to keep handy for occasions like this. I'm responsible for a thousand men; emotional control is every-thing.

With an inversion of rank I salute my dead comrade and say good-bye. I make sure his pocket is fastened securely, so his wallet won't be lost on his way to the body bag.

I look back in amazement at those months in Vietnam. I still find it difficult to believe that I not only participated in the war but did so with enthusiasm. I considered myself immune to being caught up in soldiering, but before long I was taking pride in the behaviors I had repudiated earlier. I became part of a group of men trying to survive while they did their duty, and I would have given my life and taken any risk whatever, as I did many times, to help them succeed. They knew there were no limits to my devo-tion to them, and they responded to me in the same way. This unconditional mutual support explained why, for example, during a combat assault mission, an eighteen-year-old soldier once ran across a rice paddy, braving enemy fire, *to hand me a Coke*.

Along with the dangers came the wildest sensations and most paradoxical satisfactions I have ever known. There are simply no comparisons to the emotions of war. Warriors know this, and this realization accounts in no small measure for the silent understanding that binds them.

I've long since ceased looking for rational explanations for these experiences, because there are none. The brute fact is this: the tug of war is one of the most irresistible forces humans ever encounter, a power capable of shredding any process of reasoning thrown up against it. To complicate matters, war, for all its horrors, is always studded with a profusion of virtues – not just sacrifice and heroism, which are predictable, but also love and compassion, which are not. If war brings out the worst in humans, it also elicits the best. War is the preeminent human activity in which the beastly and the divine reveal themselves side by side, in the same person.

As a result of my experiences in Vietnam, I believe that no one is safe from the seductions of war. If I, against the backdrop of antipathy and disgust for war, can embrace it, hunger for it, *love* it, then perhaps no one is immune to its attractions. I wish my experience were unique, but unfortunately it is all too common and is part of the reason wars endure.

War and the Shadow

I fell under the spell of war as a consequence of unconscious forces I did not comprehend and therefore could not control. The psychological forces compelling people to go to war constitute a universal pattern in the mind that appears across cultures and through time – what psychologist C. G. Jung called an archetype. These unacknowledged factors are part of what Jung called the shadow, the part of the psyche that contains all the unlovely, unacceptable traits we reject at a conscious level.

The most significant event in modern history forcing us to confront our individual and collective shadow was probably the Vietnam War. Harry A. Wilmer, president of the Institute for the Humanities in Salado, Texas, is a psychiatrist and researcher who is an expert in treating Vietnam veterans suffering from psychological trauma. In his book *Vietnam in Remission* he states: 'Until Vietnam, Americans were content to see the shadow and evil only in their enemies. But with

the Vietnam experience, the media – and the living-room video-war
. . . changed that. Suddenly technology not only let us see the close-
up horror of war but also let us see it as it was happening. That has
never happened before in the history of the world.'

Blaming the Warriors

The psyche is ingenious and will go to any length to avoid
confronting its dark side. This frequently involves attributing to
someone else the sordid traits we sense in ourselves – a psychological defense mechanism called projection. Following Vietnam,
the most dramatic case of projection involved Lieutenant William
Calley, who was court-martialed and found guilty of perpetrating
the atrocities at My Lai. Calley's conviction made it possible for us
to say that *we* didn't murder Vietnamese women and children, but
he and soldiers like him did. We essentially accused thousands of
United States soldiers of Calley's crimes – warriors like Tom, who
was one of the returning veterans treated by Wilmer:

> Tom prided himself on being a grunt (foot soldier) who managed
> to survive twenty-six months in Vietnam. He had survived the
> thick of battle, including the Tet Offensive at Hue, which was
> captured by Vietcong and North Vietnamese troops. Tom told
> Wilmer that, when he landed at National Airport in Washington,
> D.C., 'a lady came up to me and called me "a murderer," and
> hit me in the face with her purse. I said, "Shit! This is what I
> came home to?" I went and got a drink. I didn't want to come
> home if this was how it was gonna be.'

Another of Wilmer's patients was Cervando, a tough ex-Marine
who came back with a drawerful of medals. In an interview he said
to Wilmer, 'Look around you. There are still people who are ashamed
to say, "I'm a Vietnam veteran" because [they're] scared that people
won't talk to [them]. I've been insulted. "Sir, were you one of [those]
butchers over there? Did you enjoy killing babies and people?"'

Mike, another of Wilmer's patients, arrived in the United States
wounded, frightened, and feeling guilty for having survived when
his buddies had been killed, but happy nonetheless to be home.
He said: 'I arrived at the San Francisco airport and went to a bar.

The people at the bar said, "Well, what are you doing here? You're crazy. Why don't you get the hell out of here?" It seemed to me that the media had depicted us as being crazy and when I left the service I considered myself normal. I just wanted to get out. I did my thing, and now leave me alone.'

Eric, a returning veteran who lost his foot in an explosion, experienced shame so oppressive that he lied about his wounds: 'When they used to say to me, "Hey were you in Vietnam?" or "What happened to your leg?" I'd say I had a car accident so I didn't have to bring it up.'

The Uniform and the Garbage Can

My return flight from Vietnam landed in Seattle, Washington, in the early morning hours. As my buddies and I exited the plane, there was no joy among us. Neither were there any welcoming committees or the yellow ribbons that would festoon every town in America when the Gulf War veterans returned a generation later. As I set foot on American soil, I actually felt as if I were entering hostile territory, a feeling I knew well enough after a year in the bush. I had calculated my return for weeks. Before leaving Vietnam, I had managed to acquire some civilian clothes.

My first act in the Seattle airport was to duck into a restroom, strip off my jungle fatigues and combat boots, stuff them in a garbage can, and don the cheap civilian clothes before catching the connecting flight home. I knew that a peace march was scheduled to convene in Washington, D.C., in a few days, and that antiwar sentiment was at a fever pitch. I simply could not tolerate the prospect of being ridiculed, and I was not confident that I could control my rage if someone made a cynical remark to me. Maybe ditching the combat garb would help. I remember feeling numb as I walked out of the men's room with my new identity. Like Tom, Cervando, and Mike, I wanted to hide away somewhere.

Wilmer, summarizing how Americans projected their guilt onto returning Vietnam veterans, spoke for how I felt: 'I need not repeat the endless shameful ways in which many veterans were "welcomed" by being spit on and humiliated, stereotyped as losers, baby killers, dope fiends, and walking time bombs.'

Americans don't have a monopoly on the shabby treatment of returning soldiers. The Russians also treated their Afghanistan war veterans with disrespect. On May 9, 1990, they were left out of the parade in Moscow celebrating the forty-fifth anniversary of the World War II victory over Germany. While the festivities were in progress, the Afghanistan veterans gathered in Gorky Park to celebrate 'nothing more than survival.'

Nightmares of War

On returning from Vietnam, I reentered medical training and completed a residency in internal medicine. But at night the war was always close at hand. It dogged me in the form of a horrifying nightmare that recurred for almost twenty years.

An emergency radio call: A patrol has just been ambushed and has taken casualties. I run for the medevac chopper and scramble inside as it lifts off in a cloud of red dust. In minutes we are over the ambush site and the helicopter lands in the jungle clearing. The smell of gunfire is still in the air. On the ground are three young men who are not moving. I quickly examine them and discover that two are dead. The third soldier is alive but is ashen, clammy, and barely conscious. I can find only a single wound – a tiny dot of red over his heart, the signature of shrapnel. Has it punctured his pleura, lung, pericardium, or heart? Wasting no time, we load the young man onto the helicopter. He loses consciousness. I have no blood, intravenous fluids, or chest tubes, and I begin manual resuscitation to keep him alive. As we skim the jungle canopy en route to the evacuation hospital, I am furious that this stalwart young soldier is dying from such an insignificant-appearing wound.

We land on the helipad and two waiting medics load the young soldier onto a stretcher and dash for the receiving area. I follow but am stopped at the entry by a fellow captain who is also a physician. His pristine, starched uniform is a dramatic contrast to mine. He is gesticulating in uncontrolled anger. 'You cannot come inside this hospital!' he fumes. I don't understand; I'm a doctor and the soldier is my patient. I have kept him alive. 'Look at you!' he sneers, pointing to my uniform, which is covered with blood and the red dirt of Vietnam. My rifle and medical aid are slung over my shoulder and a .45 is at my waist. 'You're armed! This is a hospital! We don't allow weapons and filth here!' Suddenly a group of medics surround me and try to hustle me away, as if I were a criminal. I resist but am over-come. After they strip me of my rifle, pistol, and aid bag, they hurl me into the dirt. I look beyond them and see the young soldier, my patient, disappearing on a gurney down a hallway. I must get to him and help him! I try to rise but the burly medics overpower me again. 'You don't belong here!' the arro-gant physician screams. 'Get out!' Now I see that the entry to the hospital is barred. My weapons are locked inside and I cannot reach them.

Realizing I have nothing with which to defend myself, I feel helpless and begin to panic. The helicopter is waiting, its motor still running, and I climb inside. I am enraged at the physician who has just insisted that the war be aseptic and tidy. I realize he is typical of many of the hospital-based military physicians I have met, who, in spite of their safe assignments and comfort-able quarters, spend their time complaining about the inter-ruption of their careers and the indignities they are enduring. They have no idea what things are like for the 'grunts,' the real warriors, or for the medics and battalion surgeons who try to keep them alive. As we head back into the jungle, I have a morbid sense of dread.

Up to this point in the dream, the events were essentially factual: the patient was real and I had, in fact, been barred and disarmed at a MASH-type evacuation hospital on transferring wounded solders there by helicopter. But then the dream took a monstrous turn:

On the way back to the fire base where my aid station is located, my helicopter is shot down. The crew is wounded but I am unhurt. They are crying out for help, but I have no supplies. The Vietcong are closing in on the downed chopper; I can hear them moving closer through the jungle. I realize we will be captured, tortured, killed, and mutilated. Instinctively I reach for my weapons, not remembering I have none. The worst possible thing has happened: I have become totally defenseless. Waiting for the end, I awaken in terror.

Year after year the nightmare continued. In an attempt to shut it out, I avoided anything that reminded me of Vietnam. I refused to see movies about the war, I shunned books written about it, and I never talked about my experiences to anyone, including my wife. Vietnam was a closed subject that belonged to the past. Besides, I considered my demons my own and could not see the point in unleashing them on anyone else. My approach did not work. Trying to keep the lid on my psyche was like trying to hold back the sea. The nightmare would always recur, each time as terrifying as before.

A resolution occurred in a quite unexpected way. Eighteen years after my return from Vietnam, I was traveling with my wife, Barbie, in New Mexico. We were visiting Santa Fe, staying in La Fonda, a beautiful, historic hotel on the plaza. It was late at night and we were exhausted. Wanting some mindless diversion, we turned on the television and sank into bed. A made-for-TV drama about Vietnam was on. Before I could change the channel, which was my habitual way of dealing with anything related to the war, I realized that the events being portrayed on television were a reenactment of my nightmare – a downed helicopter, wounded soldiers, and the approaching enemy. I was mesmerized. The television drama became as real as the dream, and I found myself entering it fully. But instead of feeling panic and terror as in the nightmare, I began to weep. Soon I found myself sobbing uncontrollably – rivers of tears, sobs that shook the bed. Some of the television soldiers actually resembled some of my previous comrades. The thing that impressed me most was their innocence. They seemed so *young* – *children*, almost – and the compassion I felt for them was beyond description. When the program ended, my sobbing continued. Even with my wife's continual comforting, I simply could not stop. I was now in Vietnam, and for the first time in nearly twenty years I allowed my imagination to reengage the buried memories. The lid was completely off my psyche, and the repressed, painful events came spilling out unopposed. I made no attempt to monitor or censor anything. Hours later, after soaking every towel in the bathroom, my tears finally ceased.

Exhausted yet immensely peaceful, I left Barbie sleeping in the hotel room and went for a walk. It was early morning and the stars were fading. In the east, blood-red streaks announced the dawn, a symbol of an ending and a new beginning. The nightmare has never returned.

Do We 'Catch' War?

War behaves like an infection. Some societies seem to be relatively immune to being infected by the 'microbe' of war, whereas others have little resistance and are always falling prey. In her brilliant book *Blood Rites: Origins and History of the Passions of War*, biologist and author Barbara Ehrenreich suggests that following an outbreak war is 'capable of encysting itself for generations, if necessary, within the human soul,' breaking out unpredictably at a later time. Unlike a disease such as measles or chicken pox, infection by war does not result in permanent immunity. If anything, war seems to destroy a society's immune system against armed conflict. After a nation goes to war, it tends to go to war repeatedly. Has there ever been a nation that has engaged in only *one* war?

If the inoculum is great enough, war can infect any state. The infection may begin as an insult to national pride, economic oppression, or actual invasion. Once the initial provocation has occurred, war can spread from country to country, not unlike the self-replication and propagation of a living organism.

The microbe of war is apparently becoming more virulent. As evidence, the twentieth century produced 75 percent of all the war deaths inflicted since the rise of Rome. As in infectious diseases, the greatest number of casualties includes the weakest and most vulnerable: 90 percent of the deaths in modern conflicts are noncombatants, including the aged, women, and children. Like many infections, war increases one's susceptibility to other diseases. In Rwanda, cholera killed up to forty-five thousand people in only a few weeks in 1994, one of the most intense, lethal epidemics ever recorded.

A variety of opportunistic 'infections' accompany war, as they do many infectious diseases. Consider, for example, the following:

- the one hundred million land mines that currently lie in wait in sixty-four nations
- the 2.2 billion hectares of forest and farms that were denuded in Vietnam from land clearing, napalm, and defoliation with seventy-two million liters of herbicides
- the toxic wastes that result from weapons production and testing, including fuels, paints, solvents, phenols, acids, alkalines, propellants, and explosives
- the high rates of cancer around Hanford Reservation, Washington; Rocky Flats, Colorado; and Oak Ridge, Tennessee
- the forty-five hundred contaminated Department of Energy sites in the United States
- the long-term cognitive and developmental deficits and malnutrition that affect the seventeen million children who have currently lost their homes as a result of war

Origins of War: The Two Dominant Theories

There are two major theories about why we go to war: (1) war is a method by which humans seek to advance their collective political and economic interests and improve their lives, and (2) war stems from subrational drives similar to those that lead individuals to commit violent crimes – drives that may be biological. The first reason goes virtually uncontested. 'There is no doubt . . . ,' Ehrenreich states, 'that wars are designed, at least ostensibly, to secure necessaries like land or oil or "geopolitical advantage."'

Is war 'biological'? Anyone who is willing to observe nature unobtrusively might think so. In *On the Mesa*, naturalist John Nichols describes his observations at a stock pond on a high-desert mesa in northern New Mexico following a summer thunderstorm: 'Hours after the water is impounded, mosquitoes and other bugs are running rampant. I begin to see the splash rings of insects being born. It isn't long before green darning needles zip over the muddy pond, chased by aggressive blue and gray dragonflies. Tiny things grab each other, kick and fuss, chew and dismember, eat, digest, and defecate, and then look around hungrily to see if there's anybody they missed: life, elucidated by unending holocaust; the natural world as total war!'

It seems as if the Marquis de Sade (1740–1814) may have been correct when he said, 'Who else but Nature whispers to us of personal hatreds, vengeances, wars, in fact all the everlasting motives for murder? . . . It is impossible for murder ever to outrage Nature.'

Is this our inheritance? Are we driven to war by thought processes dictated ultimately by our DNA? 'There is no straight-forward biological calculation that could lead a man to kill himself in war,' Ehrenreich asserts. 'The "rational" argument for sacrificing oneself in combat is that doing so promotes the survival of one's kin and therefore genetic material similar to one's own – selfish-ness disguised as altruism. Perhaps this might apply to situations in which warriors died fighting for their immediate family or clan, but it is a stretch to suppose this sort of reasoning applies to the huge, "genetically polyglot" armies of both ancient and modern states.' Even so, the theory that human violence has biological roots is immensely influential, with a great deal of evidence in its favor. The question, it seems, is not *whether* we have biological inclinations to harm others, but how deep these roots go.

If our genes compel us toward war, we might expect forms of violence that accompany war to be embedded in nature. An example is rape.

Copulation by force is so common in nature that one might wonder whether it is the norm. The male scorpion fly is a master rapist. He will lie in wait for an unwary female and, as she passes, lash out with his flexible abdomen and grasp her leg or wing. Although she escapes most of the time, she is not always successful and is forced to yield to copulation. Aggravated sexual assault and gang rape are common among mallard ducks; occasionally the female is attacked so persistently she drowns in the process. Man-eating male blue sharks make injurious attacks on their own females and seem unable to mate without doing so. Rape is a commonplace pattern of behavior in many insects, frogs, and turtles, and homosexual rape is seen in some parasitic worms.

In spite of the fact that rape is unquestionably ubiquitous in nature, it seems animalistic, beastly, 'other.' On the human level, rape and pillage are something the evil enemy does. When Japanese forces captured the Chinese city of Nanjing in 1937, more than twenty thousand women were sexually tortured and murdered in a month – the 'Rape of Nanjing.' In 1943 Moroccan mercenaries fighting with the French were allowed to rape their way through tens of thousands of Italian women. We like to think that 'our boys' never do such things. But, writes feminist author Ruth Seifert in her essay 'War and Rape,' when Berlin was liberated, in the spring of 1945, 'Allied troops took leave of the war and of their senses, raping hundreds of thousands of German women, included among whom were victims of Nazi concentration camps.'

The Frisson of War

As people are being sucked into the black hole of war, they often become excited. In the days preceding World War I, hardly anyone could resist the attractions of the approaching conflict. Ehrenreich notes that Anatole France, though seventy years old, offered to volunteer; Isadora Duncan described being 'all flame and fire' about the war. Feminists such as England's Isabella Pankhurst set aside the struggle for suffrage in order to support the war effort. Even the young Gandhi recruited Indians to join the British army. Arnold J. Toynbee, the British historian, was caught up in the frenzy and produced several volumes of 'atrocity propaganda' as his contribution to the war effort.

The case of Sigmund Freud is particularly interesting. Like most people, he was swept up in the excitement of the war and for a while, according to Ehrenreich, gave 'all his libido to Austria-Hungary . . . Unable for weeks to work or think of anything else, Freud was eventually led to conclude that there is some dark flaw in the human psyche, a perverse desire to destroy, countering Eros and the will to live.' But if Freud really comprehended the power of the unconscious, why was he so powerless before his own?

Ehrenreich concludes that in his analysis of war, Freud had a blind spot. He 'failed to reflect on his own enthusiasm; otherwise he would never have hypothesized that men are driven to war by some cruel and murderous instinct.'

By the time war in Europe ended in 1918, it had cost approximately twelve million military lives and resulted in twenty million civilian casualties. But in 1914 no one could comprehend the magnitude of the coming slaughter. In England, says British author Oliver Thomson in *A History of Sin*, 'the imperial war image was thrust on the young through cigarette cards, jigsaws, music-hall songs, board games, biscuit tins, lantern slides and picture postcards: "Women of Britain Say Go."' Although a few groups such as the Peacettes dissented, few listened to the message in their tracts that 'the good soldier is a heartless soul-less, murderous machine.'

Amid the frenzy, no one could believe that their enchantment with the approaching conflict could possibly be due to a raw instinct to kill their fellow human beings. They preferred, rather, to describe their justifications in terms of the noblest feelings humans can experience – heroism, commitment to a worthy cause, comradeship, patriotism, selflessness, and sacrifice – the same reasons we give today.

No one seems immune from being drawn into war. Consider the Semai Senoi people of the rain forest of the Malay peninsula, one of the most peaceful tribes known. There are approximately thirteen thousand of them, and they appear never to kill each other. 'We never get angry,' they say – meaning, rather, that they have found ways of channeling anger into nonviolent forms of behavior. Violence horrifies them, is unthinkable, and apparently never happens. They have no need of a court system or police force. No single instance of murder, attempted murder, or even injury by a Semai has ever come to the attention of the Malaysian authorities.

Yet when the Semai were conscripted into the British Army to deal with Communist insurgents during uprisings in the early 1950s, the Semai were overcome by a kind of insanity they called 'blood drunkenness.' 'We killed, killed, killed,' they explained later. 'Truly we were drunk with blood.' One Semai even told how he drank the blood of a man he had just killed. When the peninsular uprisings were over, the Semai returned to their communities as gentle and nonaggressive as before, as if nothing had happened.

War as Sacrament

I can affirm from personal experience that the thrill of war is like no other. This peculiar state of awareness is described in Ehrenreich's *Blood Rites* as 'ecstasy'; an 'altered state of consciousness'; 'one of humankind's great natural "highs"'; 'social intoxication, the feeling on the part of the individual of being a part of a [greater] body'; 'the sense of self-loss, . . . of merger into some greater whole'; the satisfaction of the same psychological needs met by 'love, religion, intoxication, art'; and 'a sense of transcendent purposefulness.'

Why do we experience war in this way? Ehrenreich offers a fascinating hypothesis. A key to her thesis is that war, over the course of human history, has become invested with a deep sense of religious significance. To associate war with religion is to regard it as a *sacrament* – a holy ritual – and to experience the 'spiritual high' that accompanies the sacred. Uniting war and religion also makes possible a justification for killing and for abandoning ethical and moral norms. 'It is the religiosity of war, above all, that makes it so impervious to moral rebuke,' Ehrenreich states.

What actually constituted the connection between war and religion? Ehrenreich finds the link in the ancient ritual of *blood sacrifice*. Throughout history, even in times of peace, the religions of traditional cultures have often been knee-deep in the bloody business of killing both animals and humans dedicated to their gods. Over time, murder and the shedding of blood have come to lie at the very core of what humans consider religious and sacred.

Conventional explanations indicate otherwise. Human violence is best explained, it is claimed, as a result of our long history as hunters and killers of animals for food. As a result, we have become 'natural-born killers.' Unable to shed our old drives, we carried these habits over into the era of herding and farming. As the hunting of wild beasts for food became less necessary, a new form of 'hunting' arose – preying on other peoples' herds or the grain in their village fortresses. The name for this new form of hunting was war. Because the old type of hunting had been considered a sacred endeavor, war came to be sacralized as well.

But why did humans find the practice of blood sacrifice attractive in the first place? Ehrenreich believes the ritual was rooted in the 2.5 million years during which early humans lived in small hunting bands. Evidence suggests that during this period humans were not skilled predators but were mercilessly preyed upon. Only in the 'last thousand or so generations' did we gain the skill and cunning required to make the transition from prey to that of self-confident predator. This transition as a species, Ehrenreich maintains, has been almost entirely repressed because it is much more flattering to believe that we have always been atop the food chain. But we have only 'recently' learned 'not to cower at every sound in the night.' The gradual transformation from prey to predator was of unimaginable importance, and it required rituals to honor it:

> Rituals of blood sacrifice both celebrate and terrifyingly reenact the human transition from prey to predator, and so, I . . . argue, does war. Nowhere is this more obvious than in the case of wars that are undertaken for the stated purpose of initiating young men into the male warrior-predator role – a not uncommon occurrence in traditional cultures. But more important, the anxiety and ultimate thrill of the prey-to-predator transition color the feelings we bring to *all* wars, and infuse them, at least for some of the participants, some of the time, with feelings powerful and uplifting enough to be experienced as 'religious.'

In this view, then, war is the response to the ancestral urge of blood sacrifice, which developed as a means of celebrating the greatest transition our species has perhaps ever known – the movement from the status of prey to predator.

In *Dark Nature* Lyall Watson records many instances of human sacrifice: Pausanias, the Greek historian, tells of the dismemberment and communal eating of a child sacrificed to Zeus on Mount Lykaion. Throughout Europe, Asia, and the Pacific, there is evidence of human sacrifices at bridges, temples, houses, and forts to ensure that these structures contained the proper spirit. The penchant of the ancient Aztecs, Mayans, and Incas for sacrificing humans to their gods is well known. These grim customs persist. Following a tidal wave in southern Chile in 1960, Mapuche Indians threw a five-year-old boy into the sea to appease the ocean spirit. In 1986 in Peru an Aymara man was beheaded by cocaine traders to 'pay the earth' in an attempt to bring blessings on a new venture.

Human sacrifice is right at home in our Judeo-Christian traditions. It was enshrined with the aborted sacrifice by Abraham of his son Isaac, the sacrifice of Jephthah's daughter, and the death of the son of God himself at Golgotha. Christian sacrifice still has its appeal. In 1986 evangelical Christians in an Andean village drove a stake through the heart of a nine-year-old boy in an attempt to save the life of a sick man.

In *Fear and Trembling*, Søren Kierkegaard, the Danish philosopher, called Abraham's willingness to sacrifice his own son a 'monstrous paradox' and could find no logical justification for it. He concluded that something else must be going on, 'which no thought can grasp.'

As animal sacrifice has become an unacceptable method of shedding blood, we have taken to sacrificing each other on our altars of social violence. The principal tool in this carnage is the handgun. According to Watson, twenty of them are manufactured each second in the United States, and they find their way into seventy-one million homes. In 1992 there were 13,220 handgun murders in the United States, of which only 262 were ruled as justifiable homicides in cases of self-defense. Watson reveals that our capacity for murder led classics scholar Walter Burkert to suggest renaming our species *Homo necans*, or 'man the killer.'

As if they are finally taking revenge for being used in ritual sacrifices for millennia, animals have begun shooting us. 'Hundreds of people are killed each year by firearms accidentally discharged by domestic pets,' Watson's research reveals.

Gender and War

When males *go* to war, somebody *sends* them. This means that the masculine warrior function has evolved hand in hand with the role of those who stay behind to tend the hearth – wives, lovers, parents. The discovery of the complicit role of women in war can come as a shock to soldiers, as it did to Lieutenant Adolf Andreas Latzko, who fought for Germany during World War I. In 1918, in his book *Men in War*, he wrote:

> You want to know what was the most awful thing? The dis-illusionment was the most awful thing – the going off. The war wasn't. The war is what it has to be. Did it surprise you to find out that war is horrible? The only surprising thing was the going off. To find out that the women are horrible – that was the only surprising thing. That they can smile and throw roses, that they can give up their men, their children. That was the surprise! That they sent us – sent us! No general could have made us go if the women hadn't allowed us to be stacked on the trains, if they had screamed that they would never look at us again if we turned into murderers.

Hearth tending is generally considered a *passive* female role – waiting and worrying until 'the boys come home.' But female roles during war are often quite active. As C. E. Montague put it, 'War hath no fury like a non-combatant.' In modern times women have adopted vigorous pursuits such as encouraging popular support, selling war bonds, working in industry, growing crops, and nursing the wounded. Women have become the weapons makers for soldiers away at war, the most famous symbol of whom was Rosie the Riveter of World War II.

Although heavily gendered, war has never been a totally male endeavor. Early European explorers of western Africa encountered the female regiment maintained by the kings of Dahomey, a living equivalent of the mythical Amazons. Deborah Sampson enlisted in the American Revolutionary War and served with valor, but only after 'becoming a man' and transforming herself into 'Robert Shirtluff,' and concealing her sex (until a wound to her shoulder gave her away). Ehrenreich notes in *Blood Rites:*

> The female disadvantage in the realm of muscular strength was mitigated long ago with the invention of the bow and arrow, not

to mention that great leveler of our own era, the gun. Nor . . . do women have any innate inhibition against fighting and shedding blood. Revolutions and insurrections have again and again utilized women in combat roles, if only because revolutionary forces are generally less formal and tradition-bound than the armies of nation-states. Even as 'noncombatants,' women have played lethal roles in men's wars . . . Polynesian women had the job of selecting and cooking defeated enemies for postbattle feasts . . . There is no compelling biological or 'natural' reason why men have so exclusively starred in the drama of war.

Margaret Thatcher, the former prime minister of Britain, won the Falklands War, supplied the British military with nuclear submarines, and stocked them with nuclear-tipped ballistic missiles. Indira Gandhi led a military campaign against Pakistan and jailed her opponents. The assassination squads of Peru's Shining Path guerrillas were composed almost entirely of women.

Only a generation ago it was virtually unthinkable that we would send women into combat. In fact, this prospect was used to mobilize votes against the Equal Rights Amendment to the United States Constitution. Since then, however, women have served in a variety of combat-related roles, from directing artillery to piloting helicopters, and a few have been trained as fighter pilots and have found assignments on combat ships. When eleven women were killed and two were captured in the Gulf War, there was no special outcry, states Ehrenreich. From many women's perspective, this was not an entirely negative development.

Is War Men's Fault?

People often say that was results from some incurable defect in the masculine character. Women are wiser and more compassionate, and they know better than to make war. If only they could ascend to positions as heads of states, peace might prevail and war become obsolete. However, in view of the ferocity with which women currently are clamoring for roles in combat, this claim has a hollow ring. As Ehrenreich puts it, 'To anyone who had believed

that war could be abolished by severing its links to male privilege
. . . the end of the twentieth century can only bring gloom.'
Biologist Howard Bloom agrees. In his acclaimed book *The Lucifer
Principle*, he states:

> It is useless for women to blame violence on men, and it would
> be futile for men to blame violence on women. Violence is built
> into both of us. When Margaret Thatcher constructed a nuclear
> navy, she was not behaving in a manner distinctly male, nor
> was she behaving in a manner distinctly female. She wasn't even
> obeying a set of impulses that are uniquely human. Thatcher,
> like Rome's Livia, was in the grip of passions we share with
> gorillas and baboons, passions implanted in the primordial
> layers of the triune brain.

Is a World without War Possible?

Taking the path of the warrior was for me one of the most enlight-
ening events of my life, because it was an opportunity to dredge
unexamined areas of my unconscious mind into the light of awareness. Jung called this process 'making consciousness.' I am not
proud of a lot of the things I found scattered in my psychic base-
ment, and I consider it a great misfortune that I did not find a
less violent path toward self-understanding. Nonetheless the experience was healing and freed me in large measure from being
unconsciously and endlessly enslaved by my impulse for violence.

These are some of the reasons I am not a pacifist. To totally
obstruct deep-seated psychic drives such as the urge to warriorship seems to me sheer folly, because in the end this obstruction
leads to the very violence it seeks to avoid. Yet it is clear we cannot
afford any longer the kind of warriorship that takes place on
modern battlefields. Our world is too small and fragile, too
precious, and the weapons too destructive. How, then, are we to
deal with the old drives?

The answer is not to abolish warriorship (as if we could) but
to find less violent ways of being warriors – possibly becoming
warriors for the earth and the environment, or warriors against

poverty, illiteracy, overpopulation, and human suffering in all its forms – in other words, to practice compassion. These endeavors hold the prospect of adventure, exposure to exotic cultures and foreign lands, and even the risk of personal harm or death, which are salient features of rites of passage and participation in war.

Yet even as I write these words I am leery of them. To suggest that the drive toward war can be sublimated in socially valuable ways is to sell war short and risk being victimized by it in the future. We do not choose war, it chooses us; and if we forget this maxim we are in grave danger. Even when we describe war as a rite of passage we intellectualize it. We simply cannot *think* our way out of war. As the Israeli military theorist Martin van Creveld said in his book *The Transformation of War*, 'So elemental is the human need to endow the shedding of blood with some great and even sublime significance that it renders the intellect entirely helpless.'

War and Religion

It is useless to argue that we can escape war's grasp by becoming more religious. War has always been used as an instrument of the world's great religions, with the blessed exception of Buddhism.

Injunctions for inflicting civilian casualties in war, including rape and the slaughter of innocent children, are biblical. After Moses' troops defeated the Midianites, he commanded them, 'Now therefore kill every male among the little ones, and kill every woman that hath known man by lying with him. But all the women children, that have not known a man by lying with him, keep alive for yourselves.'

The extent to which Christianity has employed war is often denied in the West. But the imperatives of Christianity have always been militaristic: 'Onward Christian soldiers, marching as to war.' In *The Code of the Warrior*, Rick Fields informs us that Saint Bernard (whose name is derived from words that literally mean 'bold as a bear') said in the twelfth century, when the Crusades were in progress, 'The soldier of Christ kills safely: he dies the more safely. He serves his own interests in dying, and Christ's interests in killing! Not without cause does he bear the sword!'

Oliver Thomson states in *A History of Sin* that during the period of crusading activity between 1091 and 1291, the battlefield was believed to be a clear path to heaven, and the duty of war was preached from every pulpit. Of the nine million people killed during this two hundred-year span, approximately half were Christians. The other half?

> In the panoptic holocaust of the crusader's imagination, . . . the killing of Jews, the nation of Judas, was certainly not seen as inhumane . . . [But] the Jews were not the only people to suffer from the violence of the crusades. There was much gratuitous killing of Moslems also: in the siege of Nicaea in 1097, human heads were used for catapult ammunition; and Richard I (1157–99), Coeur de Lion and a man of limited moral imagination, slaughtered 2,700 prisoners of war at Acre when their ransom was delayed. He was also the first ruler to make general use of the new 'immoral weapon' of its time, the crossbow, which was condemned as such by the Lateran Council of 1397 and barred for use against other Christians. [So much for arms control.] Ironically, Richard died a lingering death from a crossbow wound.

Killing for Christ achieved great momentum when the Cathars, who were among the last European adherents of nonviolence, were targeted as heretics by Pope Innocent III in the thirteenth century and exterminated. Northern French knights, in return for indulgences, 'flayed Provence [where the Cathars lived], hanging, beheading, and burning "with unspeakable joy,"' as Roland H. Bainton states in *Christian Attitudes toward War and Peace*. When the city of Béziers was taken and the papal legate was asked how to tell the Cathars from the regular Catholics, he replied, 'Kill them all; God will know which are His.' The knights complied by slaughtering twenty thousand. The main villain at Béziers was the crusader Simon de Montfort (1165?–1218), who enjoyed gouging out the eyes and slitting the noses of his victims.

The Church was on a roll. In the fourteenth century, notes Oliver Thomson, 'Catholicism produced a morality which encouraged the slow burning of non-orthodox members of its own faith.'

The scourge of torture leaped the Atlantic to appear in Protestant New England. Thomson adds, 'The otherwise punctilious Puritans regarded it as moral to drown muddled old women whom they suspected of witchcraft.'

It is difficult to argue that the major religions are becoming less warlike. In recent years we have seen religious struggles erupt in Northern Ireland, the Middle East, Bosnia, and elsewhere. In all these examples, the adversaries have offered the same prayer to the same god: Let us be victorious over our enemies.

It is also difficult to really believe that the goal of the major religions is peace. Although Jesus appeared on earth 'to guide our feet into the way of peace' and advocated his followers to 'have peace one with another,' he also warned, 'Think not that I am come to send peace on earth: I came not to send peace, but a sword,' and 'Suppose ye that I am come to give peace on earth? I tell you, Nay; but rather division.' In the Old Testament we find similar statements from Jehovah – for example, Isaiah 45:7, 'I form the light, and create darkness: I make peace, and create evil: I the Lord do all these things.'

This is not meant to single out Christianity and Judaism. Where war is concerned, there is plenty of blood to go around, including for Islam. In the Koran, in the chapter titled 'Repentance,' we find that although Allah is forgiving and merciful, he nonetheless wishes the faithful to 'slay the idolators wherever you find them. Arrest them, besiege them, and lie in ambush everywhere for them ... Make war on them.' This includes, in particular, their original neighbors. 'The Jews say Ezra is the son of Allah, while the Christians say the Messiah is the son of Allah. Such are their assertions, by which they imitate the infidels of old. Allah confound them! How perverse they are!'

What Channel Is It On?

Shortly before the Gulf War broke out in 1991, a six-year-old boy wanted to know, 'What channel is the war going to be on?' The answer, it turned out, was all of them. There was no escaping the excitement. Across America streets filled with demonstrators both for and against our involvement in the war. Everywhere people were wondering. What is this war really about? American economic and political interests? Freedom for the Kuwaitis?

Soldiers in desert camouflage uniforms were frequently interviewed on TV. They wanted to 'kick Saddam's ass,' the sooner the better. Opposing these soldiers were protesters screaming, 'No blood for oil!' Then the scene changed to spouses and parents of soldiers who spoke through tears about American values and democracy. Mothers and fathers said they were proud their sons and daughters were 'serving.' President Bush said we were stopping 'naked aggression' and implied the war was a bargain: a limited 'engagement' now would prevent a bigger one in the future.

People said this war was going to be different. Unlike during the Vietnam War, America was now united, and we were smarter, too; this time we would not tie our soldiers' hands but would allow them to fight with all their resources from the outset. Another major difference from Vietnam was that drugs and alcohol were banned in this Islamic theater of operations. As a result of all these factors, it was predicted that the psychological problems of returning soldiers would be virtually eliminated.

It didn't turn out that way. World War I had its shell shock, World War II its battle fatigue, and Vietnam its post-traumatic stress disorder. Other terms applied to previous wars have been *war excitement, exposure, overexertion, sunstroke, homesickness,* and *nostalgia,* the last based on the French diagnostic term *nostalgie,* which has been in the medical lexicon since the seventeenth century. A Civil War veteran from Indiana lent one of the most graphic expressions when he described his experiences as being 'shook over hell.' *All* wars produce scarred minds and ravaged spirits; the conflict in the Persian Gulf was no exception.

Seven Principles for Returning Warriors

For those who suffer the consequences of war, what advice can be given to rebuild a life with meaning on return? I am hardly an authority on this question; I required nearly two decades to resolve my own difficulties, then only through pure accident. Still, I venture a few recommendations below. I follow most of these with quotes from poet Rainer Maria Rilke, who spent time in his youth in a military school and whose father was an army officer. Rilke's counsel in *Letters to a Young Poet* seemed to get to the heart of these matters and has always moved me.

First Principle: The grim and terrible reminders of war, whether they occur in nightmares, memories, or feelings of guilt or remorse, will never go away until we face them; they become stronger if we lock them away in the darkness of the unconscious. Rilke: 'You have had many and great sadnesses . . . Only those sadnesses are dangerous and bad which one carries about among people in order to drown them out; like sicknesses that are superficially and foolishly treated they simply withdraw and after a little pause break out again the more dreadfully . . . of which one may die.'

Second Principle: Facing these 'sadnesses' is one of the most difficult and lonely battles returning warriors will ever fight. Although one can engage the help of others – support groups, encounter groups, men's groups, veterans' groups, psychiatrists or other professionals – in the end the journey must be taken alone and the problem must be faced by the individual self. Rilke again:

> We *are* solitary. We may delude ourselves and act as though this were not so . . . But how much better to realize that we are so . . .
>
> There is but *one* solitude, and that is great, and not easy to bear . . . Going-into-oneself and for hours meeting no one – this one must be able to attain. To be solitary, the way one was solitary as a child, when the grownups went around involved with things that seemed important and big because they themselves looked so busy and because one comprehended nothing of their doings.

Third Principle: Healing may come suddenly, unexpectedly, and radically – in the truest sense a breakthrough: 'For him who becomes solitary all distances, all measures change; of these changes many take place suddenly, and then, as with the man on the mountaintop, extraordinary imaginings and singular sensations arise that seem to grow out beyond all bearing,' says Rilke.

Fourth Principle: Healing the wounds of war frequently involves a process of radical transformation, the nature of which cannot be fully predicted ahead of time. This healing invariably involves the turning of weakness into strength and ignorance into wisdom. 'That which . . . seems to us the most alien will become what we most trust and find most faithful. How should we be able to forget those ancient myths about dragons that at the last moment turn into princesses . . . So you must not be frightened . . . if a sadness rises up before you larger than any you have ever seen.'

Fifth Principle: Staying stuck in the 'Why me?' syndrome – hostility toward 'the system,' indignation about having had to serve, resentment over an interrupted career, or anger about the unfairness of life – guarantees failure. If one is to progress, the anger must be given up. 'You must think that . . . life has not forgotten you, that it holds you in its hand; it will not let you fall . . . Why do you want to persecute yourself with the question whence all this may be coming and whither it is bound?'

Sixth Principle: Be patient. Rilke again:

> You must be patient as a sick man and confident as a convalescent; for perhaps you are both. And more: you are the doctor too, who has to watch over himself. But there are in every illness many days when the doctor can do nothing but wait . . .
>
> *Live* the questions now. Perhaps you will then gradually, without noticing it, live along some distant day into the answer.

Seventh Principle: After your own healing, extend compassion to those fellow warriors who remain in conflict, whose understanding is not yet complete. Give something back by trying to help them – for this is also part of your healing. Rilke: 'Rejoice in your growth, in which you naturally can take no one with you, and be kind to those who remain behind, and be sure and calm before them and do not torment them with your doubts and do not frighten them with your confidence or joy, which they could not understand. Seek yourself some sort of simple and loyal community with them.'

A Way Out?

It is estimated that at this moment there are more wars in more places on the earth than at any other time in human history. What is to be done? At least in one way, 'we have gotten tougher and better prepared to face the enemy that is war,' Ehrenreich believes. 'If the twentieth century brought the steady advance of war and war-related enterprises, it also brought the beginnings of organized human resistance to war.' We have the opportunity as never before, she suggests, to fight against war itself by directing 'our incestuous fixation on combat' into new types of battles – fighting, as we've mentioned, 'the possibility of drastic climate changes, the depletion of natural resources, the relentless predations of the microbial world . . . [and meeting the challenges of] sanitation, nutrition, medical care, and environmental reclamation.'

Some of the most morbid predictions of our future come from biologists who believe we are programmed by our genes to engage forever in warlike behavior. But Howard Bloom's *The Lucifer Principle* – his name for our innate predispositions for evil behavior – suggests that we can defy nature's dictates:

> But there is hope that we may someday free ourselves of savagery. To our species, evolution has given something new – the imagination. With that gift, we have dreamed of peace. Our task – perhaps the only one that will save us – is to turn what we have dreamed into reality. To fashion a world where violence ceases to be. If we can accomplish this goal, we may yet escape our fate as highly precocious offspring, as fitting inheritors of nature's highest gift and foulest curse, as the ultimate children of the Lucifer Principle.

Our first task in resisting war is to acknowledge its grip on us. To do so, it will help to listen to the warnings of the warriors among us who have known war's horrors.

I do not mean listening to common sense – even a fool can tell us that war is horrible – but hearkening to the *dreams* of those who have been to war. This is the approach recommended in 1835 by Alexis de Tocqueville in *Democracy in America*: 'In times when the passions are beginning to take charge of the conduct of human affairs, one should pay less attention to what men of experience and common sense are thinking than to what is preoccupying the imagination of dreamers.'

If I were allowed to pick a dream worthy of our collective attention, I'd choose that of a Vietnam comrade about the city where I spent my doctor days:

> I am trying to warn people that another war is coming, and people are laughing at me. I am in Dallas and we are going in a chopper to secure a position. I am trying to warn people: 'Hey! There's a war fixing to happen! You'd better take cover and get off the street!' But they were laughing and scoffing and they wouldn't listen to me. I was trying to reason with the people when the helicopters flew off and left me there. I . . . couldn't get the people to understand what was really happening.

Part Two

MIND

Introduction

A FEW YEARS AGO my wife, Barbara, and I were invited to India to lecture on the role of the mind in health. It seemed an odd situation. India – birthplace of yoga and Buddhism – has recognized for millennia the role of the mind in healing. Why were we Westerners being asked to come there to discuss these issues?

The reasons became clear following our lectures at the country's major medical school in New Delhi. We discussed the latest mind-body research and how certain clinical interventions, such as biofeedback, imagery, and meditation were being used with great success. Afterward we were told that a group of medical students wanted to speak with us privately. The solemn, earnest young students were disturbed. Their spokesman said hesitantly, 'Do you *really* believe that the mind can influence the body?' The ideas we had presented had not meshed with their scientific training that the body was everything, the mind nothing. For a moment I was speechless and deeply sad. These students, India's best and brightest, had become so thoroughly indoctrinated with the mechanical, Western view of human function that they had lost contact with the great insights of their own culture. For them, mind-body interaction had become largely unthinkable. They were, of course, merely following our lead.

For the past century Western scientists have not been able to make up their minds about whether or not the mind exists. For example, a leading neurology textbook does not even list *mind* in the index. When the author was asked to explain why he left out the mind in a book about the brain, he said, 'It was unnecessary to introduce the concept.' For him, the mind was redundant; it just got in the way.

So it has gone in medicine in modern times. The paradox – medical scientists using their minds to deny the mind's existence – would be funny if the consequences were not so serious.

Although it has been fashionable in science to deny that the mind exists, this trend is coming to a close for several reasons. There simply are too many facts about our existence that cannot be explained merely by focusing on the workings of the brain. As we've seen, we humans derive meaning from life, and our meanings affect our health for good or ill. Indeed, the capacity to form meanings and to be conscious of them is largely what we mean by mind.

Moreover, we are faced with evidence that minds can do things that brains can't do. As we will see in part 3, the mind can act beyond the brain – at a distance, remotely, even outside the present moment. Brains are captives of space and time, the here and now; not so, minds. These stubborn facts show clearly that mind is more than brain.

As a result of the mind's new status, mind-body medicine is fast becoming an established part of the medical landscape in the Western world. Today almost everyone recognizes the role of emotional stress in heart disease; that depression can inhibit our body's immune function; and that people who attend to their mental health – their satisfaction, joy, and fulfillment – generally live longer and are healthier than people who do not. These developments indicate that the mind, after a lengthy absence, is back in medicine.

Now we will venture off the beaten path to explore some neglected aspects of the mind's role in health.

6

Reenchanting the World

*Everything is alive. What we call dead is
an abstraction.*
— DAVID BOHM —

THE ORIGINS OF LIFE are a mystery. Most scientists believe it began
as a result of interactions between simple, carbon-containing molecules in some inchoate, primordial soup. Across the aeons of evolution, these material aggregates became increasingly intricate.
Eventually they grew into single-celled organisms and higher forms
of life, and at a certain stage of biological complexity something
we now call mind or consciousness 'emerged.' There are several
varieties of this story, but it basically remains the same: the mind
is an epiphenomenon, a by-product, an emergent property of the
material brain and body.

Mind out of Matter?

If you are puzzled by how mind could pop out of matter, you are
not alone. So, too, are eminent scientists such as Sir John Eccles,
the Nobel neurophysiologist, who offers a critique of the emergent theory of consciousness in his book *The Wonder of Being
Human*. Eccles observes, 'There is no statement in the "natural
laws" that there is an emergence of this strange, nonmaterial entity,

consciousness or mind ... Any statement that consciousness emerges at a specified level of complexity of systems ... is gratuitously assumed.' Eccles also questions the widespread view that consciousness can't 'do' anything – that it is only the brain, but not consciousness, that is causal: 'If consciousness is causally impotent, its development cannot be accounted for by evolutionary theory. According to biological evolution, mental states and consciousness could have evolved and developed *only if they were causally effective* in bringing about changes in neural happenings in the brain with the consequent changes in behavior.'

Eccles also asserts that materialistic theories of the nature of consciousness are a reductio ad absurdum. He quotes philosopher Karl Popper, who stated in his Compton Lecture: 'According to determinism, any such theory, such as, say, determinism, is held because of a certain physical structure of the holder – perhaps of his brain. Accordingly, we are deceiving ourselves, and are physically so determined as to deceive ourselves, whenever we believe that there are such things as *arguments or reasons* which make us accept determinism. Purely physical conditions, including our physical environment, make us say or accept whatever we say or accept.'

Popper raises a serious question: Why should we listen to 'mental materialists' in the first place? If they are right – if the mind is completely physically determined, and if free will is an illusion – then they have not freely arrived at their conclusions but are simply saying what their brains compel them to say. Philosopher-scientist Willis Harman expresses the predicament faced by all who hold to a thoroughly materialistic view of consciousness. 'Science for three and a half centuries has been built on the premise that consciousness as a causal factor does not have to be included. Now, nobody has ever lived life on the basis of such a contrary premise. Nobody has ever said, "I'm going to live my life as though my consciousness – my mind – weren't capable of making decisions, making choices, taking action."'

The behavior of materialists suggests that they do not actually believe the implications of their own theories. They appear to think that they and perhaps a few of their colleagues, at the very least, have *some* freedom of consciousness. Why else would they energetically publish articles, write books, and give talks at conferences that are designed to bring others around to their way of thinking? Why else would they lobby representatives in Congress to vote favorably on their pet science projects? If consciousness is on automatic, why bother?

Rummaging around in the Brain

Philosopher-scientist David Darling sums up the problems with the materialist view of consciousness:

> A growing number of scientists are now busily rummaging around in the brain trying to explain how the trick of consciousness is done. Researchers of the stature of Francis Crick, Daniel Dennett, Gerald Edelman, and Roger Penrose have recently come forward with a range of ingenious theories. All purport to explain, in one way or another, consciousness as an epiphenomenon of physical and chemical processes taking place in the brain – and all fail utterly. They fail not because their models are insufficiently accurate or detailed, but because they are trying to do what is, from the outset, impossible. The truth is that *no* account of what goes on at the mechanistic level of the brain can shed any light whatsoever on why consciousness exists. No theory can explain why the brain shouldn't work exactly as it does, yet without giving rise to the feeling we all have of 'what it is like to be.' And there is, I believe, a very simple reason for this. The brain does not *produce* consciousness at all, any more than a television set creates the programs that appear on its screen.

The textbook picture of the mind that most of us get in our professional training virtually reeks with certainty. One gets the impression that the broad strokes are already on the canvas and all that remains is to fill in the details. This sort of complacency has occurred often in the history of science – usually just before the lid blows off as a result of unexpected discoveries. One of the most dramatic examples of this sort took place in physics in the waning moments of the nineteenth century. In 1894 the physicist Albert Abraham Michelson, who helped lay to rest the idea of the ether, confidently noted, 'The more important fundamental laws and facts of physical science have all been discovered, and these are now so firmly established that the possibility of their ever being supplanted in consequence of new discoveries is exceedingly remote . . . Our future discoveries must be looked for in the sixth place of decimals.'

About the same time, Lord Kelvin stated that the job of physics and physicists was almost done. He noted that there were only a few problems that needed tidying up, and he actually suggested that young scientists go into a different field. Then, in 1899, only five years following Michelson's cozy prediction, all hell broke loose in physics. Max Planck discovered that energy was not smooth and uniform in nature but discontinuous, composed of units he called 'quanta.' And when Albert Einstein published his special theory of relativity in 1905, the completely predictable, mechanical vision was never to be the same.

New Views of Consciousness

The inconsistencies of the materialist view of the mind are becoming increasingly obvious, and scientists are speaking out. An example is David J. Chalmers, a mathematician, philosopher, and cognitive scientist at the University of Arizona. In an article titled 'The Puzzle of Conscious Experience' in the December 1995 issue of *Scientific American*, he describes how the materialist view fails to account for consciousness: 'Nobody knows why these physical processes [in the brain] are accompanied by conscious experience at all. Why is it that when our brains process light of a certain wavelength, we have an experience of purple? Why do we have any experience at all? Could not an unconscious automaton have performed the same tasks just as well?'

Chalmers states that all the current work in neuroscience deals with what he calls the 'easy problems' – the physical ways in which information is processed in the brain. 'The confidence of the reductionistic view comes from progress on the easy problems,' he states, 'but none of this makes any difference where the hard problem is concerned.' The 'hard problem' is why there should be conscious experience at all, and how it could possibly emerge from physical processes studied by scientists. Until we know these answers, we will not have crossed what philosopher Joseph Levine has called the 'explanatory gap' between physical processes and consciousness. 'Making that leap,' Chalmers believes, 'will demand a new kind of theory.'

Chalmers is not alone. He cites the view of physicist Steven Weinberg, who describes the goal of physics as a 'theory of everything' from which all possible knowledge of the universe can be derived. 'But,' Chalmers observes, 'Weinberg concedes that there is a problem with consciousness. Despite the power of physical theory, the existence of consciousness does not seem to be derivable from physical laws . . . If the existence of consciousness cannot be derived from physical laws, a theory of physics is not a true theory of everything. So a final theory must contain an additional fundamental component.

'Toward this end,' Chalmers continues, 'I propose that *conscious experience be considered a fundamental feature, irreducible to anything more basic*' (emphasis added).

Physicist Nick Herbert, in his book *Elemental Mind*, also asserts that consciousness is a ubiquitous, fundamental feature of the world, like mass and energy:

One of the major mistakes of the medieval philosophers was their underestimation of the size of the physical world. This cozy earth, the seven celestial spheres, plus Dante's concentric circles of hell: that was the full extent of the universe in the medieval imagination. No one at the time even dreamed of other solar systems, let alone galaxies like dust in a vast room billions of light-years in diameter. I believe that modern mind scientists are making this same medieval mistake by vastly underestimating the quantity of consciousness in the universe. If mind is a fundamental force in nature, we might someday realize that the quality and quantity of sentient life inhabiting just this room may exceed the physical splendor of the entire universe of matter. I confess that I do think that consciousness will turn out to be something grand – grander than our most extravagant dreams. I propose here a kind of 'quantum animism' in which mind permeates the world at every level. I propose that *consciousness is a fundamental force that enters into necessary cooperation with matter to bring about the fine details of our everyday world* [emphasis added]. I propose, in fact, that mind is elemental, my dear Watson.

Other new views are emerging to counter the prevailing materialistic concepts of consciousness:

• Nobel physicist Brian Josephson of Cambridge University's Cavendish Laboratory believes there may be a connection between the causal powers of consciousness and developments in a field of fundamental physics that deals with 'nonlocality.' He proposes that distant, simultaneous, 'nonlocal' events at the subatomic level may eventually help explain various nonlocal behaviors of the mind – events such as telepathy, clairvoyance, transpersonal imagery, and distant or intercessory prayer. Josephson suggests that these distant mental connections are made possible through the unique ability of humans to find a meaning or a pattern behind our various perceptions and experiences.

• English botanist Rupert Sheldrake has also proposed, in *Seven Experiments That Could Change the World*, that consciousness is extended nonlocally. Whereas consciousness may work through the brain, Sheldrake suggests, it is not restricted to it. Sheldrake believes that the mind is not totally governed by the so-called iron-clad laws of nature. In fact, he maintains that such laws do not exist. He believes natural laws are not unchanging givens but patterns of occurrence that, like habits, become stronger as events are repeated. The more often an event happens, the more likely it is to occur in the future. Consciousness, Sheldrake maintains, is a factor that has the capacity to shape natural laws.

• Biophysicist Beverly Rubik, at the Institute for Frontier Sciences in Oakland, California, suggests that consciousness can act causally and that its activities will eventually be understood through breakthroughs in the field of information theory. The link between consciousness and information is also sanctioned by mathematician and cognitive scientist Chalmers, whom I have mentioned.

• The late David Bohm, professor of physics at the University of London's Birkbeck College, proposed the existence of several levels of order within nature. There is the manifest or *explicate* world of things and events that constitute our daily lives. In addition, several layers are unseen, which he designates as the *implicate* order. In the implicate domain, everything – including consciousness – is enfolded and in contact with everything else. 'Thus,' Bohm states, 'one is led to a new notion of *unbroken wholeness* which denies the classical idea of analysability of the world in separate and independently existent parts.' This implies that everything may be conscious, at least to some degree.

• In *Janus: A Summing Up*, Arthur Koestler, the late novelist and philosopher, also challenged the idea that nature is fundamentally made up of independent units of dead, mindless matter. He advanced the idea of a multileveled, tiered form of existence made up of 'holons' – what he called a 'holarchy.' Holons exist in two different but related ways. They function on their own as individual, quasi-independent wholes, but at the same time they are parts of larger wholes. For example, an electron has a certain independence but at the same time unites with other particles to form atoms. In the same way, a human being has a unique existence but also belongs to a larger social and cultural group. Koestler saw these self-assertive and integrative tendencies as a universal characteristic of life. He realized that these ideas are ancient – found, for example, in the Pythagorean 'Harmony of the Spheres' and the Hippocratic 'sympathy of all things,' according to which 'there is one common flow, one common breathing, all things . . . in sympathy.' Koestler observed that

the doctrine that everything in the universe hangs together, partly by mechanical causes, but mainly by hidden affinities (which also account for apparent coincidences), provided not only the foundation for sympathetic magic, astrology, and alchemy; it also runs as a *leit-motif* through the teachings of Taoism and Buddhism, the neo-Platonists, and the philosophers of the early Renaissance. It was neatly summed up by (among many others) Pico della Mirandola, A.D. 1550: 'Firstly, there is the unity in things whereby each thing is at one with itself, consists of itself, and coheres with itself. Secondly, there is the unity whereby one creature is united with the others and all parts of the world constitute one world.'

This is only a sampling of the views about the nature of consciousness that are surfacing. All these ideas imply that consciousness extends beyond humans and is a fundamental aspect of the universe. Although couched in the language of science, these views are not new. As Darling observes, 'The idea that the mind is a fundamental, all-pervasive property of the universe lies at the heart of mystical traditions stretching back over 2,000 years.'

The Enchanted World

Not so long ago, almost everyone held such a view, as philosopher of science Morris Berman describes in his book *The Reenchantment of the World:* The view of nature which predominated in the West down to the eve of the Scientific Revolution was that of an enchanted world. Rocks, trees, rivers, and clouds were all seen as wondrous, alive, and human beings felt at home in this environment. The cosmos, in short, was a place of *belonging*. A member of this cosmos was not an alienated observer of it but a direct participant in its drama. His personal destiny was bound up with its destiny, and this relationship gave meaning to his life. This type of consciousness – . . . 'participating consciousness' – involves merger, or identification, with one's surroundings, and bespeaks a psychic wholeness that has long since passed from the scene . . .

The story of the modern epoch, at least on the level of mind, is one of progressive disenchantment. From the sixteenth century on, mind has been progressively expunged from the phenomenal world. At least in theory, the reference points for all scientific explanation are matter and motion – what historians of science refer to as the 'mechanical philosophy.' Developments that have thrown this world view into question – quantum mechanics, for example, or certain types of contemporary ecological research – have not made any significant dent in the dominant mode of thinking. That mode can best be described as disenchantment, nonparticipation, for it insists on a rigid distinction between observer and observed. Scientific consciousness is alienated consciousness: there is no ecstatic merger with nature, but rather total separation from it. Subject and object are always seen in opposition to each other. I am not my experiences, and thus not really a part of the world around me. The logical end point of this world view is a feeling of total reification: everything is an object, alien, not-me; and I am ultimately an object too, an alienated 'thing' in a world of other, equally meaningless things. This world is not of my own making; the cosmos cares nothing for me, and I do not really feel a sense of belonging to it. What I feel, in fact, is a sickness in the soul . . .

For more than 99 percent of human history, the world was enchanted and man saw himself as an integral part of it. The complete reversal of this perception in a mere four hundred years or so has destroyed the continuity of the human experience and the integrity of the human psyche. It has very nearly wrecked the planet as well. The only hope, or so it seems to me, lies in a reenchantment of the world.

I suggest that we *are* in the process of a reenchantment of the world. The forces favoring reenchantment come from fields as diverse as biology, physics, cognitive science, medicine, and information theory. If we have any hope of genuinely engaging these exciting developments, we may have to reawaken a way of thinking that is not highly prized in our society. This pattern of thought has variously been called metaphoric, symbolic, poetic, or imaginative. There is always the danger that this sort of reasoning will lead to excesses such as unbridled fantasy or even hallucinations. But metaphoric, poetic, symbolic thought is not irrational; it has its own laws, albeit different from those preferred by the rational mind.

Employing this way of thinking will require us to set aside some of our biases – such as that revered idea in philosophy called the pathetic fallacy. According to this notion, to which most materialists would presumably subscribe, it is wrong to attribute human feelings to inanimate objects. Because these things are not alive they cannot have feelings. We are wrong to speak of the sea as 'angry,' a song as 'sad,' or a zipper as 'stubborn.'

Were our predecessors correct? Is the world enchanted? Can things come alive?

Under certain circumstances even the inanimate world can manifest in meaningful, intelligent ways. So-called dead things like stones, coffee cups, and automobiles may on occasion speak, as it were, in their own language, in ways that are rich with pattern and information. So, too, perhaps, might the tools we use in therapy. Our stethoscopes, acupuncture needles, tablets, herbs, and medications of all sorts may be capable of entering into meaningful exchanges with us.

I am aware that this sort of thinking is considered more typical of the schizophrenic than the physician. Indeed, you may wonder if I've gone round the bend. If I have, I at least have fine company, because an increasing number of respected scientists and other thinkers are beginning to entertain these ideas, as we will see.

Jung and Synchronicity

Physicist F. David Peat, in his book *Synchronicity: The Bridge between Matter and Mind*, discusses C. G. Jung's proposal that there is a *psychoid* or mindlike quality to the world, which links us with the natural environment in a special way. This linkage sometimes results in a *synchronicity*, a term Jung used for the first time in a lecture at London's Tavistock Clinic in 1929 and elaborated further in *The Interpretation and Nature of the Psyche* (which he wrote with the famous physicist Wolfgang Pauli), and in his *Synchronicity: An Acausal Connecting Principle*. Peat quoted Jung's definition of synchronicity as 'the coincidence in time of two or more causally unrelated events which have the same or similar meaning . . . Meaningful coincidences are unthinkable as pure chance – the more they multiply and the greater and more exact the correspondence is . . . they can no longer be regarded as pure chance, . . . [but] as meaningful arrangements.'

'Synchronicities act as mirrors of the inner processes of the mind and take the form of outer manifestations of interior transformations,' says Peat. 'Synchronicities are therefore often associated with periods of transformation; for example, births, deaths, falling in love, psychotherapy, intense creative work, and even a change of profession. It is as if this internal restructuring produces external resonances or as if a burst of "mental energy" is propagated outward into the physical world.'

Peat cites an example given by psychiatrist Arnold Mindel, in which a psychotic patient declared he was Jesus, the creator and destroyer of light. At that very moment the lighting fixture dropped from the ceiling, knocking the man out. There was a meaning, an apparent significance of this event that seems to separate it from pure chance.

Jung recorded in *Memories, Dreams, Reflections* a famous synchronicity that took place in 1909 when he visited Freud in Vienna, three years before their collaboration broke off. Jung wanted to know Freud's opinion on ESP. At the time, Freud rejected it, although in later years he became more cordial to the idea. Jung describes what happened:

> While Freud was going on this way, I had a curious sensation. It was as if my diaphragm was made of iron and was becoming red-hot – a glowing vault. And at that moment there was such a loud report in the bookcase, which stood right next to us, that we both started up in alarm, fearing the thing was going to topple over us. I said to Freud: 'There, that is an example of a so-called catalytic exteriorisation phenomenon.'
>
> 'Oh come,' he exclaimed. 'That is sheer bosh.'
>
> 'It is not, Herr Professor. And to prove my point I now predict that in a moment there will be another loud report!'
>
> Sure enough, no sooner had I said the words than the same detonation went off in the bookcase.
>
> To this day I do not know what gave me this certainty. But I knew beyond all doubt that the report would come again. Freud only stared aghast at me.

Jung's idea that an emotional state can result in a physical 'exteriorisation' closely resembles the suggestion of physicist Peat that nature can mirror our emotions – or, as Lyall Watson puts it in *The Nature of Things*, that nature can somehow take on our emotional fingerprints.'

Jung's patients were sometimes caught up in the web of synchronistic events with him:

> A young woman I was treating had at a critical moment, a dream in which she was given a golden scarab. While she was telling me this dream I sat with my back to the window. Suddenly I heard a noise behind me, like a gentle tapping. I turned round and saw a flying insect knocking against the window-pane from outside. I opened the window and caught the creature in the air as it flew in. It was the nearest analogy to a golden scarab that one finds in our latitudes, a scarabaeid beetle, the common rose-chafer (*Cetonia aurata*), which contrary to its usual habits had evidently felt an urge to get into a dark room at this particular moment.

The Library Angel

Inanimate things sometimes come to our assistance, which suggests that the world actually *cares* about us. This is illustrated in the Library Angel, Arthur Koestler's tongue-in-cheek spirit associated with 'lucky coincidences' involving libraries, quotations, references, and the like. A typical example was reported to Koestler by Dame Rebecca West, who was researching a specific incident that took place during the Nuremberg war crimes trials: 'I looked up the trials in the library and was horrified to find they are published in a form almost useless to the researcher. They are abstracts, and are catalogued under arbitrary headings. After hours of search I went along the line of shelves to an assistant librarian and said: "I can't find it, there's no clue, it may be in any of these volumes." I put my hand on one volume and took it out and carelessly looked at it, and it was not only the right volume, but I had opened it at the right page.'

Can Things Strike Back?

The reverse also happens. Sometimes the world of things behaves in ways that seem genuinely malicious. An example of such a troubling episode, reported in Peat's *Synchronicity*, involves M. F. Mansfield's 1898 novel of the magnificent ocean liner *Titan*, the largest ever built. Like the *Titanic* years later, the fictitious *Titan* sailed into the Atlantic laden with rich and famous passengers, and was similarly undersupplied with lifeboats. The *Titan* struck an iceberg and sank. Was this a mere chance correlation with the yet-to-be *Titanic*? Could Mansfield have been reading a future event – what is called precognition by parapsychologists – and transcribing this fore-knowledge into his novel? Or is the inanimate world so impressionable, so responsive, that our thoughts can inscribe and bring to life actual events that would not otherwise have occurred?

Is there a perverse side of nature? Can things strike back? Perhaps there are clues in the events surrounding another type of physical object with which humans have long had intense emotional attachments: precious stones or jewels.

The Diamond of Death

Precious stones are often more highly prized than gold. Native Americans, who placed little value on the shiny metal and could not understand the obsession of whites for it, kept highly prized stones such as quartz. 'Lithomania,' says Watson in *The Nature of Things*, 'is a human obsession. People everywhere worship and revere, cherish and collect an astonishing variety of stones. And these are not just things like jade, alabaster and turquoise which have obvious visual appeal. We sleep under and generally decorate our lives with everything from pet rocks to gravestones and should not be surprised if some of these things on which we lavish attention come to carry real emotional fingerprints, which make inorganic and inanimate things behave in some astonishingly life-like ways.'

Watson recounts the history of the seemingly cursed Hope diamond as an example of things that appear to have a malevolent mind of their own. No one knows the origins of the deep blue, heart-shaped stone, but legend has it that a thief stole it from the eye of a sacred idol. It was brought to Europe in 1669 by Jean Baptiste Tavernier and sold to Louis XIV, the Sun King. His successor, Louis XVI, gave it to Marie Antoinette. When they were both guillotined in 1793, the diamond disappeared. Eventually it showed up in Amsterdam, where it was recut and stolen. The thief took it to London, where he committed suicide in 1830, at which point it passed to the hands of a banking family called Hope. The diamond became the object of great disputes and litigation and was sold in 1901 to a French broker, who killed himself within a year. Then the diamond passed to the Russian prince Ivan Kanitowsky, who lent it to Mademoiselle Ladré, an actress at the Folies-Bergère. When she appeared onstage the next evening wearing the stone, she was shot by an ex-lover. A short time later the prince was stabbed to death by revolutionaries.

A Greek jeweler, Simon Montharides, became the next owner. He drove his carriage over a precipice while negotiating a deal with Sultan Abd-al-Hamid, or Abdul the Damned, known as the Great Assassin of Turkey. Abdul was deposed shortly thereafter, at which point the jewel passed via Cartiers of Paris to Evalyn Walsh McLean, an American heiress, in 1910. McLean reportedly wore the Hope constantly until her nine-year-old son was killed by a car, her twenty-five-year-old daughter died of an overdose of sleeping tablets, and her husband drank himself to death in a mental hospital. When McLean died in 1947 of pneumonia, she left the diamond in trust to her six grandchildren until the youngest was twenty-five. The family contested the trust and the jewel was sold to pay claims and debts against the estate. In December 1967 another Evalyn McLean was found dead in her home in Dallas – the youngest former joint-heiress to the diamond – shortly after her twenty-fifth birthday. The wake of death left by the Hope seems to have abated. After centuries of wandering, it has come to rest in the Smithsonian Institution in Washington, D.C.

What are the odds that the Hope diamond would accumulate such a record for a violent or untimely death in its owners? Is there a straightforward answer? Are those who could afford such a stone more prone to reckless behavior and more likely to die tragically as a consequence? Would such individuals have died violently anyway, even if they never heard of the Diamond of Death? Or do stones speak, and are their messages sometimes negative? Are there 'lithic hexes'?

Do Stones Speak?

Watson also relates an interesting discovery by scientists at the De Beers Research Laboratory in Johannesburg in 1965. They found that the deep blue color of the Hope diamond is due to the replacement of a few carbon atoms by boron atoms at several critical points in its crystalline lattice structure. 'The result,' Watson writes, 'is that the Hope is, and always has been, a powerful semiconductor of electricity.' Noting that there are strong similarities between our own nerves and artificial semiconductors, Watson cites the proposal of solid-state chemist Don Robins that these similarities may make possible certain feedback loops that link the energies of humans with those of buildings, stones, and artifacts. Robins implies that we may have the ability to imprint an electronic or informational trace on crystal and stone and that our bodies may contain a 'lithic memory' as well, which may be triggered and released under certain circumstances. Robins suggests that the coupling between humans and stones is most often acoustic, 'and that recording takes place as a direct result of structured sound signals such as those produced by ritual music, chant, prayer, dance, applause and song. This nicely accounts for the atmosphere, the sense of something sacred, common to temples and cathedrals, shrines and standing stones, extending very often to those long in ruin.'

This does not mean that stones are conscious in the way humans are but that stones may nevertheless carry 'a pattern that can model or induce a certain frame of mind. In other words, in the presence of such stone,' says Watson, 'we can become aware of "echoes of the past" which may lead to particular mental imagery.' In turn, do these echoes lead to certain behaviors that inevitably surround certain 'cursed jewels' such as the Hope diamond?

The Revenge of Things

On Saturday, July 8, 1995, Cecilia Dillenham, the organist for a fundamentalist Pentecostal congregation outside Amarillo, Texas, stopped by the church to practice the organ for services the next day. The organ was fairly new to Dillenham. It was an old German pipe organ that had recently been donated to the church by one of the members. Ethan Paxen, the church's forty-two-year-old pastor, was nearby in his church office preparing his Sunday sermon. Organist Dillenham spoke to him, then sat down at the organ to play. Unbeknownst to her, the organ's volume mechanism had been set at full blast by 'some idiot.' When she sat down and struck the first note – a C-sharp – the old church shook to its foundation and the windows rattled. 'It sounded like a mortar blast,' the shaken organist said. Then she heard something in Paxen's office. She went to check and found him lying on the floor clutching his chest. An ambulance was called, but resuscitation attempts were unsuccessful. 'That pipe organ killed him, there's no doubt about it,' the grieving organist said. Dillenham predicted the church would probably return the organ that put their minister in the grave. 'A big organ like that is just too dangerous for a little church like ours,' she lamented. Paxen had never had heart problems. A pathologist said he died of a heart attack, apparently triggered by extreme shock or fright.

As a physician, I am aware of the usual explanations for deaths like these. But when I let my imagination wander, questions arise. Would any loud note have resulted in the pastor's death, or was there something special about C-sharp? Music has strange powers. Specific musical passages, for example, are known by medical scientists to evoke epileptic seizures – it's called musicogenic epilepsy, reports Macdonald Critchley in *Music and the Brain*. Certain notes have been associated in the past with evil – most notably B-natural, which was known as 'the note of the devil.' Some types of music are still considered demonic. Was the old German pipe organ innocent? Was it an inert, unfeeling, unthinking machine? Was it happy in its new home? Did it resent being ripped from its German homeland and transplanted to the dreary plains of the Texas panhandle? Could it have resented Pastor Paxen's brand of spirituality? Did it resist being made an accomplice to his Bible-pounding, fire-breathing exhortations? Was it resentful of the Pentecostal musical strains Dillenham inflicted on it? Did it miss having glorious Bach played on its keys? Did the organ take revenge? Was the homicidal C-sharp the organ's way of saying, in effect, '*I won't take it anymore!*'?

Musical instruments are exposed to a greater range of human

emotions than perhaps any other object. We channel our most intimate feelings through them. As a result of their chronic exposure
to our innermost emotions, is it possible for musical instruments
to resonate with us? Can they spring to life and speak, as it were,
in their own language? When we refer to violins that weep and
strings that sing, are we acknowledging a liveliness lying dormant
in things? If we knew how to listen, could we hear their messages?

I raise these questions in all seriousness. I believe we have
underestimated the boundaries of life and consciousness. When
treated badly, things sometimes appear to strike back as if in
revenge. Consider also the golf clubs of Jean Potevan, who threw
them along with his golf bag into a lake after missing three putts
on the final hole of a disastrous round at a French golf course.
When he realized his car keys were in the bag, he waded in fully
clothed and drowned when he became entangled in weeds as he
dived under the water. According to fellow golfer Henri Levereau,
his final words were, 'I'm going back for the keys, but I'm leaving
the clubs down there.'

When Cars Turn

Perhaps the most dramatic suggestions that things can turn on
humans occur in our interactions with automobiles. 'No other arti-
fact has ever inspired such emotion or been so potent an instrument for change, reshaping human society in its image,' observes
Watson in *The Nature of Things*.

> No other machine has been so treated as a being with powers
> of its own. Automania is already endowed with many of the
> characteristics of a religious cult. Anthropologist Andrew Greeley
> points out that every motor show is a highly ritualised religious
> performance, a form of public worship complete with pomp,
> splendour, temple maidens in the form of fashion models, lights,
> music, lavish waste of money, and a congregation come to
> worship with every evidence of awe.

'*Auto*biography is evident in every bumper sticker,' Watson adds.
'"A van's got to do what a van's got to do." "You only love me for
my body," [or] the plaintive "Wash me!"'

Cars embody our emotions; they add meaning to peoples' lives. And emotion and meaning, we have seen, appear to be major stimulants for the life-like behavior of inanimate objects. Can our emotions and meanings bring autos to life? Watson reports several cases in which they appear to do so.

In Florida in 1978 a woman was leaving her car in a supermarket parking lot when it started up on its own, reversed, ran over her, and kept running over her as it repeatedly circled. It kept rescuers at bay for fifteen minutes. At her funeral one of her friends observed, 'She never liked that car.' And in Sydney, Australia, in 1981, Dorothy Woodward was trying to push over a cliff an old wreck she despised, when it dragged her two hundred feet to her death.

Or consider the open touring car built by Graf and Stift in which Archduke Franz Ferdinand was traveling when he was assassinated at Sarajevo in 1914. Two weeks later a captain in the Fifth Austrian Corps ran over two workmen and killed them and himself when he swerved into a tree while driving the same car. The car then passed into the hands of a Yugoslavian government official, who had four further accidents in it, the last of which resulted in the loss of an arm. 'Destroy it; the thing is cursed,' he said. It was sold instead to a doctor who was crushed to death when the car rolled on top of him. Then the ill-fated auto passed to a wealthy businessman who disregarded its history; later he was found dead in the car, a suicide. A Swiss auto racer then took possession; he was killed when he crashed into a wall the first time out. The vehicle was repaired and bought by a farmer. One day, after a breakdown, it was taken in tow. But the car broke loose, overturned on a curve, and killed its owner. A mechanic mended the car and borrowed it to drive four friends to a wedding. A head-on collision with an oncoming vehicle killed them all. Finally the Austrian government stopped the slaughter by purchasing the auto and restoring it. Today the four-cylinder Graf and Stift – the automobile equivalent of the Hope diamond – is on permanent display in the Army Museum in Vienna.

One of the most rebellious rampages of an inanimate object, Watson reports, was that of the Porsche Spyder purchased by actor James Dean in 1955. Following Dean's death in the car crash, the wrecked Spyder was purchased by car designer George Barris, who wanted to salvage the parts. It broke his mechanic's leg when it slipped off its carrier immediately on arrival in the mechanic's backyard. Barris sold the engine to a Beverly Hills physician who was a racing enthusiast. The first time out with the Spyder engine he crashed his car and died. The transmission of the Spyder was purchased by another doctor who was seriously injured in the same race. The Porsche's body went to Salinas as part of a display emphasizing road safety, but the truck on which it was being transported skidded, killing the driver. While on the bed of another truck in Oakland, somewhat later, the wreck broke apart. One part caused an accident when it fell onto the road; the rest continued until the brakes on the truck failed, causing it to smash into a store. The remains of the wreck were shipped by train to Miami for another display. They never arrived; presumably they were dismantled and stolen by James Dean fans along the way.

'The whole thing is ridiculous,' Watson admits. 'Nothing but freak accidents, naturally . . . But what is one to make of cars that get involved in long lines of such coincidence?'

Implications for Healing

There is a veritable 'thing apartheid' in our culture, whereby inanimate objects are not accorded the same respect as living, sensate organisms. Proposing that things can behave well or badly, or that they have any behavior at all, sounds preposterous to anyone schooled in twentieth-century science. Yet things appear to be avid accumulators of significances, particularly when they are chronically exposed to humans. They appear capable of catching our feelings, resonating with our emotions, responding to our meanings, and obtruding in our lives, often when we least expect it. And the implications for healing are profound.

Healers for millennia have cultivated the ability to interact with the world of things. This ability is illustrated in the following episode, reported in *Psychological Elements in Parapsychological Traditions* by the Greek physician Angelos Tanagras, who was also a highly decorated admiral in the Greek navy. In addition to his scholarly writings on Greek history and legend, he was keenly interested in what he termed 'psychoboly,' the action of 'man's impulses . . . upon living or inorganic matter.'

The case involves the experiences of Monsieur A. Laforest, 'a French literary man,' in the jungles of Colombia. One day Laforest went into the jungle to hunt wild pigeons, and en route he met the beadle, a minor parish officer of the church of Simiti. When Laforest inquired about the purpose of the beadle's journey, he replied, 'I am going to Joselito's to get rid of his fish worms. It is an exorcism. I go here and there in the countryside ridding fish of worms. I am the only one in the whole country who can do this.'

Laforest, not comprehending, remained silent and went along to see what would happen. They soon arrived at Joselito's wood cabin and Joselito explained to the beadle that the white worms had invaded his store of salted fish. He showed them about a hundred infested fish hanging on an iron wire. The beadle examined them, saw they were full of worms, and shook his head. 'They will only disappear by exorcism,' he announced. Then he stepped back a pace and began repeating an incantation in a low voice.

'He had hardly finished when the worms began to drop from the fish like iron filings,' Laforest reported. Joselito then thanked the beadle, as if this event were the most natural thing in the world.

'I approached the fish to examine them,' Laforest said. 'Not a single worm remained. A few words from the beadle had been sufficient to loosen them from the flesh in which they had been buried. I could not understand it at all, but the miracle had been carried out before my own eyes.'

Laforest, stunned, returned to Simiti, where he hastened to see the priest and tell him what had occurred. The good man shook his head: 'No, it is not witchcraft,' he said, 'it is simple exorcism . . . accompanied by great faith. My beadle is the simplest and most devout of all my parishioners. The words themselves are meaningless . . . Be like my beadle and you will possess the same power . . . Such things do not surprise anyone here. Sometimes flies lay their eggs in the wound of a horse, thus making the wound fatal. But my beadle heals the wound from a distance of several kilometers, provided he is told in which part of the animal's body the wound is situated.'

Tanagras reported a similar case with plants. A priest in the Caucasus was invited to visit a Russian farmer whose field of sunflowers was infested by worms that were causing great damage. The priest began to recite with great fervor prayers that were composed for such occasions by Saint Basil and other saints of the Greek Orthodox Church. The worms, present in great numbers, 'began to drop off the plants and flee like a minor torrent in the opposite direction.'

Similar methods appear to work on insects. Tanagras reported that in 1920, during the Greek occupation of Asia Minor, a Greek professor journeyed to the Turkish village of Eskisehir for the purpose of examining the local antiquities. For his accommodation an empty house was requisitioned, but in the door of this house, at a height of about six feet. a swarm of bees had built their nest. Every effort was made to dislodge the nest, without success. The maidservant, very disturbed by the proximity of the bees, advised calling in a local *hodja*, a Turkish priest, who had the ability of 'exorcising' and would therefore be able to solve the problem. 'The *hodja* . . . came in the evening and stayed for some time in order to pray. The bees were not seen again and no dead bees were found, as would have been the case if fumigation or a poison had been used.'

Sometimes the organisms get the upper hand and appear to strike back, as suggested by the events surrounding the Hope diamond and the Porsche Spyder. One such incident involved one of Brazil's most famous 'psychic surgeons,' reported to me by Stanley Krippner, Ph.D., director of research at the Saybook Institute in San Francisco. As reports of the man's healing ability grew, so did his ego. He became increasingly arrogant and proud, traits generally considered by genuine healers to be incompatible with their calling. At the height of his fame and hubris, he and a friend were paddling a boat in the middle of a wide river when they were attacked from nowhere by a swarm of 'killer bees.' Oddly, the bees attacked only the healer, leaving the other boatman unharmed. 'They want only me!' the man shouted as he tried in vain to fight off the bees. 'They are punishing me because of my pride! I have been untrue as a healer!' The man dived into the river to escape the bees, but he was unsuccessful. As his horrified companion looked on helplessly, they stung him to death.

A charming story about human-insect interaction originated several years ago from the Findhorn community in Scotland. For many years the Findhorn residents have not only survived but thrived in one of the most inhospitable regions of the country. Findhorn attributes its success in large measure to a spiritual approach to life, particularly in farming and gardening. Their beliefs bear fruit, literally; the bounty of their fields is legendary.

At one point the Findhorn kitchen became infested with cockroaches. Killing the insects with insecticides or fumigants was contrary to the community's belief that all life was sacred, and was therefore considered unacceptable. Something had to be done, but what? After much deliberation they decided to negotiate firmly with the pests. They filled several garbage cans with succulent wastes that would be the envy of any cockroach community and placed them at some distance from the dwellings. 'You cannot remain in the kitchen,' they announced to the cockroaches. 'We have a better home for you. You must vacate the kitchen by the end of the week or we shall unleash harsh methods to get rid of you.' According to reports, the cockroaches accepted the offer. By the end of the week the kitchen was insect-free, and the cockroach population in the garbage cans was thriving.

Shamans and Hospitals

The connection with shamanic healing, which has existed for at least fifty thousand years, should be obvious. Shamans consider the entire world to be alive. When they engage in healing, they journey to other dimensions where they meet benevolent spirit animals who assist them in their tasks. They also encounter malevolent entities who have caused the illness, and they bargain and negotiate with them to bring about healing in the affected individual. 'Talking out worms' from animals and plants and banishing bees and cockroaches each resemble shamanic healing to a great extent. Both involve the belief that the world is alive. If properly engaged, all things can be communicated with and may possibly come to our assistance.

I strongly suspect that the vestiges of shamanism can be found in any modern hospital. Everyone recognizes that certain nurses and physicians have uncommon talents in dealing with sick persons. Their patients simply 'do better.' They develop fewer complications, such as infections, and they recover and are discharged more quickly. I hypothesize that, in addition to whatever technical skills they may bring to the situation, they are also wheeling and dealing with the bacteria, the cancer cells, the T and B cells, and so on, like any good shaman.

There appears also to be a flip side – a natural equivalent to bad bedside manner – in which inanimate things behave negatively around certain individuals and not others. On November 4, 1924, in a woolen mill in Yorkshire, England, three spinning frames broke down simultaneously in the same room. The manager called in his best mechanics, who could find nothing wrong, so the machines were set in motion again. Before long there were several more breakdowns, one after the other. Unable to discover the cause, the manager called in experts from the Woolen Research Association. Their suggestions were heeded, but again the machines began to break down for no apparent reason. The chaos continued until a nineteen-year-old girl, Gwynne, who had just begun working in that particular section, happened to be sent to another area of the mill. The breakdowns followed her. This was pointed out to the owner of the mill, but 'that solid Yorkman poured scorn on tales of a "witch" in his works' – that is, until Gwynne was brought into a room in full production and asked simply to walk down an aisle, hands in pockets, between the spinning frames. Within seconds they malfunctioned. Then she was taken into another room, where the frames also broke down. Finally, as Gwynne was being hustled out of the mill, several more machines ground to a halt as she walked by. 'The unfortunate Gwynne was forbidden to go near a mill again and set to work instead as a maid in the company canteen.'

Most health-care professionals have probably worked with colleagues who are the medical equivalent of Gwynne. I have known doctors whose patients always seem to be getting sick and winding up in the hospital, where they stay longer. Their hospital census is always booming. I suspect that we all know doctors who, if we were sick, we would not invite to take care of us.

What about the inanimate objects we use in therapy? Are they capable of responding to our emotions, feelings, and meanings? Can inanimate things injure or kill patients, as suggested by the track record of the Hope diamond and the Porsche Spyder? Are the toxic and fatal effects of drugs and surgical procedures random events? Or might the injections, capsules, tablets, and scalpels be objecting? Why do some therapies seem to cooperate with some therapists and not others? And why, for that matter, do the outcomes in controlled studies seem to mirror the emotions and meanings of the scientists who conduct them? Marilyn Schlitz, Ph.D., director of research at the Institute of Noetic Sciences in Petaluma, California, has been involved in controlled studies that seem to clearly demonstrate that preexisting beliefs and attitudes held by the principal investigator correlate with their clinical outcomes. What is going on? As long as we continue to believe that the material world is made up of unthinking dead stuff, we may never know.

If we in the health-care professions used our 'medical things' with a sense of sacredness and respect, would they be more likely to respond with gratitude, and would side effects be fewer? If we gave thanks to our stethoscopes, retractors, and otoscopes for their service, would they give of themselves more freely? Would we find that we could hear more, see more, and do more with these tools if we accorded them greater respect?

The New Animism

Many people think we are making tremendous progress in introducing consciousness into healing. But although advances in meditation, hypnosis, mental imagery, prayer, self-responsibility, and prevention involve consciousness, they do not go far enough. The current attitude toward consciousness in healing is far too conservative.

Consider how we speak about consciousness. We talk almost exclusively in mind-body medicine about the effects of *my* consciousness on *my* body. Mind-body medicine has really become 'my mind, my body' medicine. This development is not wrong, but it is incomplete. We have not yet begun to engage fully the evidence for nonlocal or transpersonal manifestations of consciousness: the ability of *my* consciousness to affect *your* body at a distance – even when you are unaware this is going on – and the capacity of *your* consciousness to do the same.

Not only is our current attitude toward consciousness conservative, it is arrogant as well. 'Consciousness' for most of us is thoroughly anthropocentric – something for us humans and not for anything else. We continue to set ourselves apart from those so-called lower organisms and the 'inanimate' world, which we insist are unconscious by definition. So we talk a good game about consciousness – but scratch the surface of most people who believe in 'the powers of the mind' and you will usually find someone who believes in the special status of humans and the lower status of just about everything else in this world. ·

The integration of consciousness and healing involves going much further. It is not enough to accord significance to *our* mind, *our* consciousness. We also must be mindful of the consciousness of *things* – cells and tissues, bacteria, the tools we use, the medications we administer, the uniforms we wear, the buildings in which we work.

I am aware of the dangers involved here. But let us not be overcome with the fear of falling into fantasy as we begin to explore once again an animated world. Let us recall once again that, for most of the history of the human race, this point of view has seemed natural. Only lately have we lost our way, and we can find it again. Guides still exist. Let us recall also that we have an advantage our predecessors never had: the insights of creative scientists who, as we've seen, are formulating theories of the nature of consciousness – and the consciousness of nature – to help us negotiate this enchanted domain.

Let us make a space for the 'new animism' – not just because it seems intuitively right to do so, but also because our data demand it. We have not examined the empirical data supporting the view of pervasive consciousness, but they are extensive. They are manifested in the many areas of investigative science showing the capacity of consciousness to interact nonlocally with the inanimate and semianimate world – areas such as human/machine interaction; transpersonal imagery; studies in so-called bio-PK (psychokinesis) and distant, intercessory prayer, in which individuals interact with 'lower,' nonhuman organisms such as bacteria, fungi, yeast, and cells of various sorts. These empirical findings point to a nonsentient world that is nevertheless responsive to human thought and emotion, which, therefore, cannot be as dead as we have believed.

Finding the Right Channel

William James said, 'There is really no scientific or other method by which men can steer safely between the opposite dangers of believing too little or believing too much. To face such dangers is apparently our duty, and to hit the right channel between them is the measure of our wisdom.'

How can we find the right channel? At the very least, we must follow what Hermann Hesse called 'the whisperings of our blood' – our own intuitions, hunches, and best bets. This is nothing new; all good scientists do this already. Second, we must listen to the stories and experiences, such as those described in this chapter, that crop up spontaneously and unannounced in people's lives. And third, we must be willing to submit our conclusions and theories to rigorous experimental tests. If we do so, we may learn again to hear the stones speak.

7

Tickled Pink

AN APACHE MYTH TELLS how the creator endowed human beings, the two-leggeds, with the ability to do everything – talk, run, see, and hear. But he was not satisfied until the two-leggeds could do just one thing more – laugh. And so men and women laughed and laughed and laughed! Then the creator said, 'Now you are fit to live.'

Humor may reign in heaven, as this story suggests, but it has often seemed to be in short supply here on earth. Although we tolerate laughter in children, as they near adulthood we ask them, metaphorically speaking, to wipe the smiles from their faces, act their age, grow up, and be serious.

Our religious traditions have often reinforced this message. As if suffering from a pounding puritanical hangover, they frequently conveyed the message that laughter is perilously akin to sin. Brian Luke Seaward describes the stormy relations between piety and play in his book *Managing Stress*. 'Laughter has not always been looked upon with favor,' he observes. 'Europeans in the middle ages and Puritans on the eastern shores of North America, among others, perceived laughter to be the work of the devil. People caught laughing out loud were often denounced as witches or believed possessed by Satan. The expression of humor was considered a sin in many Christian denominations . . . It was not until the 20th century that people would risk a smile in a photograph.'

Psychiatrist and author Raymond Moody, in his book *Laugh*

after Laugh: The Healing Power of Humor, cites a corroborating remark by Lord Chesterfield in 1748 about the corrupting power of laughter:

> Laughter on any occasion is immoral and indecent.
>   Laughter obscures truth, hardens the heart, and stupefies understanding.
>   A man of parts of fashion is therefore only seen to smile, but never heard to laugh.

Fortunately, many influential Western thinkers were not as grim and realized that a humorless life leaves out something vital. Goethe: 'The man of understanding finds everything laughable, the man of reason, almost nothing.' Schiller: 'Man is only fully human when he is at play.' Schopenhauer: 'A sense of humor is the only divine quality of man.'

Pinning Humor Down

Attempts to define humor and laughter have occasionally been humorous themselves:

- 'Laughter is a reflex. The word reflex . . . is a . . . fiction.'
- 'Laughter [is] the behavioral response to humor.'
- 'Spontaneous laughter is produced by the co-ordinated contraction of fifteen facial muscles in a stereotyped pattern and accompanied by altered breathing.'
- 'Smiling involves a complex group of facial movements . . . the drawing back and slight lifting of the corners of the mouth, the raising of the upper lip, which partially uncovers the teeth, and the curving of the furrows betwixt the corners of the mouth and the nostrils . . . the formation of wrinkles under the eye . . . and the increased brightness of the eyes.'

Although these definitions attempt to be physiologically precise, they do not account for the *experience* of humor and laughter – what they *feel* like. To see the difference, we have only to look at a commonplace but amazingly complex phenomenon: tickling.

'The harmless game of tickling has resisted all attempts to find a unitary formula for the causes of laughter; it has been the stumbling block which made the theorists of the comic give up, or their theories break down,' observes Arthur Koestler in his landmark book, *The Act of Creation*. At one time it was believed that the laughter resulting from tickling was a purely automatic reflex in response to the physical stimulation of the skin, but this view is surely too simple. 'If a fly settles on the belly of a horse,' Koestler explains, 'a kind of contractile wave may pass over the skin – the equivalent of the squirming of the tickled child. But the horse does not laugh when tickled, and the child not always.' Darwin and other naturalists interpreted the squirming response as an innate defense mechanism to protect vulnerable areas of the body from attack – the armpits, soles of the feet, neck, belly, flank. But what is its connection with laughter?

To understand tickling, the mind must be brought in. Children will laugh only if they perceive the tickling to be 'a mock attack, a caress in a mildly aggressive disguise.' This helps to explain why children laugh only when tickled by others and not by themselves, Koestler maintains, and also why 'peekaboo' behavior is so effective in eliciting laughter. Surprise also helps bring forth laughter – delivering the tickling at an unexpected time and location, for example.

In order for tickling to cause babies to laugh, they must feel safe, observes Koestler. Experiments in tickling babies under one year of age revealed that they were fifteen times more likely to laugh if they were tickled by their mothers than by strangers. Mothers can be trusted; with strangers, one never knows if the threat is real or not.

Tickling in infants can tell us a lot about laughter in adults. In comic impersonation, for example, the 'tickler' often behaves like a mock aggressor, but we know the aggression is not real. We feel safe, and we laugh. So, too, when we consent to be victimized in horror movies and laugh when the 'horror' is most intense.

Humor and the Brain

Do we have a 'humor center'? Which part of the brain is involved when we laugh? Peter Derks, a researcher at the College of William and Mary, recorded electroencephalograms on individuals as they were presented with humorous material. While the joke was being set up, activity in the left cerebral hemisphere dominated as the subject analyzed and processed the information. Then the dominant activity shifted to the frontal lobe, the center of emotionality. Moments later, when the subject seemed to be trying to 'get' the joke, the right hemisphere's activity joined in. A few milliseconds later, prior to laughing, increased brain activity spread to the occipital lobe, where the processing of sensory information takes place. As the person 'got' the joke and laughter began, delta waves increased and reached a crescendo. Derks's findings suggest that there is no 'humor center' but that various parts of the brain work together when we experience delight and laughter.

A study of cerebral blood flow with positron emission tomography yields additional insight into how the brain functions during the experience of positive emotions. Investigators examined cerebral blood flow during states of sadness and happiness in healthy women. During happiness no detectable increase in blood flow was found anywhere in the cerebrum; in fact, there was decreased flow in the prefrontal and temporoparietal cortical areas, suggesting that positive emotion puts the brain momentarily at rest – 'precisely what appears desirable for healing.'

The Physical Effects of Humor

The past twenty years have been a golden era in humor research. Among the most provocative experimental findings are the following:

• The experience of laughter is associated with a lowering of serum cortisol level, an increase in activated T lymphocytes, an increased number and activity of natural killer cells, and an increase in the number of T cells having helper/suppressor receptors. These findings suggest that laughter quiets the body's stress response and enhances immune activity.

• After subjects viewed a humorous video or one involving trust, there was an increase in salivary immunoglobulin A (IgA), which is believed to protect against some viruses.

• Laughter appears to be a form of 'internal jogging,' as author and editor Norman Cousins put it. Laughing initially causes an increase in the heart and respiratory rate, raises blood pressure, increases oxygen consumption, gives the muscles of the face and stomach a workout, and relaxes the muscles not involved in laughing. Shortly following laughter, however, these cardiovascular indices fall to levels below previous resting values.

• When researchers asked professional actors and scientists to mimic prototypical emotional facial expressions and then to experience various emotions by reliving a past experience, they found striking differences in heart rate, hand temperature, skin resistance, and muscle tension. In contrast to the changes seen with anger and fear, happiness was associated with much lower rises in heart rate and hand temperature.

• The experience of positive emotions such as happiness during exercise appear to produce beneficial cardiovascular effects.

• Individuals who said they turned to humor as a way of coping with difficult life situations had the highest initial concentrations of salivary IgA, suggesting that a consistently cheerful approach to life enhances one's immune capacity.

• Tears in response to laughter and pain have a different composition than do those induced artificially by cutting onions. 'Emotional teardrops' have a higher concentration of proteins and toxins, suggesting that they may be helpful in ridding the body of injurious substances.

Humor and Medicine

Medicine, like religion, has often been intolerant of humor. One of my earliest memories of a medical environment is associated with solemnity and trepidation. As a child, I would often journey with my parents to visit sick relatives in Cox's Hospital, a twenty-bed facility in the small farming town of Groesbeck in central Texas. I will never forget a poster that was displayed throughout the hospital: an image of a beautiful, stern, white-capped nurse holding a finger to her lips in the universal signal for silence, with 'SHHHHHHH!' as the caption. She had a barely detectable frown that seemed to say, 'I'm not kidding!' She seemed to glower at me, like a menacing gargoyle, everywhere I turned. I could not escape her. I was thoroughly intimidated and would not have uttered a squeak in Dr Cox's facility if my life had depended on it.

There is another side to medicine's attitude toward humor, an openness and flexibility that have never died. The healing power of a light heart has been recognized since antiquity. As a single example, Henri de Mondeville, a professor of surgery in fourteenth-century Europe, advised, 'Let the surgeon take care to regulate the whole regimen of the patient's life for joy and happiness, allowing his relatives and special friends to cheer him, and by having someone tell him jokes.'

The most dramatic event in recent history that brought humor into the medical spotlight was the illness of Norman Cousins. In 1964 he was diagnosed with ankylosing spondylitis, with severe inflammation of the spine and joints. Even minimal activity, such as turning over in bed, was excruciatingly painful for him. Cousins tried to learn as much as possible about his disease. He discovered that there were apparent connections between psychological stress and certain diseases. If negative emotions correlated with illness, could one deliberately use positive emotions to restore health? With the collaboration of his physician, Dr William Hitzig, Cousins checked out of the hospital into a nearby hotel. He obtained humorous books as well as movies featuring Laurel and Hardy and the Marx Brothers. A friend, Alan Funt, donated classic clips from his popular TV show *Candid Camera*. Cousins was delighted to discover that ten minutes of solid belly laughter gave him two hours of pain-free sleep. This became a significant feature of his treatment.

Dr Hitzig was also intrigued. He monitored Cousins's sedimentation rate, a measure of inflammation in the body, testing it before and after his response to amusing situations in films and books. Hitzig found that just a few moments of robust laughter correlated with a reduction of the sedimentation rate by a few units. Importantly, the reduction held and was cumulative.

Cousins reflected on his illness in his book *Anatomy of an Illness*, which created a worldwide sensation. He clearly realized that more than laughter had been involved in his improvement. For instance, he had taken large doses of vitamin C in addition to focusing on positive emotions. And humor was not the only emotion he brought into the mix. 'I . . . tried to bring the full range of positive emotions into play,' he stated, '– love, hope, faith, will to live, festivity, purpose, determination.'

Cousins was careful not to recommend laughter as a panacea: 'Obviously, what worked for me may not work for everyone else. Accumulating research points to a connection between laughter and immune enhancement, but it would be an error and indeed irresponsible to suggest that laughter – or the positive emotions in general – have universal or automatic validity, whatever the circumstances. People respond differently to the same things. One man's humor is another man's ho-hum. The treatment of illness has to be carefully tailored to suit the individual patient.'.

Above all, Cousins did not wish to counterpose laughter to orthodox medical measures. He continues: 'I was disturbed by the impression these [newspaper] accounts created that I thought laughter was a substitute for authentic medical care . . . I emphasized that my physician was fully involved in the process and that we regarded laughter as a metaphor for the full range of the positive emotions.'

Cousins's cautions and qualifications, however, largely went unnoticed. In the public's imagination, he literally had laughed himself back to health, and a new specialty – humor therapy – was born.

Theories of Humor

What is humor? Why do people laugh? These questions are not easy ones, and no one has been able to answer them satisfactorily. In *Humor: God's Gift*, Tal D. Bonham describes four major theories about why people find things humorous.

Superiority Theory

The superiority theory is perhaps the oldest theory of humor and often is credited to Plato in the fourth century B.C.E. According to this theory, we laugh at the mistakes and misfortunes of others because it makes us feel superior and raises our self-esteem. 'Typically, the greater the dignity of the object – for example, President Ford and his golfing mishaps, Prince Charles and his Ouija Board, and Vice President Dan Quayle and his misspellings and verbal gaffes – the greater the laugh,' Brian Seaward explains in *Managing Stress*. Superiority-based humor can be painful if one is on the wrong end of it, as in sexist, racist, and ethnic jokes. We can glimpse the painful potential of superiority-based humor in sarcasm, a word derived from the Greek *sarkazein*, which means 'to tear flesh like dogs.'

Oddly, humor at the expense of others is part of our religious heritage. According to one survey, thirteen of the twenty-nine references to laughter in the Old Testament are linked to scorn, derision, mockery, or contempt, and only two are 'born out of a joyful and merry heart.'

We learn to laugh at others at a young age. 'A survey among American schoolchildren between the ages of eight and fifteen led to the conclusion (which could hardly have surprised anybody) that "mortification or discomfort or hoaxing of others very readily caused laughter, while a witty or funny remark often passed unnoticed."'

All of this suggests there is a dark side to humor. In *The Act of Creation*, Koestler calls the 'theory of superiority' the 'theory of degradation' and finds it the most persistent theory of humor in history:

> For Aristotle himself laughter was closely related to ugliness and debasement; for Cicero 'the province of the ridiculous . . . lies in a certain baseness and deformity'; for Descartes laughter is a manifestation of joy 'mixed with surprise or hate or sometimes with both'; in Francis Bacon's list of laughable objects, the first place is taken by 'deformity.' . . . In Hobbes's *Leviathan*, 'The passion of laughter is nothing else but sudden glory arising from a sudden conception of some eminency in ourselves by comparison with the infirmity of others, or with our own formerly.'

Incongruity (Surprise) Theory

According to the incongruity theory, humor arises when the mind suddenly encounters an outcome it doesn't expect – a little ambush of the intellect. When we think an event is headed one way and it suddenly veers off in another, we often think it is funny. Koestler called this phenomenon 'bisociation' – the connection of two or more things we believed were separate.

During a recent meeting of the editors of *Alternative Therapies in Health and Medicine*, we were discussing several research papers that had been submitted for publication. Sensing our need for some comic relief, Michael Villaire, our managing editor, casually circulated a sheet of paper to everyone on which was a cartoon depicting an automobile accident. The victim is lying on the pavement and is surrounded by a crowd of onlookers, and a woman is aggressively elbowing her way through them to lend a hand. The caption reads, 'Let me through! – I'm an herbalist.' Everyone howled as our rational minds collided with the unexpected – the incongruity theory of humor in action.

Release/Relief Theory

Freud believed that people laugh because they need to release nervous tensions built up from repressed thoughts, hostile urges, and sexual desires, and implied that the greater the suppression of these thoughts, the greater the laughter in response to humor. Dirty jokes fall into this category – which, incidentally, were found in a survey by *Psychology Today* to rank at the top of all jokes told worldwide.

Some people criticize this form of humor categorically, but this may be a mistake. In her epochal book *Women Who Run with the Wolves*, Jungian scholar Clarissa Pinkola Estés suggests that sexual humor can play a valuable role:

> Can we imagine the sexual and the irreverent as sacred? Yes, especially when they are medicine. Jung noted that if someone came to his office complaining of a sexual issue, the real issue was often more a problem of spirit and soul. When a person told of a spiritual problem, often it was really a problem about the sexual nature.

In that sense, sexuality can be fashioned as a medicine for the spirit and is therefore sacred. When sexual laughter is medicine, it is sacred laughter. And whatever causes healing laughter is sacred as well. When the laughter helps without doing harm, when the laughter lightens, realigns, reorders, reasserts power and strength, this is the laughter that causes health. When the laughter makes people glad they are alive, happy to be here, more conscious of love, heightened with eros, when it lifts their sadness and severs them from anger, that is sacred. When they are made bigger, made better, more generous, more sensitive, that is sacred . . . In the wild nature, the sacred and the irreverent, the sacred and the sexual, are not separate but live together.

Clifford C. Kuhn, M.D., is professor of psychiatry at the University of Louisville School of Medicine and an expert on the healing effects of humor. He is known as the Laugh Doctor and is a professional comedian. Dr Kuhn once gave me an unexpected, personal demonstration of the 'relief theory' of humor. In 1994 I was asked to give a lecture in Louisville, Kentucky, and discovered, to my delight, that Dr Kuhn would attend. We had the opportunity to meet before my talk, and he stationed himself in the front row. About five minutes into my lecture, which was a serious talk given to an even more serious audience, I glanced down from the podium to Dr Kuhn. He was sitting in rapt attention, wearing a straight face – and a huge red clown nose. I erupted in laughter! I knew the audience probably thought I had gone over the edge, but I couldn't help it. It was some time before I could contain my outburst and continue with my talk. Kuhn wasn't being disruptive or disrespectful. He sensed that both the audience and I needed to 'lighten up,' and his silliness gave us permission to relieve our tensions.

Divinity Theory

'Does God have a sense of humor?' Seaward asks in *Managing Stress*. 'Most theologians think (and hope) so.'

Laughter has always been connected with the divine. Kierkegaard once had an imaginary confrontation with Mercury, the great trickster figure of the Greeks, in which he discovered the high regard the gods have for laughter:

> Something wonderful has happened to me. I was caught up into the seventh heaven. There sat all the gods in assembly. By special grace I was granted the privilege of making a wish. 'Wilt thou,' said Mercury, 'have youth or beauty or power or a long life or the most beautiful maiden or any of the other glories we have in the chest? Choose, but only one thing.' For a moment I was at a loss. Then I addressed myself to the gods as follows: 'Most honorable contemporaries, I choose one thing, that I may always have the laugh on my side.' Not one of the gods said a word; on the contrary, they all began to laugh. From that I concluded that my wish was granted, and found that the gods knew how to express themselves with taste; for it would hardly have been suitable for them to have answered gravely: 'Thy wish is granted.'

Throughout history wise teachers have implied that spiritual understanding comes through a lighthearted attitude and that it is a mistake to take spiritual matters too seriously. As Zen Master Sengai said,

> There are things that even the wise fail to do,
> While the fool hits the point.
> Unexpectedly discovering the way to life in the midst of
>   death, he bursts out in hearty laughter.

How does humor catalyze psychological and spiritual growth? Consider the following:

• It can reveal the naked truth about ourselves, which we would not accept in other contexts.

• Humor has the power to dissolve the walls of the ego rather than intensify them. As Jewish scholar Speed Vogel puts it, 'Humor and meditation accomplish some of the same aims. Both help to let everything float away – they show you that you're not the center of the universe.'

• Humor also dissolves barriers between ourselves and others. 'Humor has an adhesive quality which connects and bonds people together, if only for the duration of a joke, and connectedness is a component of spiritual wellbeing,' Seaward states. And he quotes Victor Borge: 'A smile is the shortest distance between two people.'

• Not only do humor and laughter reduce the barriers that separate us from each other, they also help eliminate the obstructions between ourselves and the Absolute – God, Goddess, Allah, Tao, Universe. To put it more precisely, humor and laughter help us see that these barriers were never there to begin with.

Many lines of contemporary research suggest that there is some aspect of human consciousness that cannot be confined to specific points in space (brains and bodies) or time (the present moment). Such a quality of the mind is nonlocal – not localized to the here and now but spread everywhere through space and time. This implies that something about us is literally godlike and divine – omnipresent, immortal, eternal. Genuine, unrestrained laughter can be a way of contacting this awareness, because when we laugh we let go of the sense of 'the small self' that defines and limits us. Zen scholar and translator R. H. Blythe writes: 'Laughter is a state of being here and also everywhere, an infinite and timeless expansion of one's nevertheless inalienable being. When we laugh we are free of all the oppression of our personality, or that of others, and even of God, who is indeed laughed away.'

Laughter sometimes shades into ecstasy, as Blythe implies. *Ecstasy* comes from the Greek *ekstasis*, 'a being put out of its place.' Laughter puts us out of our place by reminding us we are in *all* places, that we are unlimited in space and time. Entering this boundless domain can result in indescribable pleasure. This ecstatic experience was described by the poet Tennyson, who found that he could evoke it through the repetition of his name, a method that sounds a bit humorous in its own right:

I have never had any revelation through anesthetics, but a kind of waking trance (this for want of a better term) I have frequently had, quite up from boyhood, when I have been all alone. This has often come upon me through repeating my own name to myself silently till, all at once, as it were, out of the intensity of the consciousness of the individuality, the individuality itself seemed to dissolve and fade away into boundless being; and this is not a composed state, but the clearest of the clearest, the surest of the surest, utterly beyond words, where death was an almost laughable impossibility, the loss of personality (if so it were), seeming no distinction, but the only true life. I am ashamed of my feeble description. Have I not said the state was utterly beyond words?

In *Thinking Body, Dancing Mind*, C. A. Huang and Jerry Lynch observe that in Chinese writing, laughter is depicted by a character suggesting 'a human with arms and legs flung wide apart, head up to the sky, vibrating with mirth like bamboo leaves in the wind' – the Wild Man and Wild Woman, anchored to the earth but also penetrating heaven, whose laughter echoes throughout the universe.

Here we come to the associations made throughout history between spirituality and madmen, including the silly fools, clowns, and jesters who make us laugh. *Silly* comes from the Greek *selig*, meaning 'blessed.' Jacob Boehme, Germany's great sixteenth-century mystic, described how individuals interested in spiritual pursuits are often seen as fools: 'It is true the world will be apt enough to censure thee for a madman in walking contrary to it: And thou art not to be surprised if the children thereof laugh at thee, calling thee silly fool. For the way to the love of God is folly to the world, but is wisdom to the children of God. Hence, whenever the world perceiveth this holy fire of love in God's children, it concludeth immediately that they are turned fools, and are beside themselves.'

The Bible itself supports this view: 'But God hath chosen the foolish things of the world to confound the wise' (I Cor. 1:27) and, 'If any man among you seemeth to be wise in this world, let him become a fool, that he may be wise' (I Cor. 3:18).

The connection between silliness and spirituality was not lost on the Barnum and Bailey Circus. Seaward reports that years ago, when the circus held Sunday services for its employees, the altar boys were always the circus clowns.

From Ha-Ha! to Aha!

Throughout history, scientific discovery and play have often joined hands. Koestler recounts several examples in *The Act of Creation:* The steam engine was invented as a mechanical toy in the first century C.E. by Hero of Alexandria almost two thousand years before it was reinvented and put to practical use. Dutch opticians made various 'telescopic toys,' which Galileo turned into the astronomical telescope. In the third century B.C.E., Apollonius of Perga studied the geometry of conic sections just for the fun of it; two thousand years later they gave Kepler his elliptical orbits of the planets. Passion for dice made the Chevalier de Méré approach Pascal for advice on a safe gaming system, out of which the theory of probability was born, helping form the foundation of modern science. Thus was Laplace led to observe, 'It is remarkable that a science which began with considerations of play has risen to the most important objects of human knowledge.'

Psychologist Alice M. Isen of Cornell University believes that laughter increases creativity. One of her studies challenged subjects to tack a candle onto a wall in such a way that the wax would not drip onto the floor as the candle burned. Those who had just seen a short comedy film were more likely to devise innovative solutions than were those who had not. Isen believed that the group went from 'functional fixedness' to 'creative flexibility' after seeing the film.

We often equate creativity with making something new, something that did not exist before. But 'the creative act is not an act of creation in the sense of the Old Testament,' Koestler reminds us: 'It does not create something out of nothing; it uncovers, selects, re-shuffles, combines, synthesizes already existing facts, ideas, faculties, skills . . . Man's knowledge of the changes of the tides and the phases of the moon is as old as his observation that apples fall to earth in the ripeness of time. Yet the combination of these and other equally familiar data in Newton's theory of gravity changed mankind's outlook on the world.'

The reshuffling of facts and ideas that are already present, Koestler contends, accounts for that great paradox of creativity – that the more original a discovery, the more obvious it seems afterward. This is what prompts people to say 'I knew that all along!' or 'I've had the same idea myself!' in response to innovative breakthroughs.

In the 1940s, Koestler reports, mathematician Jacques Hadamard studied the creative habits of great mathematicians. Mathematicians are often regarded as 'ice-cold logicians, electronic brains mounted on dry sticks.' Hadamard discovered that, even in this highly rational domain, 'invention or discovery . . . takes place by combining ideas.'

Why can't we control creativity? Why is it so elusive? Again, there are parallels between creativity and humor, both of which involve making unforeseen connections in the mind. As we listen to a good joke, we allow ourselves to be taken in. If we could see the punch line coming, the joke would not work. In this process we consent to enter a state of helplessness in which we *give up control*. The creative moment 'works' like a good joke. Both humor and creativity require relinquishing control and entering a momentary state of helplessness. Creativity and humor are surprises that spring from the shadows of ignorance. And there is no better staging area for these little surprises than the unconscious mind – for instance, in dreams.

One afternoon in 1865, Friedrich August Kekule von Stradonitz, professor of chemistry in Ghent, fell asleep, Alexander Findlay reports in *A Hundred Years of Chemistry*, and dreamed:

> I turned my chair to the fire and dozed . . . Again the atoms were gambolling before my eyes. This time the smaller groups kept modestly in the background. My mental eye, rendered more acute by repeated visions of this kind, could now distinguish larger structures, of manifold conformation; long rows, sometimes more closely fitted together; all twining and twisting in snakelike motion. But look! What was that? One of the snakes had seized hold of its own tail, and the form whirled mockingly before my eyes. As if by a flash of lightning I awoke . . . Let us learn to dream, gentlemen.

The serpent biting its own tail revealed to Kekule that certain organic compounds were not open structures but closed chains or rings. Kekule's dream – a rearrangement, a repatterning, a fresh vision of how things fit – proved to be one of the cornerstones of modern science and literally changed world history.

A good joke toys with us; we give up control, allow it to taunt us, and follow helplessly wherever it leads. So, too, with scientific creativity, although this point is overlooked – particularly by scientists themselves, who often equate 'science' with 'control.'

'Connections' play a role in the creative process in another important way. The lives of creative geniuses usually are not laid out by careful advance planning. They more often appear chaotic, adrift, random – a patchwork of events cobbled together without much rhyme or reason. Creative individuals tend to be interested in a great many things and sometimes have trouble staying on track. Koestler calls this quality 'multiple potential' and believes it is shared by most great scientists. Kepler planned to become a theologian until he was offered a job as a mathematician at a provincial school. Darwin, preparing to become a country curate, had the good fortune of being invited to join the expedition of the *Beagle*, without which experience he almost certainly would never have written *The Origin of Species*. Alexander Fleming, the discover of penicillin, adopted the medical profession because his brother was a doctor. He originally went to Saint Mary's Hospital, where he would spend his entire life, because he had played against their water polo team. He chose bacteriology as his branch of investigation because a particular researcher wanted to keep Fleming, who was an excellent shot, in the Saint Mary's rifle club. Pasteur's notebooks and casual remarks indicated numerous projects and hunches that, if he had had time to follow them up, would have led in equally fertile but entirely different directions. True genius, Samuel Johnson observed, 'is a mind of large general powers, accidentally determined to some particular direction, ready for all things, but chosen by circumstances for one.'

Humor, insofar as it teaches us to take ourselves less seriously, can perhaps inspire us to allow richer connections to form in our lives. If we allowed ourselves to 'lighten up,' could we escape the tyranny of that modern curse – the 'career path' – which we think we walk, but which more often walks *over us*? What would wildly diverse people like Archimedes, Galileo, Newton, Faraday,

Franklin, or Edison have thought about the typical 'degree plan'? Is the ominous trend toward overspecialization in science in general, and in modern medicine in particular, deadening to Koestler's 'the versatility, the quicksilvery mobility' of creative geniuses? If we allowed twists and turns to develop playfully in our lives – as in a good joke – would we become more creative?

Humor is a Latin word meaning 'moisture' or 'fluid.' The etymology suggests images of water, which in Buddhism and Taoism represents flowing freedom and perfect naturalness. Humor has a watery quality. To catch a subtle joke, we have to go with the flow, allowing the intellect to shift this way and that. Creative geniuses throughout history have embodied this freedom and the power it generates.

Nourishing the 'Inner Clown'

Patty Wooten, a critical-care nurse and founder and president of Jest for the Health of It Services in Davis, California, is concerned about problems of professional burnout among her nursing colleagues. She performed a study to investigate the possible role of humor in helping nurses develop a greater sense of control and personal power. Wooten assessed the locus of control – whether the subject believed he or she was in control or was controlled by outside events – in 231 nurses in Pennsylvania, Kentucky, and California, as well as their sense of humor, using standard methods. The experimental group then completed a six-hour humor training course, and subjects were given permission and techniques for appropriate use of humor with patients and coworkers. She found that there was a significant decrease in the measure for external locus of control in the experimental group, with no significant change in the control group. 'This study indicates,' Wooten states, 'that, if one is encouraged and guided to use humor, one can gain a sense of control in one's life.' She advocates 'stay[ing] in touch with our "inner clown," that playful, childlike nature we all have but perhaps fail to acknowledge because of the seriousness of our work.'

A Caution

Norman Cousins, as we have seen, cautioned against making generalizations about the healing effects of humor. For him, humor was
a metaphor for a gamut of emotions, not just jocularity. Evidence
suggests that Cousins was correct and that there is no linear, invari-
able relationship between humor and health.

Let's not kid ourselves: science raises more questions about
humor than it answers. In fact, humor is like an electron: to observe
it too intensely is to change it – humor's own uncertainty principle. I admire this quality of humor. It suggests that a bit of
mystery is present in every good joke, and to me this intuitively
feels right.

From a scientific perspective, no one has ever explained satisfactorily why we humans have the capacity to laugh. We could
presumably conduct our affairs better if we always stayed on an
even keel emotionally, like computers – no depressive lows, no
humorous highs. True, there are physiological benefits to laughter,
as we've seen, but other creatures get along fine without them. So,
too, might we.

But humor exists – improbably – and thus appears to be a
blessing, a gift bestowed against the odds.

8

Embracing the Trickster

The one-sided get blind-sided.
— JEREMIAH ABRAMS —
The Shadow in America

PROBLEM SOLVING IS ONE of the great joys of the practice of medicine, particularly when the solution enriches the life of a sick person in the process. During my medical training the surgery trainees used to call us internal medicine residents 'swamis' and 'crystal ball gazers.' These gentle jibes about our method of solving problems suggested we were hopelessly given to thinking as opposed to doing, which was their turf. There was wisdom in their observation. Most physicians are trained to be thinkers, analysts, logicians. When we encounter clinical problems such as cancer, heart disease, or AIDS, our search for solutions begins with the assumption that we need more facts and information, which form the substrate upon which reason can operate. Only an approach anchored in analysis and reason, we say, stands a chance of working.

In contrast, many cultures have recognized that an intellectual approach to life's problems can be carried to excess. They have accorded great respect to irrationality and foolishness in its many forms – play, humor, nonsense, lightheartedness. One of the most universal expressions of this point of view is the trickster figure, which has appeared in the mythology and folklore of perhaps every culture on earth.

In modern psychology *trickster* is often used to refer to a universal force or pattern within the mind – what psychologist C. G. Jung called an archetype – that represents the irrational, chaotic, and unpredictable side of human thought and behavior. This aspect of the mind is contrasted with the logical, analytical, and intellectual side that values order, precision, and control. According to the tenets of depth psychology, a balance between these two vectors of the psyche is required for optimal mental health. When either the rational or the irrational side dominates, self-correcting forces come into play to restore some semblance of harmony between the two. The countless trickster tales describe how this process plays itself out in everyday life.

We pride ourselves on order and reason in practically every area of modern life. The messy, unlovely, and foolish aspects of human nature are accorded secondary status or rejected outright. Ignoring these traits – which everyone possesses to some degree – does not dissolve them but shunts them into the unconscious part of the mind, often called the shadow. The trickster operates, therefore, largely outside conscious awareness but always from within the human mind, not from without. We *are* the trickster, and when we describe trickster phenomena we are always describing aspects of ourselves. Thus the trickster has been called a *speculum mentis*: a mirror into the mind.

The Trickster in Native North America

Trickster lore flowered in the mythology of native North America as well as in traditional cultures throughout the world. Not only does the trickster exhibit trickery, buffoonery, and crude behavior in indigenous tales, he also appears as a creator, culture hero, and teacher. He is partly divine, partly human, and partly animal and is an amoral and comic troublemaker. Although he appears most frequently as the coyote in the cultures of the Southwest, the Great Basin, California, and the Great Plains, many other creatures are also represented, including the raven, crow, blue jay, mink, rabbit, spider, raccoon, mud hen, opossum, and bear, according to Sam Gill and Irene Sullivan's *Dictionary of Native American Mythology*.

Trickster figures also abound outside native cultures, such as in ancient Greece, where they appeared as Prometheus, Epimetheus, and Hermes. In the European Middle Ages, the court jester or fool served the trickster function. In our time clowns, comedians, movie actors, and cartoon characters often fulfill the role.

According to Gill and Sullivan, *trickster* was probably first used in 1878 by Father Albert Lacombe in his *Dictionaire de la Langue des Cris*, in which he wrote that the name of the Cree figure Wisakketjak means 'the trickster, the deceiver.' *Trickster* was picked up by Daniel Brinton in his 1885 article 'The Hero-God of the Algonkins as a Cheat and Liar,' in which he cites Lacombe's use of the word. Soon afterward *trickster* was widely embraced as a character type broadly applicable in Native American mythology.

However, *trickster* is not a term or category used by any Native American culture; it is an academic invention intended to make more comprehensible various Native American figures who share common traits. Peculiarly, once invented, the term came to have a seductive power and has taken on more reality – at least for academics – than the various figures such as Coyote and Raven who are classified as tricksters. In other words, the trickster is generally referred to as though it were a person rather than a category invented to facilitate study. A list of the scholars who have written about the trickster reads like a *Who's Who* in the social sciences, humanities, and psychology.

The Trickster and Modern Medicine

The goal of modern medicine is to be scientific, which has naturally led to an overwhelming reliance on reason. The trickster principle suggests that intrinsic balancing forces come into play in the psyche when reason – or any other quality – gets the upper hand. Do trickster phenomena exist in modern medicine?

Probably everyone involved in health care sooner or later confronts the fact that all medical therapies, for all their power and popularity, can be frustratingly capricious and sometimes harmful. This is true not only for drugs and surgical procedures but also for the alternative/complementary and consciousness-based methods that are becoming increasingly popular. All therapies work only some of the time; they work sensationally for some people and not for others; they sometimes kill as well as cure. One can never predict with certainty in a given case whether any therapy will work; one can only provide a statistical probability that it will do so. Moreover, scientific studies demonstrating efficacy often give conflicting results. They sometimes show that a therapy that was previously thought to be helpful is actually harmful, and vice versa.

The trickster perspective suggests that some of these problems and paradoxes may result from too much, not too little, reliance on logic, analysis, and reason – the very bedrocks of modern science. Is the trickster afoot in medicine? Evidence for trickster effects is subjective; we have no detection devices to get a direct readout of the trickster's presence. In spite of this limitation, we can look at some specific areas in contemporary medicine where the trickster may be leaving his tracks, areas where confusion and chaos arise in frustrating degrees. We will notice that the confusion often takes the form of paradox.

• In a study reported by T. E. Strandberg in the *Journal of the American Medical Association*, 3,490 Swedish business executives were given maximum attention to reduction of risk factors for cardiovascular disease. After five years of intervention and a total of eleven years of follow-up, even though they succeeded in reducing their risk factors by 46 percent, they had a higher mortality rate than control subjects.

• In the highly publicized 'Mr Fit' (Multiple Risk Factor Intervention Trial) study, researchers at twenty-two medical research centers in the United States studied almost thirteen thousand men. Half of them received an all-out push by physicians to reduce their risk factors for heart disease. But at the end of seven years, even though they were successful in lowering their risk factors, their death rate was higher than that of the control group, for reasons that are still being debated.

• In spite of the fact that exercise is known to have many beneficial effects on the heart and circulation, 'there still is no clinical trial to demonstrate that increasing physical activity in a group of sedentary people reduces the rate of disease vs. sedentary controls,' according to a 1991 study published in the *Journal of the American Medical Association*.

• A study reported in the *Archives of Internal Medicine* points out that 'there is considerable interobserver variability in the roentgenographic diagnosis of pneumonia' – in other words, that pneumonia diagnoses from chest X rays depend very much on who's looking at them. 'This variability does not improve with increasing experience.'

• *Science News* reports on a study on calcium: 'Because most kidney stones are made of calcium, physicians often recommend that patients who have already suffered from stones reduce their calcium intake . . . A research team from the Harvard School of Public Health reports that men who ate a diet rich in calcium faced a 34 percent lower risk of developing kidney stones than did men who consumed a restricted calcium diet. "This goes against everything we had been taught," says kidney specialist Gary C. Curhan, who led the calcium investigation."'

• 'Although the periodic health examination was introduced over 80 years ago, it remains a controversy in internal medicine. There have been few data from controlled studies to document the examination's efficacy for adults; nevertheless, its popularity has become a multimillion-dollar industry in the United States,' states H. C. Mitchell in *Annals of Internal Medicine*.

• 'A new study suggests that physicians and nurses should offer this seemingly paradoxical advice to patients awaiting surgery: Don't relax, be worried.' Although relaxation training before surgery helps people feel less tense, researchers investigating anxiety before surgery found that the greatest postsurgical increases in adrenaline and cortisol, two hormones associated with the body's reaction to stress and danger, were significantly higher among patients given relaxation training prior to their surgical procedure, compared with control subjects.

• A study on men with low cholesterol published in *Science News:* 'Sometimes you can't win for losing. Case in point: New evidence indicates that elderly men boasting low cholesterol levels also suffer markedly more symptoms of depression than peers with moderate or high cholesterol levels . . . Several cholesterol-reduction trials have found unexpected jumps in suicide and other violent deaths

. . . Neither weight loss (which often lowers cholesterol) nor the presence of various medical problems accounted for the link between cholesterol and depression.'

• 'The current coronary heart disease risk factors explain only about 50% of new events,' says R. S. Eliot in the *Journal of the American Medical Association*.

• Professional working women enjoy lower blood pressure than women who stay at home, concludes a study reported in *Science News*. 'Basically, the theory that job stress will make women as susceptible as men [to high blood pressure] doesn't bear out.'

• Data on infant health presented in the *Journal of the American Medical Association* challenge the widely held assumption that United States women, who usually enjoy higher levels of education, employment, and income, have healthier infants than immigrants. According to statistics from San Diego County from 1978 to 1985, the lowest infant mortality rates were seen in Southeast Asian and Hispanic women, most of whom were foreign-born; highest rates were seen in white and African-American women, most of whom were United States – born. The United States, which prides itself on having the most advanced health-care system in the world, is number twenty-two in infant mortality when compared with other developed countries, according to a report published in *The Sciences*. In 1992 corporate health-care expenditures exceeded corporate profits. Yet we offer fewer services and have a shorter life expectancy at birth than many other industrialized countries.

• According to data published in the *Journal of the American Medical Association*, each year 225,000 people die in hospitals in the United States as a result of medical errors and the side effects of drugs. This makes hospital care the third leading cause of death in the United States, behind heart disease and cancer.

Our usual approach to paradoxes such as these is to design more and better studies to clear up the ambiguities. The problems, we say, are not a failure of reason but a lack of sufficient information to which reason can apply itself. Can we eradicate all the confusion with good studies? It would be foolish not to employ our intellect as skillfully as possible. But how fully can reason serve us without becoming susceptible to the self-correcting, intrapsy-chic forces of irrationality and unpredictability?

It is not popular to propose limits to reason in medicine. To do so sounds defeatist. But the trickster perspective suggests *not* that the problems we face are intractable or that reason is somehow 'wrong' but that the problems may not be penetrable by logic alone. We may not be able to bludgeon our way to solutions solely with reason, as we habitually try to do. The path toward clarity may lie, paradoxically, with unreason.

Alternative Medicine and the Trickster

All schools of healing conform to some sort of mythology. Modern medicine largely follows the hero myth, which is based not only on reason but also on effort, will, and courage. Alternative/comple-mentary medicine also generally follows a rational, causal frame-work: if you do X, Y will follow – whether X means taking vitamins or herbs, using a homeopathic remedy, or praying, imaging, or meditating. In alternative circles, as in orthodox medicine, heroic vigor and assertiveness are also routinely emphasized, epitomized by the frequent advice that patients 'take charge,' 'assume respon-sibility,' and 'fight' their illness.

As complementary medicine attempts to match the intellectual rigor of orthodox medicine, there is a risk that it, too, may ignore the trickster forces in the psyche. If so, it may find itself suscep-tible to the unpredictability and confusion that so often plague conventional medicine. The field of complementary medicine is not off-limits to trickster effects; it enjoys no privileged status. The trickster sows confusion *wherever* hyperintellectuality is mani-fested.

Many researchers and clinicians in alternative medicine realize that it may be impossible to subject some healing methods to the rational strategies favored in contemporary biomedical research such as double-blind methodology. Consider, for example, studies involving the effect of prayer among patients who are seriously ill. How can one establish a control group that, by definition, should receive no prayer? People facing serious illness routinely pray for themselves, whether or not they belong to a control group. Even if they did not, their loved ones pray for them. No one has yet devised a way of annulling the 'problem of extraneous prayer.' An alternative research approach has been to study the effects of prayer not on humans but on nonhumans – assessing, for example, the effects of prayerful intentionality on growth rates of bacteria or fungi or on the healing rates of surgical wounds in rats or mice. Presumably the bacteria or mice in the control group do not pray for themselves, nor are they being prayed for by their fellow creatures.

In spite of these difficulties, we should not abandon the customary forms of investigation that are based on reason in favor of an 'anything goes' policy, for this approach would lead to the opposite excess in which too little, not too much, reason is employed. We should push the limits of reason as far as possible in our research strategies, recognizing in advance that the limits are real. We should also be willing to search for creative alternatives when we encounter paradoxes we cannot penetrate.

The Trickster and the Creative Process

The trickster, therefore, suggests *not* that we abandon our rational faculties altogether but that reason must be complemented by unreason if it is to achieve full flowering. Nowhere is this lesson clearer than in the creative process of great scientists.

When Jonas Salk was researching the polio vaccine that would bear his name, he decided to distance himself from his work for a short period by going to the monastery of Assisi in Italy. Salk had a keen interest in architecture, and his encounter with the shapes and spaces, light, materials, and colors of this monastery, and its history, had a profound impact on his mind and spirit. Salk became highly energized. 'Under that influence,' he later recalled, 'I intuitively designed the research that I felt would result in the desired vaccine. I returned to my laboratory in Pittsburgh to validate my concepts and found that they were indeed correct!'

Salk's experience is not unique. Throughout history researchers have often achieved success only when they allowed play and other distractions to mingle with the intellect – in other words, when they invited the trickster to come out to play.

Arthur Koestler observes in *The Act of Creation:*

The creative act, in so far as it depends on unconscious resources, presupposes a relaxing of the controls and a regression to modes of ideation which are indifferent to the rules of verbal logic, unperturbed by contradiction, untouched by the dogmas and taboos of so-called common sense. At the decisive stage of discovery the codes of disciplined reasoning are suspended – as they are in the dream, the reverie, the manic flight of thought, when the stream of ideation is free to drift, by its own emotional gravity, as it were, in an apparently 'lawless' fashion.

The paradoxes involved in the creative process are vividly exemplified in the life of England's Michael Faraday (1791–1867), one of the greatest physicists in history. Perhaps the most remarkable fact about Faraday is that he lacked any mathematical education or gift, and was 'ignorant of all but the merest elements of arithmetic,' according to Koestler. Faraday was a visionary in the literal sense. He was able to see stress lines around magnets and electric currents as curves in space, for which he coined the term *lines of force*. For him these patterns were as real as if they were made of solid matter. These images 'rose up before him like things,' says Koestler, and proved incredibly fertile, leading to the birth of the dynamo and electric motor, and the postulate that light was electromagnetic radiation.

In the 1940s the mathematician Jacques Hadamard performed systematic research into the psychology of highly creative mathematicians, whose work generally is considered the purest example of reason and logic. In his book *The Psychology of Invention in the Mathematical Field*, he reports that 'among the mathematicians born or resident in America . . . practically all of them . . . avoid not only the use of mental words but also . . . the mental use of algebraic or any other precise signs; . . . they use vague images. . . . The mental pictures . . . are most frequently visual, but they may also be of another kind, for instance, kinetic. There can also be auditive ones, but even these . . . quite generally keep their vague character.'

Einstein was one of the individuals in Hadamard's survey. He described his creative process thus: 'The words or the language . . . do not seem to play any role in my mechanism of thought. The . . . elements in thought are certain signs and more or less clear images . . . This combinatory play seems to be the essential feature in productive thought – before there is any connection with logical construction in words or other kinds of signs which can be communicated to others.'

Such reports contradict the stereotypical view that creative research is only a dogged exercise of the rational mind. There is a tricksterish, uncontrollable, unpredictable side of creativity in which reason is flouted. This implies that 'creativity on demand,' the kind often taught in weekend workshops, is an oxymoron.

Writing in the 1950s in *Scientific American*, Frank Barron, an expert on the psychology of imagination, captured the essentially unharnessable nature of the creative process:

> Creative individuals are more at home with complexity and apparent disorder than other people are . . . The creative individual in his generalized preference for apparent disorder, turns to the dimly realized life of the unconscious, and is likely to have more than the usual amount of respect for the forces of the irrational in himself and in others . . . The creative individual not only respects the irrational in himself, but courts it as the most promising source of novelty in his own thought. He rejects the demand of society that he should shun in himself the primitive, the uncultured, the naive, the magical, the nonsensical . . . When an individual thinks in ways which are customarily tabooed, his fellows may regard him as mentally unbalanced . . . This kind of imbalance is more likely to be healthy than unhealthy. The truly creative individual stands ready to abandon old classifications and to acknowledge that life, particularly his own unique life, is rich with new possibilities. To him, disorder offers the potentiality of order.

Barron's statement might well serve as a kind of Trickster Manifesto, emphasizing as it does the central role of the irrational, chaotic elements of the psyche in the creative process.

In my practice of internal medicine, one of my colleagues was concerned with how we might nourish the creative impulse in the physicians in our group. A tireless traveler himself, he knew it was important to set the stage for creative insights – by journeying to unfamiliar surroundings, for example, just as Salk did in the afore-mentioned instance. He therefore proposed that each physician be encouraged to go periodically on an extended sabbatical outside the city, investigate a topic of personal interest, and formally report his findings back to the group. This would not only challenge the individual physician but would stimulate the other doctors as well. As an enticement, the physician would be paid for doing so. The proposal was resoundingly rejected. This example shows that we physicians, as well as practically anyone else, will go to great lengths to remain locked into familiar routines, which can have a dead-ening effect on our creative potential.

In Greek mythology the classic trickster figure is Hermes, the fleet-footed messenger of the gods and the deity of speech, communication, and writing, whose first act as a baby was to steal cattle from Apollo. Thus we see in Hermes the qualities of thievery, trickery, and deceit combined with the skill of communication.

This may appear to be an odd combination of traits, but if we look closely we can see that the pairing of deception and commu-nication makes sense. Because trickster happenings are paradoxi-cal, confusing, and chaotic, they take us off guard mentally and jolt us into seeing unexpected patterns and new meanings. G. K. Chesterton, the English writer, emphasized this 'breakthrough' potential by defining paradox as Truth standing upside down to attract attention. In the wake of paradox, we see connections and patterns to which we were previously blind. It is as if our normal modes of perception have been tricked. The logical mind, accus-tomed to following old paths of reason previously laid down, is momentarily sidetracked into a different mode of perception. A new communication channel with the universe suddenly opens and grand patterns are revealed – creativity and discovery as a prank played on the habits of reason.

'Messing Up the Mind'

Similar processes happen in healing.

Myrin Borysenko was a prominent researcher in immunology at Tufts University School of Medicine. He was intrigued by the work of Harvard's David McClelland on the impact of belief in healing. On one occasion Borysenko asked McClelland how a particular healer in the Boston area healed people. 'Oh, he messes up your mind,' McClelland replied.

One morning while at his laboratory Borysenko began to come down with symptoms of flu – fever, aches, cough, and congestion. By noon he felt miserable. Unable to function, he decided to leave work and go home to bed. On his way home he suddenly thought of the psychic healer he had discussed with McClelland. Why not give the healer a try? Besides, he told himself, no one will ever know.

He found the healer in a dilapidated part of the city. As he climbed the rickety stairs he began to have second thoughts. What if my colleagues could see me now? he worried. The door to the healer's apartment was open as if Borysenko were expected. He entered to find an enormously fat, unkempt man sprawled on a sofa watching a soap opera on TV and drinking wine from a gallon jug. Summoning his courage, Borysenko said, 'I hear you can cure people. Can you cure my flu?' Without taking his eyes off the TV, the healer reached for a small bottle of purple liquid on the floor. 'Go into the bathroom, fill the tub half full of water, pour this stuff in, and sit in it for thirty minutes. Then you will be cured.'

Borysenko did as he was told. As he sat in the tub, up to his waist in the densely purple water, he was struck by the sheer absurdity of what he was doing. He felt so silly he began to laugh uncontrollably. He was still laughing when he realized his half-hour was over. He dressed and walked to the living room to find the healer still engrossed in the soap opera. He simply said, 'Now you are healed.' Then he pointed to the door, indicating he was free to go.

Driving home, Borysenko gradually realized he felt different. He sensed no symptoms whatever. He felt well – so well that he decided to return to work. He worked late. As he recited his adventure that night to his wife while undressing for bed, she suddenly burst into laughter. Looking into the mirror, he knew why. He was purple from the waist down.

Borysenko's healer was a first-rate trickster – one who upsets expectations, creates confusion, and jumbles the normal categories of thought. Borysenko was enticed to abandon everything he believed about how healing worked, put his intellect on hold, and simply 'let it happen.'

It is perfectly natural to try to find approaches to healing that are completely objective and that can be successfully applied to all individuals who have the same illness. One might try, for example, to reduce Borysenko's experience to an algorithm whereby every patient with a diagnosis of the flu is advised to add a specific amount of the purple liquid to his bath-water. But when used in a repetitive, formulaic way, these approaches rarely work as dramatically as for Borysenko, perhaps because they do not 'mess up the mind,' as McClelland put it. This is perhaps one reason behind the adage. 'One should use a new medication as often as possible, while it still has the power to work.'

Arrogance and the Trickster

Author Richard Smoley captured the essence of the trickster in *Gnosis* magazine:

> As long as we lie to ourselves, the Trickster will be with us. He'll show up just when we least want him, to embarrass us on a first date, to prove us fools in front of the learned company we're trying to impress, to make us miss a power breakfast with that all-important business contact. Yes, he'll leave at our bidding, but he always comes back with a vengeance. The only way to get rid of him is to listen to his message – and to admit the truth about ourselves in all its beauty and ugliness.

The trickster not only deceives others; he is always himself being duped, often by pranks that backfire. Trickster tales show that humiliation is never far away; thus the trickster warns us of the dangers of arrogance and hubris.

In 1994 I had been preparing an important address for several days. The night before Halloween I had a trickster-type dream that was an important lesson about the pitfalls of pride:

> I am waiting to give a speech at a prestigious gathering. The setting is imperial – an outdoor, semicircular structure of marble Corinthian columns with a podium in the center. I am to be introduced by Albert Einstein. As Einstein rises from his seat and walks to the podium, I realize that something about him is different. He is feisty and animated, not the avuncular, shy, saintly figure I expected. I suspect something unusual may be about to happen. Einstein introduces me with a flourish, and I walk to the podium to deliver my sensationally important address. I hear murmurs from the dignified scientists seated with Einstein, who have come from around the world to hear my speech. I suddenly realize the cause of the whispers: I am naked except for a pair of shorts, which are black and white. For some reason, I am not fazed. I realize that a grievous complication has arisen, with which I must contend. I excuse myself, walk to the left of the stage, and discover that a men's room is handy. I step inside, close the door, and see that a complete set of clothes is hanging on the wall, just waiting for me – a tuxedo and shirt, black and white, matching my shorts, precisely my size. I realize this delay is only temporary and will not be fatal to my talk. I dress, reenter the stage, assume the podium, and proceed with great care.

In medicine we often find ourselves symbolically without clothes. Arrogance and recklessness often set the stage for these humiliating situations. When we make rash assurances to patients that 'everything will be fine,' that our favored therapy is sure to work, or that we can find the problem when a string of prior diagnosticians have failed, we are setting ourselves up to be tricked. 'You can think as much as you like,' a Russian proverb warns, 'but you will invent nothing better than bread and salt.'

What if modern medicine were to become all-powerful? What if healers one day were able to cure all illnesses and make people live forever? A Winnebago trickster story contains a warning about the hubris that often accompanies such fantasies:

Hare decides to help out the human beings and makes all the animals defenseless against them. 'Now the people will live peacefully and forever,' he thinks. But his wise Grandmother disagrees. 'Grandson, your talk makes me sad. How can you make the people live forever, as you do? Earthmaker did not make them thus. All things have to have an end.' Grandmother's body begins to undergo destruction before Hare's eyes. 'If all the people live forever,' she continues, 'they would soon fill up the earth. There would then be more suffering than there is now, for some people would always be in want of food if they multiplied greatly. That is why everything has an end.' Hare is disconsolate. His motives were so admirable!

In Herrymon Maurer's *The Way of the Ways*, we find a similar warning about the incessant attempts of reason to fix things from Lao-tzu, the reputed founder of Taoism in China around the sixth century B.C.E.:

> It is ominous to improve on life,
> Injurious to control breathing by the mind.

These warnings are often criticized as antiquated recommendations for a retreat into passivity, but their lessons lie deeper. Light does not come without darkness, they seem to be telling us, nor life without trouble. All opposites interpenetrate and sustain each other, as the trickster element of the psyche reminds us. We cannot have it one way. When we forget these eternal polarities, a price will be paid.

Is the Trickster Dangerous?

One of the most common ways of dealing with the trickster patterns of the psyche is to intellectualize them. According to this point of view, if we read enough books about trickster lore we can eventually decipher the meaning of the trickster tales and escape the pitfalls about which they warn. Such a project is impossible in principle, for two reasons. First, the trickster element lies so deeply in the unconscious that it is essentially beyond the reach of reason. It belongs to what has been called the *really* unconscious. Second, something of the trickster refuses to be analyzed. The more aggressively the rational mind tries to tame the trickster, the more ferociously it resists.

Anthropologist Barre Toelken describes his forty-year experience doing fieldwork with the Navajos in southeastern Utah, during which he investigated their Coyote trickster stories. At one point his Navajo informant asked, 'Are you ready to lose someone in your family?' Toelken did not understand. 'Well,' the man said, 'when you take up witchcraft, you know, you have to pay for it with the life of someone in your family.' The Navajo storyteller saw that Toelken was approaching the Coyote tales intellectually, dismembering them analytically, discussing the parts and motifs separately in a typically academic way. When the tales are disrupted this way, Navajos believe, the various elements of the stories can be used by witches to promote disharmony and thwart healing. Thus the Navajos were concerned that Toelken, against his knowledge, was flirting with witchcraft. 'My advice to you,' his Navajo informant told him, 'is: don't go deeper into this subject unless you're going to join the witches.'

After the Navajo storyteller narrated the Navajo Coyote tales to Toelken, a series of disasters befell the informant and his family. The man developed a problem with his legs; he later died from a heart attack as he emerged from a sweat lodge. An auto accident killed his granddaughter and was nearly fatal to his daughter. A son developed schizophrenia. A brother died in a rock fall. The family became scattered and largely estranged from one another. Toelken's own Navajo foster son committed suicide. Toelken raises the chilling question of whether these incidents were coincidences or retribution for divulging the Coyote tales. His answer: From the standpoint of reason, they are coincidences; from the Navajo perspective, they are punishment for misuse of the stories.

Toelken eventually decided that although a particular area of scholarly inquiry might be 'interesting' and 'important,' these reasons do not always justify continuing a research project. 'Just as a moment of enlightenment may lead a scholar to pursue a subject further,' he decided, 'it may also clarify the need to call a halt.' Thus he chose to abandon this area of fieldwork after deciding that it 'stood a strong chance of being dangerous to the informants as well as to myself and my family.' Toelken does not advise others to avoid the study of trickster phenomena. He does imply, however, that if one chooses to investigate these matters, there may be a high price for doing so.

Many psychologists who have plumbed the depths of the unconscious have come away with a reverence for this aspect of the mind. Typical was C. G. Jung, who wrote of the folly in trying to compel the unconscious to reveal its secrets. Jung wrote of the need to wait patiently, to see what the unconscious chose to deliver of its own accord. Can we imagine a future in which experiments are selected with reverence – as if research were an exploration of sacred space – and only after due reflection on what the consequences of the intellectual foray might be?

Be Aware or Beware

Why can we not function as rationally as a computer? Why does the psyche revolt when we become too logical and analytical? Why do we require a balance between reason and unreason, spontaneity and control? Why do we need irrational experiences such as laughter, play, and love?

We don't choose to be foolish, irrational, and playful; the need is innate. Foolishness is required for our psychological health; we can develop a shortage of foolishness just as we can acquire deficiencies of a vitamin.

The need for balance between the irrational and rational forces in the psyche is often rejected by 'hard' thinkers who believe there are no limits on how rational we should strive to be. People of this persuasion often say that we do not have the courage to follow the intellect, and they describe the fall into irrationality as a lack of nerve. This point of view is perhaps more heroic than wise, because it ignores the stubborn facts of human experience and the findings of modern psychology on the role of the unconscious in our mental life. Transpersonal psychologist Ken Wilber wisely wrote, 'After all, you will own [your opposites], or they will own you – the Shadow always has its say . . . We may wisely *be aware* of our opposites, or we will be forced to *beware* of them.'

Infatuated as we have become with the achievements of reason, there is always the temptation to reject everything that is irrational in favor of order and control. But we can never banish the trickster. To do so would be to amputate a vital part of ourselves, including our need to create, to frolic, to love – to be, in a word, human.

9

Trout Mind

When I was growing up in the 1940s, vitamins and trace elements were being identified right and left. Advertisers began to prey on mothers, implying that if they *really* loved their kids they'd stuff them with vitamins every day. If the vitamin marketers were right, my brother, sister, and I were drowned in love. I can still see my mother towering over me with a mammoth bottle of vitamin D-rich cod liver oil in one hand and a tablespoon in the other. I suffered through this daily ritual by invoking an inflated fantasy – that God created vitamin D expressly for Dosseys. This meant that my mother was an instrument of God's will and the least I could do was to help her fulfill her divine mission by swallowing the foul stuff.

But despite these unpleasant experiences with cod liver oil, my relationship with fish got better. Fishing was one of the few opportunities for recreation available to my twin brother and me on the prairie farmlands of central Texas, and we made the best of it. I would pray for rain as a boy – not for the crops, but because my father could not work in the fields if they were wet and he might take us fishing instead. Going fishing with Dad was a magical ritual that began with digging worms in the barnyard – long, fat, torpid worms that were monsters compared with the hyperactive, skinny, thyrotoxic-looking night crawlers sold in bait shops these days. One of my most vivid memories is of staring at the heels of my dad's boots, trying to match his giant strides as we tramped through woods and fields to some nameless fishing hole.

Fishing was our intoxicant and my brother and I became addicts. Pristine lakes and running streams did not exist; this was arid Texas prairie country, and a fishing hole was an unglamorous pond or 'tank,' a cavity gouged in the prairie at a runoff site, where cattle watered. We knew every fishing hole in our part of Limestone County, and the owners always gave us permission to fish. Almost always we were successful, returning home with strings of perch and catfish and an occasional black bass, which, we were certain, was the most majestic fish in the world.

We knew a lot of fishermen as we were growing up, and some of them let us tag along. One of my favorites was an old farmer who went fishing every Sunday morning instead of going to church, for which reason he was considered a reprobate by the devout. He laughed at the criticism, claiming that he got closer to God while fishing than he ever could in church. I believed him.

This was my first hint that fishing could collide with religion. Needing to resolve the tension between the two, I began to pay special attention to the Bible stories I heard in church having to do with fish. If one read between the lines, it seemed obvious that fish could serve as special messengers or instruments of God, which I found consoling. I was particularly impressed by the Old Testament story of Jonah and the whale (I didn't know then that whales were mammals, not fish). My rationalizations for fishing were off and running. I found it highly significant that Jesus recruited *fishermen* to be his disciples. And the food he chose to multiply to feed the hungry who had come to hear him preach? *Fish*, with a few loaves of bread thrown in. And he vowed to transform his followers into *fishers* of men, implying that a glorious destiny awaited fishermen. By the time I was finished with my analysis, Western religion was a vehicle for fishing; I considered it my Christian duty to fish as often as possible.

Fish as Messengers

I didn't realize at the time, of course, that there is an immense canon of universal mythology suggesting, as in the Bible, that fish and fishing are mediators between the sacred and the mundane.

Tales abound in which fish confer special insights, power, and transformation – the golden fish whose stomach contains a magical ring, the mermaid who awakens a poor fisherman from an ordinary to a transcendent dimension of existence, a fish who guides a sailor through treacherous waters.

These myths endure because something deep inside us answers to the mysterious powers that lurk in the dark, aquatic depths. Each time a fisherwoman sinks a line below the surface of a stream, lake, or ocean, she dimly perceives that something momentous may happen at any time. The act of fishing is always a venture into the mythic unknown. That is why it is irreverent to refer to fishing as mere 'recreation.' One might as well say that Captain Ahab was engaging in 'sport fishing' for the great white whale in Melville's *Moby-Dick*.

Fishing is suffused with mythic power, and it is one of the most common activities in which mythic reality strays into ordinary life. That is why fishing is often punctuated with events that are utterly strange and shocking. Consider what happened to fifteen-year-old Robert Johansen, who went fishing on a summer day in 1979 in Norway in Oslo Fjord. He usually did not catch anything, but that evening he landed a ten-pound cod and presented it proudly to his grandmother, Thekla Aanen, of Larkollen. As she was preparing the fish for the family dinner, she opened its stomach and found a diamond ring – a family heirloom she had lost while swimming in the fjord three years earlier.

Or consider the experience of John Cross of Newport News, Virginia, who lost a ring in 1980 while crossing Hampton Roads during a storm. Two years later it turned up inside a fish served at his favorite restaurant in Charlottesville.

This sort of thing is nothing new. In ancient times, Polycrates, the Tyrant of Samos, sacrificed his gold and emerald seal-ring by throwing it into the sea, only to have it restored to him in the belly of a fish. Saint Mungo, bishop and patron of Glasgow, saved the reputation of a married woman who was suspected of giving her lost ring to a lover. After praying all night, the Bishop asked that the first fish caught the next morning in the River Clyde be brought directly to his table. Inside the fish was the ring. Bishop Gerbold, after being driven from his palace at Bayeux, threw his episcopal ring into the sea in disgust and retired to a hermitage. Shortly thereafter a fish was caught with the ring in its stomach. The congregation that had driven him off was greatly impressed, and restored him to his previous position.

What is going on? The mythic dimensions of these strange occurrences are not lost on Lyall Watson, who reports these events in *The Nature of Things: The Secret Life of Inanimate Objects*. 'The thing about fish, apart from their tendency to swallow shiny things, is that they are heavily symbolic of motherhood and the womb – "from which all treasures flow" – and it is no surprise to find them involved in the *restoration of wholeness* [emphasis added] and acts of reunion. Such archetypal reinforcement is bound to encourage the reporting of these events, giving them deep credence even now, bringing old myths back to life.'

Fly-Fishing as Alternative Therapy

Watson's suggestion that fish can function as agents for the restoration of *wholeness* implies that they may also mediate *healing*, because wholeness and healing are related. Indeed, fish and fishing often serve as an alternative therapy in the lives of the sick.

Take the remarkable case of Mike Crockett, coauthor of a book on fly-fishing called *Flywater*. By every conventional measure, Crockett's life was a success: he had a beautiful wife, two wonderful kids, a thriving career, a vacation house in the mountains, friends he valued – 'just about everything I had ever wanted,' he says, 'and more than I expected.' Then, in the early nineties, the same week his new daughter was born, Crockett received devastating news: the lumps he had recently noticed were an incurable form of lymphoma. Although chemotherapy was begun, his physician advised him to get his affairs in order.

Crockett knew he didn't have time to waste. 'I began taking inventory and realized I was involved in a lot of activity I didn't really enjoy,' he says. He began to focus on activities that gave him fulfillment and to eliminate those that did not, resolving to 'try something new as the essence of living.'

A few months after his cancer diagnosis, during a trip to

Colorado, he prevailed upon a friend to introduce him to fly-fishing on the San Miguel River. 'It would be hard to imagine a more beautiful place for an escape or a healing experience,' Crockett says of this small river flowing through red sandstone canyons and forests of blue spruce, alder, and cottonwood. Starting out as a novice, within a couple of days he had mastered sufficient skills to catch a few brook trout. Although these were days of worry and concern about the future, Crockett became aware of a very interesting phenomenon: almost every moment on the stream was spent in relaxed contentment. He writes: 'Fishing – fly fishing – was the only enterprise I was involved in that transported me away from the considerable anxieties I felt about the difficulties that were lurking. Occasionally, it even served as an effective relief for physical pain or nausea. In time, I began to see fishing as a form of therapy . . . The activity of rigging up, wading, casting, watching the line unfold and following the float of the fly – it all flows together to become a kind of meditation, a spiritual recreation.'

Crockett survived two death sentences, half a dozen courses of chemotherapy, and several hospitalizations. At one point he became resistant to all his medications and traveled to Stanford University Medical Center for a two-month experimental treatment involving monoclonal antibodies. However, after the initial tests it was discovered that for only the second time in more than fifty similar trials, the antibody did not react with Crockett's cells, and the treatment was abandoned. He and his wife tried to make the best of things. They decided to spend the rest of the summer in Colorado on the San Miguel, doing a lot of trout fishing. By the time he saw his doctor two months later, he knew before his exam that he was better and that three years of steady decline had been reversed. His physician could not explain this unusual remission but advised him to continue whatever he was doing.

Crockett didn't really know what made the difference. He wrote:

I don't mean to suggest that fly fishing can cure cancer. When conventional medicine failed me, I tried every alternative approach that came to my attention. It is possible that any or even all of them made some contribution . . . I can say this: fly

fishing, more than any other activity, frees my mind and nour-
ishes my soul. And I do know that time spent on the river has
often provided a profound sense of well-being – that feeling of
being rooted in the present without needs or worries beyond
the moment . . . There is an old saying that one can never enter
the same river twice. The river is always new; the man is forever
changed.

'Fishfalls'

The mythic strangeness of fish reaches great heights, literally.
Sometimes fish come falling from the heavens onto humans – a
phenomenon sometimes referred to as a fishfall. Falling fish have
hit people in the face, fallen down their collars, splattered on their
windshields, clogged the gutters of their houses, and stopped
traffic. It's as if they can't wait to be caught, so they come to the
fisherman.

On an October morning in 1947, A. D. Bajkov, a marine biologist with the United States Department of Wildlife and Fisheries,
was having breakfast with his wife at a restaurant in Marksville,
Louisiana, when 'the waitress informed us that fish were falling
from the sky . . . into the streets and yards. We went immediately
to collect some of the fish.' Bajkov identified four species, including
a nine-inch largemouth bass, *Micropterus salmoides*, which came
falling from the sky and landed at his feet. This incident was
reported in *Science*, one of the most respected scientific journals
in the world. Bajkov's report is interesting because it shows that
these events have been witnessed by skilled observers, including
first-rate scientists.

Another typical fishfall occurred on May 8, 1985. At first Louis
Castoreno thought someone was playing a trick on him when
dozens of small fish fell into his backyard as a dark cloud passed
overhead. 'A whole bunch came down at one time,' he said. 'It
scared me. A local spokesman for the National Weather Service
said it has happened before in the past five years, usually just
before a tornado or heavy storm.'

Fish have been doing this for a very long time. Athenaeus,

around 200 C.E. in ancient Greece, described several fishfalls in his book *The Deipnosophists*, a summary of the work of eight hundred writers he had read at the Library of Alexandria before it was destroyed. Under the heading 'Rains of Fishes' (*De pluvius piscium*), he wrote, 'Phaenias, for example, says, in the second book of *The Rulers of Eresus* that in Chersonesus it rained fishes for three whole days. And Phylarcus in his fourth book says that certain persons have in many places seen it rain fishes, and the same thing happens with tadpoles.'

In the late nineteenth century a small number of well-known scientists began to collect cases of fish falling from the sky. Among them were the English meteorologist D. P. Thompson and the naturalist George Buist, the French astronomer Camille Flammarion, and the German naturalist G. Hartwig. In 1917 Waldo McAfee, a biologist with the United States Bureau of Biological Survey, published a widely read account of these strange events, as did J. R. Norman in a 1928 article in *Natural History Magazine* with the provocative title 'Fish from the Clouds.' The quality of the evidence is quite good, with a canon of well-observed cases. Although nobody has yet filmed or photographed falling fish, many photos have been taken shortly thereafter.

The phenomenon is universal. Cases have been documented in South Africa, India, Guam, Australia, England, North America, and many other areas and have involved quite a cast – minnows, sticklebacks, smelts, flounder, bass, crabs, snails, tadpoles, menhaden, and more. Some of the fallen fish arrive alive, unhurt, and flopping; others are smashed and dead; and some are frozen, as in the Louisiana case described by Bajkov. They usually are confined to a relatively small area. A remarkable feature of many fishfalls is that the fish are of a single species, which is perplexing if they have been lofted by tornadoes or waterspouts from a large lake or ocean, as many researchers believe.

How do the fish do it? Several theories have been offered, which is a clue that nobody really knows. Some of the potential explanations make sense, while others are bizarre and even humorous.

• The leading candidates are whirlwinds, tornadoes, and waterspouts. Falling fish sometimes arrive frozen or mixed with hail,

suggesting a stormy sojourn at high altitudes. However, these meteo-
rological conditions are not always present, as in the well-observed
Bajkov case, where the weather was 'foggy but calm.' If whirling
winds or tornadoes over water are the explanation, why then,
wonders Minnesotan Robert Schadewald, who has researched these
events, do we 'have so many fish falls from Great Britain but none
whatsoever from Minnesota, the "Land of 10,000 Lakes" that aver-
ages 17 tornado touchdowns a year?'

• The 'disgorging hypothesis' is also popular. Large fish-eating
birds sometimes swallow fish whole or carry them in their beaks,
and they occasionally vomit their catch when disturbed in flight.
This could explain single fallen fish but not fishfalls in the thousands – unless, as some have suggested, gigantic flocks of birds
disgorged their meal in a remarkable feat of coordination.

• Some fish, such as the spangled grunter of Australia, are
known to migrate across vast tracts of land, usually via pools made
by recent rains or floods. Some theorists contend, therefore, that
fish don't actually fall from the sky but move about on land. Most
fishfalls, however, involve fish not known to migrate in this way.

• Perhaps, some have suggested, the fish were teleported at a
distance through physical processes currently unknown to science.
This might explain their arrival, they say, intact and unharmed.

• Some people imagine that there may be an undetected repository of organic life somewhere in the sky, a sort of aerial Atlantis.
When shaken by violent thunder, its contents might be dislodged
and fall to the ground.

• Then there is the theory of estivation, which posits that the
fish are created spontaneously, just before they are observed, by
the fertilizing powers of rain acting on eggs that lay dormant in
great numbers in dust and dirt. This may not be as zany as it
seems. Some fish and frogs can lie dormant for long periods and
be revived with the coming of rains or floods. But this would not
account for fish actually seen falling from the sky, or fishfalls
involving fish not known to estivate, or fish of a larger size than
hatchlings.

• Finally, there is the old standby for skeptics and cynics: the
'phantom fishmonger' hypothesis. 'A prime example occurred in
1881, when great quantities of periwinkles [a type of small snail]

and crabs fell on the English city of Worcester. The authorities of the day supposed that a mad fishmonger must have traveled the byways of the city, unseen, shoveling thousands of periwinkles off the back of his cart.'

There are holes in all these ideas. For instance, Schadewald has calculated from experiments that the terminal velocity of a small falling fish is nearly thirty-two miles per hour. Although some fallen fish are smashed, fishfalls have been observed in which none of the fish are harmed. After hitting the ground at this velocity, why don't they *all* resemble anchovy paste every time?

You can judge whether these hypotheses are the products of enlightenment or desperation. If fish have a sense of humor, they must be laughing at some of them.

Although some wind-related explanation is the leading contender, no theory is adequate to account for all the observed fishfalls, particularly those that occur in calm weather. Until a comprehensive explanation arrives, we are free to allow our imaginations to probe the mythic dimensions of this strange phenomenon. The mythic imagination is at liberty to ask questions that would prove embarrassing to our practical, everyday minds: In fishfalls, are fish going 'humaning,' like humans go fishing? Why aren't fish content to stay put in their aquatic environment? Do fishfalls indicate a primordial urge to defy the limitations imposed by gravity? Do fish have a desire, like humans, to fly? Are they awaiting a sufficiently strong wind to take to the air, much like an eagle or a hawk catching a thermal and soaring? When they fall onto our heads and windshields, are they trying to get our attention? Are fishfalls some sort of piscine FedEx, by which the fish are attempting to deliver a message? What might it be? Do they want to communicate? Do fish *care* about us?

Fishing and Kids

One might think fish *do* care, judging from the therapeutic benefits humans derive from hanging out with fish.

Some of the finest descriptions of the health benefits of fishing come from psychologist Paul Quinnett's admirable book *Pavlov's Trout*. Quinnett, who lives in the Pacific Northwest, was fishing with his middle son on a trout stream in eastern Washington state on a warm spring day in 1980 when a sinister black cloud began to form in the west. The sky became increasingly menacing, and a powdery gray substance began to rain from the sky.

'Geez, Dad, we're being buried alive by this stuff,' his son protested. 'I think we should get the hell out of here. That's not a normal cloud.'

Quinnett knew that the Hanford Nuclear Reactor was less than one hundred miles southwest of their trout stream. Although his son had caught six trout, he had caught none. If Hanford had exploded, he realized, this could be his last chance.

'Just one trout, before it gets too dark to see,' Quinnett responded, as he saw a trout rise and made another cast.

Driving home, they learned from a radio news report that Mount Saint Helens had erupted and that pandemonium had gripped that part of the country. With the windshield wipers brushing away the falling ash, conversation turned naturally toward ultimates – life, death, immortality. Quinnett, who believes fishing and eschatology are first cousins, used this opportunity to tell his son about a man who died what he considered to be a good death.

'A *good* death?' his son pondered. What could be good about death? The old man, Quinnett explained, was a logger who really lived to fish. When his wife died, he sold the family home and bought a cabin along the Washington coast. He let the place go and soon it was overrun with wild blackberries, which, along with game and fish, helped feed him. One day, while fishing with a friend in the rain, he hooked a huge steelhead trout. He fought it a long time and eventually waded out to position the fish between him and the shore. Finally, with his rod arched high and the magnificent silver fish flashing in the shallows, he waved to his friend and collapsed with a fatal heart attack. His last words were, 'Get the net!'

Quinnett clearly believes that fishing can be salvific and that one's chances of being netted by the Almighty are enhanced by fishing. He deserves a hearing. In addition to being an avid fisherman, he is an authority on substance abuse and suicide, with several books to his credit. He directs Adult Services at the Community Mental Health Center in Spokane, Washington, and is on the clinical faculty in the Department of Psychiatry and Behavioral Science at the University of Washington School of Medicine. I admire his book *Pavlov's Trout* immensely, in part because it is the only fishing book I know of that does not tell you how to catch a fish.

Quinnett is particularly enthusiastic about a drug prevention program called Hooked on Fishing – Not on Drugs. 'This may be the most exciting drug prevention effort ever devised for schools and communities,' he says. This highly acclaimed program offers a kindergarten-through-twelfth-grade teacher's guide that describes activities and lessons for kids of all ages. 'The goals are simple: Hook kids on a healthy, lifetime sport that teaches the principles of conservation, sportsmanship, ethical behavior and also reduces stress while it enhances relationships with others.'

A fourteen-year-old named Matthew Deakins came up with the idea for the program. Matthew said he was too busy fishing to fool around with drugs and that fishing gave him time to 'think things out.' Perhaps, he said, fishing might also help other kids stay off drugs. 'I like this campaign,' Quinnett says. 'Our schools offer only so many slots on the basketball and football teams, only a few kids play in the band, and only a few of the very cutest make the cheerleading squad. Between the handful of attention-getting star performers at the top and the attention-seeking trouble-makers at the bottom lies the great majority of children who pass through our schools, those without much recognition, attention, purpose, or passion. In some ways, these are our most at-risk children for drug experimentation, abuse and eventual addiction.'

Why fishing? Quinnett explains: 'Fish don't care if you're talented or in a wheelchair or blind or skinny or fat or tall or short or even what color you are. Fishing can be instantly rewarding for *any* kid. Angling gives everyone a level playing field and an equal chance . . . Catching a fish won't produce a high equal to or better than crack cocaine, but the *process* by which you "hook" a kid on fishing involves something which drugs can never replace or become a substitute for: a positive relationship with another human being. It is this relationship, not fishing per se, that can save a kid.'

The only thing more powerful than drugs and booze, Quinnett asserts, is love: not just sexual love, but love of humankind, fraternal love, parental love – the sort of love that can be developed and fostered, he believes, in a fishing boat or on the banks of a stream.

The single biggest reason young people put drugs into their bodies, says Quinnett, an authority on drug abuse and rehabilitation, is that they don't like themselves very much. Can fishing help? 'I think it can,' he says, 'because fishing can become a positive addiction.' Why substitute one addiction for another? Simple, says Quinnett: drugs kill; fishing doesn't. Although you may indeed have trouble controlling how often you go fishing, or become fanatical about hook sharpness or fly patterns, or become a compulsive liar about how many fish you caught or the one that got away, these habits don't destroy one's liver, brain, family, or friends, says Quinnett, with tongue in cheek. Instead, they give kids pleasure and help them build self-esteem.

For Quinnett, however, fishing is more than a tool for psychological growth and maturity. It is ultimately a spiritual path and potentially a way to answer some of life's great questions – among which, he suggests, are the following: 'What is man's purpose? What is his place in the cosmos? What happens after death? Why do the big ones get away?' And, finally, 'To fish or cut bait . . . that is the question.'

Trout Mind: An Altered State

I know several fly fishermen who proudly call themselves fish-heads. This is their way of admitting that they have lost their minds to trout, that they are literally crazy about fishing. This may sound like an exaggeration to anyone who has never had firsthand experience of this madness. But, in fact, fishing *can* involve an altered state of consciousness, with three distinct features.

For one thing, one's sense of time slows while fishing – a hallmark of authentic meditation, contemplation, and prayer. One day an oncologist colleague of mine disarmed me when he said, 'I've just figured out why so many of my patients take up fishing after they are diagnosed with cancer.' His insight came while he was fishing the previous weekend, and he had an uncomfortable sunburn to show for it. 'If you're sitting in a boat doing nothing but waiting for a fish to bite,' he said, 'time drags. I can't think of a better way to make the days longer. It's a perfect recreation for someone who believes he's going to die and that his time is limited.'

The second major feature of the altered state of awareness experienced by fishermen is going beyond duality – ceasing to experience the world as separate or 'out there.' The word *nondual* means 'not two,' which suggests a sense of unity with all there is. Millions of dedicated fishermen and fisherwomen know this state of mind intimately, although they may not articulate it as such. They can become so absorbed, so identified with fishing that they *become* the fish – and not just the fish but the water, the forests, and the mountains as well, which are also part of their immediate experience. Often while fishing everything feels perfect and right, and one feels united with all there is. This experience keeps one returning – fish luring fisherman.

Those familiar with the tenets of mysticism will recognize that this circumstance resembles the state of oneness for which the mystic strives. To be a decent fly fisherman, it is not enough to craftily master the mechanics of casting and fly selection. One must learn to *think* like a fish and *merge* with the fish. That is why 'Trout Mind' is analogous to Buddhism's 'Big Mind,' in which one gives up the sense of an isolated self and enters a state that is transpersonal and universal. The fly fisherwoman's *fly* is a perfect metaphor for this transformation, because on entering Trout Mind she flies or soars above self-identification and loses herself in a unity that bridges species.

I have had many moments on trout streams during which the entire world seemed transformed – for example, standing in the Clark's Fork on the Montana-Wyoming border in a chill, gray dusk as a doe and her fawn came to the stream's edge, acknowledged me with their gaze, stepped lightly into the stream with me, drank their fill of the crystalline water, nodded their good-bye, and disappeared silently into the forest. And fishing a white-water section of the Pecos River in northern New Mexico, when suddenly the setting sun turned the water into such a dazzling, heart-stopping torrent of gold and turquoise that I expected it to catch fire. A similar feeling came over me late one afternoon in a remote canyon on the Río Mora, where sunlight never touches the water – a place so primeval it sent shivers up my spine and reminded me that there are places so sacred that humans should not tread there. Then there was a specimen day spent on a tributary of the Yellowstone River in Wyoming while a solitary buffalo bull grazed nearby. After landing a large cutthroat trout, I knelt beside her on a gravel bar and, with trembling hands, carefully removed the fly. Then, overwhelmed with a feeling of love for this indescribably gorgeous fish, I lifted her gently with both hands and kissed her on her nose before committing her back to the swirling waters. When I later divulged this gesture to my brother, he informed me that my action may have been more appropriate than I realized, because the scientific name for the rainbow trout, a close relative of the cutthroat, is *Oncorhynchus mykiss*.

Yet the most memorable fishing experience of my life, to which all others pale in comparison, occurred on a hot July afternoon when grandmother Dossey took my twin brother and me fishing for the first time in our lives when we were four years old. When Mamaw announced out of the blue that we were going fishing, we were perplexed. For all we knew we could have been departing for the moon, because we had no concept of what *fishing* meant. She assembled a cane pole, line, hook, and bobber, and off we went walking down a dusty country road. Our destination was a small pond under a narrow wooden bridge. Mamaw caught a grasshopper, impaled it on the hook, and lowered it into the water. The cork disappeared immediately, and with lightning reflexes she landed a small sunfish. My brother and I were mesmerized and speechless. Never had we seen such a thing! The magic that enchants young children when they are first exposed to fishing had invaded us, never to depart. As our catatonia wore off, Mamaw let us try our hand. By the end of the afternoon we had both caught fish, and our world had changed forever.

I do not pretend to understand this power, but it is surely connected with the unconscious. It seems most potent while fly-fishing, when one is standing in water, which is a symbol of the unconscious mind. Symbolically, then, fly-fishing involves standing in mystery. Thus Kitty Pearson-Vincent, a photographer and writer, sees fish as 'otherworldly . . . Trout are like dreams hovering in the elusive unconscious. In capturing one, if ever so briefly, before release, there is that sense of revelation occurring when one awakens in the night, snatching a dream from the dark portals of sleep.'

This brings us to the third connection between fishing and mystical experience – that of nonattachment, of ceasing to demand specific outcomes. Fly-fishing is a humbling reminder that one cannot *compel* things to happen. One merely selects a fly and presents it as skillfully as possible, then respectfully awaits the outcome. This is like any good laboratory experiment, which, if done properly, is a sacred invitation for nature to manifest in a particular way.

I take the invitation aspect of fly-fishing seriously, and I have a ritual I always invoke before making my first cast. Standing on the stream bank, I enter a prayerful state in which I tell the fish what I am about to do. Then I invite them to participate if they wish and tell them that I will release them if caught. Most of them, believe me, decline.

Associating fishing with nonattachment may seem contradictory, because many of those who fish take pride in the number and size of their catch. But a new ethic called 'catch and release' is emerging among fishermen of all sorts these days, which has an unmistakable affinity with the mystical ideal of nonattachment. Fisherfolk acknowledge by this action that there is something more important about fishing than keeping their catch. Perhaps they realize the truth in Henry David Thoreau's maxim – 'Many go fishing all their lives without knowing it is not fish they are after' – and choose, as a result, to release their catch.

In *Fly Fishing through the Midlife Crisis*, Howell Raines, a former White House correspondent and political journalist for the *New York Times*, describes how as a youngster he fished with one goal in mind: tonnage. The size and numbers of the fish he caught were everything. As he grew older and took up fly-fishing, however, something shifted. Eventually it became immaterial whether he caught fish or not.

Nonattachment in fishing seems to be learned by men with

great difficulty. Women, on the other hand, seem to reach this point intuitively. Dave Decker runs the Complete Fly Fisher fishing retreat in Wise River, Montana. Approximately half his clients are women, and during August he stages a women-only week. He and his guides have come to appreciate women's patience. 'Men measure success by whether they catch the big fish,' Decker says. 'Women don't care. And guess who catches the fish?'

Radiologist and research scientist Kathryn Ann Morton is a case in point. She goes back every summer to the Complete Fly Fisher to hone her skills. 'I enjoy casting, the precision it requires, and I enjoy it whether I get a result or not,' she says. 'The reward is in the act itself – though it's always nice to catch a big brown trout.' Morton's patience on the water seems to flow from her work as a professional researcher. 'I spend my time trying to find hidden patterns in complex images,' she says. 'One of the things about fly-fishing that appeals to me is that I'm able to see things: I can look across the surface of the water and see subtle changes that indicate there's a fish down there somewhere.'

For many, fishing also serves as a spiritual refuge or psychological haven – a resting point where balance and sanity can be regained. In his book *The Face of Battle*, British military historian John Keegan relates how fishing served this function in one of the most unlikely settings: war. Since the middle of the nineteenth century, the width of battlefields had been extending so rapidly that no general could hope to be present at successive points of crisis to direct his men, as Wellington had done at Waterloo. The general's primary work now had to be done in his office, before the battle began. Before World War I, one of the most popular pieces of literature in the British army was a short story by General Sir Edward Swinton called 'A Sense of Proportion.' The central character was a general who was obviously modeled after the legendary German general Helmuth von Moltke, 'who, having made his disposition on the eve of battle, spends its hours casting flies for trout, serene in the assurance . . . that he had done all he could.'

I realize that the analogies I have made between fly-fishing and religious or spiritual experience are a stretch for some people; lots of folk will think I'm suffering from an overheated, frothy imagination. Others take a dim view of fishing in general and perceive it as spiritually incorrect. To those who believe that fishing indicates spiritual bankruptcy, please take another look. Throughout history fishing has often been regarded as a legitimate spiritual endeavor. It was recommended by no less a master than Jesus Christ. 'Go thou to the sea,' he told Peter on one occasion, 'and cast a hook, and take up the fish that first cometh up.' Jesus as fishing instructor.

The Literature of Fishing

Because fishing can be a beatific experience, it is notoriously difficult to describe. I suspect this is why most of the literature on the subject is so dismal. Fishing has not yet produced its Shakespeare, which leaves the rest of us free to rail clumsily on and on about this mystifying enterprise. Perhaps this explains, as Howell Raines tells us, why there are five thousand books on fishing in the English language, which is the most extensive literature on any sport, and why every good fishing store these days has a book section.

Fishing is always in danger of being romanticized, and the egos of fishermen can become insufferably inflated, so it is not surprising that fishing and fishermen have always provided easy targets for satirists. A typical blast has been attributed both to Samuel Johnson (1709–1784) and to Jonathan Swift (1667–1745): 'Fly fishing may be a pleasant amusement; but angling or float fishing I can only compare to a stick and a string, with a worm at one end and a fool at the other.'

Not everyone is this cynical. Novelist Robert Traver, in his 'Testament of a Fisherman,' also hints at fishing's spiritual side:

> I fish because I love to; because I love the environs where trout
> are found, which are invariably beautiful, and hate the environs
> where crowds of people are found, which are invariably ugly;
> because of all the television commercials, cocktail parties, and
> assorted social posturing I thus escape; because in a world where
> most men seem to spend their lives doing things they hate, my
> fishing is at once an endless source of delight and an act of
> small rebellion; because trout do not lie or cheat and cannot be

bought or bribed or impressed by power, but respond only to quietude and humility and endless patience; because I suspect that men are going along this way for the last time, and I for one don't want to waste the trip; because mercifully there are no telephones on trout waters; because only in the woods can I find solitude without loneliness; because bourbon out of an old tin cup always tastes better out there; because maybe one day I will catch a mermaid; and, finally, not because I regard fishing as being so terribly important but because I suspect that so many of the concerns of men are equally unimportant – and not nearly so much fun.

Fishing as Protection

The fear of curses and spells is ancient, and the methods humans have devised to protect themselves against the malevolent intentions of others are wildly varied. On the surface many appear zany. Some, however, may have a rational basis when examined closely, including certain methods that may be connected with fishing.

Consider the ancient belief that a witch can be thrown off the trail by crossing running water. When I first read about this means of protection, my thoughts turned to fly-fishing in a mountain stream, which one crosses many times in the course of a day. The water is crystal clear, the scenery majestic, the air bracing. My spirits are so elevated in this setting that I feel I can resist *anything* negative – including the influence of witches, if they exist. Always looking for (yet another) reason to go fly-fishing, I have come to place great confidence in this method of protection and employ it whenever I can.

More than rationalization may be involved. We know today that a positive attitude and physical exercise set in motion a host of mind-body events that can stimulate our immune function and increase our cardiovascular fitness. Perhaps we are drawn to certain activities such as hiking and crossing the running water of mountain streams because we have learned through generations that they are somehow good for us. Crossing mountain streams makes us healthier, stronger, more resistant – more 'protected.'

Gender and Fishing

Most people consider Izaak Walton to be the father of fishing as a result of his book *The Compleat Angler*, published in England in 1653. But the first known treatise on the subject in English was written around 1496 by a Catholic nun, Dame Juliana Berners, from whom Walton borrowed (some say stole) heavily. Dame Juliana wrote 'Treatyse of fysshynge wyth an Angle,' a chapter in *The Boke of St Albans*. So fishing has a mother, not a father, and a spiritual one at that. 'All writing about fishing stems from Dame Juliana,' as Howell Raines states in *Fly Fishing through the Midlife Crisis*. '. . . Scholars, mostly male, have recently called her authorship into doubt. Perhaps we can attribute that to jealousy, as few writers have better expressed the primal joy of the sport.' Dame Juliana also provided the first written instructions in Britain on fly tying.

Raines goes on to list other important women in the history of fishing. The first American to explore how one could imitate aquatic insects by tying imitative flies was Sara J. McBride of Rochester, New York. She wrote about her experiments with nymphs in her home aquarium in 1876, thirteen years before Theodore Gordon, the 'father' of American fly-fishing, got around to catching his first brown trout, and three-quarters of a century before Ernest Schwiebert became famous for his advice about 'matching the hatch.' Mary Orvis Marbury, the daughter of C. F. Orvis, who invented the modern fly reel and whose firm is today justly famous, handled the business's fly-tying effort and published a landmark book, *Favorite Flies and Their Histories*, in 1892. Carrie Stevens, an American, invented the streamer school of fishing in the 1920s (streamers are artificial flies that imitate bait fish rather than insects), and the patterns that she created are still highly valued. Joan Wulff, who instructs women at her school on the Beaverkill River in Lew Beach, New York, is the current grandam of fly-fishing. She is the only woman ever to win a national distance-casting championship against all-male competitors.

Many people stereotypically think that fishing is a 'man thing.' However, of the fifty-three million people who fish in the United States, eighteen million are women, two hundred thousand of whom fly-fish regularly.

Fishing and Romance

John Donne (1572–1631), the English poet, spoke of fishing and romance in the same breath in his exalted poem 'The Bait':

> Come live with me, and be my love,
> And we will some new pleasures prove
> Of golden sands, and crystal brooks,
> With silken lines, and silver hooks.

The same sentiment comes through in Renoir's painting *Fisher with Rod and Line*, in which a young fisherman clad formally in coat, tie, and hat is fishing from the lush banks of a stream, while a gorgeously dressed woman (friend? wife? lover?) sits nearby, apparently sewing or perhaps reading. The painting is suffused with Renoir's characteristic tenderness and suggests that fishing can be a medium for harmony and love.

My experience assures me that Renoir is correct. Although my wife, Barbara, has never cast a fly and has no interest in learning, we have fished together for three decades in streams and lakes across the continent. She is a prolific author and often carries a small library and writing materials on our outings. Some of her most creative breakthroughs as a writer have taken place in these settings. She is also an accomplished needlepointer and has done some of her finest needlework in spectacular settings alongside alpine lakes and streams. Fly-fishing has always catalyzed a special closeness between us. So I know that Donne was not exaggerating and that Renoir was right on target.

'Now He Can Have Me'

I know a remote glacial lake in a primitive, mountainous area of central Idaho that for me has all the attributes I expect from heaven. Its shores are strewn with boulders the size of houses and it is ringed with granite spires on three sides, which are the aeries of eagles. Its crystalline waters are inhabited by cutthroat trout, who through the years have lured me far more powerfully than I have lured them. Their bodies have fed me over campfires a few times. When I die, I hope to return the gesture by having my ashes scattered on those waters, entering the food chain of those blessed cutthroats, thereby *becoming* a trout.

For years I believed this wish was an idiosyncrasy, but it may be more common than I thought. Writing in *Fly Fisherman* magazine, Nick Lyons described a friend who, when he went fishing on a remote New England river, always paused at a bridge. The man had seen, in his early fifties, what he believed was the wavering tail of a gigantic brown trout, about twenty feet out, near the first abutment – though it could have been just a weed or a shadow. The next year he saw it clearly – a six- to eight-pound brown trout, perhaps twenty-six inches long, the largest trout he'd ever seen in an Eastern river. He waded into the water and tried casting a fly, but the currents made it impossible. He knew he could climb the bridge and try to catch the great fish with bait, or he could cast a metal lure to catch him, but neither option was acceptable to him.

Each time the man fished the river, three or four times each season, he stood quietly and stared at that patch of quiet water. It became a ritual. In the off-season he dreamed of the fish often and calculated new strategies, but none worked. The fish was there for two years, disappeared, and then was back. For ten years this went on, and the fisherman began to realize he probably was not looking at the same fish. The original brown trout, old when he first saw it, was now surely dead, replaced by another huge fish.

The man never grew tired of thinking about the fish, nor of visiting it and not catching it. Eventually he grew old and began to fish less because of painful arthritis. This only caused him to think more of his fish, 'the first one and its successors melding into one, transcending themselves, becoming some sort of emblem.' In July 1997 he saw it for the last time.

The man declared he'd never fish again; he had developed cancer, which was rapidly progressing. He told his wife he wanted to be cremated, and that he wanted a friend to drop his ashes from the upstream part of the bridge so the current would carry them to the great trout:

'That fish gave me so much pleasure over the years – thinking about it, watching for it, pitching a fly toward that abutment. Every time I went I simmered with hope, and if I saw it, I returned radiant . . .' He paused for a moment. 'We were really linked, you know.'

[His] friend said he did know.

'And now, since I couldn't have him, he can have me.'

Part Three

NONLOCALITY

Introduction

SOME THINGS TAKE A BIT of getting used to.

Take the Internet and e-mail, for example. Although today I can hardly imagine getting along without them, I resisted hooking up for years, rationalizing my objections in a hundred ways. I could barely handle all my regular mail; why complicate things by adding another stream of correspondence? Moreover, the idea of electronic messaging seemed impersonal and dehumanizing; why should I degrade the quality of my interactions with friends? Most of my colleagues who already relied on e-mail laughed at my defenses, berating me for being out of touch and pressuring me to take the leap. Finally I knuckled under. Within a week I discovered that all my preconceptions were wrong. E-mail actually brought me closer to my friends and made my work more efficient, and the Internet opened up sources of information I never knew existed. However, none of my friends' earlier justifications of electronic communication had been convincing; I had to experience e-mail and the Internet personally for them to become real.

Nonlocal, or infinite, mind, which we will now examine, is like that. The idea that the mind could be infinite is so unreasonable, so irrational, that personal experience is required for it to make sense.

Nonlocal literally means 'not local' – not here, not now. *Nonlocality* has a special meaning in the world of physics, where it is used to describe subatomic particles such as electrons and photons when they behave as if they were not confined to specific points in space and time – when they appear everywhere at once, and when they seem not to travel through time.

For millennia people have observed that consciousness often behaves similarly, as if it too were unlimited in space and time. For instance, individuals often report knowing something before it happens or gaining information at great distances outside the reach of the senses. These phenomena have been called clairvoyance, telepathy, and precognition – so-called extrasensory perception, or ESP. These events have largely been dismissed in modern times because scientists hold to a local concept of the mind – mind acting only within the body and in the present moment, which in principle rules out the possibility of nonlocal mental events.

But in view of our appalling ignorance of the nature of the mind, we should be careful in saying what the mind can and cannot do. No one really knows the origin of consciousness, its destiny following death, or how it interacts with the brain. The plain fact is that the local view of the mind is an assumption, an ingrained belief, which, in view of current evidence, gives us a false view of who we are.

When I began to explore the nonlocal nature of consciousness shortly after becoming a physician, I believed I was involved merely in an intellectual and philosophical exercise. But as I opened myself to the actual scientific evidence favoring the idea that the mind can act beyond the body, I began having personal experiences that confirmed this view. Three times I had precognitive dreams revealing detailed clinical events that would actually take place only later. In the most elaborate example, I dreamed about events that concerned a sick patient I would not encounter until the following day. The dream was highly specific, down to minute details, and could hardly have occurred by chance. I soon realized that my questions about the nature of the mind were not just intellectual probes; they had down-to-earth consequences for health and healing.

Like my confrontation with e-mail and the Internet showed me, we need personal experiences for nonlocal, infinite mind to become real to us. But how? As it turns out, it really isn't too difficult. These events are already a part of the life of billions of people worldwide. They often occur as part of a spiritual discipline such as meditation or prayer. And they seek us out, ready or not. As evidence, a 1987 survey by the National Opinion Research Center of the University of Chicago found that 67 percent of Americans have had nonlocal mental experiences such as clairvoyance, telepathy, and precognition. Surveys throughout North America, Great Britain, the Middle East, Brazil, Asia, and Australasia show similar findings: more than half the population have experienced these events in their lives.

Like the blind men feeling separate parts of the elephant and coming up with different definitions of the animal, different approaches to the mind yield conflicting pictures of what it is like. That is why philosophers, neuroscientists, physicists, shamans, spiritualists, and theologians almost never agree on the nature of consciousness: they are viewing different expressions of consciousness in isolation. True, each approach can add something valuable to our understanding of the mind, but we err when we regard any single approach as complete. This is where we have taken a wrong turn in medicine during the twentieth century – considering mind-as-brain to be the full picture. This has led us to deny the possibility that the mind can act nonlocally beyond the brain and that these nonlocal actions might affect human health.

As we now examine the mind's infinite reach, let's acknowledge that there is nothing new about this view. This picture of consciousness has echoed through the great spiritual traditions since recorded history. What is new, however, as we will see, is the science that supports such a view and the evidence that nonlocal, infinite mind affects health and healing.

The nonlocal picture of consciousness is one of the most majestic and glorious views of the mind we can conceive: mind as infinite, mind as immortal. Let's take a closer look.

10

A Different Kind of DNA

*There I beheld the emblem of a mind
That feeds upon infinity.*
— WORDSWORTH —
The Prelude

ONE MORNING WHILE I was sitting in my office at the Dallas Diagnostic Association, a patient knocked on my door and, without waiting for me to answer, thrust past the nurse to the inside. She was an intelligent, middle-aged woman who was highly successful in her profession. I had cared for her for years and counted her a friend. She was distraught and near tears. Without wasting time on formalities, she got to the point.

'I need your help,' she said. 'Last night I had a dream in which I saw three little white spots on my left ovary. I'm terrified they are cancerous.'

That was all there was to it – no symptoms, just a disturbing dream. Because of my own unsettling dream experiences that I referred to in the introduction to part 3, which were also health-related and proved to be eerily prophetic, I was intrigued by her report. We proceeded to an examination room. But when her exam proved normal, she was not consoled.

'The dream was one of the most vivid I've ever had,' she said. 'I can't dismiss it. I know something is wrong.'

'Let's do a sonogram and get a picture of your ovaries,' I suggested.

She eagerly agreed, so I escorted her down the hall to the radiology department and introduced her to the radiologist, a no-nonsense colleague whose technical skills were superb. When he asked her what her problem was, she described her dream without hesitation: three little white spots on her left ovary. The radiologist was not exactly enchanted by this clinical tidbit, and he gave me his best you've-got-to-be-kidding glance. It was obvious that this was the first procedure he'd ever performed because of a dream. Nevertheless, I left them alone and walked back to my office to see other patients.

Within an hour the radiologist was in my office. The fact that he chose to deliver the sonogram report personally suggested he'd found something interesting, which was a bad sign. Moreover, he was nervous and looked pale, as if he'd seen a ghost.

'What on earth is wrong?' I asked. 'What did you find?'

'Three little white spots,' he reported hesitantly. 'On her left ovary.'

'Cancer?'

'No. They're ovarian cysts, completely benign.'

'Just like she saw in her dream?' I asked, rubbing it in.

'Yeah,' he conceded. 'Just like in her dream.'

Coincidence?

Skeptics in these matters say that the fact that my patient saw three little white spots on her left ovary in a dream, which turned out to be true, was a fluke, just one of those things. It was all a coincidence – a meaningless, chance correspondence between unrelated events. Instances such as this *must* be coincidental, skeptics insist, because humans can't see inside their bodies or into the future.

Moreover, skeptics contend that we only remember dreams of lucky hits and we forget dreams that don't pan out, and that this creates the illusion that we can gain knowledge through dreams. If we statistically compared the remembered hits with the forgotten misses, we'd see that nothing remarkable is going on and that 'valid' dreams are merely chance happenings.

But this reasoning is facile. It simply isn't correct that people remember only dreams that come true. Moreover, it is presumptuous and arrogant for one individual to declare that events in someone else's life have no pattern or meaning. 'Meaning meters' don't exist, so the perception of patterns and connections, including those in dreams, is hugely subjective. What is meaningless to one person may be highly meaningful to another. Furthermore, some people are skilled at perceiving meaning, whereas others are meaning-challenged, unable to make out connections and patterns even when they are staring them in the face.

As it is often said, 'Everything that counts cannot be counted.' And even when things *can* be counted and analyzed statistically, a false picture often arises. Nowhere is this truer than in distant nonlocal awareness, particularly in dreams. For example, according to statistics, if my patient's dream about her left ovary had been followed by several that were off base, her one accurate dream would technically be insignificant, attributable to chance. Yet she would never agree that her dream was meaningless and a matter of mere chance, and there is no statistician alive who could prove her wrong. The reason is that human experiences are often unique and so rare and idiosyncratic that they render the idea of statistical significance insignificant. For example, a great athlete may run a four-minute mile only once in his lifetime, among the hundreds of races in which he engages. A mathematical analysis would declare his singular accomplishment statistically insignificant, attributable to chance. But the athlete knows, of course, that his performance was due not to chance but to years of dedication and training. When he crossed the finish line, chance was nowhere in sight. He would probably become angry if a statistician met him at the tape and dismissed his achievement as just one of those things. Just so, a statistical approach is limited in analyzing the significance of dreams. Yet in spite of these shortcomings, statistics remains one of the favorite weapons of the dream bashers.

Many health-care professionals reject the significance of dreams as if they understood them, but this is mainly intellectual swagger. The scientific understanding of dreams is exceedingly limited. As James Pagel, M.D., chairman of the dreams section of the American Sleep Disorders Association, says, '[Dreaming is] still a very limited science. We don't even know why people sleep, let alone why they dream.'

In view of our appalling ignorance about dreams, the main reason for rejecting their significance appears to be pure prejudice. Most health-care professionals are anchored in a worldview that does not permit dreams to reveal actual events. If dreams could disclose pathology in our body or forecast illness, such professionals fear that medicine might be reduced to divination and prophecy, like the radiologist who thought my patient's dream was silly. This reflects the situation described by the eminent biologist Theodosius Dobzhansky, 'No evidence is powerful enough to force acceptance of a conclusion that is emotionally distasteful.'

Rejecting dreams puts us at odds with our own history. Greek physicians, who laid the foundations for today's medicine, regularly relied on patients' dreams in their *asklepions*, their healing temples, for insights into the nature of illness. Most modern doctors see this as a blemish on Greek medicine – not something to be taken seriously.

The main sticking points for us moderns are our assumptions about the nature of the mind and how we acquire information in the world. Attributing significance to dreams requires giving up the dictum that we know things only through the physical senses. If we could gain information nonlocally, bypassing the senses, we'd have to rewrite the textbooks and rearrange our worldview. It's a lot less trouble, and considerably less threatening, to continue attributing valid dreams to the old standbys of illusion, coincidence, and chance.

I'm not saying that coincidence and illusion don't exist where dreams, premonitions, hunches, and intuition are involved. People notoriously see patterns and connections that aren't real, particularly in matters of health. Saint Augustine, for instance, insisted that all disease among Christians was caused by demons, and he saw proof everywhere. Later, physicians abandoned Augustine's theory in favor of the notion that disease was caused by an imbalance of the four humors, and they too found evidence to support their view. Today the pendulum in science has swung to the opposite extreme, in which gullibility and lax standards of evidence have been replaced by intellectual cowardice toward certain kinds of facts, particularly about the nature of consciousness. As physicist David Bohm, one of the twentieth century's leading experts on quantum theory, observed, the great accomplishment of modern science is it's reliance on fact – and it's failing is that only certain kinds of facts are permitted.

Health Radar

I've heard hundreds of peoples' experiences suggesting that they can know things in ways that can't be explained conventionally. These messages come not only during dreams but also in the form of premonitions, intuitions, and vague hunches. I am struck by the fact that so many of these instances are health related, of which the patient's dream described above is a typical example.

Why the focus on health? The reason, I suggest, is that we possess a survival-oriented quality of consciousness that can bypass our normal senses and function remotely – nonlocally, infinitely – in space and time. It's as if we had a kind of health radar that continually probes the world for threats to our survival. We can call it distant nonlocal awareness, or DNA for short – a different sort of DNA from the deoxyribonucleic acid that makes up our genes.

I propose that my patient was invoking this capability during her dream. She perceived a threat to her survival, a derangement in one of her ovaries. Her information was not completely accurate; she suspected that the three spots meant cancer, when in fact they were benign cysts. This suggests that the ability for nonlocal knowing functions imperfectly. It exaggerates dangers, it is too sensitive – which, from a survival perspective, is better than not being sensitive enough. This may explain why dreams are often invalid. The threshold of the warning system is set low; it has a hair trigger. This results in frequent false alarms for every true alert. For every valid warning about our health, we may have to endure several that are false. Again, this is as it should be; it's the lion in the bush we *don't* see that kills us.

A challenge facing any creature with such a warning system would be to distinguish false alarms from accurate ones. People

I've known who are good at reading their own dreams say that valid dreams often have qualities that set them apart from invalid ones. Dreams that turn out to be true have a noetic or numinous quality, as if they were 'realer than real.' In contrast, during false dreams one often knows that it is 'just a dream' even while it is progressing. Also, valid dreams are often repetitive, as if they were clamoring for attention. My patient seemed able to tell the difference between ordinary and nonordinary dreams. Never before had she cried wolf as a result of a dream about her health, and she has never done so since. Her dream life seemed well calibrated, telling her when to pay attention to dream messages and when to disregard them.

The Science of DNA

From a *biological* point of view the existence of distant nonlocal awareness makes perfect sense, because this is just the sort of ability that, sooner or later, an intelligent, survival-oriented organism might develop – an early-warning process capable of informing us of threatening events lying beyond the reach of our physical senses. Any organism possessing such an ability could scan the spatial and temporal horizons remotely, assess impending dangers, and take appropriate measures. In the language of evolutionary biology, such an organism would have a distinct advantage in the high-stakes game of survival of the fittest.

The question from a *physical* point of view is, What could be the mechanism for such a facility? In recent years eminent scientists have proposed several models of consciousness that embody this quality of the mind. Here I review these proposals briefly:

• David J. Chalmers, a mathematician and cognitive scientist from the University of Arizona, has suggested that consciousness is fundamental in the universe, perhaps on a par with matter and energy. It is not derived from anything else, and cannot be reduced to anything more basic. His view frees consciousness from its local confinement to the brain and opens the door for nonlocal, consciousness-mediated events such as we have discussed.

- Physicist Amit Goswami of the University of Oregon's Institute of Theoretical Science has proposed his Science Within Consciousness (SWC) theory, in which consciousness is recognized as a fundamental, causal factor in the universe, not confined to the brain, the body, or the present.

- Physicist Nick Herbert has long proposed a similar view. He suggests that consciousness abounds in the universe and that we have seriously underestimated the 'amount' of it, just as early physicists drastically underestimated the size of the universe.

- Nobel physicist Brian D. Josephson of Cambridge University's Cavendish Laboratory has proposed that consciousness makes possible 'the biological utilization of quantum nonlocality.' He believes that nonlocal events not only exist at the subatomic level but, through the actions of the mind, can be amplified and emerge in our everyday experience as distant mental events of a broad variety.

- Rupert Sheldrake, the British botanist, has proposed a nonlocal picture of consciousness in his widely known 'hypothesis of formative causation.' Sheldrake sees great promise in his model for distant, mental events.

- Systems theorist Ervin Laszlo has proposed that nonlocal, consciousness-mediated events such as intercessory prayer, telepathy, precognition, and clairvoyance may be explainable through developments in physics concerning the quantum vacuum and zero-point field.

- The late physicist David Bohm proposed that consciousness is present to some degree in everything. 'Everything material is also mental and everything mental is also material,' he states. 'The separation of the two – matter and spirit – is an abstraction. The ground is also one.' Bohm's views, like the above hypotheses, liberate consciousness from its confinement to the body and make possible, in principle, the distant, nonlocal phenomena we have examined.

- Robert G. Jahn and his colleagues at the Princeton Engineering Anomalies Research lab have proposed a model of the mind in which consciousness acts freely through space and time to create actual change in the physical world. Their hypothesis is based on their experimental evidence, which is the largest database ever assembled of the effects of distant intentionality.

• Mathematician C. J. S. Clarke, of the University of Southampton's Faculty of Mathematical Studies, has proposed that 'it is necessary to place mind first as the key aspect of the universe.' Clarke's hypothesis is based on a quantum logic approach to physics and takes nonlocality as its starting point.

• Erwin Schrödinger, the Nobel physicist whose wave equations lie at the heart of modern quantum physics, says in his book *What Is Life?*: 'Mind by its very nature is a *singulare tantum*. I should say: the overall number of minds is just one.'

• Sir Arthur Eddington, the eminent astronomer-physicist, is quoted in Ken Wilber's *Quantum Questions*: 'The idea of a universal Mind of Logos would be, I think, a fairly plausible inference from the present state of scientific theory; at least it is in harmony with it.'

• Sir James Jeans, the British mathematician, astronomer, and physicist, says in his *Physics and Philosophy:* 'When we view ourselves in space and time, our consciousnesses are obviously the separate individuals of a particle-picture, but when we pass beyond space and time, they may perhaps form ingredients of a single continuous stream of life. As it is with light and electricity, so it may be with life; the phenomena may be individuals carrying on separate existences in space and time, while in the deeper reality beyond space and time we may all be members of one body.'

Although these views are recent, they are part of a long tradition within science. They show that a nonlocal view of consciousness is not a fringe or radical idea, as critics often claim. To the contrary: many of the greatest scientists of the twentieth century were cordial to an extended, unitary model of the mind that permits the sort of distant mental intentions we've been examining.

Empathy

Distant nonlocal awareness often involves others, particularly those with whom we share empathic, loving bonds. The following case, reported by L. A. Dale in the *Journal of the American Society for Psychical Research*, is a typical example:

A woman one afternoon experienced a strong awareness that her six-year-old son was drifting out to sea in a tiny boat. (All she knew normally at the time of her experience was that he had been playing with his sisters six miles away from home at a beach on Long Island Sound.) The [mother] heard her boy calling 'Mommie, Mommie!' She became very upset, but as she had no car she could not go to the beach. She knelt down and prayed very earnestly that her boy would be helped; that he would stay sitting in the boat, and not stand up. 'I knew,' she wrote, 'that if he stood up, he would be lost.' Before the [mother] was able to verify her experience she told it to some friends, one of whom corroborated that she had done so. Later that day she learned that at the time of her experience her son was in fact drifting out to sea in a boat, but was rescued by persons who heard him calling 'Mommie, Mommie!' They attributed his not being drowned to the fact that he had remained sitting in the boat instead of standing up.

As we've noted, most experts dismiss these happenings as coincidence. But when they happen to large numbers of people at the same time, the explanatory power of coincidence evaporates, as in the following example from biologist Lyall Watson's book *The Dreams of Dragons*:

Choir practice in the small town of Beatrice in Nebraska usually began at 7:20 P.M., but on the evening of March 1, 1950, all fifteen members of the choir were late. The minister's wife, the one who played the organ, was still ironing her daughter's dress. One soprano was finishing her geometry homework; another couldn't start her car. Two of the tenors were listening, each in his own home, to the end of a sports broadcast. The bass had taken a quick nap and overslept. There were ten separate reasons to account for the unusual fact that not one of the choir turned up on time. And at 7:25 P.M. that evening, the church was completely wrecked by a devastating explosion.

If we assume that each of the choir was late for about one in every four rehearsals, then the chance of everyone being late on the same day was about one in a billion. This is improbable, but it is not necessarily surprising. It can happen. That it should have happened on the same night as the boiler blew up is a lot more than surprising and begins to border on the uncanny. Coincidences of this order take some explaining.

But what sort of explanation? I prefer one that makes biologic sense, such as a survival-oriented faculty that can scan the future, acquire health-related information, bring it back to the present, and display it to us, allowing us to respond in ways that promote health and survival.

A Saint in the Parish: Why DNA Operates Unconsciously

None of the Beatrice choir members were actually aware that they were avoiding disaster by being late for practice, and they all had perfectly conventional explanations for being tardy. This suggests that our nonlocal survival faculty operates at the level of the unconscious.

Why would such a valuable asset function outside our awareness? There are considerable advantages. Vital bodily functions such as respiration, heartbeat, blood pressure, and immune activity tend to be automatized, outside the reach of conscious meddling. Although it is true that we can learn to exert conscious control over these processes to a limited degree through yoga or biofeedback training, they remain largely autonomic, outside of conscious control. It is a blessing that we don't have to attend to them consciously, for when we do we often make a mess of things. For example, when people pay too close attention to their breathing, they often hyperventilate, which can cause temporary incapacitation and loss of consciousness. Similarly, if we consciously tried to seize control of our nonlocal alert system, we would probably jam the works.

There are strong sociocultural reasons why distant nonlocal awareness may have been shoved from the stage of awareness. There is an old saying: 'No priest wants a saint in his parish.' Saints make the rest of us feel inferior. Just so, people who claim they can intuit the future are often resented by their peers. They may be considered weird, deviant, mentally ill, or demonic. In the West such people have consistently been shoved to the margins of society and considered outcasts; often they have been condemned as witches or heretics and have paid with their lives. (The situation is different in native cultures, of course, where nonlocal ways of knowing are a highly valued part of every shaman's repertoire.)

Because Western societies have often reacted homicidally toward such individuals, a low-profile variety of nonlocal knowing would be much safer than one that is obvious. One of the most effective ways of hiding such a trait would be if it were buried in the unconscious mind of the individual in whom it resides. This would ensure that this faculty would pass undetected not only by outsiders but also by the person possessing it – the ultimate concealment.

If distant nonlocal awareness operated at the level of the unconscious, the possessors would be unaware when this faculty was functioning. When they gained information nonlocally, they would attribute this to other factors, as was the case with all fifteen members of the Beatrice choir. Or, if no convenient surrogate reasons were at hand, one could always invoke chance as the explanation. This would avoid a backlash from the surrounding community toward the knower, who would be as ignorant of this unconscious faculty as anyone else. Thus all involved could shake their heads and marvel at the wonders of coincidence, preserving the fiction that the physical senses are everything.

The paradox is that we have so disowned a trait that is genuinely dedicated to serving us. It's as if we had denied our own heartbeat.

The Ego Fights Back

If we can gain information nonlocally, then the operations of our mind are obviously not confined to our brain and body. Acquiring information nonlocally implies that human consciousness is more than the physical brain and body and that the barriers separating us from others are not as fundamental as we imagine. This fact is obvious to anyone who has felt as if he or she had shared thoughts or emotions with a distant human being – an exceedingly common experience. When this happens, we know in a flash that our separateness from others is something of an illusion.

It's as though we were separated by a porous membrane that leaks information across space and through time, as if we were an extended organism with a single mind. This collective view of consciousness has always been repugnant to people who value individuality over connectedness. The ego resists being a part of something larger – the fear of being swallowed up, of losing one's identity. This helps explain why arguments against the nonlocal, unitary nature of consciousness are sometimes vehement, and why the facts so often get lost.

Of course, a healthy sense of individuality is crucial for normal mental health. Yet problems arise when the self or ego takes control and denies the collective, shared features of who we are. To give an adequate account of human experience, we must acknowledge the entire spectrum of consciousness, including our extended, nonlocal side.

Doing so isn't easy. Our culture places a huge premium on being individual, on being one of a kind. We Americans adore our image as the rugged trailblazer, the solitary innovator who is out front in every field, the most recent expression of which is the 'dot.com' guy who becomes, overnight, the twenty-something gazillionaire. Given our preference for individuality, it is not surprising that we prefer to believe that we only gather information from the world individually, through the senses, and that this is the only mode of perception that exists.

Sudden Infant Death Syndrome

Let's look at another example of how our minds may bypass our senses and acquire lifesaving information about future events. Sudden infant death syndrome (SIDS) is a tragic problem in which an infant dies in his or her sleep for no apparent reason. In 1993, researchers at the Southwest SIDS Research Institute in Lake Jackson, Texas, performed a survey of parents who had experienced the death of a baby from SIDS. The parents were asked if they had ever sensed that something was going to happen to their baby. Twenty-one percent of the SIDS parents reported that they'd had such a premonition; by contrast, only 2.1 percent of parents of non-SIDS infants said they'd had such a premonition. To make sure their findings were on firm ground, the researchers asked an additional control group of two hundred consecutive patients in a suburban pediatric clinic whether they had ever sensed that their baby was going to die and then it did not die. Only 3.5 percent replied yes.

The SIDS parents said that when they reported their premonition of their baby's impending death to a medical professional, spouse, or friend, they were rarely taken seriously. Despite their requests to their physicians for additional medical evaluation and intervention, nothing beyond routine measures was advised for *any* of the SIDS infants. When asked to take special precautions for the apparently healthy child, the physicians' responses ranged from 'placating denial' to 'outrage.'

The conventional explanation is that the SIDS parents picked up subtle cues that something was wrong with their infant; they did not – they could not – survey the future and detect an impending threat to their baby's health.

Picking up subtle cues has long been a favorite explanation of these types of events by skeptics. In the heyday of 'psychical research' in the mid- to late 1800s in England and Europe, 'hyperacuity of the senses' was a popular way of dismissing telepathic and clairvoyant happenings. Skeptics claimed that, just as a blind person develops a highly acute sense of touch, some people have extremely sensitive physical senses that allow distant perceptions to take place. Skeptics clung stubbornly to this hypothesis even when subjects were many miles apart, and even when subjects knew about events before they took place. In taking this position, skeptics seemed not to notice that they were attributing powers to the physical senses that were as outrageous as the magic they sought to deny. It would have been far simpler to admit that they were dealing with the capacity for distant nonlocal awareness.

Nonlocal Mind in History

The concept of distant nonlocal awareness is ancient. Many terms have been proposed in the past for this idea – Universal Mind, Cosmic Consciousness, the One Mind, God or Christ Consciousness, Buddha Mind, and so on. Central to these perspectives is an infinitely extended intelligence that unites all people in a shared existence. As Hippocrates stated, 'There is one common flow, one common breathing, all things are in sympathy.' Pico della Mirandola, the Renaissance philosopher, believed that the world was governed by a similar principle of wholeness – a 'unity whereby one creature is united with the others and all parts of the world constitute one world.' More recently, the philosopher Hegel (1770–1831) called distant mental exchanges between humans 'the magic tie.' He believed that 'the intuitive spirit oversteps the confines of time and space; it beholds things remote; things long past, and things to come.' Arthur Schopenhauer (1788–1860), the nineteenth-century philosopher, suggested that a single event could figure in two or more different chains of circumstance, linking the fates of different individuals in profound ways. He believed in a form of communication that took place between humans during dreams. Similarly, the Swiss psychologist C. G. Jung (1875–1961) coined the term *synchronicity*, in his *Structure and Dynamics of the Psyche*, to describe experiences that appeared coincidental but were highly meaningful to the individual involved. Synchronistic events, Jung asserted, illustrate an 'acausal connecting principle' that does not follow the laws of classical physics.

This philosophic lineage supports a hidden unity underlying our apparent separateness. Therefore, the possibility that the fates of fifteen church choir members in Beatrice, Nebraska, could have been intertwined or that SIDS parents could have foreseen the fate of their infants would hardly have surprised our predecessors.

Would History Have Been Different?

Many tantalizing examples suggest that history might have been considerably different if people had paid attention when their health radar gave warnings of impending problems. In his seminal book *Our Dreaming Mind*, Robert L. Van de Castle, former director of the Sleep and Dreams Laboratory at the University of Virginia Medical School, provides extensive descriptions of 'dreams that have changed the world,' dating to antiquity, as well as those that *could* have changed the world had they been taken seriously. One variety is prophetic dreams involving assassinations. Van de Castle describes President Lincoln's dream of his own assassination about two weeks prior to his murder; the dream of Bishop Joseph Lanyi of Hungary involving the assassination of Archduke Franz Ferdinand of Austria, which triggered World War I; the well-documented dream of George Wallace Jr of the attempted assassination of his father in 1972; and many others.

Another fateful dream is reported by Dean Radin in *The Conscious Universe*. Although Lincoln's dream of his own death has drawn considerable attention, it is less well known that on the night of Lincoln's assassination, General Ulysses S. Grant and his wife, Julia, were supposed to accompany President and Mrs Lincoln to Ford's Theater in Washington. Grant was then the toast of the city; only days earlier he had accepted the surrender of Confederate general Robert E. Lee, ending the Civil War. Accompanying President Lincoln was a great honor, which Grant would hardly have refused. That morning, however, Mrs Grant felt a tremendous sense of urgency that General Grant, their child, and she should not go to the theater that night but should leave Washington immediately for their home in New Jersey. For obvious reasons, General Grant argued that he could not do so. But Mrs Grant's anxiety and urgency increased throughout the day, and she repeatedly sent word to her husband that they must depart. Grant finally relented. When they reached Philadelphia, news of the President's assassination caught up with them. Later they learned that they would have been seated in the same box as the president and that the general was also on actor John Wilkes Booth's list of intended victims.

Van de Castle reveals another little-known but vividly detailed assassination dream, reported by John Williams, a Cornishman, on May 3, 1812. He dreamed he was in the lobby of the House of Commons when he saw a small man enter dressed in a white waistcoat and blue coat. Then he observed an individual in a snuff-colored coat with peculiar metal buttons fire a pistol, and saw a large bloodstain erupt over the left breast of the small man's white waistcoat before he sank to the ground. The assassin was captured by several bystanders. The dreamer asked them the identity of the victim, and was told that it was Mr Spencer Perceval, the chancellor of the exchequer.

Williams awoke and revealed the dream to his wife, who urged him to ignore it. He went back to sleep and had the same dream a second time. Again his wife told him it was just a dream and to disregard it. When he had the dream a third time that night, Williams became very agitated. He consulted several friends about whether he should alert someone in authority. They urged him to keep quiet lest he be ridiculed and considered a fanatic. About a week later, on May 11, 1812, Perceval was assassinated in the lobby of the House of Commons. 'The details of the assassination.' Van de Castle reports, 'including the colors of the clothing, the buttons on the assassin's jacket, and the location of the bloodstain on Perceval's white waistcoat, were identical to those Williams said had appeared in his dream.'

Beyond Anecdote: What Experiments Show

Science has begun to go beyond anecdotes in documenting distant nonlocal awareness. Over the past thirty years or so, for example, many studies have been done to determine whether people can transfer information between each other, at a distance, during sleep and dreams – so-called dream telepathy. In *The Conscious Universe* Dean Radin reports a meta-analysis of 450 dream telepathy sessions published in journals between 1966 and 1973. When all the individual experiments were combined and the evidence was taken as a whole, there was a 63 percent success rate in the 450 sessions. The odds against chance for this outcome are 75 million to 1.

Replication is vital in any controversial area of science, particularly where the nonlocal manifestations of consciousness are concerned. Replication is a strength, not a weakness, of much of this research. In 'Ordinary State ESP Meta-Analysis,' a presentation at the thirty-sixth annual convention of the Parapsychological Association, British psychologist Julie Milton of the University of

Edinburgh, Scotland, reported her analysis of seventy-eight studies, published from 1964 to 1993, in which people attempted to acquire information by extra-sensory perception, or ESP, bypassing the physical senses. These experiments had been reported in fifty-five publications by thirty-five different investigators and involved 1,158 subjects, most of whom were volunteers not known to be gifted. Milton found the overall effects to be highly positive, with odds against chance of 10 million to 1.

Retroactive Influence

The evidence indicated above suggests that distant nonlocal awareness operates independently of space. Other data suggest that it functions outside of time as well, such as studies in remote viewing conducted over two decades at the Princeton Engineering Anomalies Research (PEAR) Laboratory. According to the PEAR protocol, an individual attempts to convey mentally a specific image to a distant individual, who may be stationed as far away as the other side of the earth, and the recipient attempts to record the information that is sent. The image that is mentally sent is selected from a random data bank by a computer, and the scoring of whether there is a hit or a miss is done by a computerized method of evaluation. Hundreds of remote viewing trials have been conducted at PEAR with considerable success, showing odds against chance of 100 billion to 1. Radin reports that in most of the trials, the receiver 'gets' the information from the sender precognitively – up to several days *before* it is sent, and *before* the image has been selected by the computer. These studies have been replicated in several institutions by many different investigators, Radin indicates, among them Stanford Research Institute (odds against chance of 1 billion billion to 1) and Science Applications International Corporation (SAIC). These results have been published in prestigious scientific journals such as *Nature, Proceedings of the IEEE*, and the *Journal of Scientific Exploration*. Following his evaluation of the government-sponsored SAIC tests, Ray Hyman, the University of Oregon psychologist who is the most prominent critic of this field, conceded, 'I cannot provide suitable candidates for what flaws, if any, might be present.'

Our everyday assumptions about time have also taken a beating as the result of studies in retroactive intentional influence. William Braud, professor and director of research at the Institute of Transpersonal Psychology in Palo Alto, California, and codirector of the institute's William James Center for Consciousness Studies, has reviewed all the experiments in this field. In them people try to 'reach back' in time to influence events that presumably have already happened but that may not be fixed. In five experiments involving inanimate objects, such as electronic random-event generators, people were able to successfully influence their output *after* the machine had already run, if the earlier output of the machine had not actually been observed. There was less than 1 chance in 10,000 that the successful results could be explained by chance. Braud also reviewed the results of nineteen similar experiments involving living systems, both human and nonhuman. Odds against chance were 32 in 100 million.

Holger Klintman of the Department of Psychology at Sweden's Lund University began a series of experiments in the early 1980s in which a person was shown a patch of color – green, red, blue, or yellow – followed by the name of the color (that is, the words *green, red, blue,* or *yellow*). He asked the participants to speak aloud the name of the patch of color shown to them as quickly as possible, and then to speak aloud the name that followed as fast as they could. Klintman found that if the initial color patch matched the succeeding name, participants could say the subsequent name quickly and accurately. But if the initial color patch mismatched the subsequent color name, the task became surprisingly difficult and frustrating and participants spoke the subsequent color name more slowly.

Then Klintman decided to analyze the time it took for people to speak aloud the name of the color patch, the first stimulus. He was astonished to find that the initial reaction time was faster if the color patch matched the name that was to follow, and slower when they were mismatched. But how could the person have known whether the two were *later* going to be matched? Klintman believed this effect represented what he called time-reversed interference, in which a later event somehow traveled backward in time, causing cognitive interference when the future stimulus was mismatched, and slowing down the first reaction time. He devised a further double-blind experiment to test his hypothesis that involved twenty-eight subjects. It produced odds against chance of 67 to 1. He ran a total of five successful experiments, each with a somewhat different design, resulting in overall odds against chance of 500,000 to 1.

Responding to the Future

Researcher Dean Radin and his colleagues at the University of Las Vegas explored whether the central nervous system responds to future events – events that have not yet happened. They took advantage of the well-known 'orienting response,' which is displayed by an organism in a fight-or-flight situation. When humans face a crisis or an unknown, fearful situation, there is a characteristic response of the autonomic nervous system: pupils dilate, brain waves alter, sweat gland activity increases, a rise/fall pattern in the heart rate ensues, and there is a blanching of the extremities as blood vessels constrict. These physiological changes make biological sense, because when we are in danger these modifications sharpen our perceptions, increase our physical strength, reduce the danger of external hemorrhage, and in general make it more likely that we'll survive whatever threat we face.

Subjects in Radin's experiment sat in front of a computer screen. On participants' left hands, Radin and his team measured three physiological responses that indicate physiological arousal: heart rate, the amount of blood in a fingertip, and electrodermal activity or skin conductance, which is an indicator of sweating. In their right hands subjects held a computer mouse. When subjects pressed the mouse, the computer randomly selected an image from a pool of 120 high-quality digitized photographs. The computer waited five seconds while the screen was blank, then showed the image for three seconds. Then the screen went blank for five seconds, followed by a five-second rest period. Then another trial would begin. Twenty-four subjects participated, viewing a total of nine hundred pictures. The photos were of two kinds, calm and emotional. The calm photos were pleasant images of natural scenes, landscapes, and cheerful people. Emotional photos were disturbing, shocking, or arousing, such as erotic, sexual pictures and grisly autopsies.

During the five seconds after the subjects pressed the mouse and the screen was blank, their electrodermal activity began to rise in anticipation of the subsequent photo: nothing surprising there. The stunning finding, however, was that the electrodermal activity increased *more* if the future picture was going to be emotional. In other words, the participants 'preacted' to their own future emotional states *before* the emotional pictures were seen. Radin and colleagues called this a presentiment effect, meaning 'a prior sentiment or feeling.' Professor Dick Bierman, a psychologist at the University of Amsterdam, replicated Radin's results, using the same photos.

In summarizing these studies, Radin states, 'Klintman's reaction-time studies and the physiological presentiment experiments . . . suggest that under certain circumstances we can consciously or unconsciously respond to events in our future, events that we have no normal way of knowing.'

It is interesting that the two future stimuli that most aroused Radin's and Bierman's subjects were photos that were sexual or violent in nature. This makes biological sense. If an organism were aware that sexual activity lay ahead, he or she could prepare to procreate; or if violence or danger were about to happen, he or she could prepare for or avoid it. This foreknowledge would be an advantage in staying alive and reproducing, in meeting our evolutionary imperative.

These studies are like a 'time tenderizer' that softens up our rigid categories of past, present, and future, and there is considerable debate among researchers about how to interpret them. Are they really telling us that the future acts backward to affect the present? If so, what does time mean? How can effects come before causes? And what about free will? If we know what lies ahead, is the future determined? Commenting on these sorts of questions, researcher Radin confesses, 'They make my brain hurt.' Mine too.

Although we don't fully understand the meaning of these various experimental findings, it seems clear that there are enough data on the table in science to shred forever our ideas of the brain-limited nature of consciousness. These conventional notions are morphing into a model of consciousness that is nonlocal, because only a nonlocal model of the mind can accommodate the space-time independence demonstrated in actual experiments, and in our own experience as well.

It is mainly 'academic bombast,' says physicist Russell Targ, that prevents this information from being widely acknowledged. No matter; the wheels of science grind slowly, but they grind surely. Nonlocal mind will have its official day, and because of the rapidly accumulating evidence, we can confidently predict that the time is not far off.

Bypassing the Senses

Professor David Ray Griffin believes that the role of the physical senses is vastly overestimated. Griffin is a distinguished figure in contemporary philosophy. He is professor of philosophy of religion and theology in the School of Theology at Claremont and Claremont Graduate School, Claremont, California, and one of the most respected authorities on the works of mathematician-philosopher Alfred North Whitehead, a giant of twentieth-century Western thought.

Griffin contends that the most fundamental way we gain information from the world is not *through* the senses but through *bypassing* them. As he argues in his book *Parapsychology, Philosophy, and Spirituality*: 'Sensory perception is a rather rare form of perception, being exemplified only by the minds of animals with central nervous systems . . . Sensory perception is not our only or even our basic mode of perception . . . Nonsensory perception is . . . a more fundamental mode . . . In nonsensory perception we are always directly perceiving not only contiguous events . . . but also remote events. That is, perception at a distance is going on all the time.'

If Griffin is correct – if a nonlocal, nonsensory mode of perception is our basic way of knowing – how might we enhance its function? If we could step outside our everyday assumptions, our habitual way of seeing things, would distant nonlocal awareness be more obvious and more powerful?

Hypnosis

For decades, researchers in the field of parapsychology have used hypnosis to do just that – to bypass our biases and ingrained habits in the hope of gaining fuller access to nonlocal perceptions. In 1994 psychologists Rex Stanford and Adam Stein, from Saint John's University in New York, published a meta-analysis of extrasensory perception (ESP) studies contrasting the use of hypnosis with ordinary states of awareness. They found twenty-nine relevant studies, twenty-five of which provided sufficient information to analyze the experimental outcomes. These studies were published by eleven different investigators in journals from 1945 to 1982. Hypnosis resulted in significant ESP effects, with odds against a chance explanation of 2,700 to 1. By comparison, the ordinary-awareness studies yielded odds against chance of only 8 to 1. This meta-analysis suggests that when we remove our mental filter, such as through hypnosis, nonlocal ways of knowing are more prone to surface.

Sheep and Goats

Some individuals consider nonlocal ways of knowing so implausible that no amount of evidence would change their mind. As one skeptical research scientist huffed, 'Not 1000 experiments with ten million trials and by 100 separate investigators giving total odds against chance of one-thousandth to 1' could make him accept ESP. Researchers have investigated whether beliefs for or against nonsensory perceptions actually influence their occurrence. Parapsychology researcher Dean Radin describes these findings in his book *The Conscious Universe:* 'This turns out to be one of the most consistent experimental effects in psi [parapsychology] research. It was whimsically dubbed the "sheep-goat" effect by psychologist Gertrude Schmeidler, who in 1943 proposed that one reason that confirmed skeptics do not report psi experiences is because they subconsciously avoid them. People who do report such experiences Schmeidler called the "sheep," and the skeptics she called the "goats."'

In 1993 University of Edinburgh psychologist Tony Lawrence

published a meta-analysis of all the sheep-goat experiments conducted between 1943 and 1993 that involved the selection of limited numbers of choices, as in a card-guessing experiment. He found seventy-three published reports by thirty-seven different investigators, which involved more than 685,000 guesses produced by forty-five hundred subjects. The results strongly favored a sheep-goat effect, with believers performing better than disbelievers with odds greater than 1 trillion to 1. Were these results due to the fact that researchers failed to publish studies to the contrary, which might have annulled the findings (the so-called file-drawer effect)? Analysis showed that it would have required about 1,726 unpublished, nonsignificant studies for each published experiment to eradicate the sheep-goat differences. Lawrence further found that the results could not be explained by differences in the quality of the studies or by a few studies with exceptionally large results. He concluded, 'The results of this meta-analysis are quite clear – if you believe in the paranormal you will score higher on average in forced-choice ESP tests than someone who does not.'

I know about resistance to nonlocal awareness from personal experience. My precognitive dreams that I referred to earlier occurred in a cluster over a period of only a few weeks. Then they stopped, and I haven't had one since. I have often wondered why. Did my mental filter against these experiences start working over-time in an attempt by my ego to shore up my personal bound-aries? I have often told myself that I'd like to have more of these experiences, yet I have to admit that I'm terribly hypocritical on this point. For example, I could have engaged in hypnosis, which, as the research discussed earlier shows, is a way of stimulating these happenings, but I haven't done so. I have to concede that I am hesitant – as most people are – to plunge fully into the nonlocal dimensions of the psyche. I wear my local, sensory-bound personal identity quite comfortably. But my personal experiences of nonlocal knowing, limited though they were, were highly beneficial. They opened for me a side of reality that profoundly affected the way I saw the world and prompted me to remove my blinders to the excellent research in this area.

Shared Feelings

Distant nonlocal *awareness* sometimes shades into distant nonlocal *feeling*. For example, when an individual knows nonlocally that a loved one is in crisis, he or she often experiences the same physical symptoms that are occurring in the distant individual. Usually, however, the physical exam of the 'receiver' is unremarkable.

Psychiatrist Ian Stevenson of the University of Virginia has pondered the clinical implications of this phenomenon. Consider the fact that many people who go to physicians and psychiatrists have no obvious cause for their symptoms. Could their complaints be originating in some distant individual with whom they are empathically and nonlocally united? Stevenson believes the answer may be yes. He writes in *Telepathic Impressions:* 'I believe that if psychiatrists would think more often of the possibility of paranormal influences on their patients they might account for some otherwise inexplicable changes in their patients' condition.'

The Dark Side

We cannot engineer crises in peoples' lives and study their distant effects on others under controlled conditions. By their very nature, these events are spontaneous and anecdotal. Still, they deserve notice. Stevenson describes a patient of his whose clinical course suggests that mental symptoms may be linked nonlocally to distant events. The patient was a forty-five-year-old professor who had become so depressed he required hospitalization. One reason for his depression was disagreements with colleagues in his department. He was on a steady course of medication, and the outward circumstances of his life did not change during Stevenson's period of observation. Although the patient seemed to be gradually improving, one day he became much worse and complained of deteriorating feelings. 'It turned out later,' Stevenson says in *Telepathic Impressions*, 'that this worsening of his condition coincided temporally with meetings of his opponents in his department who were, in effect, plotting to oust him from his position.'

Paranoid persons often claim that hostile feelings are being communicated to them by extrasensory means. Psychoanalyst Jan

Ehrenwald suggested in *Telepathy and Medical Psychology* that they, like Stevenson's patient, might be picking up on the negative wishes and thoughts of others through distant nonlocal awareness.

The nonlocal sharing of thoughts and feelings occasionally takes on macabre dimensions, as in the lives of male twins born in the spring of 1962 to Rozalia Cosma in Brasov, Romania. She named them Romulus and Remus, after the legendary infant twins left to die in the Tiber who were rescued and suckled by a she-wolf. Romulus became the founder and first king of Rome.

As is often the case with twins, the Romanian twins experienced the sharing of sensations at a distance. When one had an accident, the other felt the pain.

On growing up, Remus settled in Cluj in central Romania and Romulus in the Black Sea port of Constanta, five hundred miles away. As adults their sharing of symptoms continued. They became ill with jaundice at the same time. When Romulus broke his leg during an excursion into the Carpathian Mountains, Remus fell downstairs in Cluj and broke his leg as well.

In the fall of 1987, Remus began courting Monika Szekely. Romulus, a week later, started courting a girl also named Monika. The following spring Remus married his Monika and in 1989 they moved to a new apartment. The marriage soon fell on hard times and they quarreled daily. At 10:00 P.M. on May 16, 1993, Remus came home drunk and his wife screamed to him that she planned to take a lover. He shoved her against a wall, whereupon she grabbed a knife from the table. Remus wrested it from her and stabbed her twelve times. At midnight he went to the police station and turned himself in.

At 11:00 P.M. that same evening, Romulus had a talk with his Monika. Although their relationship up to this time had been smooth, Romulus was inexplicably seized with rage and strangled her. He told police in Constanta, 'I don't know why I committed this monstrous crime. When I began to strangle my girlfriend, I felt impelled by an invisible force. I couldn't, or perhaps didn't want to, resist it.' Investigators discovered that Remus had committed his crime only a few minutes before that of his twin.

Why Not Joy?

Why is the information that is nonlocally shared between distant individuals so often negative? The reason may relate to the greater survival value of negative perceptions as opposed to positive ones, as Stevenson suggests in *Telepathic Impressions:* 'Is it a failing of human beings that they do not more often communicate news of . . . happy events by means of extrasensory processes? Or is it that the communication of joy has no survival value for us, while the communication of distress has?'

Stevenson reports that Gerhard Sannwald, in his analysis of information that is shared nonlocally, found that only 15 percent of spontaneous cases involved positive emotional content, while 85 percent involved negative affect. In the 15 percent of cases involving positive feelings, the nonlocal communication was often of the 'I'm all right' variety.

A famous case of this sort involved General John C. Frémont, one of the early explorers of the American West, Stevenson recounts. In the winter of 1853–54, he was involved in a hazardous expedition in the Rocky Mountains, which involved risks from starvation and great physical danger. Meanwhile his wife, who was living in Washington, D.C., was so worried she was wasting away from lack of appetite and sleep. This had been a typical reaction for her when General Frémont had been away on expeditions in the past. Suddenly, out of the blue, she had the unmistakable impression that her husband was no longer in danger. She was so consoled she fell into a profound sleep that left her much recovered from her previous weakness.

News eventually reached her that at the time of her sense of relief, General Frémont had led his party into a settlement where they found food, warmth, and rest, after a long period of near starvation. The general affirmed that Mrs Frémont's experience coincided quite closely to the moment when he, having seen the rest of his party taken care of, sat down to rest and write in his journal. At the time he wished somehow that 'Mrs Frémont could only know that all danger was past and that it was well with me.'

Individuality: The Price We Pay

Coincidence? Many people hope so, because they find reprehensible the idea that an individual's actions may be influenced by the behavior and thoughts of a distant person. Our legal system rests on the premise that each person is responsible for his or her actions. If we are all linked nonlocally in our thoughts and actions, who gets indicted? In a society where everybody is responsible, nobody is responsible. Therefore, if we took seriously the idea of nonlocal interconnectedness, this would unleash an orgy of self-indulgence and an epidemic of social disorder – so the warnings go.

The fallacy in this sort of thinking is the assumption that we must choose between two incompatible alternatives – either being responsible individuals or sinking into a faceless, homogenized, social goo in which individual responsibility evaporates. This choice is false, of course, because each of us has *both* individual and collective characteristics.

If we openly acknowledged our nonlocal unity with one another, the result might be *greater* self-responsibility and social harmony, not less. We pay a huge price for denying the unity that is betokened by our nonlocal connectedness. The great wars of the twentieth century and the conflicts that still rage – in Northern Ireland, the Balkans, the Middle East – are fueled by the belief in the specialness, uniqueness, and superiority of a single religion, race, or political system and the individuals that constitute them. It is not nonlocal oneness but uncompromising individuality that may be our ruin. Without a sense of unity with others, empathy, compassion, and charity go out the window and are replaced by unremitting selfishness and intolerance.

Ironically, acknowledging our transindividuality strengthens us as individuals. We are made hardier by linking with others. As writer Elizabeth Berg expresses this paradox, 'There is incredible value in being of service to others. I think if most people in therapy offices were dragged out to put their finger in a dike, take up their place in a working line, they would be relieved of terrible burdens.'

Nonlocal interconnectedness does not depend on our permission. We are linked nonlocally whether we realize it or not, and we continually influence one another for good or ill. Denying our nonlocal connections does not eradicate them; denial means only that they operate outside our awareness and therefore outside our control. Admitting their existence permits us to bring them into conscious awareness and exercise some measure of control over them when they push us in pathological directions, as with the Romanian twins.

To be influenced by something is not the same as being controlled by it. We can be influenced nonlocally by others without being controlled by them and without giving up self-responsibility – but *only* if we recognize that these influences exist in the first place. The surest way to lose self-control is by denying that we are nonlocally connected, and by adopting the social fiction that we are individuals who always act independently.

Honoring our nonlocal unity requires that we steer clear, however, of that rapturous, New Age call to 'oneness' – that fictional state in which all our precious differences are smoothed out in favor of some blissful sameness. The promise of nonlocal interconnectedness is neither bliss nor sameness but wholeness.

The Brain as Transmitter

Currently, most paid-up scientists believe that the brain somehow *produces* the state we call consciousness. This view restricts consciousness to the physical brain and body and the present and does not permit the distant nonlocal awareness we've been exploring. From time to time, however, a few scholars have suggested that the brain does not produce consciousness but *transmits* it. Transmission theories contend that consciousness exists beyond the brain and body, and they are therefore cordial toward distant nonlocal awareness.

One example was Harvard psychologist William James (1842–1910), who is considered the father of American psychology. James did battle with the materialists of his day over the nature of consciousness. His arguments are still relevant. In 1898, in the annual Ingersoll Lecture at Harvard, titled 'Human Immortality: Two Supposed Objections to the Doctrine,' James said: 'The plain truth is that *one may conceive the mental world behind the veil in as individualistic a form as one pleases, without any detriment to the general scheme by which the brain is represented as a transmissive organ.*'

Neuropsychiatrist Peter Fenwick is another example. Fenwick is now Britain's leading clinical authority on near-death experiences (NDEs), but he began exploring this area as a skeptic. When he first learned of the intense interest in these cases in the United States, and how Americans traveled through a tunnel and met beings of light, he was dubious. He suspected that a strong 'California factor' was involved, and he doubted whether these experiences would cross the Atlantic to staid Britain. But Fenwick became increasingly intrigued by these accounts, and when he publicly announced his interest in them he was flooded with stories that were virtually identical to those in America. He and his wife, Elizabeth, obtained the details of 350 near-death experiences from people all over England, Scotland, and Wales. Their findings are reported in their book *The Truth in the Light*. It is a compelling work because it is written through the eyes of an expert neurologist who knows a great deal about consciousness and the workings of the brain.

Fenwick tackles the various hypotheses put forward to account for NDEs. Are NDEs induced by drugs, oxygen starvation, or the buildup of carbon dioxide? Are they hallucinations, dissociative experiences, or dreams? Are they produced by fear, or by a subtle malfunction of the brain's temporal lobes? Are they caused by a flood of endorphins, the naturally occurring opiates in the brain? Fenwick methodically examines the pros and cons for each possibility and concludes that all these mechanisms fall short:

> Clearly there must be brain structures which mediate the NDE and they are probably the same structure that mediates any mystical experience ... But the major question still remains unanswered. How is it that this coherent, highly structured experience sometimes occurs during unconsciousness, when it is impossible to postulate an organised sequence of events in a disordered brain? One is forced to the conclusion that either science is missing a fundamental link which would explain how

organised experiences can arise in a disorganised brain, or that some forms of experience are transpersonal – that is, they depend on a mind which is not inextricably bound up with a brain.

Fenwick gives serious consideration to the hypothesis that the brain somehow transmits, but does not produce, consciousness. He too credits William James as one of the most lucid proponents of the transmission theory, and he believes that James's theory 'is as relevant to our science today as it was almost one century ago.'

Underlying the transmission theory is the supposition, as we've noted, that there is a form of consciousness that is external to the brain. The brain is in contact with this source, receiving and modifying information from it. Fenwick proposes that although memories are held partly in the brain, a large part of memory is stored external to the brain. This off-site repository of consciousness is compatible with its survival following the death of the brain and body. It may also help explain why many people feel that they are part of a larger whole.

Fenwick acknowledges the problems with this sort of model. He states, 'We come up against the difficulty that at present there is no known mechanism which would link brain to mind in this way, or which would allow memory to be stored outside the brain.' Fenwick adds:

> Another weakness of transmission theories in general is that even if they are correct, they are difficult to test. A transmission theory would argue that as mind is transmitted through the brain, disturbances in brain function will produce disorders of mind because their transmission is interrupted. But a similar argument can equally well be used if it is argued that mind is located in and is a function of the brain. Then too a disorder of brain function will produce a disorder of mind. There is no experiment which can easily distinguish between these two possibilities.

Although all transmission theories are speculative, it is easy to fall into a double standard in evaluating them. Conventional scientists often discard these theories because, as Fenwick acknowledges, they offer no explanation of how an external mind would interact with the material brain. Yet the idea that prevails in current science – that consciousness is produced by the brain – is also pure speculation. As philosopher Jerry Fodor soberly states, 'Nobody has the slightest idea how anything material [such as the brain] could be conscious. Nobody even knows what it would be like to have the slightest idea about how anything material could be conscious. So much for the philosophy of consciousness.'

Even though all theories of consciousness are speculative, transmission theories have a distinct advantage. They can accommodate the empirical data affirming distant nonlocal awareness, and they do not force us to deny our own experience.

Transmission theories of consciousness, however, are misnamed. *Transmission* comes from Latin words meaning to 'send over or across.' There is no evidence that anything is actually transmitted or sent during nonlocal experiences, and there are good reasons why. If consciousness is genuinely nonlocal, as the evidence suggests, it is infinite or omnipresent in space and time. There is therefore no place consciousness is *not*, which means that there is no necessity for anything to be transmitted from point A to point B: it's already there. Moreover, if the mind is genuinely nonlocal, the idea of an off-site, outside-the-brain storage depot for consciousness is meaningless. To store something is to confine it, and the essence of nonlocality is *un*confinement, or the absence of localization. In a nonlocal model of consciousness, therefore, there is no need to agonize over how consciousness is transmitted and where an extracranial repository of memory may be located, because nonlocality renders these sorts of questions superfluous.

'Transmission,' then, is a concept drawn from the classical, mechanical view of world. When applied to nonlocal phenomena, it gives a misleading impression about the nature of consciousness. Still, transmission theories are an improvement over the brain-based images of consciousness, because they release consciousness from its enslavement to the brain. One day, when we learn to think and speak with ease about nonlocal phenomena, we will create a vocabulary that can stand on its own without being contaminated by inappropriate terms drafted from the classical worldview. Until then, perhaps we should keep 'transmission' in quotes in order to emphasize its tentative, qualified usage.

If we are to have a ghost of a chance of understanding the relationship between mind and brain, we are going to have to learn to think nonlocally, not locally. Otherwise we will forever be chasing problems that simply don't apply in a nonlocal world.

Getting Nonlocal

I used to believe that the best way for health-care professionals to overcome their hang-ups about the existence of distant nonlocal awareness was to have one of these uncommon experiences themselves. But this is not quite right. These experiences are not rare; they are going on all the time – they are the norm. To emphasize philosopher David Griffin's view, nonsensory knowing is our *fundamental* way of acquiring information. This means we don't have to go out of our way to *have* nonlocal experiences, we have only to *notice* them.

William B. Steward, M.D., is the medical director of the Institute for Health and Healing and the Health and Healing Clinic at San Francisco's California Pacific Medical Center. Bill has long been a leader in reintroducing genuine healing and caring into medicine. A few years back, someone got wind of the exciting developments at California Pacific and phoned for more information. Bill happened to answer the phone. The individual asked, 'Do you have a visionary on your staff?' Bill, an ophthalmologist, responded, 'I don't know about a visionary, but would a plain ole eye doctor do?'

I love Bill's response. We don't need exotic visionaries to help us tap into the nonlocal dimension of consciousness, to know who we are. We need only to wake up.

11

The Return of Prayer

MARGARET MEAD, THE NOTED anthropologist, once said, 'Prayer does not use any artificial energy, it doesn't burn up any fossil fuel, it doesn't pollute.' It has another attribute Mead didn't mention, which should be of interest to all health-care professionals: it apparently works. An impressive body of evidence suggests that prayer and religious devotion are associated with positive health outcomes.

As this information has become increasingly known, prayer is returning to medicine after sitting on the sidelines for most of the twentieth century. This phenomenon has evoked a variety of responses, ranging from elation to confusion to horror.

'Prayer Actually Works?'

I encountered one such response in 1996 when I was invited to lecture and consult at a large hospital in New York City. The day began with an address to the house staff, in which I discussed the emerging scientific evidence for the effectiveness of intercessory prayer. I reviewed several of the salient experiments that had captured the attention of the medical profession, and I summarized some of the studies that were currently in progress. Later in the day I met with the staff of the hospice department in a follow-up meeting. Before our discussion could begin, I was approached by a clergyman who was obviously quite disturbed. He worked full-time in the hospice area and devoted his life to offering spiritual guidance and prayer for dying patients and to providing psychological and spiritual support for the hospice staff. He said, 'Look. I need to get something straight. I heard your lecture this morning – and if I understand you correctly, you're claiming that intercessory prayer actually *works?*'

For a moment I was speechless and did not know how to respond. Although this man's life was immersed in prayer, he obviously harbored deep doubts about whether his prayers had any effect whatever. When confronted with evidence that intercessory prayer might actually be effective, he was astonished and confused. We chatted privately for a few moments, and I affirmed my earlier comments. I admired his honesty; most of us aren't as courageous as he was in expressing our doubts about prayer.

This experience confirmed my belief that even 'true believers' often doubt, at some level of the mind, the effectiveness of prayer, and that even religious professionals can be shocked to discover that science has something positive to say about prayer. The reasons are no doubt complex but are related to the stormy relations that have existed between science and religion for the past two centuries, particularly since the time of Darwin. When battles between these two camps have arisen, religion usually has not fared well. As a result, most religious believers are understandably leery of what science says about their faith.

Another reason many religious folk object to the entry of science onto their turf is the stereotypical attitude toward science that most of us have developed during the process of becoming educated and socialized in twentieth-century America. The following message has been driven home to almost all of us in our colleges and universities: 'There are two ways to live your life. You can choose to be intellectual, rational, analytical, logical, and scientific, or on the other hand, you can choose to be intuitive, spiritual, and religious. These two vectors of the psyche are incompatible and cannot be brought together; you cannot have it both ways.'

Most of us choose one path or the other and suffer the rest of our life as a result of this artificial, schizophrenic split. Developments in prayer research show, however, that these choices are not incompatible. Science and spirituality *can* come together; we *can* have it both ways.

What Is Prayer?

I have discussed with thousands of Americans what they believe prayer is. I have concluded that the most common image of prayer in our culture, if we were really honest with ourselves, is: 'Prayer is talking, either out loud or silently, to a white, male, cosmic parent figure.'

Of course, this is an extremely limited and culturally conditioned view of prayer. It disenfranchises large proportions of the world's population as well as those in our own society who do not share this perspective. For example, many people believe that prayer is more a matter of *being* than *doing* – such as Thomas Merton, who once remarked that he prayed by *breathing*. Also, many people who pray are not fond of the idea of a male god or a personal god of any kind. Consider Buddhism, one of the world's great faiths: Buddhism is not a theistic religion, yet prayer is central to the Buddhist tradition. Buddhists offer their prayers to the universe, not to a personal god. Buddhism therefore violates most of the cultural assumptions we make about the nature of prayer. Shall we inform Buddhists and others who differ from our cultural norm that they aren't really praying?

In the following discussion I want to employ a deliberately broad and ambiguous definition of prayer: 'Prayer is communication with the Absolute.' This definition is inclusive, not exclusive; it affirms religious tolerance; and it invites people to define for themselves what 'communication' is and who or what 'the Absolute' may be. This definition is broad enough to include people of the various faiths who have participated as subjects in prayer research.

What is *intercessory* prayer? *Intercessory* comes from the Latin *inter*, 'between,' and *cedere*, 'to go.' As discussed earlier, intercessory prayer is therefore a go-between – an effort to mediate on behalf of, or plead the case of, someone else. Intercessory prayer is often called distant prayer, because the individual being prayed for is often remote from the person who is praying.

There is a significant difference of opinion as to how much of the experimental data supports intercessory prayer, and part of the problem in identifying work in this field is the lack of agreement on language. If one performs an electronic database search using *prayer* as a keyword, one will probably retrieve around a half dozen studies of dubious quality. On the other hand, physician Daniel J. Benor has written a four-volume work, *Healing Research* (the first two volumes of which have been published), which cites nearly 150 studies in this field, many of which are of excellent quality and over half of which show statistically significant results.

Many researchers shy away from using the word *prayer* in favor of a more neutral term such as *distant intentionality*. Even though their experiment may actually involve prayer, they often do not use this term in the titles of their papers. If their subjects pray, researchers may say instead that the subject 'concentrated' or applied 'mental effort' to produce the effect being studied, or they may use terms such as *mental healing, psi healing*, or *spiritual healing* to describe their work.

Perhaps we should not be too critical of researchers on this point. Research into the distant effects of consciousness is generally considered to be the domain of parapsychology. This field is sufficiently controversial without adding the furor surrounding the concept of distant, intercessory prayer. But the aversion of experimenters to using *prayer* comes with a price: the difficulty of identifying prayer-and-healing studies and the underestimation of the number of prayer experiments that exist.

Conversely, many religious people are exceedingly uncomfortable about 'parapsychology,' and they deplore parapsychologists' practice of equating prayer with mental intentionality, focused attention, concentration, or even meditation. They often feel that parapsychologists dishonor prayer and are disrespectful of the spiritual traditions in which prayer is embedded. I sympathize with these reservations, but after exploring prayer and parapsychology for several years, I feel that a clean separation between these fields does not exist and is impossible to achieve. In experiments in parapsychology in which individuals attempt to influence living things at a distance, participants often actually pray or enter a sacred, reverential, prayerlike state of mind to accomplish their task. On the other hand, when people pray, they often have paranormal experiences such as telepathy, clairvoyance, precognition, and so on. Anyone doubting this would do well to read philosopher Donald Evans's scholarly work *Spirituality and Human Nature* or historian Brian Inglis's classic book *Natural and Supernatural: A History of the Paranormal.*

As a single example of how parapsychology (often called 'psi') and prayer are difficult if not impossible to keep separate, consider a study by Erlendur Haraldsson and Thorstein Thorsteinsson in which subjects attempted mentally to cause increases in the growth rate of yeast cultures. The title of the paper, 'Psychokinetic Effects on Yeast: An Exploration Experiment,' gives no hint that spiritual healers and prayer were involved. The researchers recruited seven subjects – two spiritual healers who used prayer, one physician who employed spiritual healing and prayer in his practice, and four students with no experience or particular interest in healing. The subjects were asked to 'direct their healing effects' to increase the growth of yeast in 120 test tubes. The study was well designed and employed appropriate controls. The results indicated that 'mental concentration or intention' indeed affected the growth of the yeast. The bulk of the scoring was done by the two spiritual healers and the physician; the odds against obtaining the same result by chance were less than 14 in 100,000. In contrast, the students, who had little interest in either prayer or healing, scored at chance levels.

The title of this paper suggests that it was a study in parapsychology and psychokinesis ('mind over matter'), but a closer look shows that it was clearly an experiment in the effects of prayer. Because of this study's title, however, a survey of the prayer-and-healing literature would probably not identify it. This experiment is a typical example of why the boundaries between prayer and experimental parapsychology are artificial.

Fortunately, the long-standing antipathy between religion and parapsychology appears to be diminishing. The *Journal of Religion and Psychical Research*, published in the United States, and the *Christian Parapsychologist*, published in Great Britain, are notable examples of bridge-building between these fields. The latter publication was begun in 1953 by a group of British clergy and laymen who were, the journal's mission statement says, 'convinced that psychical phenomena [have] great relevance to the Christian faith, both in life and death . . . [but that] psychical studies are as likely to lead to harm as to good if pursued outside the realms of the spiritual life . . . through the practice of prayer, worship and service to [our] fellow creatures.'

As further evidence of the emerging religion-and-parapsychology dialogue, Michael Stoeber, assistant professor in the Department of Religion and Religious Education at the Catholic University of America, and Hugo Meynell, professor in the Department of Religious Studies at the University of Calgary, have coedited a critically acclaimed book, *Critical Reflections on the Paranormal*, that examines issues of mutual interest to both parapsychology and religion.

Surveying the Field

Studies in distant, prayerful intentionality of living systems involve not only humans, but nonhumans as well. William G. Braud, director of research at the Institute of Transpersonal Psychology in Palo Alto, reports that 'persons have been able to influence, mentally and at a distance, a variety of biological target systems including bacteria, yeast colonies, motile algae, plants, protozoa, larvae, woodlice, ants, chicks, mice, rats, gerbils, cats, and dogs, as well as cellular preparations (blood cells, neurons, cancer cells) and enzyme activity. In human "target persons," eye movements, gross motor movements, electrodermal activity, plethysmographic activity, respiration, and brain rhythms have been influenced.' As mentioned, Benor has identified about 150 of these studies in his four-volume analysis of this area.

The most celebrated twentieth-century prayer study involving humans was published in 1988 by physician Randolph Byrd, a staff cardiologist at UC San Francisco School of Medicine. Byrd randomized 393 patients in the coronary care unit at San Francisco General Hospital either to a group receiving intercessory prayer or to a control group. Intercessory prayer was offered by groups outside the hospital; they were not instructed how often to pray but only to pray as they saw fit. In this double-blind study, in which neither the patients, physicians, nor nurses knew who was receiving prayer, the prayed-for patients did better on several counts. There were fewer deaths in the prayer group (although this factor was not statistically significant); they were less likely to require endotracheal intubation and ventilator support; they required fewer potent drugs, including diuretics and antibiotics; they experienced a lower incidence of pulmonary edema; and they required cardiopulmonary resuscitation less often.

Byrd's study illustrates some of the difficulties in studying the effects of intercessory prayer in humans. In one variation of a controlled study – the testing of a new drug, for example – the control group does not receive the treatment being evaluated. But in prayer studies involving humans who are seriously ill, subjects in the control group may pray for themselves or their loved ones and friends may pray for them – introducing the problem of 'extraneous prayer.' Even though the degree of outside prayer may equalize between the treatment and control groups, a major problem remains. If both groups are prayed for, the experiment becomes not a test of prayer versus no prayer but a test of the *degree* or the *amount* of prayer. 'It could be that the efforts of these strangers [who are recruited to pray for the "prayer treatment" group] will be swamped by the heart-felt prayers of those directly involved with the patients,' says professor of physics Russell Stannard of the Open University in England. If so, both groups might benefit equally from prayer, with no significant differences detectable between them. In technical jargon this is called 'reduction of the effect size' between the two groups. This can be a vexing methodological problem because it means that prayer can appear ineffective even when it works. Although this problem can be dealt with through sophisticated research methods, it is a significant obstacle in perhaps all prayer studies involving sick people.

Researchers have considered ways of overcoming the problem of self-prayer by individuals in the control group – for example, using as subjects sick infants or newborns, or unconscious, brain-damaged adults who do not or cannot pray for themselves. But this still does not eliminate the confounding effect of prayer by loved ones and friends.

Critics have therefore charged that controlled studies of prayer are impossible, because extraneous prayer cannot be eliminated from the control group. However, a controlled study does not always require that the control group not be exposed to the variable being tested. An example is the controlled testing of high-dose versus low-dose treatment regimens of a particular drug, in which *both* the control and treatment groups receive the drug being evaluated. This is analogous to most of the human studies involving intercessory prayer.

These research difficulties can be completely overcome if non-humans instead of humans are used as subjects. If bacterial growth rates are being manipulated through prayer, for example, the organisms in the control group presumably do not pray for themselves, nor do their fellow bacteria pray for them. This makes it possible to achieve great precision in nonhuman prayer studies and may account for why the effect sizes of these studies often dwarf those seen in human experiments.

Although the design of Byrd's study could have been improved, he deserves immense credit for undertaking the experiment. He established a principle: that distant, intercessory prayer can be studied like a drug in humans, in a controlled fashion in a sophisticated medical environment. Byrd's contribution is monumental – not because it was the first prayer study (many others preceded it) or because it was flawless, but because it helped break a taboo against prayer as a subject of medical research.

Objections to Prayer Research

The Religious Community

When I began to research experiments involving prayer, I thought that religious people who believed in prayer would be uniformly delighted to discover the scientific evidence that prayer worked. I was therefore surprised to find that some religious groups responded to these findings with vehement objections. There were several main reasons for this.

Many people believe that prayer is more appropriate to religious ceremony than to the nitty-gritty world of scientific experimentation, as though prayer were wrapped in some celestial halo and easily sullied when used for secular purposes. The Benedictine order would probably have disagreed with this restriction. They chose as their ancient motto *Orare est laborare, laborare est orare* – 'To pray is to work, to work is to pray.' What if one works in a lab? Can't prayer be part of lab work, as the Benedictine attitude suggests? Why should prayer be genuine in church but bogus in the lab?

Sometimes a slight shift in perspective can help us see how prayer can be used in the most unlikely situations. Jean Kinkead Martine describes a conversation between two Zen monks. Both were prodigious smokers who were concerned whether it was permissible to smoke during their prayer time. They decided individually to ask the abbot of the monastery his opinion and then compare notes. One said, 'I asked "Is it permitted to smoke while praying?" and I was severely reprimanded.' The other said, 'But I asked, "Is it permitted to pray while smoking," and the abbot gave me a pat of encouragement.'

Martine says, 'To pray while typing, while answering the phone – would it require a very different way of praying; a way that Zen monks must come to through their training – something like that wordless beseeching one discovers in trying to guide a car along an icy road or in performing any exacting piece of work under all but impossible conditions?' I like Martine's image – 'that wordless beseeching . . . in trying to guide a car along an icy road.' Subjects in studies in distant intentionality use a kind of 'wordless beseeching.' They try to coax, nudge, help, and somehow guide the experiment toward a certain outcome, often through prayer.

In my book *Healing Words* I advanced the concept of 'prayerfulness' to describe how prayer can become a natural part of our daily tasks. Prayerfulness is more a matter of *being* than *doing*. I discovered that this makes sense to a lot of physicians. An eminent surgeon wrote me that after his medical and surgical training he abandoned prayer and never formally prayed for his patients. Yet after thinking about the concept of prayerfulness, he realizes that he prays continually for his patients through his feelings of empathy, caring, and compassion for them – that, in fact, surgery for him is a continual exercise in prayer.

Others who object to prayer research see these experiments as the work of unbelieving heretics bent on 'testing God.' I believe this is a mischaracterization of researchers involved in prayer and is irrational as well. Does anyone really believe that a die-hard skeptic would spend valuable time and scarce research funds investigating a phenomenon that he bitterly opposed in the first place? Researchers usually choose topics toward which they feel cordial, not those they consider fallacious.

In fact, the attitude of most prayer researchers appears to be precisely the opposite of 'testing God.' One prayer researcher says that when she performs a prayer experiment, she is not setting a trap but opening a window through which the Almighty can manifest. Another prayer experimenter imagines that arranging a prayer experiment is like preparing an elegant meal in his home. When the table is set and the food is served, he opens the door of his house and waits patiently to see if anyone shows up. If a guest appears (if the experiment works), the meal is a success; if not, it's back to the drawing board to design a more inviting situation. Again, I know most of the researchers in this area, and I believe they are some of the most spiritually grounded people I have ever met. I believe all of them would agree that one can conduct prayer experiments with a profound sense of sacredness, reverence, and respect.

I discovered that there was a more subtle objection against prayer experiments from some religious groups. They seemed troubled by the absence of any correlation between the *effect* of the prayer and the *religious affiliation* of the person praying. The prayer experiments showed clearly that no religion has a monopoly on prayer and that prayer is a universal phenomenon belonging to all of humankind and not to any specific religion. Some fundamentalist groups found this implication offensive and chose to condemn all the experimental evidence favoring prayer in an attempt to preserve their own sense of specialness.

Still others object specifically to the practice of praying for animals: this attitude is quite widespread, even among devout practitioners of prayer. I recently received a letter from a woman in Italy. Her cat had been run over by an auto and was paralyzed in its hind limbs. When she asked the local friars if they would pray for her cat's healing, they told her it was fruitless to pray for animals because they don't have souls and could not respond to prayer. She was heartbroken to consider that her beloved cat was outside the reach of prayer. It is paradoxical that this opinion originated not far from Assisi, the home of Saint Francis, who would probably have been appalled at the discriminatory attitude of the modern friars toward animals.

Susan J. Armstrong, professor of philosophy and women's studies at Humboldt State University, has extensively examined these questions in a provocative essay, 'Souls in Process: A Theoretical Inquiry into Animal Psi.' She notes that Pope John Paul II has recently reaffirmed the early Christian doctrine that animals have souls, which presumably implies that they are fit subjects for prayer. She notes, 'In a homily at the Vatican in 1989 the Pope quoted Ps. 104, in which animals are said to have the breath of life from God, and called for "solidarity with our smaller brethren." '

Part of the resistance to praying for animals in formal experiments is due to the growing gulf between animals and humans that has developed with increasing urbanization. When America was more rural, prayer for animals was widespread and seemed natural. I grew up on a farm in Texas, and though we never prayed for mice or bacteria, we prayed incessantly for cows, pigs, horses, germinating seeds, and growing plants, as do farmers worldwide. Even in urban America, millions of vegetarians feel so intimately connected with animals that they find it unthinkable to eat them. Many pray and work diligently for the welfare of animals and for the preservation of endangered species. Many veterinarians consider it quite natural to pray for their patients. I have attended churches in the United States that help place homeless animals and feature 'pet prayer' as part of the worship program. Feelings of compassion, love, and bondedness toward nonhumans, though highly variable, are nonetheless widespread and support the idea that the power of prayer can be studied experimentally in nonhumans and humans alike.

Cows are one thing; bacteria are another. Many people are puzzled how anyone could love bacteria, fungi, germinating seeds, rats, or mice sufficiently to pray for them, or believe that studies dealing with invisible microorganisms cannot possibly involve prayer because there is no biblical injunction to pray for or against microbes. But of course the Bible is mute on this question because the concepts of bacteria, fungi, yeast, and viruses did not exist in biblical times. Therefore, we must decide for ourselves whether it is fitting to apply prayer to these creatures.

There are indirect biblical sanctions to pray both for and against microbes. For example, when we pray for the sick, as we are instructed to do, this often includes those suffering from infections. A prayer *for* someone with an infectious disease is a prayer *against* the microorganisms involved, whether we realize it or not. Likewise, when we pray that our food, which is never sterile, be blessed, we are presumably asking that the bacteria it contains be put out of commission. A sanction to pray *for* microbes can be found in the Lord's Prayer. When we pray for our daily bread, this presumably includes praying for the yeast cells that make it rise.

Microbes are *not* insignificant when compared with humans, because without them human life could not exist. All ecological systems are microbe dependent. How could prayer involving microorganisms be trivial, when our life is inextricably linked to theirs?

When confronted with experimental evidence that prayer can indeed enhance or retard microbial growth, some people dedicated to an anthropocentric view of prayer resort to a last-ditch objection – that these effects are not really due to prayer but to 'mind over matter' or some 'mental force' (though they have never been able to clarify what this force might be). Others condemn these effects as 'the work of the devil' and let it go at that. Some engage in ad hominem attacks on the pray-ers, claiming that those who would be willing to engage in such an experiment must be trying to demonstrate their personal power instead of God's, which is further evidence that these studies are corrupt and blasphemous.

Perhaps the strongest evidence that these studies involve genuine, authentic prayer is the fact that respected spiritual healers often serve as the subjects, as we have already seen in the Haraldsson and Thorsteinsson experiment. As a further example, consider a study involving the well-known spiritual healer Olga Worrall, who for years conducted prayer-based healing services at the New Life Clinic at Baltimore's Mount Washington United Methodist Church. Mrs Worrall was revered as a humble servant of God by all who knew her. On one occasion she accepted the invitation of physicist Elizabeth A. Rauscher and biophysicist Beverly A. Rubik to participate in a laboratory experiment involving bacteria. The study originally called for Worrall to inhibit bacterial activity in a particular phase of the experiment. When she objected to using prayer to harm God's creatures, the study was redesigned to allow her to help, not hurt, the microorganisms by protecting them from the killing effects of antibiotics. The results showed that she was able to do so. It is difficult to dismiss this study as not involving genuine prayer, with which Mrs Worrall was intimately familiar.

Are the pray-ers in these experiments glorifying themselves instead of the Almighty, as often charged? Are they putting their ego first? For all I know, this objection may have merit in some cases. But if it does, it surely applies to prayers offered in church as well as in the laboratory. We cannot fully know the heart of another person. This fact should make us hesitant to pass judgment on the sincerity of the prayers of others, whether they take place inside or outside the lab.

The Scientific Community

There appears to be a growing attitude within the scientific community that intercessory prayer can be researched just as any other phenomenon, as evidenced by the studies now in progress at several academic centers. Yet opposition from scientists exists, most of it coming from a small but vocal minority.

Those who oppose the idea of intercessory prayer do so mainly because of the prevalent belief that human consciousness can generally be equated with the workings of the brain, which means that the effects of the mind are confined to the physical brain and body. According to this view, consciousness cannot in principle cause things to happen at a distance, whether of its own accord or by acting through a transcendent agency. From this standpoint, intercessory prayer raises the old bugaboo of 'spooky action at a distance' and is considered outrageous.

If distant mental phenomena and intercessory prayer are as nutty as some skeptics insist, why are an increasing number of prominent scientists investigating them? According to one theory, either the researchers are incompetent, they are liars and cheats, or their brains aren't working right. This view was expressed by G. R. Price in an article in *Science:* 'My opinion concerning the findings of [these researchers] is that many of them are dependent on clerical and statistical errors and unintentional use of sensory clues, *and that all extrachance results not so explicable are dependent on deliberate fraud or mildly abnormal mental condition*' (emphasis added).

Probably all skeptics who are opposed to intercessory prayer are also opposed to the field of parapsychology, which deals with distant mental phenomena such as telepathy, clairvoyance, precognition, psychokinesis, and so on. Indeed, skeptics oppose intercessory prayer and parapsychology for virtually the same reasons. They seem convinced that these phenomena so profoundly violate the laws of physics that they should be dismissed a priori.

The eminent physicist Gerald Feinberg disagreed. Speaking of precognition – knowing something before it happens, which is probably the most challenging parapsychological event of all, bearing a strong resemblance to prophecy – he wrote, 'If such phenomena indeed occur, no change in the fundamental equations of physics would be needed to describe them.' In addition, psychologist Paul Meehl and philosopher of science Michael Scriven have pointed out that many of the objections of skeptics toward distant mental intentionality rest on two highly questionable assumptions: that current scientific knowledge is complete and that ESP – and, we might add, intercessory prayer – necessarily conflicts with it. Epidemiologist Jeffrey S. Levin, one of the foremost authorities on the correlations between religious practice and health, has advanced a theoretical model of how prayer heals that places this phenomenon fully within scientific respectability.

The skeptical complaint that the distant effects of prayer simply *cannot* happen because there is no accepted theory within science that would permit them is a peculiar objection. In science, as everyone knows, the demonstration of empirical facts often precedes the development of an accepted, explanatory theory. In his *Introduction to the History of Medicine*, Fielding H. Garrison records the example of the practice of washing one's hands before delivering babies or doing surgery. When Ignaz Semmelweiss in

1848 produced overwhelming evidence for the effectiveness of hand washing, his colleagues could not believe it. At that time the germ theory of disease did not exist and the idea of hand washing was considered preposterous. Semmelweiss was hounded out of Vienna, fled to Budapest, and became mentally ill in the wake of the unremitting criticism. A fully developed theory supporting hand washing came later and Semmelweiss was vindicated.

Similar events took place in America. Garrison reports that when the Boston physician Oliver Wendell Holmes also proposed hand washing and scrupulous cleanliness to his colleagues in 1843, he was violently opposed by the prominent Philadelphia obstetricians Hugh Hodge and Charles Meigs.

Events such as these show that it is possible for medical science to progress in a thick theoretical fog. Consider many therapies that are now commonplace, such as the use of aspirin, quinine, colchicine, and penicillin. For a long time we knew *that* they worked before we knew *how*. Today we are in a similar situation with intercessory prayer: data suggesting its effectiveness have arisen prior to the development of a generally accepted theory. This should alarm no one who has even a meager understanding of how medicine has progressed through the ages.

Sometimes scientific facts are accepted but never explained. In the 1600s, when Newton invoked the idea of universal gravity, he was attacked by his contemporaries as surrendering to mysticism. They disapproved of the mysterious force of gravity because Newton could not explain *why* bodies behaved in accordance with his proposed laws or *how* physical bodies could act at a distance on one another. 'This sort of worry no longer bothers us, but not because we have answered it,' observes philosopher Eugene Mills of Virginia Commonwealth University. We've simply gotten used to the idea. So it may turn out with intercessory prayer.

On the flip side, some object that speaking out about the evidence favoring intercessory prayer will induce hordes of sick individuals to take up prayer, use it exclusively, and abandon the use of 'real medicine' – with lethal consequences. This worry appears irrational. Surveys from the Gallup organization and the National Opinion Research Center of the University of Chicago reveal that the vast majority of Americans (80 to 90 percent) *already* pray regularly; they don't 'take up prayer' when sick. Neither are they likely to bail out of orthodox medicine when they confront a health crisis. Although certain religions such as Christian Science do favor the exclusive use of prayer during illness, surveys consistently show that the vast majority of Americans are extremely pragmatic when they are sick. They generally employ *both* standard and complementary methods of health care, including prayer, and do not opt for a single approach.

Debunking the Debunkers

In addition to charges of sloppy methodology, deliberate deception, and abnormal brains, skeptics often charge that these studies are done by rogue scientists functioning outside academic settings, that the studies are not published in peer-reviewed journals, that negative findings are not reported (the 'file-drawer effect'), and that no studies have been replicated. Most of these perennial complaints are blatantly false.

As we've seen, the evidence for intercessory prayer is not limited to a single type of organism, 'targets' include a spectrum of creatures such as humans, a variety of animals, bacteria, fungi, healthy and cancerous tissue from both humans and animals, and enzyme preparations. The variety of targets is immensely important. Critics claim that these effects are due only to psychological processes such as suggestion and expectation – the placebo response. However, the fact that nonhumans are used in these studies refutes this argument – unless skeptics wish to maintain that microbes, enzymes, and cells have an emotional life similar to that of human beings.

Researchers in the field of distant intentionality and prayer often hold faculty appointments at prestigious institutions, including major medical schools. Many of their studies embody the highest scientific standards – including proper randomization and control procedures – and many have been replicated. Moreover, it is the most rigorous studies, those involving nonhumans, that generally produce the most robust and significant results – exactly opposite the charge of most skeptics.

This does not mean that all the studies in this field are perfect.

The quality of experiments varies in any field of science, and this area is no exception. In assessing this or any other field, one should look at the very best studies and try to discern the general direction in which they point. This contrasts with the strategy of many skeptics, who often cite the very worst study they can find and generalize to condemn the entire field.

There is no single 'killer study' that makes an irrefutable case for intercessory prayer. In this field, as in most other areas of medical science, it is the concatenation, or linking together, of many strands of evidence that builds the case, not what any single study shows.

The Changing Face of Skepticism

Some of the best-informed skeptics about distant mental effects seem to be taking a defensive posture. As skeptical psychologist Ray Hyman acknowledges, 'the case for psychic functioning seems better than it ever has been. The contemporary findings . . . do seem to indicate that something beyond odd statistical hiccups is taking place. I . . . have to admit that I do not have a ready explanation for these observed effects.'

This concession is important because it tends to shift the debate from *whether* these events happen to *how* they take place. Still, Hyman and many of his skeptical colleagues are unwilling to admit that these phenomena are real. He also states, 'Inexplicable statistical departures from chance, however, are a far cry from compelling evidence for anomalous cognition' – and, presumably, for intercessory prayer as well. This response seems capricious and arbitrary in the extreme and suggests a double standard. Which statistics are acceptable and which are not? Can we pick and choose? If one denies the validity of the statistical approach in parapsychology or prayer, how can one defend its use in other controversial areas of science?

'The most important indication of a shift [in favor of these controversial phenomena] . . . can be seen in the gradually changing attitudes of prominent skeptics,' says researcher Dean Radin of the Boundary Institute of Los Altos, California, in his book *The Conscious Universe*. Radin, who had done cutting-edge research in parapsychology for AT&T, Contel, Princeton's Department of Psychology, the University of Edinburgh, and the United States government, cites the example of the late Carl Sagan, who had a life-long mission of educating the public about science. Radin notes that in Sagan's 1995 book, *The Demon-Haunted World*, which is 'saturated with piercing skepticism' toward alien abductions, channelers, faith healers, the 'face' on Mars, and 'practically everything else found in the New Age section of most bookstores,' we find an astonishing admission in one paragraph among 450 pages:

> At the time of writing there are three claims in the ESP field which, in my opinion, deserve serious study: (1) that by thought alone humans can (barely) affect random number generators in computers; (2) that people under mild sensory deprivation can receive thoughts and images 'projected' at them; and (3) that young children sometimes report the details of a previous life, which upon checking turn out to be accurate and which they could not have known about in any other way than reincarnation.

Sagan's acknowledgment, like Hyman's, implies that the resistance among scientists toward the nonlocal behaviors of human consciousness – among which we might include distant, intercessory prayer – is softening.

For several years the favorite charge of critics has been that evidence for intercessory prayer and distant mental effects does not exist. But as the experimental evidence has increased and its quality has improved, critics now seem to be resurrecting an old complaint – that, as we've seen, there is no accepted scientific theory to explain these phenomena. This charge ignores significant developments within science that lend theoretical support to the events we have been examining, including intercessory prayer. The model of consciousness that is needed to accommodate distant mental intentions is one that, in my opinion, recognizes a nonlocal quality of the mind. *Nonlocal mind* is a term I introduced in 1989 in my book *Recovering the Soul*. According to this concept, as we have seen throughout this book, consciousness cannot be completely localized or confined to specific points in space, such as brains or bodies, or to discrete points in time, such as the present moment.

Some Cautions

Many of the theories hypothesized to explain distant nonlocal awareness rely on developments and interpretations within quantum physics. But let us bear in mind that physics – quantum or otherwise – does not explain consciousness or prove the effectiveness of prayer. The word *quantum* has recently been applied to everything from psychology to healing to golf. No doubt we will soon hear about 'quantum prayer.'

There is not now, nor has there ever been, a consensus among physicists – or scientists in general – about the nature of consciousness. Some respected researchers in the field of neurophysiology, such as William H. Calvin, doubt whether physics can contribute *anything* to understanding consciousness. He asserts in his book *How Brains Think:* 'Consciousness, in any of its varied connotations, certainly isn't located down in the . . . sub-basement of physics . . . [These] consciousness physicists use mathematical concepts to dazzle rather than enlighten . . . Such theorists usually avoid the word "spirit" and say something about quantum fields . . . All that the consciousness physicists have accomplished is the replacement of one mystery by another.'

Some prominent physicists are dubious about how much their field can contribute to our understanding of spirituality. For example, the late John S. Bell, whose famous theorem has generated immense interest in quantum nonlocality, said, 'In my opinion physics has not progressed far enough to link up with psychology or theology or sociology . . . I don't think Bell's theorem moves you nearer to God.'

But when viewed in the context of the growing research in intercessory prayer, perhaps this point of view is too conservative. In the opinion of an increasing number of scientists, physics opens an important window to those interested in distant intentionality and prayer. At a minimum, physics grants us *permission*, as it were, to entertain the possibility that consciousness may manifest non-locally in the world. Why? Physics now recognizes the existence of quantum-scale events that are decidedly nonlocal, such as spin correlations between distant subatomic particles. These events share three salient characteristics, according to Nick Herbert in his *Quantum Reality*. They are said to be *immediate* (that is, they occur simultaneously), they are *unmediated* (they do not depend on any known form of energy for their 'transmission'), and they are *unmitigated* (their strength does not diminish with increasing spatial separation). *Distant, intercessory prayer bears a strong resemblance to these events*. Therefore, if physicists have discovered the existence of nonlocal events in the subatomic domain, we are fully justified in exploring our macroscopic world, as well, for evidence of nonlocal events, such as distant, intercessory prayer. The importance of this contribution from physics is monumental, for it helps legitimize the debate about 'mental action at a distance' and intercessory prayer, which has been essentially closed within science for three centuries.

Another caution: We must recognize that controlled experiments test only one aspect of prayer and are therefore exceedingly limited. To quote British physicist Russell Stannard once more, 'Prayer in its totality is multifaceted consisting as it does of worship thanksgiving, contrition, self-dedication, contemplation, meditation, etc. Intercession is but one component. Not only that, the experiment is concerned solely with those intercessory prayers offered up on behalf of strangers. Like many others, I suspect that the central core of intercessory prayer has more to do with the agonising, involved prayers of loved ones and intimate friends . . . than with those of distant strangers.'

But let us not be *too* modest in assessing our harvest. As physician Daniel J. Benor states in a summary of the current status of this field, 'There are a sufficient number of well-designed, well-executed studies demonstrating statistically significant effects to support an assertion that healing is a potent intervention.'

A Look to the Future

Although we need more experimental data (scientists in every field say this), the major obstacle in taking intercessory prayer seriously is not, I think, a lack of empirical evidence. Our major difficulty is that we seem to be suffering from a failure of the imagination. Unable to see how prayer *could* work, too many people insist that it *cannot* work. Unless we learn to see the world in new ways, we will remain unable to engage the evidence for intercessory prayer that already exists, and we will be tempted to dismiss future evidence no matter how strong it proves to be. Physician-researcher Jan Ehrenwald, writing in *The Journal of Nervous and Mental Disease*, describes what we're up against:

> It is paradoxical that more than one-half century after the advent of relativistic physics and the formulation of quantum mechanics, current theories of personality are still steeped in the classical Judeo-Christian, Aristotelian, or Cartesian tradition. Our neurophysiological models of the organism, our psychological and psychoanalytic concepts about the 'mind,' are located in Euclidean space and conform to essentially mechanistic, Newtonian, causal-reductive principles.
>
> What are the hallmarks of the classical model? It conceives of personality as a closed, self-contained, homeostatic system operating in a universe extended in prerelativistic space and time and subject to the ironclad laws of cause and effect. It found its classical pictorial representation in Leonardo da Vinci's figure of a male of ideal proportions, safely anchored in the double enclosure of the circle and the square, setting him apart from the rest of the world.

Even those who believe in intercessory prayer generally seem wedded to the classical images to which Ehrenwald refers, which seem hopelessly flawed. They generally conceive of prayer as some sort of energetic signal that is sent up and out to the Almighty, who functions as a kind of satellite relay station that passes on the effect to the recepient of the prayer. There is no evidence whatever in studies of prayer and distant intentionality that these images apply. Still, the cherished hope of many seems to be that some sort of 'subtle energy' will one day be detected to explain the distant effects of prayer. Although this could conceivably happen, current evidence suggests that the old energy-based, classical concepts will remain unable to explain the workings of intercessory prayer, and new images will be necessary.

Of course, the instant we acknowledge the data that indicate we can affect living systems *positively* at a distance through prayer, the possibility is raised that we may be able to *harm* them as well. This consideration prompts almost everybody to run for cover, including believers in prayer – because, as philosopher Alan Watts once put it, we want to keep God's skirts clean. It is going to be difficult to do so. Several studies in distant intentionality using bacteria and fungi strongly suggest that we can not only increase their growth rates but *inhibit* them as well. This prospect should not horrify us. Sometimes we *need* prayer to be injurious – as when we pray for a cancer to be destroyed, for an obstruction in a coronary artery to be obliterated, or for AIDS viruses to be killed.

Until adequate scientific explanations of intercessory prayer arrive, we need not suspend our belief in prayer nor deny the evidence for it. Even when future explanations are in place, 'God does it!' will remain a perfectly reasonable alternative, because any new theory is certain to raise more questions than it will answer. After all, it is impossible in principle for any scientific theory to disprove the existence and workings of the Absolute.

Let us recall, too, that prayer does not *require* science to validate it. There is no need to hold our breath in anticipation of the results of the next double-blind study on prayer. People test prayer in their individual lives, and one's life is the most important laboratory of all. However, self-deception is possible, and science is an effective safeguard against some forms of illusion. In our culture, science has undeniably become a potent arbiter of how we construct our worldview and how we live our lives. Therefore, if science says something positive about prayer, even those who already believe in prayer may feel empowered in their convictions.

The Respiritualization of Medicine

The studies in intercessory prayer and distant intentionality represent a major opportunity for a genuine dialogue between science and spirituality. This debate desperately needs to go forward, particularly within medicine.

Modern medicine has become one of the most spiritually malnourished professions in our society. Because we have so thoroughly disowned the spiritual component of healing, most healers throughout history would view our profession today as inherently perverse. They would be aghast at how we have squeezed the life juices and the heart out of our calling. Physicians have spiritual needs like anyone else, and we have paid a painful price for ignoring them. It simply does not feel good to practice medicine as if the only thing that matters were the physical; something feels left out and incomplete.

André Malraux, the late French novelist and minister of culture of France, said that the twenty-first century will be spiritual or it will not be at all. I often feel the same way about medicine. It *will* be respiritualized, or it may not be at all – at least not in any form we would desire. Yet there is great hope, and the scientific research into the healing effects of prayer, empathy, and love bode well for a respiritualization of medicine.

12

What's Love got to Do with It?

I do not ask how the wounded one feels,
I, myself, become the wounded one.
— WALT WHITMAN —
Leaves of Grass

When Love Gets Lost

To GLIMPSE LOVE'S IMPORTANCE in healing, we have only to see what happens when it gets lost, as it does in the following incident described by medical ethicist Eric Cassell: 'During the 1930s, my grandmother saw a specialist about a melanoma on her face. During the course of the visit when she asked him a question, he slapped her face, saying, "I'll ask the questions here. I'll do the talking." Can you imagine such an event occurring today? Melanomas may not have changed much in the last 50 years, but the profession of medicine has.'

A similar incident took place in a coronary care unit to which an eighty-year-old man had been admitted for what proved to be a fatal heart attack. An hour following his admission, the man's no-nonsense cardiologist stormed through the swinging doors into the waiting area where the patient's elderly wife, realizing her husband was dying, sat weeping. The doctor was in a rage. 'Your husband is doing terribly!' he blustered. 'He refuses to cooperate with anything I'm doing for him!' The woman did not know how to respond. Eventually she managed to offer through her tears, 'Doctor, I'm sure he doesn't mean it. He's such a good man. Please don't feel badly toward him.'

It's tempting for doctors to turn away from these incidents and say they are uncharacteristic and unusual. We would never behave this way toward our patients. But in the everyday hustle of high-tech medicine it is all too easy to take our eyes off love. When we do, the hospital can become a house of horrors – as in the following case from an article with the intriguing title 'Death by Destruction of Will,' reported in the *Archives of Internal Medicine*:

A 93-year-old woman was admitted involuntarily to a psychiatric hospital's geriatric unit for increasing impairment in memory and deterioration of the conditions of her home, where she lived alone. She was functionally independent in the unit, and was bright, cheerful, and loving toward the staff. After 2 uneventful weeks in the unit, she was moved to a medical hospital for evaluation and management of anemia and stools positive for occult blood. When seen by the examining team, she denied symptoms of illness, telling them, 'I'm as healthy as you are.' Findings from the physical examination revealed a hard, 4 cm abdominal mass in the right lower quadrant.

Laboratory investigations revealed [significant anemia] . . . [and] plans were made for a [colon x-ray] and transfusion. Almost immediately, problems began to develop with the patient's desire to move about and her tendency to forget about her IV lines. A vest restraint was first applied, which led to agitation and struggling . . . Leather restraints were applied to her hands and feet . . . An altercation occurred when [she] got out of her restraints, bit her IV line in two, and moved quickly down the hall. Security guards were called . . . and she was subdued after a significant struggle. She was again placed in four-point restraints.

After this altercation, a dramatic change in her affect and demeanor was noted. She appeared despondent and broken. She told the house officer she was dying 'because God willed it.' The next morning, her restraints were removed, her medical orders were revised, and a sitter was hired to eliminate the need for restraints. Her son visited that day and was distraught at the psychological change he saw in his mother. [He] stated that he believed that the hospital was killing her, and that she had lost her will to live.

Later on the third hospital day, an initial attempt at a barium enema was unsuccessful . . . [She was transfused.] . . . A repeated chest [x-ray] showed an [abnormal area] in the right upper lobe with a suggestion of cavitation [suggesting tuberculosis]. The patient was then placed in isolation, and . . . empiric treatment for possible pulmonary tuberculosis [was suggested] . . .

She seemed minimally ill and was eating reasonably well and moving about in her room. On the fifth hospital day . . . however, her statement . . . was, 'I am going to die.' She was found without pulse and respiration [3 hours later] . . .; cardiopulmonary resuscitation was attempted but was unsuccessful.

At autopsy, a . . . carcinoma of the cecum was identified without evidence of local or remote spread. A small area of consolidation was identified in the right upper lobe of the lung . . . Cultures . . . were negative . . . No evidence of heart disease was found. Examination of the brain revealed no occlusions, softening, tumor, or hemorrhage.

When the case was later discussed, the members of the house staff involved in her care demonstrated no awareness of any potential link between the events of her treatment, her changes in affect and behavior, and her death [emphasis added].

The author of this report, Bruce E. Robinson, M.D., of the University of South Florida College of Medicine, Tampa, describes how this case could have been handled more compassionately each step of the way. He concludes with a sobering comment: 'This woman's story serves to remind us of the critical link between mind and body, and of the mortal consequences that are possible when we forget.' And we will keep on forgetting unless we are able to make a place in healing for love and empathy.

Empathy 'refers specifically to the ability of physicians to imagine that they are the patient who has come to them for help.' It is the ability to share in another's emotions and feelings. If empathy had been present, it would have allowed the team caring for the ninety-three-year-old woman to ask, What did *she* want? What was the hospital experience like for *her*? Would it have been more compassionate to allow her to pass her remaining days peacefully and not subject her to the rigors of a 'workup'? Because the house staff was unable or unwilling to share her feelings, their evaluation took on all the sensitivity of a runaway freight train.

In modern medicine there is a tendency to view love as a frill or luxury, or as something that gets in the way of a rational approach to patient care. This is a serious miscalculation. The presence or absence of love can be associated with life-and-death consequences. This was dramatically demonstrated in a report from the Oklahoma Medical School Hospital, where Drs Stewart Wolf and William Schottstaedt were conducting metabolic studies examining the role of human interaction on serum cholesterol levels. One of their patients was a forty-nine-year-old man who had had several heart attacks and a history of chaotic relationships. During the hospitalization,

> the patient seemed happy and reasonably relaxed, although very eager to please during the first few days of the study while receiving daily visits from his new woman friend. When she left town for a few days without telling him, however, he became anxious. Serum cholesterol concentration rose somewhat until she returned, revisited, and reassured him. During this visit, however, she had met another man whom she preferred. Her daily visits to the patient fell off and . . . she told him that she had abandoned the plan to marry him and would not see him again. He became intensely depressed. Again the serum cholesterol rose and the following day he had a recurrent myocardial infarction. Four days later he died.

A Lesson in Love

Of course, it isn't just physicians who forget the importance of love and empathy – educators, lawyers, politicians, law enforcers, and perhaps every other professional group could be added to the list. Despite our frequent lapses in love, I believe that medicine remains one of the most caring professions in contemporary culture. An unbroken lineage of healers who have always known the importance of love and compassion in healing continues to exist in medicine.

I was given a lesson by one of them during my training in internal medicine at a large Veterans Administration teaching hospital. The workload was burdensome – a steady, unending stream of new patients, day and night. After a particularly grueling day, I bumped into a fellow intern around 2:00 A.M. in the on-call room as we were collapsing into bed. Blind with fatigue and in a foul mood, I began to complain about how the patients used the hospital as a revolving door. After they were discharged following treatment for a particular medical problem, they would resume destructive behaviors such as unbridled smoking and drinking, which inevitably would lead to further hospitalizations for heart disease, emphysema, cirrhosis, and worse. My colleague listened patiently while I vented. When I finished he said thoughtfully, 'You're right; they *are* unredeemable. But I *love* them. In fact, I could work here all my life.' I was speechless. Had sleep deprivation overcome his good judgment? 'I like the old patients the best,' he continued. 'Even their little problems. Their hemorrhoids are just as important to me as their heart failure. When their bowels won't work right, I'll be there to help. When their nails get too long, I'll trim them. If they need a haircut or a bath, I'll give it to them.' I was beginning to feel like a sinner in the presence of a saint. 'Some of them will never change their habits. They'll always keep coming back. It doesn't matter. They're wonderful.'

When we completed our training, my colleague and I went into medical practice together. He has remained for me an icon in many ways – the consummate physician who embodies not only technical competence but wisdom, compassion, empathy, and love as well.

Is Love Real?

Can the experience of love be explained biochemically? Is it only a by-product of the physical brain? Although we have no 'emotion meters' that can measure our feelings directly, we know that a variety of emotional states have definite physical correlates in the body. Rage, hostility, and anxiety are associated with fluctuations of specific neurotransmitters and hormones in the brain and blood. Feelings of love have been linked to chemicals in the brain such as norepinephrine, serotonin, and phenylethylamine. (Interestingly, the latter chemical is also found in high concentration in chocolate – the reason, some unromantic materialists say, that on Valentine's Day we give chocolates to those we want to love us.)

Yet the more we learn about the physical correlates of emotions, the wider the gap between the two seems to become. As consciousness theorist David J. Chalmers has pointed out, no one knows why electrochemical events in the brain give rise to any conscious experience whatsoever – to love or anything else. When we see the light of the wavelength that is associated with the color purple, why do we have the experience of seeing purple? When my colleague was confronted with all his patients' problems, why did he experience love? Why did he not simply attend to the hemorrhoids and heart failure automatically, like a dependable, unconscious machine? Why does consciousness crop up? Why love?

In spite of questions such as these, the tendency in modern neuroscience has been to ignore them, or to assume that consciousness, emotional experiences, and brain chemistry are identical and interchangeable. Identifying consciousness with chemistry is one way to deny the existence of the former, so that at the end of the day it's chemistry – not consciousness – that is real. A sampling of this point of view comes from Lawrence LeShan's book *The Dilemma of Psychology:*

> A leading psychotherapist, Lawrence Kubie, writes, 'Although we cannot get along without the concept of consciousness, actually there is no such thing.'
>
> A leading neurophysiologist, Karl Lashley, puts it: 'The knower as an entity is an unnecessary postulate.'
>
> A leading psychologist, D. O. Hebb, writes: 'The existence of something called consciousness is a venerable hypothesis, not a datum, not directly observable.'

For an increasing number of thoughtful scientists, however, consciousness cannot be dismissed so easily. An example is Nobel physicist Steven Weinberg, who writes about a 'theory of everything' from which all there is to know about the universe can be derived. Weinberg concedes that there is a problem with fitting consciousness into a 'theory of everything' because consciousness does not seem derivable from physical laws. Because consciousness won't fit, a physically based theory of everything cannot be complete. A final theory must contain some additional, fundamental element. 'Toward this end,' Chalmers states, 'I propose that conscious experience be considered a fundamental feature, irreducible to anything more basic.' Chalmers and others have suggested that consciousness take its place alongside matter and energy as fundamental features of our universe. These developments in contemporary thought are crucial for medicine: unless we can find a place for consciousness, love will never have a home in our modern models of healing.

In addition to whatever theoretical and philosophical justifications there may be for addressing the role of consciousness in medicine, there are practical reasons as well. For the past several decades, evidence has gradually accumulated that conscious mental intent can influence events not just in the body but also in 'the world out there,' and that these events can be empowered by love.

Love in the Lab

In the late sixties and early seventies pioneering work began in the field of biofeedback. Researchers discovered that ordinary individuals could learn to control their heart rate, muscle tension, and skin temperature if given moment-to-moment feedback by electronic instruments that measured these events. Although biofeedback is now considered commonplace, at the time it was heretical. It contradicted the conventional wisdom that these bodily functions were always silent, controlled by the autonomic nervous system.

Soon reports began to surface from various biofeedback labs that something strange was going on. When researchers asked subjects 'how they did it,' they were unable to explain. But when subjects were asked *how they felt* when they were successful, they often responded with statements such as 'I felt at one with the instruments.' Some went further, saying that they felt inseparable from the instructor, the room, 'and everything else.' Some researchers realized the subjects were expressing the universal experience of mysticism, which has been defined as 'becoming one' or uniting with everything there is.

Similar observations have cropped up in other types of laboratories as well. Along with his team, Robert G. Jahn, director of the Princeton Engineering Anomalies Research (PEAR) laboratory, has observed millions of trials in which individuals attempted to influence the performance of sophisticated electronic instruments such as random-event generators. Their results indicate that ordinary individuals can mentally exert a statistically significant effect on the machines' performance under controlled conditions. How do they feel when they do it? According to Jahn, 'The most common subjective report of our most successful human/machine experimental operators is some sense of "resonance" with the devices – some sacrifice of personal identity in the interaction – a "merging," or bonding with the apparatus. As one operator put it: "I simply fall in love with the machine." And indeed, the term "love," in connoting the very special resonance between two partners, is an apt metaphor.' Interestingly, the highest scores are seen when emotionally bonded couples, who share unusually deep love and empathy, interact *together* with the electronic devices. They achieve scores up to eight times higher than those of individuals who try to influence the devices alone.

Some scientists believe that love has no place in objective science. Jahn disagrees: 'Allusions to [love] can be found in scientific literature, none more eloquent than that of Prince Louis de Broglie, one of the patriarchs of modern physics,' he writes, and quotes from de Broglie's book *New Perspectives in Physics:*

> If we wish to give philosophic expression to the profound connection between thought and action in all fields of human endeavor, particularly in science, we shall undoubtedly have to seek its sources in the unfathomable depths of the human soul.

Perhaps philosophers might call it 'love' in a very general sense – that force which directs all our actions, which is the source of all our delights and all our pursuits. Indissolubly linked with thought and with action, love is their common mainspring and, hence, their common bond. The engineers of the future have an essential part to play in cementing this bond.

Love and Resonance

Resonance is a widespread feature in nature. Jahn again:

> All manner of physical systems, whether mechanical, electro-magnetic, fluid dynamical, quantum mechanical, or nuclear, display capacities for synergistically interactive vibrations with similar systems, or with their environment. Coupled harmonic oscillators, all common musical instruments, radio and television circuitry, atomic components of molecules, all involve this 'sympathetic' resonance, from which strikingly different properties emerge than those that characterize their isolated components.

What does it mean to say that all manner of physical systems are in 'sympathetic resonance' with each other or their environment? *Sympathy* comes from the Greek *sympatheia*, 'feeling together'; *resonance* is derived from the Latin *resonantia*, 'an echo.' Is the universe one immense echo of feeling and sensitivity?

Lyall Watson suggests in *The Nature of Things* that a general kind of resonance may pervade the natural world to an almost unthinkable degree. He describes how inanimate objects and lower organisms – stones, cars, bacteria – may 'resonate' with humans by taking on our 'emotional fingerprints,' as he puts it, as a result of prolonged, intimate contact with us. When they do so, they may behave in surprisingly lifelike ways and lead to what Jung called synchronicities – those meaning-filled, unpredictable events we often call 'funny coincidences.'

Love Is Nonlocal

The resonance referred to by Jahn, Watson, and others has unusual qualities. It appears to operate without regard to distance. In the controlled experiments Jahn and his team have performed, the subjects are sometimes separated from the apparatus they are trying to influence by global distances – situated, literally, on the other side of the earth. The findings are consistent: the effects of mental effort do not diminish with increasing spatial separation. As we've seen, these experiments and scores of others conducted in laboratories around the world point to a nonlocal quality of consciousness, to some aspect of the mind that is not confined to specific points in space or time.

Love is often involved when the mind behaves nonlocally. One of the most common examples is the distant, loving resonance that exists between humans and their pets. Researchers J. B. Rhine and Sara Feather collected dozens of accounts of returning animals – pets who found their way back to their owners, sometimes across colossal distances. These instances cannot be explained by 'homing'; the animal often 'returns' to places it has never been. An example is that of Bobbie, a collie who was traveling with a family from Ohio to their new home in Oregon, where Bobbie had never been. During a stop in Indiana, Bobbie got lost. After a diligent attempt to find her, the family finally gave up and proceeded westward. Months later, Bobbie appeared at the new home in Oregon. This was not a look-alike animal: she still had her name tag and several identifying marks and scars.

I am particularly fascinated by instances in which animals find their way to owners who are ill. These cases suggest that the capacity to love and care for someone who is sick is not just a human trait but is widespread in other species. One such instance is recounted by Vida Adamoli in *The Dog That Drove Home*:

A boy named Hugh Brady, who kept homing pigeons as pets, once found a wounded pigeon in the garden of his home. He nursed the bird back to health, ringed him with identity tag no. 167, and kept him.

The following winter Hugh was suddenly taken ill and rushed

to a hospital 200 miles away, where he underwent an emergency operation. He was still recovering when, on a bitter, snowy night, he heard a persistent tapping at the window. He called for the nurse and asked her to open it. When she did, a pigeon flew in and landed with a joyful flutter of wings on Hugh's chest. Hugh knew immediately that the visitor was his bird and a look at the number on its tag confirmed it.

Pigeons are famous for their homing instincts, but on this occasion the bird wasn't returning home – he had tracked his master down to a place he had no knowledge of and had never been to before. How he did it remains a mystery.

In *Everyday Miracles*, Dr Gustav Eckstein describes a small spitz dog who doubled as a night nurse for his mistress, who was a diabetic. Each night the dog would curl up in the angle of the woman's arm. He would awaken immediately if her breathing pattern changed, which is one of the telltale signs of ketoacidosis, one of the most dreaded complications of diabetes. Though not a nonlocal event (the dog was in sensory contact with his owner), this event illustrates what every pet owner knows: love and caring are not confined to *Homo sapiens*.

If we are to understand how love functions in healing, we must confront the concept of nonlocality. Although this idea is little appreciated in modern medical science, physicists have gradually made their peace with it in recent decades. Rigorous experiments over the past twenty years have confirmed the existence of nonlocal phenomena in the subatomic domain. For example, if two particles that have once been in contact are separated, a change in one results in a change in the other – immediately and to the same degree. The degree of separation between the particles is immaterial; they could theoretically be placed at opposite ends of the universe. Apparently no energetic signal passes between them, telling one particle that a change has taken place in the other, because the changes are instantaneous; there is no time for signaling. The distant particles behave as though they were united as a single entity – paradoxically, separate but one.

Telesomatic Events: The Tug of Love

F.W.H. Myers, one of the most prominent scholars and researchers in the budding field of parapsychology around the turn of the century, was impressed by how often love seemed to be involved when individuals communicated across great distances. 'Love is a kind of exalted but unspecialized telepathy,' he said, 'the simplest and most universal expression of that mutual gravitation or kinship of spirits.'

Love has an adhesive quality. Under certain circumstances it functions as a veritable glue that binds together distant people. This is nowhere more evident than in telesomatic events. *Telesomatic*, a term coined in 1967 by neurologist Berthold E. Schwarz to describe events he observed in the lives of his patients, comes from words meaning 'the distant body.' The term is appropriate because distant individuals often behave as a single body and mind, sharing emotions and physical symptoms at a remote distance. When these events occur, the distant individuals are ignorant of what is happening to each other, which makes these events impossible to explain in terms of expectation and suggestion.

Schwarz collected approximately three hundred telesomatic cases. Hundreds have cropped up in a variety of publications over the years, some of which have been reported in medical journals. Examples:

• A mother was writing a letter to her daughter, who was away at college. Suddenly her right hand started to burn so severely she could not hold the pen. Less than an hour later, she received a phone call from the college telling her that her daughter's right hand had been severely burned by acid in a laboratory accident, at the same time the mother had felt the burn.

• A man and his wife were attending a football game in Berkeley, California. The man got up suddenly in the middle of the game and said they had to return home at once because their son had been hurt. When they arrived home, they discovered that the boy had shot a BB into his thumb, which required emergency surgery to have it removed.

• A woman suddenly doubled over, clutching her chest as if in severe pain, and said, 'Something has happened to Nell, she has been hurt.' Two hours later the sheriff came, stating that Nell had died on the way to the hospital. She had been involved in an auto accident, in which a piece of the steering wheel had penetrated her chest.

Sometimes telesomatic events involve more than two people. Multiple individuals, whole families, and entire communities have been involved, which makes it difficult to brush off these phenomena as 'mere coincidences.' Researcher Ian Stevenson of the University of Virginia cites a case in which a woman had a strong impression during the night that her mother was seriously ill. Despite her husband's protests, she traveled to her mother's house. As she approached the dwelling she met her sister, who had also had the same impression and had acted on the impulse to see their mother. The sisters discovered that their mother had suddenly become very ill, was dying, and was asking to see her daughters.

Stevenson cites another case in which all eight members of a farm family in upstate New York seem to have been affected nonlocally. They arose one morning, had their breakfast, then dispersed to various points on the farm to begin their day's work. Later in the morning, about ten o'clock, they each began to experience a strange feeling – an intense awe, a feeling of foreboding as if something terrible were about to happen. Thinking they were becoming ill, the family members independently stopped working and returned to the kitchen, unaware of the feelings of the others. This unusual behavior coincided in time with the accidental death in Michigan of a son in the family.

Telesomatic events don't qualify as 'lab science.' They crop up unpredictably in people's lives and cannot be engineered and studied at our convenience. Why take them seriously? There are two main reasons. First, they are quite common; almost everyone seems either to have experienced them or to know someone who has. Second, they demonstrate a striking internal consistency: not only do they occur between individuals at a distance but they take place between persons who are loving and empathic with each other – parents and children, siblings (particularly identical twins), spouses, and lovers.

Telesomatic events are nonlocal expressions of consciousness. They demonstrate the ability of love to reach out through space and time and unite us as one. They show that 'connectedness' and 'becoming one' are not just poetry or metaphor but concrete reality. They reveal that, at some level of the mind, unity – not separation – is fundamental.

Although we cannot compel telesomatic events to happen so they can be studied under controlled situations, something very much like them can be observed in the laboratory. In a series of experiments, the encephalograms, or EEGs, of distant individuals were measured and compared. In the baseline state there was no correlation between the two EEG patterns. But when the researchers asked the distant subjects to allow a feeling of empathy to develop between them, the EEG patterns frequently took on striking correlations, often becoming almost identical.

Whether we call these shared feelings resonance, empathy, or love, such findings seriously challenge what it means to be an individual – indeed, whether, at some level of mind, there is such a thing.

A Universal Spectrum of Love?

One of the greatest discoveries of our century – perhaps any century – may be the nonlocal connectedness that exists between the spectacular variety of entities that make up our universe. As we've seen, this connectedness is manifested between subatomic particles, mechanical systems, humans and machines, humans and animals, and humans themselves. When this nonlocal bond operates between people, we call it love. When it unites distant subatomic particles, what should we call this manifestation? Should we choose a safe, aseptic term such as *nonlocally correlated behavior*, or bite the bullet and call it a rudimentary form of love? I am not suggesting that people and electrons experience love and empathy to the same degree, but we are free to wonder whether the unity of distant subatomic particles may be a primordial kind of empathy

– a protolove – that swells in intensity with increasing biological complexity, emerging fully formed as love and compassion in people. Is there a spectrum of love spanning the entire organization of the physical universe, from the subatomic to the macroscopic, human dimension (see table)?

Are Love and Empathy Innate?

Not everybody believes that love is innate in nature. Storms of controversy have existed for decades in psychology, for example, about whether our capacity to love and empathize is inborn, or whether these are learned behaviors that develop in response to challenges from our environment. In his admirable book *The Immune Power Personality*, Henry Dreher has reviewed evidence that our capacity for love and empathy, though influenced by learning and environmental factors, has a biological basis. Jean Piaget, the influential Swiss psychologist, contended otherwise. He maintained that children do not feel empathy until their brains are sufficiently developed, around age seven or eight. Before this time, he maintained, they cannot make sense of other people's experiences. But beginning in the 1970s and 1980s, evidence began to accumulate that Piaget may have been wrong. Psychologist Martin L. Hoffman of New York University showed that newborn babies will cry in response to the cries of another infant but barely respond to equally loud computer simulations of babies' cries or even to tape recordings of their own cries. 'Virtually from the day they are born, there is something particularly disturbing to infants about the sound of another infant's cry,' Hoffman states. 'The innate predisposition to cry to that sound seems to be the earliest precursor of empathy.'

Carolyn Zahn-Waxler, a developmental psychologist at the National Institute of Mental Health, brought together mothers and their infants or toddlers in the lab to observe the children's responses when the mothers or other children were distressed. She asked the adults to drop things or bump their heads to see if the children would comfort them. In a variant of this study, conducted in the home, she trained mothers to simulate pain, fake a cough, act angry or cry, and then rate their own children's reactions. In

The Universal Spectrum of Love

Interacting Systems	Evidence of Interaction	Expression of Interaction
Humans and humans	Humans interact with each other nonlocally – at a distance, without benefit of sensory- or energy-based exchanges of information. Many controlled studies deal with distant/intercessory prayer and other types of distant mental intent. Hundreds of telesomatic events have been reported. Numerous controlled studies have documented nonlocal forms of gaining or conveying information (clairvoyance, telepathy).	Love, empathy, compassion, caring, unity; collective consciousness, the Universal or One Mind; God ('God is love'), Goddess, Allah, Tao, the Absolute
Humans and animals	Scores of studies involving various types of distant healing intent have been done using higher animals as 'targets.' These studies often involve prayer or 'bio-PK' (psychokinesis). Lost pets return to owners across vast distances to places they have never been.	Love, Empathy
Humans and living organisms	Scores of controlled studies have dealt with the distant effects of prayer and other types of positive, distant healing intent, in which various 'lower organisms' – bacteria, fungi, yeasts – are the targets, as well as seeds, plants, and cells of various sorts.	Love, Empathy

COMPLEXITY

The BIOLOGICAL axis (arrow pointing upward) runs along the rows.

Humans and complex machines	Humans can mentally influence the behavior of sophisticated electronic biofeedback devices – affirmed by the collective record of more than 30 years of biofeedback research in hundreds of laboratories. Humans also can mentally influence random event generators and other electronic instruments at a distance, as demonstrated in studies conducted at the Princeton Engineering Anomalies Research (PEAR) lab and many other institutions.	'Becoming one' or 'falling in love' with the machine; interconnection; unity
Humans and simple machines	Humans can interact with and influence the behavior of freely swinging pendulums, mechanical cascade devices, and other relatively simple apparatuses, at a distance – affirmed by studies conducted at the PEAR lab and elsewhere	'Becoming one' or 'falling in love' with the machine; interconnection; unity
Complex physical devices/systems	According to commonly accepted principles in physics, coupled harmonic oscillators, all common musical instruments, and radio and television circuitry interact and resonate with each other. In general, all manner of physical systems – whether mechanical, electromagnetic, fluid dynamical, quantum mechanical, or nuclear – display synergistically interactive vibrations with similar systems or with their environment.	Sympathetic or harmonic resonance
Subatomic particles	Subatomic particles such as electrons, once in contact, demonstrate simultaneous change – no matter how far apart – to the same degree. Bell's theorem, the Aspect experiment, and many other developments affirm these possibilities at the quantum-mechanical level.	Nonlocally correlated behavior; rudimentary or proto-love?

each instance children acted upset, and with sounds and gestures tried to comfort their distressed parents. According to Zahn-Waxler, 'We couldn't be sure whether the 1-year-old was giving reassurance or seeking it, or both. But in children only a few months older we'd see unmistakable expressions of concern for the other person. The floodgates of altruism open along with the development of language.' Summarizing these findings, Dreher states, 'What begins in infancy as a reflex develops into the fully formed response we call empathy – a complex cluster of feelings, thoughts and actions . . . By the second year of life, children demonstrate not only empathy but the altruistic behavior that follows.'

The capacity for empathy and love, it seems, is written into our biology.

Love's Larger Lessons

Love is useful in healing. It alleviates pain and suffering, and it sometimes sets the stage for physical improvement or cure. As a result of these effects, there is a frequent tendency to try to 'put love to work' in the service of healing. But problems can arise as a result of this utilitarian approach. Love's larger lessons can be obscured – lessons that, in my opinion, dwarf the question of whether love can be 'used' to diminish pain, cure a heart attack or cancer, or heal relationships.

A far greater benefit is that *love provides evidence of who we are*. Love unmasks the illusion of isolation. It subsumes (but does not eradicate) individuality by making possible the experience of a collective, unitary consciousness – what Nobel physicist Erwin Schrödinger called the One Mind. Through love we see that at some level human consciousness is nonlocal – unconfined to specific points in space such as brains and bodies, or to specific moments in time such as the present moment. In this service, love reveals our hidden identity by showing us that in some sense we are infinite, eternal, immortal, and one. As Jan van Ruysbroeck (1293–1381), one of the most sublime mystics the world has ever known, said, 'When love has carried us above all things . . . we receive in peace the Incomprehensible Light, enfolding us and penetrating us. What is this Light, if it be not a contemplation of the Infinite, and an intuition of Eternity?'

But love is not without hazards. There is always the risk of 'getting lost in love' – of losing one's grounding and becoming vaporized, as it were, in the infinite. If we are to stay balanced as individuals, we must always remain aware of love's great paradox: love not only transcends our individuality, it also affirms it. The infinite can be known only through the finite. As Blake wrote, 'Eternity is in love with the productions of Time.' Thus love fills us with a sense of being that Evelyn Underhill says in *Mysticism* is 'great enough to be God, intimate enough to be me.' As Jung put it:

> The decisive question for man is: Is he related to something infinite or not? . . . The feeling for the infinite, however, can be attained only if we are bounded to the utmost . . . Only consciousness of our narrow confinement in the self forms the link to the limitlessness of the unconscious. In such awareness we experience ourselves concurrently as limited and eternal, as both the one and the other. In knowing ourselves to be unique in our personal combination – that is, ultimately limited – we possess also the capacity for becoming conscious of the infinite. But only then! Uniqueness and limitation are synonymous. Without them, no perception of the unlimited is possible.

Just as the finger that points to the moon is not the moon, all of our scientific papers and ruminations will never truly capture love. The more we explore it, the more its mysteries deepen. No one knew this better than Jung, with whose words I close:

> In all my medical experience as well as in my own life I have again and again been faced with the mystery of love, and have never been able to explain what it is . . . No language is adequate . . . Whatever one can say, no words can express the whole. To speak of partial aspects is always too much or too little, for only the whole is meaningful. Love 'bears all things' and 'endures all things' (1 Corinthians 13:7). These words say all there is to be said; nothing can be added to them.

13

Creativity and Cosmic Soup

I COMMITTED MY FIRST crime at age seventeen – breaking and entering the office of my high school principal late at night to steal a test score. You might say it was the perfect crime, because my three accomplices and I were never caught. But in fact I paid a terrible penalty.

It all started when the secondary schools throughout the state of Texas became caught up in a frenzy of IQ testing. On one fine spring day, every kid in Groesbeck High, including the thirty-five in my class, was subjected to the lengthy exam. The purpose of the test, the teachers said, was 'to see how smart you are.' Why this was a good idea was never explained. With typical teenage arrogance, I was confident that I had scored high. I didn't know for sure, however, because the test scores were confidential and the teachers refused to reveal them. This drove my friends and me crazy. We *had* to know our scores! So one night four of us broke into the principal's office through an unlocked window (this was the pre-security-system era), rummaged his files, and discovered our IQs.

It was one of the worst mistakes of my life. My score was not nearly as high as I expected and I was devastated. The fact that I was top in my class was clearly a dubious achievement, obviously made possible only because I worked harder to make up for my innate intellectual handicap. Overnight I was plunged into an abyss of inadequacy, inferiority, and self-doubt. To make matters worse, I could do nothing to improve myself, because the teachers had already explained to us that 'your IQ never changes.' Once cursed, always cursed.

I developed an immediate loathing for IQ tests and vowed never to take one again. Over the years, however, my academic achievements remained substantial and I began to wonder whether my high-school IQ score might have been incorrect. Eventually my curiosity got the better of me.

During my final year in medical school, a close friend of mine was doing graduate work in psychology and needed subjects for IQ testing as part of her research. When she invited me to take the test, I initially refused. She continued to badger me, however, and, after considerable harassment I consented, on one condition – that I be allowed to take the test inebriated. This would help me get my nerve up and would provide me with a perfect excuse if I scored low. By the time the exam started I was in an upbeat, lighthearted mood. The test was delightful, even fun. When my friend told me my score, I was shocked to discover that my IQ had risen nearly forty points beyond high school level. I had mysteriously gotten a lot smarter! I didn't know whether to feel jubilant about the new score or angry about the old one.

Is Your Brain Really Necessary?

The IQ test is no longer regarded as infallible, as it used to be. One reason is that people such as Nobel physicist Richard Feynman keep turning up. His IQ was 122, which is merely respectable and probably on the low side for physicists in general. No one would have predicted on the basis of his IQ that Feynman would turn out to be one of the greatest creative geniuses of twentieth-century science.

Some scientists actually make light of a biological explanation for intelligence, an assumption on which the IQ test is based. An example is Albert Einstein, who is said to have remarked, 'The secret to creativity is knowing how to hide your sources.' Most neuroscientists disagree with Einstein, however – something they demonstrated by assaulting his brain following his death. Histologists subjected tissue samples from various areas of

Einstein's brain to microscopic analysis, hoping to find some anatomical secret to his stunning originality. But aside from a few findings of equivocal significance, Einstein's brain has not yielded any major breakthroughs. Somewhere Einstein must be saying, 'I told you so,' still hiding his sources.

In an article provocatively titled 'Is Your Brain Really Necessary?' British neurologist John Lorber questions whether an intact cerebral cortex is needed for normal mentation. Lorber did computed tomography scans on hundreds of individuals with hydrocephalus, in which an excessive amount of cerebrospinal fluid accumulates inside the skull, crowding out normal brain tissue. He found that many of them had normal or above-normal intellectual function, even though most of the skull was filled with cerebrospinal fluid. Humans normally have a cerebral cortex measuring 4.5 centimeters thick, containing around fifteen to twenty billion neurons. In one patient, however, a college mathematics student who was referred to Lorber because his physician suspected that his head was slightly enlarged, the brain scan revealed a cerebral cortex only *one millimeter* thick. Functioning with only a tiny rim of cortical brain tissue of around 2 percent normal thickness, this student proved to have an IQ of 126. He was not only gifted intellectually, he was normal socially as well.

'As Darwin himself once pointed out about science, the smartest people do not tend to make the most important discoveries,' notes social scientist Frank J. Sulloway in his book *Born to Rebel: Birth Order, Family Dynamics, and Creative Lives*. 'IQ is only weakly related to achievement among people who are smart enough to become scientists . . . A scientist who has an IQ of 130 is just as likely to win a Nobel Prize as a scientist whose IQ is 180.' Where was Darwin's moderating voice when I needed it that fateful night, when those three meager digits gave a terrible thumbsdown on my mind?

Emotional and Healing Intelligence

Fortunately, in recent years IQ has been taken down a few notches as a monolithic oracle of intelligence. For example, science writer

Daniel Goleman, in his acclaimed book *Emotional Intelligence*, argues that our IQ-idolizing view of intelligence is far too narrow. Emotional intelligence – Goleman's term for self-awareness, altruism, personal motivation, empathy, and the ability to love and be loved by friends, spouses, partners, and family members – also plays a crucial role. People who possess high emotional intelligence are likely to succeed professionally and build lasting, meaningful relationships. Emotional intelligence is not fixed at birth and can be cultivated at any stage of life. Similar messages are found in psychologist Howard Gardner's book *Multiple Intelligences*, in which he argues that students have been shortchanged by the traditional, IQ-based view of intelligence and its near-total emphasis on linguistic and logical abilities.

Although patients want their physician to be smart enough to do the job at hand, they never inquire how their doctor ranked on an IQ test. They are more concerned about whether their physician *cares* about them. This reflects the importance they place on emotional intelligence – the empathy, altruism, compassion, and love they feel from their doctor.

We physicians often regard these concerns as frills. Our primary goal is to be intellectually accurate in dealing with a specific problem, not to be empathic. But even when raw brainpower is important – in making complex diagnoses or in designing intricate treatment programs – sheer intelligence is not everything. The correct answers often burst into a physician's awareness out of the blue in dreams, visions, intuitions, and hunches that seem utterly unrelated to reason.

Most of us health-care professionals are afflicted, to one degree or another, with a stereotypical view – that intelligence and emotions are opposed to each other and that empathy, compassion, and love get in the way of objective reasoning. This attitude is reflected in our medical schools, where emotional intelligence is given a low priority in the selection process for medical students. Medical schools continue to select candidates mainly on the basis of the good grades in chemistry, physics, biology, and mathematics they earned in their undergraduate years. This is the sort of achievement related to high IQ. Many medical schools are not merely blind to emotional intelligence, they are actually hostile to it. As

I explored in the chapter 'Whatever Happened to Healers?' these schools manage to extinguish whatever emotional intelligence young doctors bring along with them. It's as if a war were going on between reason and emotion and the medical schools have to choose which side they are on. Like most wars, this one is based on a profound misunderstanding. The opposition is false, because the best healers have always been individuals with *both* a head *and* a heart – a highly developed intellect and a mature emotional side.

I'm not suggesting that we abandon intellect and IQ and wing it with emotions. One extreme is as silly as the other. 'Healing intelligence' requires a balance between reason *and* intuition, between intellect *and* feeling. To achieve balance, however, we must create something that has lately been missing in health care: a space for the nonrational, intuitive side of the mind.

I'd like to try creating some space by asking, What do we really know about creativity and intelligence? In so doing, I'll explore some areas I wish I'd known about when I stole my IQ score.

Savants

Author and educator Joseph Chilton Pearce believes that people often derive creative ideas by dipping into what he calls the cosmic soup. This is a term for what throughout history has been called the collective consciousness, Universal Mind, God Consciousness, cosmic consciousness, and so on. Pearce's cosmic soup contains all the ingredients anyone could ever need to formulate a new idea. He suggests that creative breakthroughs and discoveries often occur when people dip mentally into the cauldron and ladle out what they need.

How could the existence of this hypothetical soup be proved? One way would be to find individuals who possess knowledge they could not possibly have acquired on the basis of their experience or genetic heritage and could not have formulated on their own. Good candidates are savants, from a French word meaning 'learned one.' This term has traditionally been used to describe individuals who are mentally or socially impaired but possess awesome creative and intuitive powers of obscure origin in areas such as mathematics, art, or music. The 'savant syndrome' was popularized a few years ago in the movie *Rain Man*.

The abilities of savants are often thought to be curiosities with little practical value, but this was not always true. During World War II the British government employed two mathematical savants who were reportedly infallible to serve as human computers.

Psychologist David Feinstein reports that at least one hundred savants with prodigious mental abilities have been identified in the past century. Darold Treffert, in his book *Extraordinary People*, describes a savant whose conversational vocabulary was limited to some fifty-eight words but who could accurately give the population of every city and town in the United States with more than five thousand people; the names, number of rooms, and locations of two thousand leading hotels in America; the distance from any city or town to the largest city in its state; statistics concerning three thousand mountains and rivers; and the dates and essential facts of more than two thousand leading inventions and discoveries.

Joseph Chilton Pearce gives several examples of the accomplishments of savants in *Evolution's End:* One mathematical savant was shown a checker-board with a grain of rice on the first of its sixty-four squares and was asked how many grains of rice there would be on the final square if the grains of rice were doubled on each square. Forty-five seconds later he gave the correct answer, which exceeds the total number of atoms in the sun.

A blind musical savant could 'repeat, on the piano, a complex piece heard only once, in a perfect mirroring, including every emotional nuance of expression,' says Pearce.

George and Charles are identical twins who are known as 'calendrical savants.' They are incapable of taking care of themselves and have been institutionalized since age seven. If you ask them on which date Easter will fall ten thousand years into the future, they answer immediately – not just with the date for Easter but also with other calendrical data such as the time of the tides on that day. If you ask them for the date of an event prior to 1752, when Europe shifted from the Gregorian to the Julian calendar system, their answers accommodate to the switch. They can tell you the day of the week of any date you choose, ranging forty thousand years into the past or the future. Give them your birth date and they can tell you what years your birthday will fall on a Thursday. In addition to their calendrical skills, they enjoy swapping twenty-digit prime numbers, thereby showing a parallel ability that is uncommon in savants. In spite of these prodigious abilities, they cannot add the simplest numbers. If you ask them how they knew to switch from one calendrical system to the other in 1752, they will be confused by such an abstract question; indeed, they don't know what 'calendrical system' means. Pearce states:

> Savants are untrained and untrainable, illiterate and uneducable . . . few can read or write . . . Yet each has apparently unlimited access to a particular field of knowledge that we know they cannot have acquired . . . Ask . . . [mathematical] savants how they get their answer and they will smile, pleased that we are impressed but unable to grasp the implications of such a question . . . The answers come through them but they are not aware of how – they don't know how they know . . . The ones sight-reading music can't read anything else, yet display this flawless sensory-motor response to musical symbols.

And here is the crux of the mystery. 'The issue with these savants is that in most cases, so far as can be observed, the savant has not acquired, could not have acquired, and is quite incapable of acquiring, the information that he so liberally dispenses.'

How do they do it? The usual explanations rely on not-yet-understood genetic propensities. If ever there were a promissory note in science with little redemption value, this may be it, because no one has a clue how genes could code for these abilities. Pearce proposes that there are nonlocal sources of information – invisible information fields – that savants (or anyone else) can tap into, obtaining the information needed.

Events in early life may set the stage for dipping into this cosmic soup. For example, the mother of George and Charles, the calendrical savants, had a perpetual calendar, a little brass gadget with various cogged cylinders. When one cylinder was turned, they all turned until the proper alignment was made, allowing one to determine a future or past date over a long span of time. The gadget fascinated the twins and they played with it continually. Although they were incapable of reading its coding, Pearce believes that the device may have 'acted as a stimulus that activated the corresponding 'calendrical field,' in much the same way that a mother's speech activates the phoneme response in an infant.' The low intelligence of savants may confer an advantage by narrowly focusing their attention and screening out extraneous stimuli. This might increase the 'signal-to-noise' ratio from the information field and heighten the reception of 'what comes through.' As Pearce states:

> The savant has a direct line of communication with one soup-category but only one, usually, while the rest of us can access a near-infinite number of categories . . . Our generality is bought at the price of precision . . . Almost surely the savant's failure to develop multiple intelligences is what allows such direct openness to the single one he can access. His expertise digs its channel deep from lack of competition. His potential doesn't have to accommodate to anything and can come through with pristine purity – and profound limitation. The savant's lack of personal intellect-intelligence shows that the field accessed is intelligence itself, that intelligence does indeed group in compatible aggregates and is, on some level, independent of us, a 'non-localized' conscious energy.

Young children, like savants, also appear to dip into the cosmic soup on occasion. Consider what happened to Pearce, who, in his thirties, was thinking and reading about theological questions 'to the point of obsession':

> One morning as I prepared for an early class, my five-year-old son came into my room, sat on the edge of the bed, and launched into a twenty-minute discourse on the nature of God and man. He spoke in perfect, publishable sentences, without pause or haste, and in a flat monotone. He used complex theological terminology and told me, it seemed, everything there was to know. As I listened, astonished, the hair rose on the back of my neck. I felt goose-bumps, and, finally, tears streamed down my face. I was in the midst of the uncanny, the inexplicable . . .

Here a bright, normal child underwent a kind of 'savant experience' as he responded to a field of information he could not have acquired. Terms such as telepathy are misleading; he wasn't picking up his materials from me. I hadn't acquired anything like he described and would, in fact, be in my mid-fifties and involved in meditation before I did.

Prodigies

Systems theorist Ervin Laszlo has hypothesized the existence of fields of information that function like Pearce's cosmic soup. 'We raise the possibility,' he wrote in his *Interconnected Universe*, 'that the minds of exceptionally creative people would be in spontaneous, direct, though not necessarily conscious, interaction with other minds within the creative process itself.' Under the right circumstances, a person might dip into this field and partake of the collective insights of individuals past and present. What is collectively known could be individually known, and vice versa. Laszlo says that 'to call individuals such as . . . a Mozart, a Michelangelo, or a Shakespeare . . . "gifted" and their achievements "works of genius" is not to explain their abilities, but only to label them.' He proposes that some acts of creativity, particularly when sudden and unexpected, 'are not due to a spontaneous and largely unexplained stroke of genius, but to the elaboration of an idea or a pattern in two or more minds in interaction.'

Throughout history, people have cultivated nonordinary states of awareness such as meditation to nudge the creative process along. Laszlo believes these methods help people gain access to the nonlocal, collective source of wisdom. During highly creative moments, 'there is almost always some element of transport to another plane of consciousness, a deep concentration that approaches a state of trance,' he notes. 'In some (relatively rare) cases these "inspired states" are artifically induced – by drugs, music, self-hypnosis or other means. Mostly, however, they come spontaneously to the "gifted" individual.' Samuel Taylor Coleridge described composing his celebrated poem 'Kubla Khan' in an opium-induced sleep; Milton's *Paradise Lost* was dictated, he said, by the Muse as an 'unpremeditated song.' Usually, however, when people use drugs to boost creativity, though they may feel they have connected nonlocally with 'all there is,' there is little or nothing to show for it when the drug wears off. Most 'art' produced under the influence of mind-altering chemicals winds up in the wastebasket – which, Einstein once remarked, is the creative scientist's most important tool.

A sense of profound urgency may catapult one into a state of heightened creativity. As Samuel Johnson wrote: 'Depend upon it, sir, when a man knows he is to be hanged in a fortnight, it concentrates his mind wonderfully.' Evariste Galois, for instance, at the age of twenty-three, wrote down his fundamental contributions to higher algebra in the three days before a duel in which he correctly believed he would be killed. Urgency, Laszlo suggests, gives rise to 'a subtle dialogue' between individuals 'whether or not they are physically in the same location . . . [or] whether or not they consciously know of each other.' This is affirmed in so-called telesomatic events, in which an individual shares the actual physical symptoms of a distant loved one who is involved in some type of crisis.

Unity with the Infinite

The urge to become absorbed into something greater – God, Goddess, Allah, Brahman, Universe, the One – underlies the drive of the great saints and mystics of all spiritual traditions and is also typical of many highly creative individuals. As John Briggs writes in his fine book about creativity, *Fire in the Crucible*: 'For the creative genius, the ancient perception that it is possible to invoke an identity between the universal and particular, between the personal and the vast impersonal, the part and the whole, is pervasive. It burgeons at all levels of the creative process and dominates creative vision. [In their] many moods and meanings, [creative individuals are involved in] a search for wholeness and a personal/universal identity.'

Novelist Joseph Conrad saw his connection with the whole. He spoke of 'the latent feeling of fellowship with all creation – and to the subtle but invincible conviction of solidarity that knits together the loneliness of innumerable hearts.' Painter Piet Mondrian also spoke of the artist's communion with something greater than the individual self, noting that 'art has shown that universal expression can only be created by a real equation of the universal and the individual.' Painter Paul Klee saw that the whole speaks through the part. The artist's 'position is humble,' he said. 'He is merely a channel.' In *Creativity and Its Cultivation* psychologist Erich Fromm sanctions Klee's view. For Fromm, the creator 'has to give up holding on to himself as a thing and begin to experience himself only in the process of creative response; paradoxically enough, if he can experience himself in the process, he loses himself. He transcends the boundaries of his own person, and at the very moment when he feels "I am" he also feels "I am you," I am one with the whole world.'

The creative individual also often feels nonlocally united with his medium. As virtuoso pianist Lorin Hollander describes: 'By the time I was three, I was spending every waking moment at the keyboard, standing, placing my hands on the keyboard and pushing notes. And I would choose very carefully what tones I would choose because I knew that when I would play a note I would become that note.' Hollander also describes becoming identical with the great composers. I once had the opportunity to ask his opinion of the movie *Amadeus*, which depicts the life of Mozart. He replied, 'That wasn't Mozart.' How did he know, I asked. 'Because when I play Mozart, I *become* Mozart,' he responded.

Mysticism and Creativity

For many creators, *creation* is a misnomer because the creative act does not involve making something new but linking with a complete and timeless wisdom that already exists – God, Goddess, the Absolute, Pearce's cosmic soup, Laszlo's field of information. Whatever term is used, this dimension is often considered sacred by the creative individual. Thus Einstein considered science the outlet for what he called the 'cosmic religious feeling' and what Briggs calls 'quintessential mysticism.' One of Edison's biographers notes: 'Through much of his life Edison was attracted by mysticism. After the phonograph came into existence, he could almost sense a mystic force moving about in the universe.' Two Nobelists and patriarchs of quantum physics became fascinated with Eastern mystical precepts, Briggs tells us. Erwin Schrödinger believed our scientific perspective needed to be 'amended, perhaps by a bit of blood transfusion from Eastern thought.' When it became necessary for Niels Bohr to design a family crest, he chose the ancient Chinese symbol of yin and yang, illustrating the interpenetration of opposites as well as his famous principle of complementarity. Nobel geneticist Barbara McClintock was also intrigued by the paradoxes of Buddhism and Taoism, says Briggs, and declared she was proud to think of herself as a mystic.

Mystery writer Sue Grafton believes her creative process involves mystical elements. Her views reveal the interplay between the local, individual mind and a nonlocal process that transcends the personal self or ego. She states:

> In order to get in touch I have to block out ego. Ego is the piece of me that's going, How am I doing, champ? You know. Is this good? Do you like this? Do you think the critics will like this? Because that has nothing to do with creating . . . And that's a question of not being self-conscious, not being cute, not thinking I'm so hot. Not thinking anything. Not making judgments about myself. Not sitting critiquing myself but being still enough to hear the voice that'll tell me what I'm supposed to do next. Which is maybe the unconscious, maybe the subconscious. Maybe it's right brain. Maybe it's the soul. I'm not real sure.
>
> I think there's a sort of mystical process of getting information . . . Sometimes I have dreams that I believe are not mine. I have dreams in which images and the landscape and the interior architecture are so alien that I am convinced it is somebody else's dream material.

Reverie

Concert artist Rosalyn Tureck is the first woman ever invited to conduct the New York Philharmonic Orchestra and the author of many books, including one in which she connects the structure of Bach's music to two physical theories. At certain moments in her creative life as a musician, as Stefi Weisburd reported in *Science News*, Tureck's mind seemed to be part of something larger:

> One day shortly before her seventeenth birthday, she was playing the Bach fugue in A minor from Book I of the *Well-Tempered Clavier* when she lost all awareness of her own existence. She saw Bach's music revealed in a totally new light, with a new structure that required the development of a novel piano technique. Over the next couple of days she worked out this technique on four lines of the fugue and then played it at her next piano lesson. Her teacher marveled at her break-through, saying that it was marvelous but impossible.
>
> 'All I knew,' says Tureck, 'was that I had gone through a small door into an immense living, green universe, and the impossibility for me lay in returning through that door to the world I had known.'

Into what world did that 'small door' lead Tureck? Into a transpersonal, nonlocal, preexisting pool of information?

Originality

If our consciousness is nonlocal and unbounded, it cannot be put in a box and isolated from other minds but extends infinitely throughout time and space to link with all other minds, past, present, and future. But if so, how can we determine the source of any new idea? Is the insight originating in the individual in the present or coming from someone in the past or future to whom he or she is nonlocally connected?

Baron Carl Friedrich von Weizsäcker, the renowned physicist who was a student of the legendary Werner Heisenberg, has thought deeply about creativity and discovery in science. His view, expressed in the introduction to Gopi Krishna's book *The Biological Basis of Religion and Genius*, helps us make sense of experiences such as Tureck's:

> A great scientific discovery is the recognition of a particular simple and fundamental form which heretofore had been hidden in a chaos of appearances and misunderstood theories. It is often described as an inspiration or a special gift of grace which comes to the researcher when and as it pleases, like the answer from 'another authority' and then almost without effort on his part. It is never viewed as the inevitable result of his research effort. Here we find the often disturbing and happy experience: 'It is not I; I have not done this.' Still, in a certain way it is I – yet not the ego of will but of a more comprehensive self.

The Speed of Creativity

Some individuals create things so quickly they defy our imagination. Sometimes they seem to see something that is already fully formed, as if taking down dictation. According to Brewster Gheslin in his book *The Creative Process*, Mozart said that a composition would grow in him until 'the whole, though it be long, stands almost complete and finished in my mind, so that I can survey it, like a fine picture or a beautiful statue, at a glance. Nor do I hear in my imagination the parts *successively*, but I hear them as it were, all at once.'

Mozart spilled the overture to *Don Giovanni* onto the page in the few hours before the premiere. Tiepolo painted the *Twelve Apostles* in ten hours. The great twentieth-century mathematician John von Neumann could sometimes puzzle out a complex problem in a matter of seconds. Yet some great creators dip slowly into the cosmic soup – Bach, for example, who said, 'ceaseless work . . . analysis, reflection, writing much, endless self-correction, that is my secret.' Beethoven literally worked on some of his compositions for years; Darwin took almost two decades to write *On the*

Origin of Species; and Flaubert was known to spend an entire day on a single sentence.

Play

'And so I began to travel – of course in my mind.' Thus did Nicola Tesla (1856–1943), one of the greatest scientists of all time, describe his youth. Tesla's inventions virtually transformed life in the early twentieth century, as did the discoveries of Edison, to whom Tesla is often compared. 'Every night (and sometimes during the day), when alone,' he wrote, 'I would start on my journeys – see new places, cities and countries – live there, meet people and make friendships and acquaintances.'

This is a picture of youthful exuberance, of someone having fun. Tesla engaged in these journeys 'constantly until I was seventeen when my thoughts turned seriously to invention.' Then he found to his delight that he could visualize with the greatest of ease. He needed no models, drawings, or experiments. He could picture all these things in his mind as utterly real, drawing on his facility to 'travel.' Tesla knew he was onto something important – that he had 'been led unconsciously to evolve . . . a new method of materializing inventive concepts and ideas, which is radically opposite to the purely experimental and . . . ever so much more expeditious and efficient.'

Sometimes his 'facility' seemed to take him over completely, as if it possessed a life of its own. He described the process as follows: 'Ideas came in an uninterrupted stream and the only difficulty I had was to hold them fast. The pieces of apparatus I conceived were to me absolutely real and tangible in every detail, even to the minutest signs of wear. I delighted in imagining the motors constantly running, for in this way they presented to the mind's eye a more fascinating sight . . . In less than two months I evolved virtually all the types of motors and modifications of the system which are now identified with my name.'

The 'travel' that Tesla spoke of sounds as though it were straight out of the New Age lexicon – astral travel, out-of-body experiences, or soul projection, in which, proponents say, the mind actually takes a trip to some distant place. But this literal explanation is not at all consistent with the nonlocal nature of the mind. *Nonlocal* implies *infinitude* in space and time, and therefore omnipresence. If the mind is genuinely nonlocal, it is already everywhere. This means that there is no need for it to go anywhere, because there is no place it isn't. This was captured in a bumper sticker I once saw: NO MATTER WHERE YOU GO, THERE YOU ARE. Or as Gertrude Stein remarked about Oakland, California, her hometown, 'There is no there there.'

Physical Activity

When I was writing my first book, *Space, Time & Medicine*, I was heavily involved with running. I discovered, quite by accident, that some of my most original ideas popped up while I was in that altered state of consciousness that runners know well – a nearly thoughtless condition in which the rational mind is temporarily put on hold. This happened so frequently that I would not run without a pen and paper stuffed inside my jogging shorts. I incurred many strange glances from other runners when I stopped to scribble a thought that suddenly erupted from nowhere.

I believe this experience must be fairly common, though I have heard few writers speak about it. An exception is filmmaker and novelist John Sayles, whose second novel, *Union Dues*, was nominated for the National Book Award. Sayles also discovered how to unlock the doors of creativity by altering his consciousness through swimming and running. 'One of the reasons that I like to swim,' he states, 'is that I get good ideas then. Or when I'm running. With that physical activity and lack of other input, I can put myself in kind of a trance. I fall into a state that's not totally conscious fairly easily. And I think that physical exercise usually helps you to do that, especially swimming.' Water is an ancient symbol for the unconscious mind, so it is particularly apt that fresh ideas for Sayles bubbled up during swimming.

Music

Jack Prelutsky has written more than three dozen books of poetry for children and has edited several anthologies along these lines. Dreams provide him with some of his best poems. In them, the boundaries between people, plants, and things often blur, and the world becomes enchanted and magical – the kind of world children understand and respond to. 'After watching an episode of "The A Team" on television I had a nightmare about Mr T,' he wrote. 'He was covered with vegetables. Of course the poem that resulted has nothing to do with Mr T now. I just kind of fantasized what kind of creature would want to spend its life submerged in vegetables.'

Music catalyzes some his most creative moments:

I was looking out the window of my studio one day and I fell asleep. I usually keep the radio on while I'm working – usually to classical music . . . something like Mozart or Brahms. I was thinking of the plants and the flowers that were growing there and I dreamt that they had all changed to musical instruments. The trees, instead of being trees were oboes and cellos and bassoons. Maybe it was a combination of looking at the garden and listening to the music, but when I woke up after a little nap, I immediately wrote a poem called 'I Am Growing a Glorious Garden.'

Does music's power to catalyze creative breakthroughs depend on the music itself? Composer John Cage suggests that music may point beyond itself. 'My favorite piece of music,' he says, 'is the one we hear all the time if we are quiet.' Bruce Springsteen has alluded to a nonlocal, time-transcendent quality of music: 'Music can seem incidental, but it ends up being very important. It allows you to suggest the passage of time in just a couple of quiet beats. Years can go by in a few bars, whereas a writer will have to come up with a clever way of saying, "And then years went by . . ." Songwriting allows you to cheat tremendously. You can present an entire life in a few minutes.'

Author Jill Purce points to the power of music to bring order and structure to the world, which is a kind of creativity. 'In India, Greece, and China, music represented the order of the universe,' she notes. 'No Chinese emperor would come to power without making sure that music was in order, because he knew that if music wasn't in order there would be chaos and revolution.'

Musicians have often looked to the order they see in nature as a guide in creating music – a way, again, that the creator strives to connect with a larger whole. The eighth-century pilgrim Wu-k'ung related a charming legend according to which the strains of Tokharian music were actually derived from the songs of water-falls. 'In those mountains,' Wu-k'ung reported, 'there is a spring which falls drop by drop producing musical sounds. Once a year on a certain date these sounds are gathered together to make a musical air.'

Chaos

Nonlocal ways of knowing are a mess. Chapter 8 has already noted psychologist Frank Barron's observation that

> creative individuals are more at home with complexity and apparent disorder than other people are . . . The creative individual, in his generalized preference for apparent disorder, turns to the dimly realized life of the unconscious, and is likely to have more than the usual amount of respect for the forces of the irrational in himself and in others . . . The creative individual not only respects the irrational in himself, but courts it as the most promising source of novelty in his own thought . . . The truly creative individual stands ready to abandon old classifications and to acknowledge that life, particularly his own unique life, is rich in new possibilities. To him, disorder offers the potentiality of order.

Actor and writer Spalding Gray deliberately employs chaos in his creative efforts. He is widely known for his monologues. In constructing them, he keeps a cardboard box next to his desk and throws 'everything that's unanswered, disturbing, or relevant to some of the things I'm thinking about, into the box. Then, when I have time, maybe a year later, I'll dump it out and begin to put together the puzzle of a new monologue.' He also relies on order to emerge from chaos when writing:

> I'm not working specifically with a conscious mind. I'm not at all a person who works through contrivance and manipulation of reality where you think, What would make a good story? But rather I work very passively with dreams, mistakes, serendipity, coincidence, synchronicity.
>
> Synchronicity plays a big part in my life. I like synchronicity. It gives me chills. The major synchronicity that I experience is while I'm writing. I'll often have the radio on – background classical music. The news will come on, or some spoken event, and the worlds will begin to hitch up. I'm in the midst of writing the word when I hear the word on the radio . . . Something like *languishing* really gives me the chills when I'm hearing it the same time I'm writing it. That will happen as often as one or two times a week. Which is a lot. I used to keep a record of those but I just don't any more. There are too many of them . . . It centers me in a way. It's like a mystical confirmation.

Although Gray does not consider himself particularly prone to extrasensory-perception-type events, he often has experiences that reveal to him the nonlocal connections between people. On one occasion the telephone rang in the middle of the night, awakening him from a dream. As his future wife was running to answer the phone, he lay in bed contemplating the dream, in which he was being called to Amsterdam. 'It's Amsterdam calling,' she said. It was a friend wanting him to come teach storytelling at a mime school. 'That is strong stuff,' Gray comments. 'I wonder if it is . . . simply that his message overflowed . . . and he was much more telepathic than he realized. All of a sudden there were no boundaries and his need to get me to Amsterdam was coming . . . ahead of time.'

Who makes the better chess player, scientist and philosopher Jacob Bronowski once asked, the one who makes fewer mistakes or the one who makes more? The mark of a truly great chess player, he observed, is that he allows himself the freedom to make imaginative mistakes. He continually thinks of something that by all norms of the game is an error. 'Therefore,' Bronowski stated, 'we must accept the fact that all imaginative inventions are to some extent errors with respect to the norm.'

Science and the Unconscious

We have already seen in 'Embracing the Trickster' how great scientists like Albert Einstein and Michael Faraday opened themselves up to sources of inspiration that lie outside the realm of conventional logic. Scientific inspiration has often come in the form of dreams. In dreaming, our belief in a local self confined to the here and now is suspended, replaced by nonlocal experiences that know no personal, spatial, or temporal bounds. In dreams one is not fettered by contradiction, paradox, or reason. Koestler believed dreams were as valuable as food and water. In his *Act of Creation* he called them an 'essential part of psychic metabolism . . . Without this daily dip into the ancient sources of mental life, we would probably all become desiccated automata. And without the more spectacular exploratory dives of the creative individual, there would be no science and no art.'

A spectacular exploratory dive into the unconscious was taken one night by Elias Howe (1819–1867), the inventor of the sewing machine. For years Howe had struggled unsuccessfully to perfect his machine, but he was plagued by problems with the needle. Then one night he dreamed he had been captured by savages who dragged him mercilessly before their king. The king issued an ultimatum: if within twenty-four hours Howe did not come up with a machine that could sew, he would die by the spear. The tormented Howe could not do it! His time ran out and he saw the menacing savages approaching. As they raised their spears high, towering over him for the kill, he saw that each of the spear points had an eye-shaped hole near the tip. Howe immediately awakened and realized that the hole in the sewing machine needle must go at the bottom, not at the top or middle where he had been trying to place it. He raced from bed to his workshop, filed a needle to the proper size, drilled a hole near its tip, and inserted it in the machine.

Early in the twentieth century researcher Edmond Maillet sent a questionnaire to a group of mathematicians who had worked in their profession for at least ten years. Four of his respondents described 'mathematical dreams' in which a solution actually occurred during the dream; eight acknowledged finding the beginnings of a solution or useful idea while dreaming; and another fifteen described how on waking they had achieved complete or partial solutions to questions posed the previous night.

In his monumental book *Our Dreaming Mind*, sleep-and-dreams researcher Robert L. Van de Castle cites several instances in which the minds of scientists frolicked nonlocally during dreamtime, sometimes with stunning consequences. Srinivasa Ramanujan, the twentieth-century mathematician, for example, is considered a giant in the history of mathematics. Originally a clerk in southern India, he astonished the dons of Cambridge – where he was eventually transplanted – with his insights. Ramanujan seemed to enjoy an advantage: his dreams included an otherworldly mentor. He reported how the Hindu goddess Namakkal would appear in his dreams and reveal to him mathematical formulas that he would verify on waking – a pattern that continued all his life.

A world-changing dream occurred in 1869 to Dmitri Mendeleyev, a professor of chemistry at Saint Petersburg. He had gone to bed after trying without success to categorize the chemical elements according to their atomic weights. 'I saw in a dream,' he reported, 'a table where all the elements fell into place as required. Awakening, I immediately wrote it down on a piece of paper. Only in one place did a correction later seem necessary.' The result was the periodic table of the elements. The dream also enabled Mendeleyev to predict the existence and properties of three new elements that were discovered within the next fifteen years.

The most famous example of a dreaming scientist is probably that of Friedrich A. Kekule von Stradonitz, recounted in chapter 7. After Kekule woke from the dream in which he saw a snake seize its own tail in its mouth, he began to work out the implications of the dream images, which led to the idea that benzene was a six-carbon *ring* structure and thereby revolutionized organic chemistry. In an address to a scientific meeting in 1890, Kekule concluded his talk to his colleagues by honoring his process of discovery with the advice to them: 'Let us learn to dream, gentlemen, and then we may perhaps find the truth.'

Albert Szent-Gyorgyi, a Nobel Prize winner in physiology and medicine, acknowledged the value of dreams in solving research problems. 'My brain must continue to think about them when I sleep,' he noted, 'because I wake up, sometimes in the middle of the night, with answers to questions that have been puzzling me.'

One of the legendary discoveries in modern medical research, insulin, is dream related. Frederick Banting, a Canadian physician, was conducting research on diabetes. Awakening from a dream one night, he wrote down the following words: 'Tie up the duct of the pancreas of a dog. Wait for a few weeks until the glands shrivel up. Then cut it out, wash it out and filter the precipitation.' This procedure led him to discover the hormone insulin, which proved lifesaving for millions of diabetics. It also led to Banting's being knighted – an interesting word, considering his nocturnal revelation.

The list of scientific discoveries influenced by dreams is quite long: James Watt's discovery of how to make spherical pellets that could be used as shot; D. Parkinson's discovery at Bell Laboratories of the all-electric gun director known as the M-9 device, the precursor of guidance systems used later in antiaircraft and antiballistic missiles; Ernst Chladni's invention of the euphonium, a new musical instrument – and on and on.

What Skeptics Say

Given the revelations that have come to scientists through dreams, you'd think researchers would honor and perhaps cultivate them. This was precisely the advice given by Kekule, who, as we saw, discovered the structure of benzene during a dream that he shared with his colleagues at a scientific convention in 1890. Yet many of the scientists felt not inspiration but embarrassment about the Kekule affair. When some were asked to comment on the famous discovery, they were quick to point out that Kekule's story presented 'a damaging picture of scientists' because scientists 'get hard facts' and 'don't dream things up.'

Critics often say that the dreaming scientists described above already knew the answers to their questions at an unconscious level. The components to the solutions were there all along, they argue, and merely fell into place while the scientist was dreaming. But this does not explain where the crucial knowledge came from in the first place. In some dreams the vital information seems to have no precursor.

In 1893 Dr Herman V. Hilprecht, professor of Assyrian at the University of Pennsylvania, was working late one evening in an attempt to decipher the inscriptions on two agate fragments he believed were from Babylonian finger rings. In the ruins of the temple of Bel at Nippur, dozens of similar fragments had been discovered. Hilprecht was tentatively able to assign one fragment to the Cassite period, whereas the other he placed with a great many other unclassified fragments. But he was not satisfied with these classifications. That night, reports Robert Van de Castle, Hilprecht had the following dream:

A tall, thin priest of the old pre-Christian Nippur, about forty years of age and clad in a simple abba, led me to the treasure chamber of the temple, on its southeast side. He went with me into a small, low-ceilinged room without windows, in which there was a large wooden chest, while scraps of agate and lapis lazuli lay scattered on the floor. Here he addressed me as follows: 'The two fragments which you have published separately on pages 22 and 26 belong together, are not finger rings and their history is as follows: King Kurigalzu (ca. 1300 B.C.) once sent to the temple of Bel, among other articles of agate and lapis lazuli, an inscribed votive cylinder of agate. Then we priests suddenly received the command to make for the statue of the god of Ninib a pair of earrings of agate. We were in great dismay, since there was no agate as raw material at hand. In order to execute the command there was nothing for us to do but cut the votive cylinder into three parts, thus making three rings, each of which contained a portion of the original inscription. The first two rings served as earrings for the statue of the god;

the two fragments which have given you so much trouble are portions of them. If you will put the two together you will have confirmation of my word. But the third ring you have not found in the course of your excavations and you never will find it.' With this the priest disappeared.

Hilprecht explained what then happened: 'I woke at once and immediately told my wife the dream that I might not forget it. Next morning – Sunday – I examined the fragments once more in the light of these disclosures, and to my astonishment found all the details of the dream precisely verified in so far as the means of verification were in my hands. The original inscription on the votive cylinder reads: "To the god Ninib, son of Bel, his lord, has Kurigalzu, pontifex of Bel, presented this."'

Van de Castle asks: 'How did Hilprecht come to know that the fragments had been part of a single votive cylinder presented by King Kurigalzu, dedicated to Ninib, and subsequently made into a pair of earrings? What could account for the presence of the extraordinarily accurate details in the dream? Perhaps there was a psychic, or "extrasensory," element involved. Perhaps logical, associative reasoning, assembling bits and pieces of subliminal information, is the explanation. If so, such superb deductive skill would put Sherlock Holmes to shame.'

The Creativity of Cultures

If information can be exchanged nonlocally between single individuals, why not between groups of individuals? Systems theorist Ervin Laszlo has considered how the great breakthroughs of classical Hebrew, Greek, Chinese, and Indian culture developed. These occurred at almost the same time in widely scattered areas among people not likely to have been in communication with each other, Laszlo states in *The Interconnected Universe*.

The major Hebrew prophets flourished in Palestine between 750 and 500 BC; in India the early Upanishads were composed between 660 and 550 BC and Siddharta the Buddha lived from

563 to 487 BC; Confucius taught in China around 551–479 BC; and Socrates lived in Hellenic Greece from 469 to 399 BC. At the time when the Hellenic philosophers created the basis of Western civilization in Platonic and Aristotelian philosophy, the Chinese philosophers founded the ideational basis of Oriental civilization in the Confucian, Taoist and Legalist doctrines. While in the Hellas of the Post-Peloponnesian Wars period Plato founded his Academy and Aristotle his Lyceum, and scores of itinerant sophists preached to and advised kings, tyrants, and citizens, in China the similarly restless and inventive 'Shih' founded schools, lectured to crowds, established doctrines, and manoeuvred among the scheming princes of the late Warring States Period. Space-leaping of this kind is either a sociocultural variant of action-at-a-distance, or it occurs by means of a medium of transmission.

The typical explanation for similar developments in cultures that are remote from one another is 'similar experiences, similar brains, similar breakthroughs.' But why at the same time? Laszlo points out that on the whole, simultaneous transformations of cultures were not unusual in ancient times. For his part, he believes something nonlocal is going on, but it is not easy to test the idea that cultures might dip into a nonlocal mind pool and emerge with similar knowledge and wisdom sufficient to transform their society, because cultures are no longer isolated, as a result of the modern communications revolution that instantly links our entire globe.

Can *species* make sudden transformative leaps through nonlocal influences? Today the concept of 'punctuated equilibrium' is in vogue in certain circles in the field of evolutionary biology. According to this idea, evolution does not proceed smoothly but in starts and stops. Long periods of near stagnation are interspersed with radical change. Might there be a common pool of information for species as well as cultures and individuals, into which they dip, emerging with information on how to advance suddenly toward greater complexity?

Fields and Archetypes

A field is an invisible region of influence that cannot be observed directly but that is presumed to exist in physical reality because of its effects. For example, we do not actually see a magnetic field around a bar magnet; but because iron filings arrange themselves in a certain pattern, we know the field exists.

Today science is buzzing with ideas about how fields may be involved with consciousness or even with the nonlocal behaviors of the mind. British biologist Rupert Sheldrake has proposed 'morphic fields' that 'influence organisms toward characteristic patterns of organization.' Psychologist David Feinstein has proposed 'mythic fields' as a subset of Sheldrake's morphic fields, which become established when new patterns of understanding and motivation are initiated and repeated. Stanford neurophysiologists Erin M. Schuman and D. V. Madison have proposed quantum-based 'neural fields' within the brain as part of their 'neural broadcasting' theory. According to this idea, information can be transmitted from a single neuron to neighboring neurons, bypassing the synapse that physically connects two nerve cells.

Neurologist Benjamin Libet has proposed a 'mental field' that is 'produced by, but is biologically distinct from, brain activity.' Anesthesiologist Stuart Hameroff suggests that quantum fields operate in tiny brain structures called microtubules, and that this may be the site where mind and brain are linked through quantum mechanics. Stanford materials scientist William Tiller has proposed that the quantum vacuum gives rise to field-like subtle energies that are invisible and undetectable until they are transformed by living systems. Princeton researchers Robert Jahn and Brenda Dunne and their colleagues propose information fields that mediate the nonlocal acquisition and transfer of various mental phenomena. In varying degrees, all of these hypotheses provide ways for nonlocal phenomena to take place, both in the world and inside the brain.

Psychoanalyst Stainslav Grof has proposed the idea of a Universal Mind as a result of his work with patients in altered states of consciousness resulting from their use of LSD (lysergic acid diethylamide) or forced breathing techniques. He writes in *The Holotropic Mind*:

It has been remarkable to find that people raised in one culture, or belonging to a particular race, are not limited to the archetypes of that culture or race. In our research we have seen, for example, that white, urban, middle class Americans can have meaningful encounters with such legendary heroes as the Polynesian Maui or Shango, the Bantu god of sex and war. Over the years I have, on many occasions, witnessed European and American women who became the Hindu Goddess Kali . . . Conversely, during workshops in Japan and India, we witnessed several participants, born and raised in those traditions, who had powerful identifications with Christ.

It is particularly interesting to note that in many cases, where people had no previous knowledge of certain mythological figures, they were not only able to *experience* them accurately and with great detail but they were able to draw pictures with details that perfectly matched ancient descriptions of those figures.

The idea of a nonlocal source of information that influences people worldwide was developed by psychologist C. G. Jung. Jung called the eternal patterns within the psyche *archetypes*. His views on the nature and origin of archetypes changed throughout his career. In his early, more orthodox perspective, he favored a genetic basis in which archetypes arise from a vast, limitless unconscious process shared by all humankind, emerging from the accumulated experience throughout the span of shared history. Later, however, he gave up trying to give a physiological explanation. In a letter shortly before his death in 1961, Jung wrote:

We might have to give up thinking in terms of space and time when we deal with the reality of archetypes. It could be that the psyche is an unextended intensity, not a body moving in time. One could assume that the psyche arises gradually from the smallest extension to an infinite intensity, and thus robs bodies of their reality when the psychic intensity transcends the speed of light. Our brain might be the place of transformation, where the relatively infinite tensions or intensities of the psyche are tuned down to perceptible frequencies and extensions. But in itself the psyche would have no dimension in space and time at all.

Something like archetypal influences also seems to occur in animals. As David Feinstein points out, when a wooden model of a soaring hawk is pulled over the head of a newly hatched chick, the chick will crouch down and emit cries of alarm. Even if the next ten generations are never exposed to a hawk, the chick's descendents will still cringe. British ornithologist David Lack trapped thirty finches on the Galapagos Islands in 1939, where there are no large birds of prey, and sent them to his colleague Robert Orr in California. When a predatory bird came into sight they cringed and emitted cries of alarm, even though they and their ancestors for thousands of years had never seen a predatory bird and had never exhibited that kind of response.

The usual way of explaining these types of behavior in animals is to call them instincts – but, again, this is merely a label and not an explanation. If nonlocal fields – archetypal, morphic, mythic – influence what birds do, might they help explain how we humans behave as well?

Psychologist Michael Conforti relates his experience with John, a male client of Sicilian descent. The patient's ethnicity interested Conforti because Conforti's family was from Sicily and Naples. During the initial stages of treatment, John complained that his previous analyst never seemed to understand his Sicilian temperament. Failing to understand John's way of seeing the world and conducting his business, the analyst diagnosed him as excessively paranoid. John realized that the cultural differences separating him and his Anglo-Saxon therapist would limit the effectiveness of his treatment, so he decided to change therapists. Conforti, who succeeded the original therapist, discovered that 'he was not paranoid, he was a Sicilian!' Conforti adheres to the influence of archetypal fields. To understand John, he maintains, one has to recognize the Sicilian psyche and the Sicilian archetypal field. Sicily is an island and therefore isolated from the mainland, which imbues islanders with a corresponding psychological disposition. Importantly, Sicilians have seen their island home invaded by many different nations, all bent on exploiting it. Sicilians quickly learned the art of intrigue, and for their own survival they cultivated a keen suspicion and cynicism toward outsiders. Luigi Barzini, in his book *The Italians*, expresses the essence of what Conforti calls 'the Sicilian field': 'The Sicilian's best virtues . . . are obviously not those of the anonymous organization man of today, but those of the ancient hero fighting with his little group, the rest of the world . . . He can even accept death with open eyes or deal death impassively, without hesitation or regret . . . in defense of his particular, strictly Sicilian ideals.'

Three Stages of the Creative Process

During the nineteenth century, scientists believed that if they dissected an event thoroughly enough, they could eventually understand what caused it. They extended this idea of reductionistic analysis to the process of creativity and discovery. One of the foremost leaders in this attempt was Hermann von Helmholtz, the great nineteenth-century physicist. Helmholtz divided the creative process into three stages. The first he called *saturation*, in which one immerses oneself fully in the topic of concern by gathering information through reading, consulting others, research, and so on. Then comes the stage of *incubation*, in which the work is set aside, along with all attempts at purposeful analysis. This is not a do-nothing period; the information gathered in stage one is presumably being processed by one's unconscious mind. Then follows Helmholtz's third stage of creativity, *illumination*, which may arrive suddenly as a breakthrough or 'Eureka!' experience. One often cannot deduce logically how the conclusion was reached. As one famous mathematician said, 'I know the answer, but I do not yet see how to get it.' Following illumination, there remains the leg-work of testing and verifying one's discovery.

Helmholtz was onto something important. Dreams of radical creativity do indeed tend to happen to people who are ready for them. In *The Courage to Create*, Rollo May observed that 'insight never comes hit or miss, but in accordance with a pattern of which one essential component is our own commitment.' Commitment, education, and training prepare the ground for the seed to germinate and grow.

Examples in which dreams and readiness reinforce each other are legion. William Blake, already a skilled engraver, tried many times to devise a cheaper way to engrave the illustrations for his poems but was baffled until Robert, his younger brother, appeared to him in a dream and showed Blake a method of copper engraving that he immediately verified and put to work. Similar events happened to great composers whose preparation rendered them receptive. Beethoven composed a canon in his sleep. Giuseppe Tartini heard 'the devil' play a stunningly beautiful violin sonata and transcribed it, as best he could, on waking. Wagner revealed that *Tristan und Isolde* emerged straight from a dream.

Physiologist Otto Loewi experienced one of the longest periods of incubation on record. He had a hypothesis early in his career that nerve impulses were chemically transmitted, but he could not devise an experiment that would prove this and eventually forgot about his hunch. Seventeen years later he had a dream of how to test his idea, awoke, jotted down notes, and returned to sleep. He was horrified to discover in the morning that he could not read his writing. 'His dream source was generous,' historian Robert Moss writes in *Conscious Dreaming*. 'Loewi dreamed the experiment again the following night. This time he took no chances; he rushed to his laboratory at 3 A.M. and performed an experiment on a frog's heart, as indicated in the dream. This dream-directed experiment inspired the work for which Loewi was awarded the Nobel Prize.'

Mystery writer Sue Grafton deliberately incubates ideas, exemplifying all three stages of the creative process described by Helmholtz:

> I reach a point in many of my books, when I'm very heavily engaged in the process of writing, where I have a problem that I can't solve. And as I go to sleep I will give myself the suggestion that a solution will come. Whether this is from a dream state I'm not certain. I know that I will waken and the solution will be there. I attribute it to right brain activity. I don't know the relationship between right brain activity and dreams but I know when the analytical self, the left brain, finally releases its

grip on us and gets out of the way, the creative side of us, which often surfaces in sleep, comes to the fore and in its own playful and whimsical manner will solve many creative problems . . .

If I am very blocked or very confused or frustrated I will drink coffee late in the day, knowing that it's going to wake me up in the dead of night. So I get to sleep perfectly soundly and then, at three A.M. when left brain is tucked away, not being vigilant, right brain comes out to play and helps me . . .

I write letters to right brain all the time. They're just little notes:

Dear Right Brain,

Well, sweetie, I've asked you for a little help with this and I notice you're not forthcoming. I would really appreciate it if tonight you would solve this problem.

Your pal,
Sue

Helmholtz's three stages have become part of the lore of the creative process. Particularly courageous was his contention that the rational, analytical side of the mind is supplemented by unconscious thought processes. This was a radical suggestion in the 1800s, when scholars prided themselves on the muscular nature of purposeful mental effort.

But Helmholtz's three-stage process is a thoroughly local model, in which all the information needed for a breakthrough is acquired through the physical senses and subsequently processed by the physical brain. As helpful as it is, it has a problem: it cannot account for those examples in which, as we've seen, people acquire information and insights that cannot easily be explained on the basis of prior experience, memory, or previous information.

Why didn't Helmholtz make a place in his theory of creativity for nonlocal mental functioning? This possibility was unthinkable for him and most of his colleagues. They lived and worked during a period when scientists believed passionately in the laws of classical physics. The quantum-relativistic developments lay well into the future, and nonlocal physical events had not been discovered. If nonlocal events did not exist in physics, how could they exist for the mind? Consequently, Helmholtz was a man of his time. He simply could not abide the possibility that information could be acquired nonlocally. 'The transmission of thought from one person to another independently of the recognized channels of sensation,' he wrote, '. . . is clearly impossible.'

Creativity and Mental Illness

These days, creativity isn't looking so good. There has been an increasing tendency to link various creative impulses with madness and ultimately to pathological brain chemistry, neuroendocrine disorders, and genetic factors. Psychiatrist Arnold Ludwig of the University of Kentucky Medical Center in Lexington, author of *The Price of Greatness: Resolving the Creativity and Madness Controversy*, found that around one-third of the eminent poets, musical performers, and authors of fiction suffered from psychological problems as teenagers. By adulthood the rate mushroomed to three-fourths. Even prominent scientists – who suffered from less mental disease than artists – demonstrated a steep rise in suicide rates in old age.

Examples suggesting a link between madness and creativity abound. 'There is quite definitely something or other deranged in my brain,' van Gogh said. Dostoevsky had epilepsy and gave epilepsy to at least four of his fictional characters.

Even the feeling among creative individuals that they have tapped into a higher, transcendent reality is being connected with the flux of chemicals in the brain. Researchers M. A. Persinger and C. M. Cook of Laurentian University call these feelings 'sensed presence' – basically a sense of the Almighty. This feeling, they claim, originates in the right side of the brain and can be produced artificially. In their laboratory, they exposed the brains of subjects to an electromagnetic field and asked them to press a button when they felt 'a mystical presence.' The subjects did not know when the exposure occurred. More often than chance would predict, mystical presences (button pushes) correlated with application of magnetic fields. Results such as these lead some people to conclude that religious and spiritual experiences are all brain-based.

V. S. Ramachandran, of the University of California-San Diego's

Center for Brain and Cognition, studies patients with epilepsy, brain lesions, and head injuries to find out about the relation of mind and brain. By testing individuals with temporal lobe epilepsy, he and his team have found neural tissue in the brain's temporal lobe that is involved in how intensely someone responds to mystical or spiritual experiences. People with temporal lobe epilepsy often exhibit an obsession with religious issues and may feel an overwhelming feeling of union with the universe or the divine during seizures. 'Something has happened in their temporal lobes that heightened their response to religious terms and icons,' Ramachandran says. 'There may be a selective enhancement of emotions that are conducive to religious experience.' He cautions, however, that his work 'does not prove' that brain mechanisms have evolved to respond to religion.

Other researchers are not so restrained. 'Mind has properties – self-consciousness, wonder, emotion and reason – that make it seem more than merely material,' says Michael A. Arbib, an expert on brain theory at the University of Southern California's Center of Neural Engineering. 'Yet I argue that all of this can be explained eventually by the physical properties of the brain. In 20 years we will understand what happens in the brain when people have religious experiences.' In his book *Genius*, a biography of Richard Feynman, one of the most creative physicists of the twentieth century, James Glieck agrees with the idea that the brain spawns mystical and spiritual feelings. He writes: 'That feeling of divine inspiration, the breath of revelation seemingly from without, actually came from within . . . the brain.'

Mystical and spiritual geniuses – 'religious creatives' – have long been suspected of having brain ailments such as epilepsy. The apostles Luke and Paul both agreed that Paul suffered from what he called his 'thorn in the flesh.' Distinguished biblical commentators have attributed this to either migraine headaches or epilepsy. Similar maladies crop up in all religions, as Clifford Pickover wrote in his book *Strange Brains and Genius*. When Muhammad first had visions of God, 'he felt oppressed, smothered, as if his breath were being squeezed from his chest. Later he heard a voice calling his name, but when he turned to find the source of the voice, no one was there. The local Christians, Jews, and pagan Arabs called him insane. Legend has it that Mohammad was born with excess fluid around his brain, and that as a child he had fits.' (Pickover views these legends with caution. 'I am not certain,' he says, 'they could know about excess fluid at that time in history.') Just prior to a seizure, epileptics often have a sense of impending doom. This may explain, Pickover contends, why 'the overriding emotion experienced by Mohammad, Moses, and St Paul during their religious visions was not one of rapture and joy but rather of fear.' Pickover further speculates that this was the reason Moses hid his face and was frightened when he heard the voice of God from a burning bush in 1300 B.C.E.

Along these lines, neurologists have linked hyperreligiosity – heightened interest in religion – with temporal lobe epilepsy. Van Gogh, who demonstrated classical signs of this disease, said: 'I often feel a terrible need of – shall I say the word? – religion. Then I go out at night to paint the stars.' In her book *Seized*, Eve LaPlante finds further evidence of van Gogh's hyperreligiosity in his habit of wearing rags, of punishing himself while preaching Christianity, in his mystical visions including the resurrected Christ, and in frequent attacks of rage.

Surveys show that the great majority of Americans believe in God and have a 'sensed presence' of a nonlocal, infinite Almighty. Do most of our citizens have low-grade temporal lobe epilepsy or bad genes?

Hypergraphia – excessive writing or drawing – is also a symptom of temporal lobe epilepsy. If we combine hyperreligiosity and hypergraphia, we have a caricature of many highly creative writers and artists – spiritually sensitive individuals who produce a lot, quickly.

Scientists have been writing off religious states of consciousness to abnormal processes in the brain for more than a hundred years. Harvard psychologist William James felt the need to respond to this tendency in his 1902 classic, *The Varieties of Religious Experience*:

To plead the organic causation of a religious state of mind in refutation of its claim to possess superior spiritual value, is quite illogical and arbitrary [because] none of our thoughts and feelings, not even our scientific doctrines, not even our *dis*-beliefs, could retain any value as revelations of the truth, for every one of them without exception flows from the state of the possessor's body at the time. Saint Paul certainly once had an epileptoid, if not an epileptic, seizure, but there is not a single one of our states of mind, high or low, healthy or morbid, that has not some organic processes as its condition.

Creativity has also been linked to bipolar disorder (manic depression), a genetically linked disease in which individuals oscillate between depression and euphoria. Established artists and writers experience up to eighteen times the rate of suicide seen in the general population, ten times the rate of depression, and ten to twenty times the rate of bipolar disorder. When in their manic phase, they have sharpened and unusually creative thinking, heightened productivity, grandiose moods, and expansive thoughts. They make bold assertions, take risks, and are immune to fear of consequences. They work long hours without sleep and can focus intensely. Bipolar writers rhyme more often than do unaffected individuals, use alliteration and idiosyncratic words more frequently, and have a greater command of synonyms. Some creative individuals with bipolar disorder stop taking their medication, as do some patients with temporal lobe epilepsy, because they feel the drugs dampen their emotional and perceptual range. They are willing to pay a high price for their creative spark.

Some authorities question a causal link between bipolar disorder and high creativity in the arts. Psychiatrist Arnold Ludwig contends that creative people who are mentally ill drift quite naturally into the arts rather than, say, business or the sciences. The latter fields require rationality, persistence, and level-headedness, whereas the arts are more indulgent to unreason, flamboyance, and idiosyncrasy. Mental illness can also make people feel like outsiders, and the arts can accommodate the need for isolation better than other fields.

If we take these scientific findings seriously, it may appear as though all our creative impulses were rooted solidly in the brain. Yet *none* of the research alluded to above is incompatible with nonlocal factors in creativity – sharing thoughts with distant minds, participating in various mental fields, dipping into a universal cosmic soup of intelligence, obtaining insights from a higher source of wisdom, and so on. Accepting a view of creativity that is totally brain based is bad science because it forces us to give up too much evidence favoring a nonlocal side of the mind. This evidence comes in many flavors – controlled studies of the influence of intercessory prayer on humans, plants, and animals; experiments in remote viewing; studies demonstrating the ability to affect electronic devices nonlocally; the precognitive acquisition of information; and so on. But perhaps the most monumental problem in equating creativity with the brain is that no one in the entire history of science has ever proved how the physical brain *could* produce a thought, creative or otherwise.

Again, a helpful analogy is that of the brain as a transmitter, not an originator, of consciousness. As mentioned earlier, this comparison was used by William James himself, and it still holds appeal for many consciousness researchers. The key idea is that, whereas the brain affects the *contents* of consciousness, as so many studies show, there are no data whatever indicating that it actually *produces* consciousness. The picture on the television screen may be affected by changing channels or by 'kicking the box,' just as our mental images, thoughts, and emotions can be affected by pathological brain states such as epilepsy or neuroendocrine abnormalities. But the fact that these conditions can *affect* the contents of the mind is no proof that the brain actually *produces* the mind.

Many scholars are adopting similar thinking about religious feelings. 'I would not be surprised that there were parts of the brain that were involved in religious experience,' says physicist and theologian Robert John Russell, director of the Center for Theology and Natural Science in Berkeley. 'But [religious experience] is not just those parts of my brain twitching and nothing else.' If the correlations between brain activity and religious experience become even more tightly established, will this eventually get rid of God? Not likely, says Nancey Murphy, philosopher of religion at the Fuller Seminary in Pasadena, California. 'If we recognize the brain does all the things that we [traditionally] attributed to the soul, then God must have some way of interacting with human brains.'

Neurological research can be seen, she states, as an attempt to give 'an account of divine action . . . – how God acts in the brain.'

IQ Revisited

Our tour through the lore and literature of creativity has taken many twists and turns. I hope you can see by now that there are significant problems with ascribing creativity totally to the physical brain, and therefore many reasons to look beyond IQ as an explanation for creativity and intelligence.

But although IQ is not everything, I have never met anyone who wanted to trade for a lower one. So let us be grateful for the brainpower we're blessed with, but let us not prize it too highly; for if we do so, we are likely to undervalue other factors that also make up intelligence, as we've seen.

Is it a good thing to know your IQ? I've often asked myself whether, if I could go back in time, I'd break into my high school principal's office and steal my IQ score. In spite of the grief my little theft caused me, I think I probably would. Learning my measly IQ made me pay closer attention to the relationship between mind and brain – what they have in common and how they differ. And I can't overlook the irony that discovering I wasn't smart made me a hell of a lot smarter.

'If the brain were so simple we could understand it, we would be so simple we couldn't,' biologist Emerson Pugh said. Just so, if creativity were so simple we could understand it, perhaps we would be so uncreative we couldn't.

Something tells me that the mystery of creativity will be safe for a long time to come.

14

Immortality

The decisive question for man is:
Is he related to something infinite or not?
That is the telling question of his life.
— C. G. JUNG —
Memories, Dreams, Reflections

IT IS NOW APPARENT that spiritual concerns help form the foundation of complementary and alternative medicine (CAM) in America. A 1998 national survey found that 'users of alternative health care are more likely to report having had a transformational experience that changed the way they saw the world . . . They find in [alternative therapies] an acknowledgment of the importance of treating illness within a larger context of spirituality and life meaning . . . The use of alternative care is part of a broader value orientation and set of cultural beliefs, one that embraces a holistic, spiritual orientation to life.'

A great many health-care professionals thought that the reason people use CAM is simply because they believe these therapies work, rather than because of psychological or spiritual motives. But these findings show that psychospiritual factors are crucially involved in how people choose a therapy. For too long, even CAM professionals have considered spiritual and religious issues as matters to be addressed by the minister, priest, or rabbi but not by the nurse, internist, or surgeon. This view is changing rapidly, however, because a compelling body of evidence – more than sixteen hundred published studies – now shows that the hope and meaning people find in religious and spiritual beliefs affect health outcomes and can make the difference in life and death.

The possibility of an afterlife is one of the most enduring components of the great religions, and the belief in immortality has been a source of strength and meaning throughout history. In spite of the impact of spiritual meanings on health, however, immortality is not a topic that is generally discussed in health circles.

Immortality: The 'Name of Man'?

Immortality is a tattered topic, worn ragged through the ages by the countless writers and thinkers who have offered their views on this subject. Immortality has thus become a cipher of the human psyche. Perhaps no other area of discourse so dramatically reveals the extremes of human thought and feeling. The subject of immortality lays bare our fascination with the heavenly and the hellish, the divine and the demonic. Concealed in our views of immortality are our capacity for love, compassion, and forgiveness on one hand and our penchant for hatred, revenge, punishment, and torture on the other.

Poet David Whyte describes the 'Balkanization' that has occurred in language in recent times – the breaking up of language into rigid categories like the little Balkan states that are at each other's throats. 'And so you have the jargon of, say, fundamental Christianity and of politics and of the work world and of the New Age movement,' Whyte says. 'And they are all equally pernicious because they do not speak to reality . . . You no longer see a person anymore, but someone who is "dysfunctional," "alcoholic," "needy."' The language around immortality has been Balkanized in the same way. People no longer see 'immortality' but a religion or a philosophy. As a result, there is not much real dialogue going on about immortality – just a recitation of hardened views.

After immersing myself in the literature of immortality, I find myself dazed and worn down by the arrogance, certainty, and narrowness that characterize the positions of most theologians – and, yes, scientists as well. The worst aspect is the widespread tendency of both groups to ignore recent experimental evidence of the nonlocal nature of the human psyche. This is unfortunate because this evidence transforms the debate about immortality. It is the mother lode for anyone wanting empirical validation for that timeless, immortal aspect of consciousness that has been glimpsed by visionaries throughout human history.

'I have heard that when we pronounce the name of man, we pronounce the belief in immortality,' Emerson wrote. Yet, he cautioned, 'The real evidence is too subtle, or is higher than we can write down in propositions.' But perhaps subtle proof is the best kind where immortality is concerned. We have been hemmed in too long by heavy-handed, literal visions of immortality that describe the afterlife in agonizing detail, from admission policies to music. In contrast, subtle visions leave the details to a higher wisdom, bypassing our preferences and prejudices. Perhaps it might be helpful to examine some of these and how they affect our thinking on the subject.

Images of the Afterlife

Television is particularly revealing of what our culture thinks about the afterlife. While channel surfing one day, I stumbled onto a discussion of immortality on an afternoon talk show. 'Do they wear clothes over there?' the hostess asked her invited expert. I was immediately riveted. The guest had written a monster bestseller about her near-death experience, which involved what she believed was a visit to heaven. She replied thoughtfully that, although she couldn't speak for everyone, *she* certainly wasn't naked during her journey. Then someone from the audience asked, without a hint of humor, whether the clothes they wore in heaven were togas or something a bit more contemporary. In this amazing conversation, the *fact* of survival was completely taken for granted; how people *looked* was the hot topic. You've got to admire that sort of attention to detail.

On balance, however, I'm not all that interested in the nitpicking details of the hereafter. My main concern is whether consciousness survives, period. It's the big picture that counts. I assume that a universal intelligence that would provide for the continuation of consciousness can also handle the dress code, the menu, and the activity schedule.

In fact, I find the traditional images of heaven a turnoff, and I'm not alone. As a result of my writings about spiritual issues in medicine, people often share with me their most intimate thoughts of the afterlife. I've discovered that people think a lot about heaven, and some of them are troubled. One man told me he dreads the thought of being eternally exposed to harp music, which he loathes. One woman who is afraid of heights is phobic about floating around on porous clouds. Some of the most interesting letters I receive are from prisoners. One inmate in a federal prison wrote of his concern about those *keys* to the pearly gates. This image suggests to him a state of perpetual lockdown, and this bothers him tremendously. One of the most unsalvageable type A individuals I know is concerned whether he can adjust to the *boredom* of heaven, should he be fortunate enough to wind up there. Several pet lovers say they've been told by their priests that animals don't have souls and are therefore not candidates for heaven. Because the pet owners consider their animals more deserving than most humans they know, this suggests to them that the divine is unjust. A mom said that her child, who suffers from an allergy to feathers, asked whether this poses a problem if she goes to heaven and finds herself surrounded by angels with wings.

Don't think that these concerns are limited to the common folk. Many intellectuals are so concerned about the details of the afterlife that they prefer annihilation to eternal life. David Ray Griffin provides a few examples in *Parapsychology, Philosophy, and Spirituality*. One is the Cambridge philosopher C. D. Broad, who was thoroughly informed about research in the field of parapsychology and the implications of these findings for an afterlife. He figured the odds were at least fifty-fifty for some form of survival following death, yet he did not find this a happy thought. He considered this world a nasty place and fretted that the next one might be even worse. Consequently he wryly observed that if he died and found himself still conscious, he would be 'slightly more annoyed than surprised.'

Karl Popper, arguably the most influential philosopher of science of the twentieth century, also believed that the next world might be terrifying and found the prospect of immortality 'utterly frightening.'

Karl Barth, the Swiss theologian, seemed concerned that the admission policy of heaven might be too liberal. He once asserted that God did not create heaven for geese. One wonders how he knew.

Some intellectuals seem to think that hoping for immortality implies a weakness of character or a philosophical sellout. There is a hint of this attitude in Bertrand Russell, who made the famous comment 'I believe that when I die I shall rot, and nothing of my ego will survive . . . I should scorn to shiver with terror at the thought of annihilation. Happiness is nonetheless true happiness because it must come to an end, nor do thought and love lose their value because they are not everlasting.'

The disdain of many intellectuals toward the afterlife implies that there is something wrong with the rest of us: we are too scared and weak-willed to face our impending doom. It may be the other way around: there may be something wrong with *them*. I have long suspected that people who are repelled by the idea of immortality may be suffering from subclinical agoraphobia. Just as agoraphobics are horrified of open spaces, the immortality haters seem terrified of the *infinitude* that is suggested by immortality – all that space and time. As a permanent treatment for their disorder, they prefer confinement in a cozy grave where they stay put forever without being disturbed by even a glimmer of consciousness.

Alternately, those who are repelled by the traditional images of heaven may be hard-core, incorrigible introverts, among whom I number myself. You've got to admit that heaven sounds a lot like a permanent social event designed by and for extroverts, with all that strolling, chatting, and singing – thus Tennyson's line, 'Heard the heavens fill with shouting.' 'For people who like this sort of thing,' Abe Lincoln once quipped in another context, 'this is the sort of thing they will like.' But what if one doesn't like this sort of thing? It concerns me that no one ever emphasizes privacy in heaven. Is heaven the end of solitude? Can you still go to your room up there? In all the religious and spiritual literature dealing with the afterlife that I've read, I can't recall a single instance in which privacy issues were discussed. It's as if you've got to take the Meyers-Briggs personality test and be branded an extrovert before being admitted.

Some philosophers find the idea of life after death morally repellent, if the main reason to be moral is the anticipation of rewards and punishments following death. Even spiritual teachers have criticized people's motives for desiring heaven. An example was the eighth-century Sufi poet Rabia Basri, who once walked the Arabian desert with fire in one hand and water in the other. She said she would quench the fires of hell and set fire to heaven so that humans would love God neither from fear of hell nor from hope of paradise, but only from pure love.

Others are repulsed by the idea that people who behave poorly through no fault of their own or because of extenuating circumstances might be barred from heaven. Many find it irrational that some type of hellish punishment might go on forever. There comes a point, they say, where even the most heinous crime is paid off, the scales of justice are balanced, and punishment should cease. Lots of people resent how certain organizations have co-opted heaven as their own special turf, so that being in good standing with their religion is a precondition for consignment to heaven instead of hell. Many resent the way televangelists prey on people's consciences by implying that donating to their cause is a way of currying favor with God in the afterlife. Another common objection to life after death is that this belief is an opiate; if people have their attention fixed on the hereafter, this may undermine their passion to achieve justice for everyone in this existence. Similarly, a fixation on the future might make people complacent about the fate of the earth in the face of nuclear, environmental, and other threats. Some say that belief in eternal life leads to apocalyptic thinking and that those who believe in immortality might try to bring down the curtain on this existence in order to usher in the next one.

Afterlife or Prelife?

But even if we combine all the objections to the afterlife that have ever been offered, they are swamped by the overwhelming conviction of humans worldwide, in all eras, that — following death — there's something more. Scholars have attributed this universal belief to the human struggle against biological extinction: unable to accept our demise, we invent a rosy picture for after death.

In most visions of the hereafter, people tend to see themselves as pale versions of the way they were on earth – ethereal spirits, immaterial souls, and so on. It's as if *this* existence were real and the afterlife less real. But Dennis Stillings, director of the Archaeus Project in Kamuela, Hawaii, suggests that the worldwide belief in an afterlife may indicate that it is *this* existence that is not fundamental. The evidence is everywhere, Stillings believes, that we don't really belong on Earth. On this planet we behave as if we were strangers in a strange land, fish out of water. Although we call ourselves the most highly evolved species, when we look at our situation from the widest possible perspective, we humans are a greater mess than any other form of life. We are chronically unhappy, anxious, and malcontent, unable to rest in the moment, always looking to the past or into the future. It's as if we were trying to reclaim the memory of whence we've come and where we're headed. We are only dimly aware that we don't belong here, because over the aeons the certainty of who we really are has faded dramatically. What remains is a vast uneasiness and the gnawing sense that we are better suited for some other form of existence than this one. But the old whisperings of our blood have not totally disappeared. From time to time humans arise who know how to listen to them – the great saints and mystics, poets and artists who periodically catch fire and bring back messages about another realm.

Psychotherapist Sukie Miller, Ph.D., is founder and director of the Institute for the Study of the Afterdeath. In her book *After Death: How People around the World Map the Journey after Life*, she describes and analyzes afterdeath beliefs in India, Brazil, Indonesia, West Africa, and the United States. She offers a poem that captures the idea that our earthly existence is not really fundamental. It is by an unknown poet and is about Mexico's Day of the Dead:

> We only come to dream, we only come to sleep;
> It is not true, it is not true
> That we come to live on Earth.
>
> Where are we to go from here?
> We came here only to be born,

As our home is beyond,
Where the fleshless abide.

Perchance, does anyone really live on Earth?
The Earth is not forever, but just to remain a short while.

If we honored the possibility that some other dimension is more fundamental than this one, perhaps we'd stop calling it the afterlife and start calling our current stage of existence the prelife.

The Response from Science

Immortality implies that the mind is more than the physical body and extends beyond it. Some scientists consider this idea so dangerous that it must be put down at all costs. As a leading biologist once told William James: 'Even if such a thing were true, scientists ought to band together to keep it suppressed and concealed. It would undo the uniformity of Nature and all sorts of other things without which scientists cannot carry on their pursuits.' Here we have a recommendation that scientists collectively engage in a deliberate cover-up to thwart perceived threats to the scientific enterprise. Paranoid patients have been put on antipsychotic medications for delusions that were a lot less grandiose than this.

Laypersons unfamiliar with the workings of science may find it difficult to believe that scientists would actually try to stamp out an idea out of sheer bigotry, but where the idea of an extended form of consciousness is concerned, this bigotry is often evidenced. An example is related by physicists Hal Puthoff and Russell Targ in their book *Mind-Reach*. While at Stanford Research International in the 1970s, they undertook remote viewing investigations, in which individuals attempted to gain information about a remote location without employing the physical senses. Several prominent scientists wrote angry letters to the president of SRI in an effort to get Puthoff and Targ fired, which would have meant professional death. And when a distinguished scientist had an opportunity to review their data suggesting that consciousness extends beyond the body, he huffed, 'This is the kind of thing that I would not believe in even if it existed.' In this instance the 'thought police' did not prevail. Puthoff and Targ's findings were eventually published in the prestigious *Proceedings of the Institute of Electrical and Electronics Engineers* (IEEE).

Throughout history, wise individuals have occasionally recommended shading the truth or hiding it altogether. Dante, for example, said that 'we should conceal, as far as possible, those truths which resemble lies, because they wrong us, without our being responsible for them.' And Emily Dickinson stated, 'Tell all the Truth/but tell it slant—/ . . . The Truth must dazzle gradually/ Or every man be blind.' But scoffers of the sort who attacked Puthoff and Targ are recommending something different from Dante and Dickinson. They are convinced they are suppressing lies, not slanting the truth. Their worst offense is that they wish to shut down the scientific investigation of the ideas they oppose and put their opponents out of business. A process of selective blindness is operating in them – the sort of thing described by the spiritual teacher Baba Ram Das: 'When a pickpocket looks at a saint, all he sees is pockets.' Just so, when materialists look at humans, all they see is matter.

The reason for all this hostility is simple. If the mind is more than the brain, then some of the most cherished concepts in modern science are wrong. Philosopher Colin McGinn poses the issue this way:

> What we call 'the mind' is in fact made up of a great number of sub-capacities, and each of these depends upon the functioning of the brain. [The facts of neurology] compellingly demonstrate . . . that everything about the mind, from the sensory-motor periphery to the inner sense of self, is minutely controlled by the brain: if your brain lacks certain chemicals or gets locally damaged, your mind is apt to fall apart at the seams . . . If parts of the mind depend for their existence upon parts of the brain, then the whole of the mind must so depend too. Hence the soul dies with the brain, which is to say it is mortal.

Novelist Arthur Koestler, who took seriously the scientific evidence for an extended form of consciousness, stated that there is no hope for immortality 'as long as we remain captives of that materialist philosophy which proclaimed – as [Sir Cyril] Burt ironically phrased it – that the chemistry of the brain "generates consciousness much as the liver generates bile."'

Near-Death and Out-of-Body Experiences

The survival debate has been tremendously invigorated in the past three decades by an outpouring of research in the field of near-death experiences (NDEs). (*Immortality* and *survival* are not synonymous. *Immortality* implies the *eternal* existence of a timeless aspect of consciousness while *survival* implies continued existence for an unspecified period following bodily death. In this essay, however, I use these two terms interchangeably.) When near death, people commonly experience being outside their body. Far more commonly, however, this feeling is experienced spontaneously by normal, healthy people. Surveys show that around 10 percent of the population have at least one out-of-body experience (CBE) during their lives. In some of these reports, they apparently gain information they could not possibly have known about while 'embodied.'

One such case is described by Kenneth Ring, professor amaritus of psychology at the University of Connecticut, and NDE researcher Evelyn Elsaesser Valarino. It involved 'Maria,' a migrant worker who had a heart attack while visiting friends for the first time in Seattle. She was rushed to the coronary care unit at Harborview Hospital, where, a few days later, she had a cardiac arrest and was resuscitated.

The next day Kimberly Clark, a critical-care social worker, was asked to look in on Maria. During their conversation Maria told Clark that while being resuscitated she was able to look down on her body from the ceiling and view what the medical team was doing. Clark had heard of NDEs but was skeptical of them, and she feigned empathy as Maria's bizarre story unfolded. Maria described how she was suddenly not merely at ceiling level in the coronary care unit but outside the hospital altogether, having been distracted by an object on the ledge of the third floor of the north wing of the building. She 'thought herself up there,' she told Clark, and when she 'arrived' she found herself peering at a tennis shoe on the ledge of the building. Maria described it in minute detail, including a worn place in the little toe and that one of the laces was tucked underneath the heel. Finally, Maria implored Clark to locate the shoe to make sure she had really seen it.

At this point Clark experienced profound metaphysical uncertainty. What if she went looking for the tennis shoe and found it? Researcher Kenneth Ring reported on the case in *Lessons from the Light: What We Can Learn from the Near-Death Experience*, 'I have been to Harborview Hospital myself and can tell you that the north face of the building is quite slender, with only five windows showing from the third floor. When Clark arrived there, she did not find any shoe – until she came to the middlemost window on the floor, and there, on the ledge, precisely as Maria had described it, was the tennis shoe.'

Was this just 'one of those things'? Ring continues: 'What is the probability that a migrant worker visiting a large city for the first time, who suffers a heart attack and is rushed to a hospital at night would, while having a cardiac arrest, simply "hallucinate" seeing a tennis shoe – with very specific and unusual features – on the ledge of a floor *higher* than her physical location in the hospital? Only an archskeptic, I think, would say anything much other than "Not bloody likely!"'

Ring and another colleague, Madelaine Lawrence, have investigated three cases of NDEs in which at least one independent witness is able to verify a patient's out-of-body perceptions. Like Maria's case, two of them involved shoes.

One involved Cathy Milne, who in 1985 was working as a nurse at Hartford Hospital in Connecticut. One day Milne was talking to a woman who had recently been resuscitated and had had an NDE.

She told me how she floated up over her body, viewed the resuscitation effort for a short time, and then felt herself being pulled up through several floors of the hospital. She then found herself above the roof and realized she was looking at the skyline of Hartford. She marveled at how interesting this view was, and out of the corner of her eye, she saw a red object. It turned out to be a shoe . . .

I was relating this to a [skeptical] resident, who, in a mocking manner, left. Apparently, he got a janitor to get him onto the roof. When I saw him later that day, he had a red shoe and became a believer, too!

Why do *shoes* keep cropping up in NDEs? It's ironic, because the shoe symbolizes our contact with the physical earth and the material side of existence, while OBEs point toward the immaterial and the infinite. Perhaps the shoe image is an attempt by the unconscious to keep us *grounded* following OBEs.

Near-Death Experiences and Atheists

British philosopher A. J. Ayer was one of the most influential philosophers of the twentieth century. In 1988 he had an NDE during a cardiac arrest while hospitalized with pneumonia. His account, 'What I Saw When I Was Dead,' created quite a stir when it was published in London's *Sunday Telegraph*. Ayer's story was hardly unique; NDEs were widely reported by the time he got around to having one. The reason this particular NDE generated such passionate interest was that Ayer was a famous atheist, not the sort of person whose experience could be attributed to wishful thinking. The story leapfrogged the Atlantic and was published in the United States by the *National Review* as a cover story: 'A. J. Ayer's Intimations of Immortality: What Happens When the World's Most Eminent Atheist Dies.'

While unconscious and on a ventilator, Ayer was confronted by a red light that was so bright it was painful. This light seemed responsible for the government of the universe. He saw two creatures who appeared as ministers in charge of space. Part of their job was to carry out inspections on space itself, which they had recently done, but they had done their job so poorly that space did not fit together properly and was slightly out of joint. Moreover, Ayer felt that the laws of nature had stopped functioning as they should and that it was up to him to set things right. If he could do so, maybe the painful bright red light would be extinguished. All this time Ayer was aware of the close association of space and time that Einstein's discoveries had revealed in the twentieth century, and that he could cure space by operating upon time. He tried to get the attention of the ministers by hailing them, but they did not respond. Thinking they might be interested in the measurement of time, he started waving his watch, but this did not work. He became more and more desperate, and finally the experience ended.

'So there it is,' Ayer said. 'My recent experiences have slightly weakened my conviction that my genuine death, which is due fairly soon, will be the end of me, though I continue to hope that it will be. They have not weakened my conviction that there is no god.'

In an apparent attempt at damage control, several prominent scientists put their spin on Ayer's report. Cambridge physiologist Colin Blakemore proclaimed, 'What happened to Freddie Ayer was that lack of oxygen disordered the interpretative methods of his cortex, which led to hallucinations' – the old standby 'explanation' of the materialists. And the distinguished Cambridge physicist Sir Herman Bondi, president of the Rationalist Press Association, announced that he was 'totally unimpressed' and sniffed that 'it is difficult enough to be wise when one is well.'

Ayer seemed chastised by these responses and published what amounted to a public retraction. He explained that his experience had not weakened and 'never did weaken' his certainty that death equals annihilation. Moreover, he was practically sure his images were fantasies produced by his stressed brain. 'I said in my article,' he stipulated, 'that the most probable explanation of my experiences was that my brain had not ceased to function during the four minutes of my heart arrest . . . No other hypothesis comes anywhere near to superseding it.'

The events that followed Ayer's account show how nervous committed materialists get about NDEs and how they try to keep the lid on things. The Ayer episode also shows that people find in NDEs what they want to find and that it is unlikely that NDEs will ever settle the debate about postmortem survival.

Why Materialist Explanations of NDEs Fall Short

Are the materialists correct? Were Ayer's experiences due to an oxygen-deprived, sick brain? 'This suggestion . . . faces various difficulties,' states David Ray Griffin in a careful analysis in *Parapsychology, Philosophy, and Spirituality*. 'Most OBEs do not occur under such circumstances.' This is an important point. Most people who experience OBEs aren't sick. They do so under normal conditions, not in hospitals and intensive care units.

Griffin examines the claim of some skeptics that OBE imagery is produced not by too little oxygen but by too much carbon dioxide (hypercarbia).

Experiments have indeed shown that hypercarbia can produce experiences similar to those found in OBEs, especially in their transcendental phases, such as bright lights, ecstasy, and revival of past memories. This theory, however, is likewise undermined by the fact that most OBEs, even those with vivid transcendental imagery, do not occur in hypercarbic situations . . . Hypercarbia also produces a range of experiences that are dissimilar to OBEs, such as 'stained-glass window effects,' animated fantasized objects (such as moving musical notes), seeing everything in duplicate or triplicate, and feelings of horror.

Since OBEs occur in hospitalized patients, materialists often claim that they are due to drugs. 'However,' Griffin stipulates, 'most OBEs, even most near-death OBEs, occur to people who have not taken drugs. Also, OBE visions seldom if ever have the kind of bizarre imagery that occurs in drug-induced hallucinations, and the latter are recognized as unreal at the time, or at least in retrospect, while OBEs are taken to be real both during their occurrence and in retrospect.'

Another common 'explanation' is that the OBE is something like an epileptic event, resulting from a temporal lobe seizure. 'The main connection here,' Griffin states, 'is with the life-review that occurs in some OBEs . . . An immediate problem with this attempted explanation, however, is that the reliving of memories caused by malfunctions of the temporal lobe are usually limited to a single event of no special significance; it is nothing like the life-review of myriad events of great significance. Also, these neurological hallucinations typically involve taste and smell, which are usually absent in OBEs; the perception of the immediate environment is often distorted; and subjects experience forced thinking.'

A well-known suggestion is that OBEs are caused by the release of endorphins into the person's blood, which might account for the pleasant emotions and absence of pain during these events. 'However,' Griffin states, 'injections of endorphins produce sleepiness, not the hyperalertness reported in OBEs. Also, an endorphin injection gives relief from pain for many hours (from 22 to 73), whereas OBEers . . . report that their pain returns suddenly, as soon as they reenter their bodies.'

Susan J. Blackmore is a British psychologist who believes that NDEs and OBEs reflect disordered brain metabolism. She places great emphasis on the well-known experience of traveling down a tunnel during these events. In a paper entitled 'Near-Death Experiences in India: They Have Tunnels Too,' she suggests that the fact that the tunnel experience is universal is evidence that it is due to abnormal physical events going on in the brain. But, states Griffin, 'Even given the results of her study and a couple others suggesting that something like 38 percent of NDErs experience tunnels . . . , it is hard to see how a physiological explanation of the tunnel experience, even assuming its adequacy, could provide the key to the OBE itself, as it would leave about 62 percent of the OBEs without an explanation.'

Near-death experiences and OBEs have captured the popular imagination as a result of several blockbuster best sellers in recent years, and many people believe these experiences constitute the very best evidence for an afterlife. But the case for the persistence of consciousness following bodily death goes far beyond NDEs and OBEs, as meaningful as they may be to those who have had them. These experiences are but single elements in a much larger picture. Other, more convincing lines of evidence, in my opinion, are available showing that consciousness reaches beyond the limits of the physical body and that it is nonlocal or infinite in space and time. Many of the pieces of this puzzle are dealt with dazzlingly by Griffin, whose arguments I admire. I recommend his book

Parapsychology, Philosophy, and Spirituality to anyone wanting a panoramic, in-depth look at the case for survival of bodily death. I agree with his conclusion: 'The question [of survival] should not be posed in terms of absolute proof, as such is not possible: One cannot prove either the truth or falsity of the belief in life after death. The question should be posed instead in terms of the most plausible theory, Plato's "most likely account." [Still,] . . . *there is formidable evidence for life after death*' (emphasis added).

Physician Resistance

In general we physicians are obsessively dedicated to the materialist assumption that mind equals brain, as cardiologist Michael Sabom discovered.

In his book *Recollections of Death*, Sabom reports that when he first read psychiatrist Raymond Moody's accounts of NDEs in his seminal book *Life after Life*, he thought they were 'ridiculous' and that Moody's book was a work of fiction. Like most of his colleagues, he assumed that physical death meant extinction. But when Sabom began asking his own patients who had nearly died if they had experienced anything like Moody described – moving down a tunnel toward a light, feeling inexpressible joy, reviewing one's life history in a flash, meeting helpful guides, and returning with a transforming sense of serenity and a commitment to live a more meaningful life – he found that 27 percent had in fact had such an experience.

Richard S. Blacher, a physician, wrote a commentary in the *Journal of the American Medical Association* disparaging the NDE as a 'fantasy of death' and warned physicians against 'accepting religious belief as scientific data.' Sabom, who by then was impressed by the experiences of his own patients, wrote a response. He argued that none of the popular scientific and medical explanations could fully account for NDEs and that caution should be exercised to prevent confusing scientific belief with scientific data. Blacher responded in his rebuttal, 'Dr Sabom takes me to task for describing the episodes as "fantasy." By using this word, I locate the phenomenon with the patient's psyche . . . The alternative to the intrapsychic location would be one of something (the soul?) leaving the person in reality and hovering over the table. I do not think one has to apologize for scientific belief if one does not accept the ideas of spirits wandering around the emergency room.'

Ridiculing a colleague in a professional journal may score points with fellow cynics, but it is often a last-ditch defense by someone who has run out of ammunition. In any case, Blacher's objections don't annul the fact that 10 percent of the United States population – more than twenty-five million people – have had OBEs. How can we justify turning a blind eye to such a frequent event? Even if Blacher were correct in claiming that these experiences are only fantasies, they are so common they should command our attention on mental health grounds alone.

The Divine Within

Mythologist Joseph Campbell championed the idea that every human is inherently divine. He pointed out that this teaching is virtually universal, including within Christianity. Campbell observed that Christians believe that 'the kingdom of heaven is within.' 'Who's in heaven?' Campbell asked. 'God. So if heaven is within me, so is God!' This universal concept, that God (Goddess, Allah, the Tao – take your pick) lies within, is relevant to immortality – for, *if this indwelling god is immortal, so, too, in some sense, are we*.

The idea that we are *already* immortal has been embraced by the field of transpersonal psychology. Philosopher Ken Wilber describes this view in *Beyond Health and Normality*:

At this point, we can hardly speak of potentials. What could one say, when the deepest potentials of *your* soul are already the very ones that move the planets and radiate as light from the stars; that explode as the thunderous crack of lighting and echo as the rain through the mists; that hurl the comets through the skies and suspend the moon in blackness of night? The little potentials of the persona, ego, and centaur which we nurture so carefully and of which we are so pleased, dare to stand up as candles in the sunlight. Dame Julian of Norwich cried out in her enlightenment: 'See! I am God; see! I am all things; see! I do all thing [sic]; see! I never lift mine hands off my works, nor ever shall, without end; see!'

Nevertheless we have to be careful how we understand this ultimate potential, this divine cosmic potential. It is not that the deepest I . . . stands back from the cosmos and orders it around . . . [but that] this I *is* the cosmos. For as the very depths of the transpersonal self are pushed through, the transpersonal self gives way to the ultimate or universal self – the Self that *is* all realms of existence, manifest and unmanifest, in all directions and all dimensions.

The 'divine within' is a shortcut to immortality – *too* short and easy, say some theologians, who equate it with 'cheap grace.' Other theologians equate the idea of inner divinity with blasphemy. Yet this concept has been championed by eminent Western scholars such as physicist Erwin Schrödinger whose quantum wave equations won him the Nobel Prize. Schrödinger disagreed with the tendency of Westerners to regard 'the divine within' as out-of-bounds theologically:

In Christian terminology to say: 'Hence I am God Almighty' sounds both blasphemous and lunatic. But please disregard these connotations . . . In itself, the insight is not new . . . [That] the personal self equals the omnipresent, all-comprehending self . . . was in Indian thought considered, far from blasphemous, to represent the quintessence of deepest insight. The striving of all the scholars of Vedanta was, after having learnt to pronounce with their lips, really to assimilate in their minds this grandest of all thoughts . . . that can be condensed in one phrase: DEUS FACTUS SUM (I have become God).

Paul Brunton was a Western spiritual seeker who spent many years in Asia and whose voluminous writings have become widely known posthumously. He agreed that the idea of inner divinity is not blasphemous. For when the spiritual goal is realized – the absorption of the ego or self into the divine – there is no remaining entity that *could* blaspheme. In *The Quest of the Overself*, Brunton wrote:

> Those who mistrust this mysterious teaching [of the god within] sometimes allege that its deification of self is an attempt to equate God with the human personality, and to depose Deity in order to enshrine a part of His creation. This is a misunderstanding. Whoever enters into the experience of contacting the depths of his inmost being can emerge only with deeper reverence for God. He realizes his helplessness and dependence when he thinks of that Greater Being from whom he draws the very permit to exist. Instead of deifying the personal self, he has completely humiliated it. Self, in its ordinary sense, must indeed be cast away that God shall enter in.

Too often we Westerners regard 'the divine within' as an exclusively Eastern idea. There is plenty of scriptural evidence to the contrary. Consider, for example, Psalms 82:6: 'I have said, Ye are gods; and all of you are children of the most High'; John 10:34: 'Jesus answered them, Is it not written in your law, I said, Ye are gods?'; and Ephesians 4:6: 'And God and Father of all, who is above all, and through all, and in you all.'

Ralph Waldo Emerson, America's great nineteenth-century essayist and poet, spoke of 'the Divine Presence within [one's] own mind' and cited with approval the belief of Quaker founder George Fox, who said that although he read of Christ and God, he knew them only from the like spirit of his own soul.

Emerson, a former Protestant minister, clearly saw the connection of inner divinity with immortality. In his 1865 essay 'Character' he wrote, 'He [Jesus] affirms the Divinity in him and in us – not thrusts himself between it and us,' and points to 'the presence of the Eternal in each perishing man.'

There was not much of a market among Emerson's countrymen for the idea that they possessed an eternal, divine element. Then, as now, they were more likely to believe they were inherently sinful. Emerson ran into this wall of belief. Although James T. Fields, publisher of the *Atlantic*, originally agreed to publish Emerson's essay 'Character,' he changed his mind because he believed readers would consider Emerson's view as blasphemous. The essay was finally published eight months later in the *North American Review* – anonymously, as if to shield Emerson from the contemptuous backlash from readers. By this time Emerson was famous both at home and abroad, particularly in England, where he was lionized. The fact that America's most celebrated literary figure had to go underground on the subject of indwelling divinity and eternality is a telling commentary on the Western resistance to this nearly universal idea.

Immortality and Physics

Physicist Frank J. Tipler has a lot of nerve. In his book *The Physics of Immortality*, he has mixed particle physics, computer science, general relativity, and theology and has come up with what he considers evidence affirming the existence of God, the soul, the resurrection of the body, and immortality.

Tipler is a heavyweight in the field of global general relativity, the rarefied branch of physics inhabited by well-known scholars such as Stephen Hawking and Roger Penrose. Tipler is as shocked as anyone about the directions he's taken. 'I never imagined when I began my career as a physicist,' he says, 'that I would one day be writing, qua physicist, that Heaven exists, and that we shall each and every one of us enjoy life after death. But here I am, writing what my younger self would regard as scientific nonsense. Here I stand – as a physicist, I can do no other.'

Tipler's arguments rely on computers and information processing:

A human being is a special type of computer program. Now, what you can show using physics is that it's possible to completely code a human being inside a computer, to write a human being in all his or her environment as a computer simulation. The key point is that a human being is not infinitely complicated . . . A computer of sufficient power would be able to emulate perfectly – to make an absolutely perfect copy of – a person now existing. In the far future . . . there will eventually become [*sic*] a time in which the life in the far future can emulate the entire present universe and every person therein.

Thus the resurrection. As for the soul, 'If you define your soul to be something immaterial which contains the essence of a human being, I claim [it] . . . will be brought back into existence. Let me define that: A human soul is a computer program being run on the human brain.'

Tipler says that science is such a dominant force in modern culture that 'if science continues in an atheistic vein, sooner or later everyone will have to be an atheist.' He therefore contends that in order for religion to survive, it must become a branch of science. This suggestion has not made theologians happy.

Theologians aren't the only people who are not embracing Tipler's views. Most folks want a warmer, fuzzier version of the soul than Tipler offers. They have the idea they're a lot more than the 1s and 0s that make up the computer code in their laptops, and they are dubious that they could be completely reassembled after death as a string of 1s and 0s by some future supercomputer.

I admire Tipler's courage in taking such a controversial stand, but some of the problems he leaves untouched are formidable. For instance, he never explains how you go from being a reassembled bunch of 1s and 0s to being conscious. How does Tipler know that a human who is reconstituted from computer code would not merely be an automaton or zombie? Where does consciousness come in? Tipler doesn't seem interested in questions like this. *Mind* and *consciousness* are not even listed in the index of his voluminous book. He *assumes* that consciousness would automatically crop up in a human who was reassembled from computer code, but this is a matter of faith – which is just the factor he is dedicated to eradicating from religion. At least the religions *admit* they're based on faith.

One day while I was writing about immortality on my computer, it crashed. It took me several hours to restore function. I think I heard it say, 'Do you *really* want to rely for immortality on something mortal like me? What happens to your immortality if the electricity fails, my batteries run down, or the power surges?'

Immortality, Space, and Time

For most of us, as well as for classical physics, time is a flowing entity – the 'river of time' – that passes in an irreversible, one-way direction. We carve this river up into segments we call past, present, and future. We live only once, and death is final because we cannot go backward in time and recapture life. As composer Hector Berlioz put it, 'Time is a great teacher, but unfortunately it kills all its pupils.' But immortality presumes a different view of time. Immortal things are outside of time; they have no beginning and no end and are not 'running down.'

Modern physics, in contrast to the classical view, has abandoned the idea of time as an external, objective, flowing entity in favor of, well, a picture that is still being debated. What will physics tell us about time in the future? Physicist Paul Davies says, 'Some new theory, a new model, is necessary . . . What this new theory will be like, can only be guessed. It may not even employ the concepts of space and time at all. It could be that a future society will not use these words or notions. Perhaps, like the ether, they will pass out of the interest and the language of mankind.'

If you think it unnecessary to put time under the microscope, think again. Our assumptions about the nature of time touch every niche of our lives and bring us either pleasure or torment. Our distaste for timelessness makes us unable to rest in the moment and contributes to stress and anxiety. The sense that time flows and is running out can be lethal, as shown by the increased rate of cardiac deaths at younger ages in time-aware, type A individuals. Our entire culture is obsessed with 'saving' time, as our enslavement to pagers, e-mail, faxes, and cell phones shows. The uneasiness of Western religions toward timelessness contributes to their preference for a time-limited, seven-day version of creation and underlies the greatest struggle in history between science and religion – the clash over biological evolution and its endless aeons. And our inability to conceive of timelessness blocks progress in engaging the evidence of a nonlocal aspect of consciousness, a quality of the mind lying outside of time. *All* our experiences in life, including the scientific data we encounter, are filtered through our assumptions about time. These beliefs are almost always unexamined, yet they exert tremendous influence on how we see the world.

One thing seems clear: the view of time that is emerging from science, though not fully formed, is more cordial to the idea of a nonlocal, timeless conception of consciousness than the older views and is therefore more favorable for the prospect of immortality.

Psychologist C. G. Jung realized this. Perhaps no one has applied the quantum-relativistic views of space and time to psychology as thoroughly as he, as we can see in the advice he gave to patients and friends.

In January 1939 Jung responded to an inquiry from Pastor Fritz Pfäfflin, who had lost his brother in an accident in Africa. At the time of the accident, Pfäfflin, in Europe, spontaneously experienced a conversation with his brother, and the grieving man wrote to Jung for help in understanding this event. In Jung's reply he expressed sympathy and affirmed his belief that 'spatial distance is, in the psychic sense, relative . . . [and] psychically contractile . . . This nullification of space proceeds with great speed, so that perceptions of this kind occur almost simultaneously with the accident. We can therefore speak of a psychic nullification of time as well.' The parallel with the space-time continuum of modern physics is striking. Not that Jung believed that the laws of physics always dictate how the psyche functions; indeed, he thought that, under certain conditions, it was more likely the other way around.

Could the dying man have telepathically transmitted the information to his brother via some sort of subtle energetic signal from his brain? Jung doubted this possibility. He mentioned one example in which information was received at a distance from an individual who had been decapitated. 'In that event,' Jung stated, 'there can be no question of a transmission by a dying man' from his brain, because it had been chopped off. This suggests that the psyche is not brain-dependent and that 'the psyche does not exist wholly in time and space.'

Parapsychology

It would be convenient if the question of an afterlife were resolved unambiguously by someone who 'came back,' appeared on the White House lawn, gave a press conference, and cleared things up. It hasn't turned out that way.

Instead, we must look for subtler, indirect evidence, such as that offered by the eminent French physicist O. Costa de Beauregard. He finds evidence in mathematics and physics that is cordial to 'the existence of an all-pervading "collective unconscious,"' which is suspiciously akin to a timeless, immortal mind. De Beauregard believes these developments provide a rational basis for parapsychological experiences such as precognition, psychokinesis, and telepathy, which point to a nonlocal, timeless aspect of consciousness.

Parapsychology should be a part of any current discussion of immortality because this field involves the space-time independence of the mind. Unfortunately, for decades both scientists and theologians have been tripping over one another in an attempt to flee the parapsychology scene as quickly as possible. This is an example of intellectual cowardice rooted in fear and ignorance – because, as philosopher Griffin remarks in *Parapsychology, Philosophy, and Spirituality*, 'probably not one intellectual in a thousand, including college and university professors, is conversant with the kinds of evidence' in this field. The influential British philosopher C. D. Broad, who was not an intellectual coward, immersed himself in parapsychological research and came away impressed. He was practically overrun by the stampede of his colleagues opposed to parapsychology. His stern words, offered in the 1960s, still apply: 'Anyone who at the present day expresses confident opinions, whether positive or negative, on ostensibly paranormal phenomena, without making himself thoroughly acquainted with the main methods and results of the careful and long-continued work may be dismissed without further ceremony as a conceited ignoramus.'

Since this 'Broadside,' the strength of parapsychological research has increased dramatically. For those unafraid to go there, I recommend three books: *The Conscious Universe: The Scientific Truth of*

Psychic Phenomena, by Dean Radin, Ph.D.; *Parapsychology: The Controversial Science*, by Richard S. Broughton, Ph.D., director of research at the Rhine Research Center; and David Ray Griffin's *Parapsychology, Philosophy, and Spirituality: A Postmodern Exploration*.

The Afterlife: A Finished Product or a Work in Progress?

The afterlife is usually described as a version of paradise – perfect in every way. Jung, however, believed he saw evidence to the contrary in dreams.

One patient of Jung's was a sixty-year-old woman who, about two months before her death, had a dream in which a class was going on. Several of the woman's deceased friends sat in the front row with rapt attention. The woman looked around to see who was teaching the class and saw that it was she herself. She realized that immediately following death people had to give accounts of the total experience of their lives. The dead were intensely interested in the life experiences the newly deceased brought with them, as if they had much to learn from them. This dream suggested to Jung that heaven was not a finished product; those who went there were still involved in acquiring wisdom.

Jung believed that the afterlife, though perhaps not perfect, was nevertheless blissful. He nearly died from a heart attack in January 1944 and experienced an NDE. Afterward he wrote, 'What happens after death is so unspeakably glorious that our imagination and our feelings do not suffice to form even an approximate conception of it . . . The dissolution of our time-bound form in eternity brings no loss of meaning.' Jung felt such immense peace and fulfillment that he did not wish to return to normal life.

Nonetheless, Jung identified aspects of his experience that were not entirely blissful. In his autobiography, *Memories, Dreams, Reflections*, he wrote,

> The conception people form of the hereafter is largely made up
> of wishful thinking and prejudices. Thus in most conceptions

the hereafter is pictured as a pleasant place. That does not seem so obvious to me. I hardly think that after death we shall be spirited to some lovely flowering meadow . . . The world, I feel, is far too unitary for there to be a hereafter in which the rule of opposites is completely absent. There, too, is nature, which after its fashion is also God's. The world into which we enter after death will be grand and terrible, like God and like all of nature that we know. Nor can I conceive that suffering should entirely cease. Granted that what I experienced in my 1944 visions – liberation from the burden of the body, and perception of meaning – gave me the deepest bliss. Nevertheless, there was darkness too, and a strange cessation of human warmth. Remember the black rock to which I came! It was dark and of the hardest granite. What does that mean? If there were no imperfections, no primordial defect in the ground of creation, why should there be any urge to create, any longing for what must yet be fulfilled?

In Jung's concept of the afterlife, heaven pushes back. There is bliss, to be sure, but also a dark side. This is the idea of the co-incidence of opposites, the *coincidentia oppositorum*, that is central to Jung's thought – light and shadow, birth and death, mortality and immortality, the finite and the infinite. As he expressed this interplay:

The feeling for the infinite . . . can be attained only if we are bounded to the utmost . . . Only consciousness of our narrow confinement in the self forms the link to the limitlessness of the unconscious. In such awareness we experience ourselves concurrently as limited and eternal, as both the one and the other. In knowing ourselves to be unique in our personal combination – that is, ultimately limited – we possess also the capacity for becoming conscious of the infinite. But only then! . . . It is a supreme challenge to ask man to become conscious of his uniqueness and his limitation. Uniqueness and limitation are synonymous. Without them, no perception of the unlimited is possible – and, consequently, no coming to consciousness either.

The Practical Benefits of the Belief in an Afterlife

A common objection to a belief in the afterlife is that if people focus on the hereafter they will become unbalanced, dreamy mystics. They may forget to eat or change the baby's diapers. Philosopher David Griffin doesn't agree, and offers several practical benefits of a belief in an afterlife:

- Such a belief can help overcome the fear of death and extermination.
- If people are convinced they are ultimately not subject to any earthly power, this can increase their courage to fight for freedom, ecologically sustainable policies, and social justice.
- If people believe that this life is not the final word, and that justice will prevail in the next life, this can help them withstand the unfairness they encounter in the here and now.
- The idea of life as an ongoing journey that continues even after death can lead to a greater sense of connection with the universe as it unfolds into the future.
- The belief in life after death can help counter the extreme degree of materialism that has invaded every niche of modern civilization.
- The belief that we are on a spiritual journey, and that we have time to reach our destination, can motivate us to think creatively about what we can do now – socially, internationally, and individually – to move closer to what we should be in the here and now.

Spiritual Medicine: A Look to the Future

Is it premature to put immortality on the table in medicine?

No one would have predicted a decade ago that almost all the medical schools in the United States would currently be offering courses in complementary and alternative medicine. Likewise, it may seem unthinkable that spiritual issues could find a place in the curricula of our medical schools in the not-too-distant future. That they will do so is, I believe, inevitable because of the strong linkage of spiritual beliefs and religious practices with health outcomes.

Some decry this development. They warn that physicians and nurses should not get involved with spirituality because they are not trained to do so. The same sort of warning was issued a few years ago about physician involvement in sexuality. The sexual lives of our patients were too sensitive and personal for us to enter, it was said, and we had no skills in this area. But the proliferation of AIDS and sexually transmitted diseases swept away these objections almost overnight.

No one is suggesting that health-care professionals usurp the role of hospital chaplains, ministers, priests, and rabbis. Their expertise in spiritual matters will probably always exceed ours. However, there is no reason we can't work collaboratively with our clerical colleagues. We don't have to be experts in spiritual care to deliver a bit of it. Just as we teach laypersons a basic level of competence in cardiopulmonary resuscitation without expecting them to be heart surgeons, health-care professionals can acquire basic levels of competence in 'spiritual medicine' without becoming pros.

Writing in the *Journal of the American Medical Association* in 1997, J. S. Levin and colleagues noted, 'Three years ago, only 3 US medical schools taught courses on religious and spiritual issues; there are now nearly 30.' Currently, approximately eighty of the nation's 125 medical schools teach courses on religious and spiritual issues. This shows dramatically that the taboo on spirituality in medicine has been broken.

Looking back, we may well wonder how the taboo got there in the first place – and why we ignored for so long the relevance of immortality to the healing arts. Throughout history, the fear of death and annihilation may have caused more human suffering than all the physical diseases combined. The vision of consciousness that we have explored in this book offers a relief from this dread because it suggests the existence of an infinite, eternal aspect of human consciousness. The prospect of immortality has been there all along. It is time we claimed it.

SOURCES

PART 1: INTRODUCTION

The information on the study of women with breast cancer who also use alternative medicine was downloaded from HealthMall at http://www.healthmall.com, January 11, 2001. The source was the Eleventh International Congress on Women's Health Issues, San Francisco, California, January 2001.

For studies on the relationship of job and marriage stress to health, see *Work in America: Report of a Special Task Force to the Secretary of Health, Education, and Welfare*; K. Orth-Gomér et al., 'Marital Stress Worsens Prognosis in Women with Coronary Heart Disease,' *Journal of the American Medical Association* 284, no. 23 (2000): 3008–13.

CHAPTER 1:
WHAT DOES ILLNESS MEAN?

For a discussion of the role of meaning in health and illness, and how health-care professionals might address issues of meaning in clinical practice, see Larry Dossey, *Meaning and Medicine*.

For the Idler and Kasl study on health perceptions and survival, see Ellen L. Idler and Stanislav Kasl, 'Health Perceptions and Survival: Do Global Evaluations of Health Status Really Predict Mortality?' *Journal of Gerontology* 46, no. 2 (1991): S55–65.

Instances of 'emotional sudden death' are reported in George L. Engel, 'Sudden and Rapid Death during Psychological Stress: Folklore or Folk Wisdom?' *Annals of Internal Medicine* 74 (1971): 1325–35; M. Ferguson and E. Ferguson, 'Low Death Rate for Jewish Men at Passover Shows Will to Live,' *Brain/Mind Bulletin* 14, no. 4 (1989): 4.

Sir Arthur Eddington's wry observations on the practical impossibility of living life as if devoid of meaning were quoted in Ken

Wilber, *Quantum Questions*, 207. Eddington's longing for the comforts of the physical view expressed in his quotation on 'homesickness' also appeared in Wilber, *Quantum Questions*, 200–201.

C. G. Jung's discussion of the sensitive nature of meaning appeared in C. G. Jung, *Psychology and the Occult*, trans. R. F. C. Hull (Princeton, N.J.: Princeton University Press, 1977), 136–37.

C. G. Jung's 'pendulum of the mind' quotation is from C. G. Jung, *Memories, Dreams, Reflections*, 154.

Studies elucidating the role of meaning in health can be found in the following sources: Idler and Kasl, 'Health Perceptions and Survival'; J. H. Medalie and U. Goldbourt, 'Angina Pectoris among 10,000 Men: Psychosocial and Other Risk Factors as Evidenced by a Multivariate Analysis of Five-Year Incidence Study,' *American Journal of Medicine* 60 (1976): 910–21; *Work in America: Report of a Special Task Force to the Secretary of Health, Education, and Welfare*; D. Ornish et al., 'Effects of Stress Management Training and Dietary Changes in Treating Ischemic Heart Disease,' *Journal of the American Medical Association* 249 (1983): 54–59; D. Ornish, 'Can Lifestyle Changes Reverse Coronary Artery Disease?' *Lancet* 336 (1990): 129; S. J. Schliefer et al., 'Suppression of Lymphocyte Stimulation Following Bereavement,' *Journal of the American Medical Association* 250 (1983): 374–77; R. A. Karasek et al., 'Psychosocial Factors and Coronary Heart Disease,' *Advances in Cardiology* 29 (1982): 62–67; R. A. Karasek et al., 'Job Characteristics in Relation to the Prevalence of Myocardial Infarction in the US: Health Examination Survey (HES) and the Health and Nutritional Examination Survey (HANES),' *American Journal of Public Health* 78 (1988): 910–18; D. Spiegel et al., 'Effects of Psychosocial Treatment on Survival of Patients with Metastatic Breast Cancer,' *Lancet* 2, no. 8668 (1989): 888–91.

The David Bohm quotation was in David Bohm, 'Meaning and Information,' in *The Search for Meaning*, ed. Paavo Puylkkänen, 51.

The C. G. Jung quotations were in C. G. Jung, *Memories, Dreams, Reflections*, 340.

CHAPTER 2:
WHATEVER HAPPENED TO HEALERS?

For issues of medical student abuse and the effect on students, see H. K. Silver and A. D. Glicken, 'Medical Student Abuse: Incidence, Severity, and Significance,' *Journal of the American Medical Association*

263 (1990): 527–32; H. D. Sheehan et al., 'A Pilot Study of Medical Student "Abuse,"' *Journal of the American Medical Association* 263 (1990): 533–37; J. A. Richman et al., 'Mental Health Consequences and Correlates of Reported Medical Student Abuse,' *Journal of the American Medical Association* 267 (1992): 692–94; D. J. Benor, 'The Louisville Programme for Medical Student Health Awareness,' *Complementary Therapies in Medicine* 3 (1995): 93–99; C. B. Thomas, 'Precursors of Premature Disease and Death: The Predictive Potential of Habits and Family Attitudes,' *Annals of Internal Medicine* 85 (1976): 653–58. See also S. R. Daugherty, D. C. Baldwin, and B. D. Rowley, 'Learning, Satisfaction, and Mistreatment during Medical Internship,' *Journal of the American Medical Association* 279, no. 15 (1998): 1194–99.

For a report on how medical education can be made healthier, see M. Horning-Rohan, 'Making Medical Education Healthier: A Student's View,' *Advances* 4, no. 2 (1987): 24–28.

Excerpts from the report 'Physicians for the Twenty-first Century: Report of the Panel on the General Professional Education of the Physician and College Preparation for Medicine' were published in *Annals of Internal Medicine* 101 (1984): 870–72. The full report may be obtained from the Association of American Medical Colleges, One Dupont Circle NW, Washington, DC, 20036. See also W. C. Rappley, *Medical Education: Final Report of the Commission on Medical Education*.

The quotation from the Iglulik Eskimo shaman is from K. Rasmussen, 'Intellectual Culture of the Iglulik Eskimos: Report of the Fifth Thule Expedition,' *Nordisk Forlag* (Copenhagen) 7, no. 1 (1921): 118–19.

'American Medical Education: Has It Created a Frankenstein?' by T. J. Iberti appeared in *The American Journal of Medicine* 78 (1985): 179–81.

For the *Lancet* article on acting, see H. M. Finestone and D. B. Conter, 'Acting in Medical Practice,' *Lancet* 344 (1994): 801–2.

For the study of empathic emergency room care of homeless people, see D. A. Redelmeier, J-P. Molin, and R. J. Tibshirani, 'A Randomised Trial of Compassionate Care for the Homeless in an Emergency Department,' *Lancet* 345 (1995): 1131–34.

Neil Postman's quotations are from Neil Postman, 'Currents,' *Utne Reader* (July/August 1995): 35–39.

Helene Smith is quoted in M. Toms, 'Roots of Healing: The New

Medicine,' *Alternative Therapies in Health and Medicine* 1, no. 2 (1995): 46–52.

The Thomas Kelting quotations are from Thomas Kelting, 'The Nature of Nature,' *Parabola* 20, no. 1 (1995): 24–30.

For studies on religion and spirituality in medicine see Jeffrey S. Levin, 'Religion and Health: Is There an Association, Is It Valid, and Is It Casual?' *Social Science and Medicine* 38 (1994): 1475–82; J. S. Levin, D. B. Larson, and C. M. Puchalski, 'Religion and Spirituality in Medicine: Research and Education,' *Journal of the American Medical Association* 278, no. 9 (1997): 792–93. See also Harold G. Koenig et al., *Handbook of Religion and Health*, where more than sixteen hundred studies connecting religious/spiritual practice and health are reviewed. For an account of the number of medical schools that have developed courses or lecture series emphasizing the connections of spirituality and health, see A. B. Astrow, C. M. Puchalski, and D. P. Sulmasy, 'Religion, Spirituality, and Health Care: Social, Ethical, and Practical Considerations,' *The American Journal of Medicine* 110 (2001): 283–87.

Paul Ehrlich's observation was quoted in 'Sunbeams,' *Sun* 237 (1995): 40.

For Dickstein and Elkes's report on the Health Awareness Workshop at the University of Louisville Medical School, see L. J. Dickstein and J. Elkes, 'Health Awareness and the Medical Student: A Preliminary Experiment,' *Advances* 4, no. 2 (1987): 11–23.

The Malcolm Muggeridge quotation is from 'Sunbeams,' *Sun* 235 (1995): 40.

CHAPTER 3:

SUFFERING ON THE JOB

I have greatly benefited from and relied heavily on the insights of Edward Tenner in his remarkable book *Why Things Bite Back: Technology and the Revenge of Unintended Consequences* for the discussion of job suffering.

Thomas Edison's description of his method of creativity and invention was in a November 18, 1878, letter to Theodore Puskas, quoted in Matthew Josephson, *Edison: A Biography* (New York: John Wiley and Sons, 1992), 198.

For a discussion of how inanimate objects appear to behave in animate ways, see Lyall Watson, *The Nature of Things: The Secret Life of Inanimate Objects*.

Corporate downsizing and survivor guilt are discussed in S. Griffin, 'Workers' Fears Mount as Economy Tumbles,' *San Diego Union-Tribune*, Sunday, May 3, 1992, D2.

Job stress is discussed in 'Dying to Work,' *U.S. News and World Report*, March 18, 1991.

For discussions of the Sisyphus syndrome and the effects of job strain, see L. S. Syme, 'Control and Health: A Personal Perspective,' *Advances* 7, no. 2 (1991): 16–27; J. G. Bruhn et al., 'Psychological Predictors of Sudden Death in Myocardial Infarction,' *Journal of Psychosomatic Research* 18 (1974): 187–91; Peter L. Schnall et al., 'The Relationship between "Job Strain," Workplace Diastolic Blood Pressure, and Left Ventricular Mass Index,' *Journal of the American Medical Association* 263, no. 14 (1990): 1929–35; Robert L. Karasek et al., 'Job Characteristics in Relation to the Prevalence of Myocardial Infarction,' *American Journal of Public Health* 78, no. 8 (1988): 910–16; M. A. Hlatky et al., 'Job Strain and the Prevalence and Outcome of Coronary Artery Disease,' *Circulation* 2 (1995): 327–33.

The discussion of the effects of John Henryism can be found in R. M. Sapolsky, 'The Price of Propriety,' *Sciences* 36, no. 4 (1996): 14–16.

J. R. Blackaby's discussion of managing tools appears in J. R. Blackaby, 'How the Workbench Changed the Nature of Work,' *American Heritage of Invention and Technology* (Fall 1986), 26–30.

For the study on low back pain see D. M. Spengler, 'Back Injuries in Industry: A Retrospective Study – Overview and Cost Analysis, Injury Factors, and Employee-Related Factors,' *Spine* 11, no. 3 (1986): 241–56.

For a discussion of the importance of social networks and other social contact to health, see L. F. Berkman and S. L. Syme, 'Social Networks, Host Resistance, and Mortality: A Nine-Year Follow-up of Alameda County Residents,' *American Journal of Epidemiology* 109 (1979): 186–204; R. M. Nerem, M. J. Levesque, and J. F. Cornhill, 'Social Environment as a Factor in Diet-Induced Atherosclerosis,' *Science* 208 (1980): 1475–76.

Measures for counteracting job isolation are discussed in 'Low Pay, No Say Adding Stress at Work Worldwide,' *Santa Fe New Mexican*, March 23, 1993, sec. B. See also Jim Polidara, 'Mind-Body Wellness at Work,' in *Mind-Body Wellness*, 85–93, for an excellent annotated guide to research and resources in the area of work and health.

The John Searle quotation is from John Searle, 'Minds, Brains, and Science: The 1984 Reith Lectures,' *Advances* 2, no. 6 (1984): 4.

CHAPTER 4:

THE EATING-PAPERS

The young Spaniard who pricked himself with an awl is an example of deliberately caused bodily damage, or DCBD. In such rituals, people may puncture, lacerate, or burn themselves without suffering pain, bleeding, or infection, and they heal with astonishing rapidity. DCBD almost always takes place in a setting that is highly charged with spiritual meaning as in the case of the Spaniard. For a discussion of this subject, see Larry Dossey, 'Deliberately Caused Bodily Damage (DCBD),' *Alternative Therapies in Health and Medicine* 4, no. 5: 11–16, 103–11.

The information about *Esszettel* ('eating-papers') comes from Dennis Stillings, vice president of the Archaeus Project, Kamuela, Hawaii. Mr Stillings has translated from Hanns Bächtold-Stäubli and E. Hoffman-Krayer, *Handwörterbuch des Deutsehen Aberglaubens*, vol. 2 (Berlin and Leipzig: Walter de Gruyter, 1929/1930), 1055–58. I am grateful for Mr Stillings's invaluable assistance.

. For reports of the potency of Bayer aspirin and other evidence of the placebo effect, see S. H. Bodem, 'Bedeutung der Placebowirkung in der praktischen Arneitherapie,' *Pharmazeutsche Zeitung* 139, no. 51–52 (1994): 9–19; G. S. Kienle and H. Kiene, 'Placebo Effects from Packaging, Formulation, Color, and Size of the Placebo,' in 'Placebo Effect and Placebo Concept: A Critical Methodological and Conceptual Analysis of Reports on the Magnitude of the Placebo Effect,' *Alternative Therapies in Health and Medicine* 2, no. 6 (1996): 39–54; B. Blackwell, S. S. Bloomfield, and C. R. Buncher, 'Demonstration to Medical Students of Placebo Responses and Non-drug Factors,' *Lancet* 1, no. 7763 (1972): 1279–82.

Tim's story was related to me by Barbara Dossey in July 1998. Tim is not the patient's actual name.

For experiments exploring the role of intermediary objects in healing, see Bernard R. Grad, 'Some Biological Effects of Laying-on of Hands: A Review of experiments with Animals and Plants,' *Journal of the American Society for Psychical Research* 59, no. a (1965): 95–127.

Florence Nightingale's report 'Note on the Aboriginal Races of Australia' was presented at the annual meeting of the National

Association for the Promotion of Social Sciences, York, England, September 1864.

For reasons why both practitioners and patients choose alternative medicine, see Judith J. Petry, 'Healing the Practice of Surgery,' *Alternative Therapies in Health and Medicine* 4, no. 4 (1998): 103 ff.; John A. Astin, 'Why Patients Use Alternative Medicine: Results of a National Study,' *Journal of the American Medical Association* 279, no. 19 (1998): 1551–53.

For examples of nutritional anomalies and apparent good health, see N. Baldwin, 'The Lesser Known Edison,' *Scientific American* (February 1997): 62–67; René Dubos, 'Nutritional Ambiguities,' *Natural History* (July 1980): 14–21.

For the study on atherosclerotic changes in rabbits, see R. M. Nerem, M. J. Levesque, and J. F. Cornhill, 'Social Environment as a Factor in Diet-Induced Atherosclerosis,' *Science* 208 (1980): 1475–76.

The Joan Gussow, Paul Rozin, and Mary Douglas quotations, the study by Richard Stein and Carol Nemeroff, and a discussion of the modern relation to food, nutritional correctness, and food morality are in Paul Roberts, 'The New Food Anxiety,' *Psychology Today* (March/April 1998): 30 ff.

The efficacy of oat bran is discussed in J. Raloff, 'Oat Bran Is Not Special?' *Science News* 137 (January 20, 1990): 26.

The deliberations of the participants in the 'National Impacts of Recommended Dietary Changes' session at an annual meeting of the American Association for the Advancement of Science is reported in 'Proper Diet Saves Lives, Land, Oil . . ., *Science News* 119 (January 17, 1981): 39–40.

CHAPTER 5:

WAR: A VIETNAM MEMOIR

Treatment of Afghanistan veterans is reported in M. Edwards, 'Mother Russia: On a New Course,' *National Geographic* 179, no. 2 (February 1991): 2–37.

For war deaths and consequences of modern conflict, see Barry S. Levy and Victor W. Sidel, eds., *War and Public Health*, as well as P. R. Epstein's book review of *War and Public Health* in *Journal of the American Medical Association* 277, no. 18 (1997): 1479–80.

Accounts of rape among animals and in wartime are reported in Lyall Watson, *Dark Nature: A Natural History of Evil*, 177; D. P. Barash. 'Sociobiology of Rape,' *Science* 197 (1977): 788; H. J. Pratt,

'Reproduction in the Blue Shark,' *Fishery Bulletin* 77 (1979): 445; L. G. Adele and S. Gilchrist, 'Homosexual Rape and Sexual Selection,' *Science* 197 (1977): 81; L. Friedmann, *The Law of War*; Michael Walzer, *Just and Unjust Wars*; Ruth Seifert, 'War and Rape,' in *Mass Rape*. A recommended book that deals with the biological roots of violence is Howard Bloom, *The Lucifer Principal: A Scientific Exploration into the Forces of History*. For a more mainstream view from the field of evolutionary biology, see Richard Wrangham and Dale Peterson, *Demonic Males: Apes and the Origins of Human Violence*.

For a description of the Semai and their blood drunkenness, see C. A. Robarchek and R. K. Dentan, 'Blood Drunkenness,' *American Anthropologist* 89 (1987): 356; Robert Knox Dentan, *Semai: A Nonviolent People of Malaya*.

The thumbnail sketch of the transition of humans from prey to predator does not do justice to Barbara Ehrenreich's sweeping, carefully argued thesis; those interested in her arguments should consult her book *Blood Rites: Origins and History of the Passions of War.*

A description of the female regiment of Dahomey can be found in Antonia Fraser, *The Warrior Queens* (New York: Vintage Books, 1988). An account of Deborah Sampson is in Julie Wheelwright, *Amazons and Military Maids* (London: Pandora, 1989), 75.

PART 2

CHAPTER 6:

REENCHANTING THE WORLD

Willis Harman was quoted by E. Ferguson in his review of Kay Redfield Jamison, *An Unquiet Mind: A Memoir of Moods and Madness*, in *Brain/Mind Bulletin* 21, no. 3 (December 1995): 4.

For reflections on the problems of the materialist view of consciousness, see David Darling, 'Supposing Something Different: Reconciling Science and the Afterlife,' *OMNI* 17, no. 9 (December 1995): 4; David J. Chalmers, 'The Puzzle of Conscious Experience,' *Scientific American* 273, no. 6 (December 1995): 82–83.

Albert Abraham Michelson was quoted in Deno Kazanis, 'The Physical Basis of Subtle Bodies and Near-Death Experiences,' *Journal of Near-Death Studies* 14, no. 2 (Winter 1995): 101–16.

For sources on the new views of consciousness, see Brian D. Josephson and F. Pallikara-Viras, 'Biological Utilization of Quantum

Nonlocality,' *Foundations of Physics* 21 (1991): 197–207; Beverly Rubik, 'Energy Medicine and the Unifying Concept of Information,' *Alternative Therapies in Health and Medicine* 1, no. 1, 1995, 34–39; David Bohm, *Wholeness and the Implicate Order*; David Bohm and Basil Hiley, 'On the Intuitive Understanding of Non-Locality as Implied by Quantum Theory' (preprint, Birkbeck College, University of London, 1974).

Jung and Pauli's book *The Interpretation and Nature of the Psyche* is out of print. Jung's contribution to this work can be found in C. G. Jung, 'Synchronicity: An Acausal Connecting Principle,' in *The Structure and Dynamics of the Psyche*.

Jung's account of the scarab tapping against the window can be found in C. G. Jung, *The Structure and Dynamics of the Psyche*, 438.

Dame Rebecca West's encounter with the Library Angel was reported in Alister Hardy, Robert Harvie, and Arthur Koestler, *The Challenge of Chance*, 173.

The account of the pastor's death by organ blast can be found in Joe Berger, 'Pipe Organ Blast Scares Minister to Death!' *Weekly World News*, November 1, 1995 (information provided by Don Campbell, director of the Institute for Music, Health, and Education, Boulder, Colorado, December 1995).

For a report of the French golfer who drowned, see *Fortean Times* (October/November 1995): 20.

The story of the Findhorn cockroaches was reported to the author anonymously by a Findhorn resident.

The incident of the breakdowns of the spinning frames in the woolen mill in Yorkshire is recounted in J. H. McKenzie, 'The Haunted Millgirl,' *Quarterly Transactions of the British College of Psychic Science* 182 (1925), quoted in Watson, *Nature of Things*, 152–53.

For a report of the effects of investigators' attitudes on their controlled studies, see Marilyn J. Schlitz, 'Intentionality and Intuition and their Clinical Implications: A Challenge for Science and Medicine,' *Advances* 12, no. 2 (1996): 58–66.

The capacity of consciousness to interact nonlocally with the inanimate world is discussed in Larry Dossey, 'How Should Alternative Therapies Be Evaluated?' *Alternative Therapies in Health and Medicine* 1, no. 2 (1995): 6–10, 79–85.

William James's quotation on finding the right channel first appeared in 'The Will to Believe,' reprinted in *The Will to Believe and Other Essays in Popular Philosophy* (New York: Longmans, Green, 1927).

CHAPTER 7:

TICKLED PINK

The Apache myth of the creation of the two-leggeds is recounted in R. Lewis, 'Infant Joy,' *Parabola* 12, no. 4 (1987): 44.

Goethe, Schiller, and Schopenhauer were quoted in the following sources, respectively: L. Kisley 'Focus,' *Parabola* 12, no. 4 (1987): 3; H. M. Luke, 'The Laughter at the Heart of Things,' *Parabola* 12, no. 4 (1987): 13; Barbara Hannah, *Jung, His Life and Work: A Biographical Memoir*, 40.

The humorous descriptions of humor appear respectively in Arthur Koestler, *The Act of Creation: A Study of the Conscious and Unconscious in Science and Art*, 29; D. Strickland, 'Is Humor Healing?' *Bridges: Magazine of the International Society for the Study of Subtle Energies and Energy Medicine* 6, no. 3 (1995): 11; Koestler, *Act of Creation*, 29; J. Sully, *An Essay on Laughter*, quoted in Koestler, *Act of Creation*, 29.

For the studies on humor and the brain see J. R. Dunn, interview of P. Derks in *Humor Health Letter* 4 (1992): 1–7; C. C. Kuhn, 'Healthy Humor Is Good Medicine,' *Bridges: Magazine of the International Society for the Study of Subtle Energies and Energy Medicine* 6, no. 3 (1995): 1–10; M. S. George, 'Brain Activity during Transient Sadness and Happiness in Healthy Women,' *American Journal of Psychiatry* 152, no. 3 (1995): 341–51. See also P. Wooten, 'Humor: An Antidote for Stress,' *Holistic Nursing Practice* 10, no. 2 (1996): 49–56.

The experimental findings of humor research are recorded in L. S. Berk, 'Neuroendocrine and Stress Hormone Changes during Mirthful Laughter,' *American Journal of Medicine* 298 (1989): 390–96; L. S. Berk, 'Eustress of Mirthful Laughter Modifies Natural Killer Cell Activity,' *Clinical Research* 37 (1989): 115; L. S. Berk et al., 'Humor Associated Laughter Decreases Cortisol and Increases Spontaneous Lymphocyte Blastogenesis,' *Clinical Research* 36 (1988): 435A; K. Dillon and K. Baker, 'Positive Emotional States and Enhancement of the Immune System,' *International Journal of Psychiatry in Medicine* 15 (1985): 13–17; H. Lefcourt, K. Davidson-Katz, and K. Kueneman, 'Humor and Immune System Functioning,' *International Journal of Humor Research* 3 (1990): 305–21; D. C. McClelland and C. Kirshnit, 'The Effect of Motivation Arousal through Films on Salivary Immunoglobulin A,' *Psychology and Health* 2 (1989): 31–52; W. Fry, 'Health Briefing' section, *Insight* (May 25, 1987): 59; P. Eckman,

'Autonomic Nervous System Activity Distinguishes among Emotions,' *Science* 221 (1983): 1208–10; G. E. Schwartz, D. A. Weinberger, and J. A. Singer, 'Cardiovascular Differentiation of Happiness, Sadness, Anger, and Fear Following Imagery and Exercise,' *Psychosomatic Medicine* 43 (1981): 343–64; K. M. Dillon and M. C. Totten, 'Psychological Factors Affecting Immunocompetence and Health of Breastfeeding Mothers and Their Infants,' study unpublished at time of citation in Norman Cousins, *Head First: The Biology of Hope*, 139; W. Fry and W. Salameh, eds., *Handbook of Humor and Psychotherapy*, 1986.

Henri de Mondeville was quoted in James Walsh, *Laughter and Health* (New York: Appleton, 1928), 147–48.

Norman Cousins's debilitating illness and his experience of humor and health are recorded in Norman Cousins, 'Anatomy of an illness,' *New England Journal of Medicine* 295 (1976): 1458–63, in 'The Laughter Connection' in his book *Head First: The Biology of Hope, and in Anatomy of an illness as Perceived by the Patient*.

Examples of derisive humor in the Old Testament were reported in J. C. Gregory, *The Nature of Laughter* (London: Kegan Paul, 1924), cited in Koestler, *The Act of Creation*, 52–53.

The survey of American schoolchildren and their mortification of others was reported by B. Foss, *New Scientist* 6, no. 7 (1961), cited in Koestler, *The Act of Creation*, 53.

The *Psychology Today* survery on dirty jokes appeared in J. Hassett and J. Houlihan, 'Different Jokes for Different Folks,' *Psychology Today* 12 (1979): 64–71.

Kierkegaard's imaginary confrontation with Mercury is recorded in Soren Kierkegaard, *Parables of Kierkegaard*, ed. Thomas C. Oden (Princeton, N.J.: Princeton University Press, 1978).

Zen Master Sengai's verse appears in D. T. Suzuki, *Sengai, the Zen Master* (New York: New York Graphic Society, 1971), 147.

Speed Vogel was quoted in the interview 'Meditations on a Joyful Year: Speed Vogel Talks to Moshe Waldoks,' *Parabola* 12, no. 4: 67.

R. H. Blythe was quoted in R. Lewis, 'Infant Joy,' *Parabola* 12, no. 4 (1987): 47.

Tennyson's account of his ecstatic experience when repeating his name was quoted in Justin Kaplan, *Walt Whitman: A Life* (New York: Bantam, 1980), 200.

Jacob Boehme was quoted in 'Holy Laughter' *Parabola* 4, no. 1 (1979): 51.

For the Alice Isen study of laughter and creativity, see Alice M. Isen, K. A. Daubman, and G. P. Nowicki, 'Positive Affect Facilitates Creative Problem Solving,' *Journal of Personality and Social Psychology* 52 (1987): 1122–31.

CHAPTER 8:
EMBRACING THE TRICKSTER

The male pronoun is used throughout the discussion of the trickster because the trickster is 'usually male but occasionally female or disguised in female form' according to the *Columbia Encyclopedia*, 5th ed.

Reports on the evidence of trickster tracks – areas of confusion and chaos – in contemporary medicine appeared in the following sources: T. E. Strandberg, 'Long-Term Mortality after 5-Year Multifactorial Primary Prevention of Cardiovascular Diseases in Middle-Aged Men,' *Journal of the American Medical Association* 266, no. 9 (1991): 1225–29; Leonard A. Sagan, 'Family Ties: The Real Reason People Are Living Longer,' *Sciences* (March/April 1988), 21–29; 'Exercise, Health Links Need Hard Proof, Say Researchers Studying Mechanisms,' *Journal of the American Medical Association* 265, no. 22 (1991): 298; M. Young and T. J. Marrie, 'Interobserver Variability in the Interpretation of Chest Roentgenograms of Patients with Possible Pneumonia,' *Archives of Internal Medicine* 154 (1994): 2729–32; R. Monastersky, 'Kidney Stones: Don't Curb the Calcium,' *Science News* 143 (March 17, 1993): 196; H. C. Mitchell, 'The Periodic Health Examination: Genesis of a Myth,' *Annals of Internal Medicine* 95 (1981): 733–35; B. Bower, 'Anxiety before Surgery May Prove Healthful,' *Science News* 141 (June 20, 1992): 407; B. Bower, 'Depressing News for Low-Cholesterol Men,' *Science News* 143 (January 16, 1993): 37; R. S. Eliot, 'Community and Heart Disease,' *Journal of the American Medical Association* 272, no. 7 (1994): 566; B. Bower, 'Blood Pressure Lower for Working Women,' *Science News* 148 (July 1, 1995): 6; R. Voelker, 'Born in the USA: Infant Health Paradox,' *Journal of the American Medical Association* 272, no. 23 (1994): 1803–4; R. Jerome, 'Whither Doctors? Whence New Drugs?' *Sciences* (May/June 1994): 20–25; B. Starfield, 'Is U.S. Health Really the Best in the World?' *Journal of the American Medical Association* 284, no. 4 (2000): 483–85.

For reports on the effect of prayer on humans and nonhumans, including bacteria, fungi, and mice, see R. C. Byrd, 'Positive Therapeutic Effects of Intercessory Prayer in a Coronary Care Unit Population,' *Southern Medical Journal* 81 (1998): 826–29; C. B. Nash, 'Psychokinetic Control of Bacterial Growth,' *Journal of the American Society for Psychical Research* 51 (1982): 217–21; J. Barry, 'General and Comparative Study of the Psychokinetic Effect on a Fungus Culture,' *Journal of Parapsychology* 32 (1968): 237–43; William H. Tedder and Melissa L. Monty, 'Exploration of Long Distance PK: A Conceptual Replication of the Influence on a Biological System,' in *Research in Parapsychology 1980*, ed. W. G. Roll et al., 90–93; Bernard R. Grad, 'Some Biological Effects of Laying-on of Hands: A Review of Experiments with Animals and Plants,' *Journal of the American Society for Psychical Research* 59 (1965): 95–127; Bernard R. Grad, R. J. Cadoret, and G. I. Paul, 'The Influence of an Unorthodox Method of Treatment on Wound Healing in Mice,' *International Journal of Parapsychology* 3 (1961): 5–24.

Jonas Salk's sojourn in Italy is recounted in 'Dr Jonas Salk, 1914–1995: A Tribute,' AAF (American Architectural Foundation) News, *AIARCHITECT* (September 1995): 20.

Frank Barron's insights on the unharnessable nature of the creative process appeared in Frank Barron, 'The Psychology of Imagination,' *Scientific American* (September 1958).

Myrin Borysenko's experience with the healer in Boston is recounted in Larry Dossey, *Meaning and Medicine*, 159–60.

Richard Smoley's description of the trickster appeared in Richard Smoley, 'My Mind Plays Tricks on Me,' *Gnosis* 19 (Spring 1991): 12.

The Winnebago trickster story was reported in S. M. Wilson, 'Trickster Treats,' *Natural History* (October 1991): 4–8.

Barre Toelken describes his fieldwork experience in 'From Entertainment to Realization in Navajo Fieldwork,' in Bruce Jackson and Edward D. Ives, eds., *The World Observed: Reflections on the Fieldwork Process* (Urbana: University of Illinois Press, 1996.)

The Ken Wilber quotation on being aware of our opposites is from Ken Wilber, *The Spectrum of Consciousness* (Wheaton, Ill.: Theosophical Publishing House, 1977), 216.

CHAPTER 9:

TROUT MIND

The accounts of fishfalls and the theories behind them can be found in the following sources: A. D. Bajkov, 'Do Fish Fall from the Sky?' *Science* 109 (1949): 402; *Fort Worth Star-Telegram*, May 9, 1985; Athenaeus, *The Deipnosophists*, 11–13; W. McAfee, 'Showers of Organic Matter,' *Monthly Weather Review* 45, no. 5 (May 1917): 217–24; J. R. Norman, 'Fish from the Clouds,' *Natural History Magazine* 1, no. 8 (October 1928): 286–91; R. J. M. Rickard, 'Everything You Ever Wanted to Know about Fishfalls: The Theories,' *Fortean Times* 106 (January 1998): 37–39. See also the encyclopedic work of William Corliss, *The Catalog of Anomalies*, vol. 1, *Tornados, Dark Days, Anomalous Precipitation, and Related Weather Phenomena*, section GWF 10; Lyall Watson, *The Nature of Things*, 47.

The Hooked on Fishing – Not on Drugs program was started by the Future Fisherman Foundation, with the help of the United States Department of Education; the Harrison County, West Virginia, School District; the United States Fish and Wildlife Service; the American Fishing Tackle Manufacturers Association; and the Aquatic Resources Education Council. For information, contact the United States Department of Education or Paul Quinnett, director of adult services at Community Mental Health Center in Spokane, Washington.

For discussions of fly-fishing as mystery and spiritual endeavor, see Larry Dossey, 'Personal Glimpses,' *Quest* 7, no. 2 (1994): 94–96; Larry Dossey, 'Larry Dossey Responds to Critics of Fly-Fishing,' *Quest* 7, no. 4 (1994): 4–8.

The Kitty Pearson-Vincent quotation is from Howell Raines, *Fly Fishing through the Midlife Crisis*, 107.

For the article on women and fly-fishing, see R. Cox, 'Unwinding at Full Speed,' *Working Woman* (April 1995): 72–80.

For a discussion of methods of protection against curses, hexes, and negative prayers, see the chapter 'Protection' in Larry Dossey, *Be Careful What You Pray For . . . You Just Might Get It*, 195–217. The belief that a witch can be eluded by crossing running water is described in Dion Fortune, *Psychic Self-Defense* (London: Rider, 1930), 177.

The fisherman's attempts to catch the great brown trout at the bridge is recounted in Nick Lyons, 'Going and Coming Back,' *Fly Fisherman* 28, no 6 (September 1997): 95–96.

PART 3: INTRODUCTION

The author's precognitive dream and its significance are described in detail in Larry Dossey, *Reinventing Medicine* (San Francisco: HarperSanFrancisco, 1999), 1–3.

Results of world surveys of nonlocal mental experiences can be found in Elisabeth Targ, Marilyn Schlitz, and Harvey J. Irwin, 'Psi-Related Experiences,' in *Varieties of Anomalous Experience: Examining the Scientific Evidence*, ed. Etzel Cardeña, Steven J. Lynn, and Stanley Krippner (Washington, D.C.: American Psychological Association: 2000), 219–52.

CHAPTER 10:

A DIFFERENT KIND OF DNA

James Pagel was quoted in Ann Japenga, 'Can Dreams Diagnose Illness?' *USA Weekend*, September 3–5, 1999, 4.

Theodosius Dobzhansky was quoted in F. L. Marsh, 'Review of *Evolution, Creation, and Science*,' *American Scientist* 79 (1945): 73.

The analogy of consciousness to radar is limited. Here are some of the reasons:

• A radar unit sends out radio waves that are deflected by physical objects and return to the source, indicating the presence of a physical object out there. The human mind can detect the presence of physical objects remotely – nonlocally – without using a physical signal to probe the environment.

• Radar is limited to the present; consciousness can scan not only the present but the past and the future as well.

• Radar can detect only physical objects. Consciousness can acquire information about nonphysical things as well, such as the ideas, thoughts, and feelings of distant individuals.

For models of consciousness proposed by eminent scientists in recent years, see Larry Dossey, 'Lessons from Twins: Of Nature, Nurture, and Consciousness,' *Alternative Therapies in Health and Medicine* 3, no. 3 (1997): 8–15; David J. Chalmers, 'The Puzzle of Conscious Experience,' *Scientific American* 273, no. 6 (1995): 80–86; David J. Chalmers, *The Conscious Mind*; Amit Goswami, *The Self-Aware Universe: How Consciousness Creates the Material World*; Amit Goswami, 'Science within Consciousness: A Progress Report' (talk delivered at a seminar on consciousness, University of Lisbon, Lisbon, Portugal, 1996); Nick Herbert, *Quantum Reality*; Nick Herbert, *Elemental Mind*; Brian D. Josephson and F. Pallikara-Viras, 'Biological Utilization of Quantum Nonlocality,' *Foundations of Physics* 21 (1991): 197–207; Rupert Sheldrake, *A New Science of Life*; Rupert Sheldrake, *The Presence of the Past*; Ervin Laszlo, *The Interconnected Universe: Conceptual Foundations of Transdisciplinary Unified Theory*; Robert G. Jahn and Brenda J. Dunne, *Margins of Reality*; C. J. S. Clarke, 'The Nonlocality of Mind,' *Journal of Consciousness Studies* 2, no. 3 (1995): 231–40.

David Bohm was quoted in Renée Weber, *Dialogue with Scientists and Sages*, 101, 151.

L. A. Dale's account of the mother's distant awareness of her small son adrift on the sea can be found in L. A. Dale, 'Spontaneous Cases,' *Journal of the American Society for Psychical Research* 46 (1952): 31–35.

The survey of parental premonition of SIDS death was reported in J. A. Henslee, 'The Impact of Premonitions of SIDS on Grieving and Healing,' *Pediatric Pulmonology* 16 (1993): 393.

Studies on remote viewing have been published in the following prestigious journals: Russell Targ and H. E. Puthoff, 'Information Transmission under Conditions of Sensory Shielding,' *Nature* 251 (1974): 602–7; H. E. Puthoff and Russell Targ, 'A Perceptual Channel for Information Transfer over Kilometer Distances: Historical Perspective and Recent Research,' *Proceedings of the IEEE* 64 (1976): 329–54; H. E. Puthoff, 'CIA-Initiated Remote Viewing Program at Stanford Research Institute,' *Journal of Scientific Exploration* 10, no. 1 (1996): 63–76; Russell G. Targ, 'Remote Viewing at Stanford Research Institute in the 1970s: A Memoir,' *Journal of Scientific Exploration* 10, no. 1 (1996): 77–88.

Ray Hyman's evaluation of the SAIC replications appeared in Ray Hyman, 'Evaluation of Program on Anomalous Mental Phenomena,' *Journal of Scientific Exploration* 10, no. 1 (1996): 31–58.

William Braud's report of experiments in retroactive intentional influence can be found in W. Braud, 'Wellness Implications of Retroactive Intentional Influence: Exploring an Outrageous Hypothesis,' *Alternative Therapies in Health and Medicine* 6, no. 1 (2000): 37–48.

For Holger Klintman's experiments in time-reversed interference, see Holger Klintman, 'Is There a Paranormal (Precognitive) Influence in Certain Types of Perceptual Sequences?' part 1, *European Journal of Parapsychology* 5 (1983): 19–49; Holger Klintman, 'Is There a

Paranormal (Precognitive) Influence in Certain Types of Perceptual Sequences?' part 2, *European Journal of Parapsychology* 5 (1984): 125–40.

Radin's and Bierman's experiments on the response of the central nervous system to future events were published in D. I. Radin, 'Unconscious Perception of Future Emotions,' *Journal of Consciousness Studies Abstracts* (Tucson II Conference, University of Arizona, Tucson, April 8–13, 1996), abstract no. 430: 163; D. J. Bierman and D. I. Radin, 'Anomalous Anticipatory Response on Randomized Future Conditions,' *Perceptual and Motor Skills* 84 (1997): 689–90. See also Dean Radin, *The Conscious Universe*, 125.

Russell Targ's comments on the 'academic bombast' that prevents acknowledgment of findings on nonlocal awareness appears in Russell Targ and Jane Katra, 'The Scientific and Spiritual Implications of Psychic Abilities,' *Alternative Therapies in Health and Medicine* 7, no. 3 (2001): 143–49.

For the meta-analysis of ESP studies, see R. G. Stanford and A. G. Stein, 'A Meta-analysis of ESP Studies Contrasting Hypnosis and a Comparison Condition,' *Journal of Parapsychology* 58, no. 3 (1994): 235–70.

The skeptical scientist's views on ESP can be found in G. R. Price, 'Science and the Supernatural,' *Science* 122 (1955): 359–67.

The attitude of skepticism about nonsensory perception and the sheep/goat effect are discussed in Tony Lawrence, 'Bringing in the Sheep: A Meta-analysis of Sheep/Goat Experiments,' in *Proceedings of Presented Papers: Thirty-sixth Annual Parapsychological Association Convention*. See also Gertrude Schmeidler, 'Predicting Good and Bad Scores in a Clairvoyance Experiment: A Preliminary Report,' *Journal of the American Society for Psychical Research* 37 (1943), 103–10.

Larry Dossey's precognitive medical dreams are discussed in Larry Dossey, 'Dreams and Healing: Reclaiming a Lost Tradition,' *Alternative Therapies in Health and Medicine* 5, no. 6 (1999): 12–17, 111–17. See also Larry Dossey, Reinventing Medicine, 1–3.

The story of Romulus and Remus Cosma is recounted in 'Romania's Murderous Twins,' *Fortean Times* 130 (January 2000): 10. See also Larry Dossey, 'Lessons from Twins: Of Nature, Nurture, and Consciousness,' *Alternative Therapies in Health and Medicine* 3, no. 3 (1997): 8–15.

The account of General Frémont reported by Ian Stevenson first appeared in R. Hodgson, 'Case,' *Journal of the Society for Psychical Research* 5 (1891): 54–61.

Elizabeth Berg was quoted in 'Sunbeams,' *Sun* 239 (November 1995): 40.

The William James quotation from the Ingersoll Lecture was quoted in Paul Edwards, *Immortality*, 290.

For a critique of the materialistic explanations of NDEs, see Larry Dossey, 'Immortality,' *Alternative Therapies in Health and Medicine* 6, no. 3 (2000): 12–17, 108–15.

The Jerry Fodor quotation is from Jerry A. Fodor, 'The Big Idea,' *Times Literary Supplement*, July 3, 1992, 20.

CHAPTER 11:

THE RETURN OF PRAYER

The Margaret Mead quotation is in 'Sunbeams,' *Sun* 228 (December 1994): 40.

For an article on the relationship of prayer and religious devotion to positive health outcomes, see D. B. Larson and M. A. Greenwold Milano, 'Are Religion and Spirituality Clinically Relevant in Health Care?' *Mind/Body Medicine* 1, no. 3 (1995): 147–57.

The Haraldsson and Thorsteinsson study is reported in E. Haraldsson and T. Thorsteinsson, 'Psychokinetic Effects on Yeast: An Exploration Experiment,' in W. G. Roll, R. L. Morris, and J. D. Morris, eds., *Research in Parapsychology 1972*, 20–21; E. Haraldsson, 'Research on Alternative Medicine in Iceland,' *MISAHA Newsletter* (Monterey Institute for the Study of Alternative Healing Arts) (April – June, 1995): 3–5.

The *Journal of Religion and Psychical Research* is published by the Academy of Religion and Psychical Research, P.O.B. 614, Bloomfield, CT 06002. The *Christian Parapsychologist* is published by the Churches' Fellowship for Psychical and Spiritual Studies, South Road, North Somercotes, North Louth, Lincolnshire LN11 7PT, England.

Studies in distant, prayerful intentionality of living systems are reported in W. G. Braud, 'Conscious Interactions with Remote Biological Systems: Anomalous Intentionality Effects,' *Subtle Energies* 2, no. 1 (1991): 1–40.

For reports on the power of prayer and the methodological problems associated with it, see Randolph Byrd, 'Positive Therapeutic Effects of Intercessory Prayer in a Coronary Care Unit Population,' *Southern Medical Journal* 81, no. 7 (1988): 826–29; Russell Stannard, 'The Power of Prayer,' *Christian Parapsychologist* 12, no. 7 (1997):

196–99. See also Larry Dossey, 'Prayer in the Coronary Care Unit,' in *Healing Words*, 179–86.

Jean Kinkead Martine's reflections on everyday prayer are reported in J. K. Martine, 'Working for a Living,' *Parabola* 21, no. 4 (1996).

Susan Armstrong's investigation of whether animals have souls is reported in S. J. Armstrong, 'Souls in Process: A Theoretical Inquiry into Animal Psi,' in Michael Stoeber and Hugo Meynell, eds., *Critical Reflections on the Paranormal*, 133–58.

For reports on animals and prayer, see Larry Dossey, 'Four-Legged Forms of Prayer'; 'A [Veterinarian] Doctor Tests Prayer,' in Dossey, *Prayer Is Good Medicine*, 112–23.

The negative side of prayer – it's potential to cause harm in biological systems – is discussed extensively in Larry Dossey, *Be Careful What You Pray For*.

For reports of the experiments with Olga Worrall, see A. A. Worrall and O. N. Worrall, *Explore Your Psychic World*; Beverly Rubik and Elizabeth Rauscher, 'Effects on Motility Behavior and Growth Rate of *Salmonella typhimurium* in the Presence of Olga Worrall,' in W. G. Roll, ed., *Research in Parapsychology 1979*, 140–42; Elizabeth Rauscher, 'Human Volitional Effects on a Model Bacterial System,' *Subtle Energies* 1, no. 1 (1990): 21–41.

The opinions of scientists who willingly entertain the notion of distant mental intentionality and the like are reported in Gerald Feinberg, 'Precognition: A Memory of Things Future,' in Laura Oteri, ed., *Quantum Physics and Parapsychology*, 54–73; P. E. Meehl and M. Scriven, 'Compatibility of Science and ESP,' *Science* 123 (1956): 14–15; Jeffrey S. Levin, 'How Prayer Heals: A Theoretical Model,' *Alternative Therapies in Health and Medicine* 2, no. 1996: 66–73.

Eugene Mills's views on the unresolved mystery of gravity are recorded in Eugene Mills, 'Giving Up on the Hard Problem,' *Journal of Consciousness Studies* 3, no. 1 (1996): 26–32.

For articles describing patient use of both prayer and conventional medicine when ill, see D. J. Hufford, 'Cultural and Social Perspectives on Alternative Medicine: Background and Assumptions,' *Alternative Therapies in Health and Medicine* 1, no. 1 (1995): 53–61; B. R. Cassileth et al., 'Contemporary Unorthodox Treatments in Cancer Medicine: A Study of Patients, Treatments, and Practitioners,' *Annals of Internal Medicine* 10 (1984): 105–12.

The major criticisms against distant mental phenomena, including intercessory prayer, have in my opinion been firmly refuted. This is not the place to address these issues in detail; I have done so else-where, as have many respected scholars. For a review of these refutations, I suggest the following sources: Larry Dossey, 'Response to Gracely,' *Alternative Therapies in Health and Medicine* 1, no. 5 (1995): 104–8; Larry Dossey, 'How Good Is the Evidence? Prayer, Meditation, and Parapsychology,' in *Healing Words*, 243–47; Dean I. Radin and Roger D. Nelson, 'Evidence for Consciousness-Related Anomalies in Random Physical Systems,' *Foundations of Physics* 19 (1989): 1499–1514; Dean I. Radin, 'A Field Guide to Skepticism,' in *The Conscious Universe*, 205–27; Jessica Utts, 'An Assessment of the Evidence for Psychic Functioning,' *Journal of Scientific Exploration* 10, no. 1 (1996): 3–30; Charles Honorton, 'Rhetoric over Substance: The Impoverished State of Skepticism,' *Journal of Parapsychology* 57, no. 2 (1993): 191–214; Mark B. Woodhouse, 'Why CSICOP Is Losing the War,' in *Paradigm Wars*, 116–21.

The changing attitudes of skeptical scientists are reflected in the following articles: R. Hyman, 'Evaluation of a Program on Anomalous Mental Phenomena,' *Journal of Scientific Exploration* 10, no. 1 (1995): 43; M. J. Schlitz, 'Intentionality in Healing: Mapping the Integration of Body, Mind, and Spirit,' *Alternative Therapies in Health and Medicine* 5, no. 5 (1995): 119–20.

William H. Calvin was quoted in Marcia Bartusiak, 'Mechanics of the Soul' (review of Calvin's *How Brains Think*), *New York Times Book Review*, December 29, 1996.

John S. Bell was quoted in an interview in *OMNI* (May 1988).

Russell Stannard was quoted in Russell Stannard, 'The Power of Prayer,' *The Christian Parapsychologist* 12, no. 7 (1997): 198–99.

The Daniel J. Benor quotation is from Daniel J. Benor, '"Healing" in Great Britain,' *Advances* 12, no. 4 (1996): 75.

Jan Ehrenwald's description of the failure of the imagination of science appeared in Jan Ehrenwald, 'A Neurophysiological Model of Psi Phenomena,' *Journal of Nervous and Mental Disease* 154, no. 6 (1972): 406–18.

For further discussion of energy-based, classical concepts in relation to prayer, see Daniel J. Benor, 'Survey of Spiritual Healing Research,' *Complementary Medical Research* 4, no. 1 (1990): 9–33; Lawrence LeShan, *The Medium, the Mystic, and the Physicist*; Larry Dossey, 'Energy Talk,' *Network: The Scientific and Medical Network Review* (England) 63 (1997): 3–7.

The reasons 'energy' is inadequate to explain nonlocal, distant healing are discussed in Larry Dossey, 'The Forces of Healing: Reflections on Energy, Consciousness, and the Beef Stroganoff Principle,' *Alternative Therapies in Health and Medicine* 3, no. 5 (1997): 8–14.

For studies on the effect of distant intentionality on bacteria and fungi, see C. B. Nash, 'Test of Psychokinetic Control of Bacterial Mutation,' *Journal of the American Society for Psychical Research* 78, no. 2 (1984): 145–52; C. B. Nash, 'Psychokinetic Control of Bacterial Growth,' *Journal of the American Society for Psychical Research* 51 (1982): 217–21; J. Barry, 'General Comparative Study of the Psychokinetic Effect on a Fungus Culture,' *Journal of Parapsychology* 32 (1968): 237–43; W. Tedder and M. Monty, 'Exploration of Long-Distance PK: A Conceptual Replication of the Influence on a Biological System,' in W. G. Roll et al., eds., *Research in Parapsychology 1980*.

CHAPTER 12:
WHAT'S LOVE GOT TO DO WITH IT?

E. J. Cassell was quoted in C. Laine and F. Davidoff, 'Patient-Centered Medicine,' *Journal of the American Medical Association* 275 (1996): 152–56.

The account of the eighty-year-old man who was dying of a heart attack is from a verbal communication with Barbara Dossey, R.N., M.S., August 1995.

The article 'Death by Destruction of Will,' by Bruce E. Robinson, appeared in *Archieves of Internal Medicine* 155 (1995): 2250–51.

Empathy in relation to physicians is discussed in D. Gianakos, 'Empathy Revisited,' *Archives of Internal Medicine* 156 (1955): 135–36.

The account of the role of human interaction on serum cholesterol levels appeared in Stewart Wolf, 'Changes in Serum Lipids in Relation to Emotional Stress during Rigid Control of Diet and Exercise,' *Circulation* 26 (1962): 379–87. See also James J. Lynch, *The Broken Heart: The Medical Consequences of Loneliness*, 132–33, for this account. Lynch's work remains a classic on the devastating health consequences of a lack of love and failed human interaction.

The Kubie, Lashley, and Hebb quotations appeared in Lawrence LeShan, *The Dilemma of Psychology*, 84, quoting Michael Polanyi, *Knowing and Being* (Chicago, Ill.: University of Chicago Press, 1969), 42. Although Karl Lashley's comment resembles the insight of esoteric wisdom traditions that maintain that there is no separate self, no 'I,' no substantive ego that exists apart from the rest of creation, I suspect the resemblance is superficial and that he was questioning the existence of consciousness, as were Kubie and Hebb.

David Chalmers discusses the relation of electrochemical events in the brain to conscious experience and describes Steven Weinberg's 'theory of everything' in David J. Chalmers, 'The Puzzle of Conscious Experience,' *Scientific American* 273, no. 6 (1995): 80–86.

Studies of individuals attempting to influence the performance of electronic instruments are reported in R. G. Jahn, 'Information, Consciousness, and Health,' *Alternative Therapies in Health and Medicine* 2, no. 3 (1996): 32–38; R. G. Jahn, 'Report on the Academy of Consciousness Studies,' *Journal of Scientific Exploration* 9, no. 3 (1995): 393–403.

The de Broglie quotation is from Louis de Broglie, 'The Role of the Engineer in the Age of Science,' in *New Perspectives in Physics*, trans. A. J. Pomerans (New York: Basic Books, 1962), 231, quoted in Robert G. Jahn, 'Report on the Academy of Consciousness Studies,' *Journal of Scientific Exploration* 9, no. 3 (1995): 393–403.

For a fuller discussion of the nonlocal nature of the psyche and its relevance to healing, see Larry Dossey, *Recovering the Soul*; Larry Dossey, *Healing Words*.

For reports of the feats love prompts in animals, see J. B. Rhine and S. R. Feather, 'The Study of Cases of "Psi-Trailing" in Animals,' *Journal of Parapsychology* 26, no. 1 (1962): 1–21; V. Adamoli, *The Dog That Drove Home, the Snake-Eating Mouse, and Other Exotic Tales from the Animal Kingdom*; Gustav Eckstein, *Everyday Miracles*.

F. W. H. Meyers was quoted in Robert G. Jahn and Brenda J. Dunne, *Margins of Reality*.

Discussion of telesomatic events can be found in B. E. Schwarz, 'Possible Telesomatic Reactions,' *Journal of the Medical Society of New Jersey* 64 (1967): 600–3; Larry Dossey, 'Loading at a Distance,' *Advances* 11, no. 4 (1995): 48–49; J. H. Rush, 'New Directions in Parapsychology Research,' in *Parapsychological Monographs*, 18–19; Ian Stevenson, *Telepathic Impressions*, 70, 144; L. E. Rhine, 'Psychological Processes in ESP Experiences, Part 1: Waking Experiences,' *Journal of Parapsychology* 29 (1962): 88–111.

Reports of the correlation of encephalograms of distant individuals can be found in J. Grinberg-Zylberbaum and J. Ramos, 'Patterns of Interhemispheric Correlation during Human Communication,' *International Journal of Neuroscience* 36, nos. 1 and 2 (1987): 41–55;

J. Grinberg-Zylberbaum et al., 'Human Communication and the Electrophysiological Activity of the Brain,' *Subtle Energies* 3, no. 3 (1992): 25–43.

The empathy studies of Martin Hoffman and Carolyn Zahn-Waxler are detailed in Daniel Goleman, 'Researchers Trace Empathy's Roots to Infancy,' *New York Times*, March 28, 1989. The work of Hoffman and Zahn-Waxler is also described in Morton Hunt, *The Compassionate Beast: What Science Is Discovering about the Human Side of Humankind*.

Carolyn Zahn-Waxler was quoted by Henry Dreher in *The Immune Power Personality*, 272.

Jan van Ruysbroeck was quoted in Evelyn Underhill, *Mysticism*, vi.

The Jung quotations are from *Memories, Dreams, Reflections*, 325, 353, 354.

CHAPTER 13:

CREATIVITY AND COSMIC SOUP

Richard Feynman's IQ was reported in M. Michalko, 'The Art of Genius,' *Utne Reader* (July/August 1998): 73–76.

John Lorber's article 'Is Your Brain Really Necessary?' appeared in *Science* 210 (1980): 1232–34.

David Feinstein's report on savants appeared in David Feinstein, 'At Play in the Fields of the Mind: Personal Myths as Fields of Information,' *Journal of Humanistic Psychology* 38, no. 3 (summer 1998): 71–109.

Ervin Laszlo develops his hypothesis of the existence of fields of information in his 'hypothesis of interactive creativity' and his 'quantum/vacuum interaction (QVI) hypothesis,' which are too complex to review here.

The Conrad, Mondrian, and Klee quotations are from the following sources: Joseph Conrad, *Typhoon and Other Tales* (New York: New American Library, 1925), 21; Piet Mondrian, 'Plastic Art and Pure Plastic Art,' in Robert L. Herbert, ed., *Modern Artists on Art* (Englewood, N.J.: Prentice-Hall, 1964), 116; Paul Klee, 'On Modern Art,' in Herbert, *Modern Artists on Art*.

Lorin Hollander was quoted in 'Child's Play: Prodigies and Possibilities,' a *Nova* program on WGBH television, Boston, 1985.

Sue Grafton's quotation is from Naomi Epel, *Writers Dreaming*, 70–73.

Rosalyn Tureck's breakthrough with Bach's music is recounted in

Stefi Weisburd, 'The Spark: Personal Testimonies of Creativity,' *Science News* 132 (1987): 298.

The Bach quotation is from Radoslav A. Tsanoff, *The Ways of Genius* (New York: Harper and Row, 1949), 74.

The Nicola Tesla quotations are from 'Higher Creativity in Art and Science,' *Institute of Noetic Sciences Newsletter* 12, no. 1 (spring 1984): 7.

John Sayles's quotation is from Naomi Epel, *Writers Dreaming*, 224.

Jack Prelutsky's quotation is from Naomi Epel, *Writers Dreaming*, 191.

The John Cage and Bruce Springsteen quotations were from the following sources, respectively: Kim Wolinsky, *Letting Go with All Your Might*, 130; Bruce Springsteen, *Doubletake* (Spring 1998).

Jill Purce was quoted in Mary Buckley, ed., *Wise Words*, compiled from *New Dimensions* radio interviews by Michael Toms (Carlsbad, Calif.: Hay House, 1997)

The legend related by Wu-k'ung was recorded in René Grousset, *In the Footsteps of the Buddha*, trans. J. A. Underwood (New York: Grossman, Orion, 1971), 234.

Frank Barron's observations on creativity appeared in Frank Barron, 'The Psychology of Imagination,' *Scientific American* (September 1958).

Spalding Gray's quotation is from Naomi Epel, *Writers Dreaming*, 82.

The Jacob Bronowski quotation is from Jacob Bronowski, *The Origins of Knowledge and Imagination* (New Haven, Conn.: Yale University Press, 1978), 111.

Elias Howe's solution to the sewing machine problem is recounted in John Chesterman et al., *An Index of Possibilities: Energy and Power* (New York: Pantheon Books, 1974), 187.

Edmond Maillet's survey of dreaming mathematicians was recounted in Raymond De Becker, *The Understanding of Dreams and Their Influence on the History of Man* (New York: Hawthorn Books, 1968), 85.

Srinivasa Ramanujan and his otherworldly mentor are described in Robert Van de Castle, *Our Dreaming Mind*, 35.

Dmitri Mendeleyev's dream of the periodic table of elements was reported in K. Kedrov, 'On the Question of Scientific Creativity,' *Voprosy Psikologii* 3 (1957): 91–113.

The dreams of Friedrich Kekule, Albert Szent-Gyorgyi, Frederick Banting, James Watt, and Herman Hilprecht were reported in Robert Van de Castle, *Our Dreaming Mind*, 34–39.

Ideas about how fields may be involved with consciousness may be found in the following sources: David Feinstein, 'At Play in the Fields of the Mind,' 71–109; Rupert Sheldrake, *The Presence of the Past*; E. Schuman and D. Madison, 'Locally Distributed Synaptic Potentiation in the Hypocampus,' *Science* 263 (1994): 532–36; Benjamin Libet, 'A Testable Field Theory of Mind-Brain Interaction,' *Journal of Consciousness Studies* 1, no. 1 (1994): 119–26; Stuart Hameroff, 'Quantum Coherence in Microtubules: A Neural Basis for Emergent Consciousness?' *Journal of Consciousness Studies* 1, no. 1 (1994): 91–118; William Tiller, 'What Are Subtle Energies?' *Journal of Scientific Exploration* 7 (1993): 293–304; Robert G. Jahn and Brenda J. Dunne, *Margins of Reality: The Role of Consciousness in the Physical World*.

Jung's letter discussing archetypes was published in Marie-Louise von Franz, *Psyche and Matter* (Boston: Shambhala Publications, 1992), 161.

The account of the Galapagos Islands finches is in, Anthony Stevens, *Archetypes: A Natural History of the Self* (New York: William Morrow, 1982), 48.

The story of John, the Sicilian patient, is reported in Michael Conforti, 'On Archetypal Fields,' *Round Table Review* 4, no. 2 (1996): 1–8.

The examples in which dreams and readiness reinforced each other for Blake, Tartini, and Wagner are in the following sources, respectively: Stephen Brook, ed., *The Oxford Book of Dreams* (London: Oxford University Press, 1992), 134–35; Havelock Ellis, *The World of Dreams* (London: Constable, 1911); Robert L. Van de Castle, *Our Dreaming Mind*, 34–39.

Sue Grafton's quotation is from Naomi Epel, *Writers Dreaming*, 62–63.

Hermann von Helmholtz was quoted in Michael Murphy, *The Future of the Body* (Los Angeles: Jeremy P. Tarcher, 1992), 345.

The van Gogh quotation is from Clifford A. Pickover, *Strange Brains and Genius*, 262.

The experiments linking electromagnetic exposure to experiences of 'mystical presence' are reported in C. M. Cook and M. A. Persinger, 'Experimental Induction of the Sensed Presence in Normal Subjects and an Exceptional Subject,' *Perceptual and Motor Skills* 85 (1997): 683.

V. S. Ramachandran's findings regarding temporal lobe epilepsy and spiritual experience and Michael A. Arbib's opinion are reported in

R. L. Hotz, 'Seeking the Biology of Spirituality,' *Los Angeles Times*, April 26, 1998.

For a discussion on the relationship of bipolar disorder and creativity, see K. R. Jamison, 'Manic-Depressive Illness and Creativity,' *Scientific American* 272, no. 2 (February 1995): 62–67. See also Clifford Pickover, *Strange Brains and Genius*, 273; Kay R. Jamison, *Touched with Fire: Manic-Depressive Illness and the Artistic Temperament*.

Robert John Russell and Nancey Murphy were quoted in R. L. Hotz, 'Seeking the Biology of Spirituality,' *Los Angeles Times*, April 26, 1998.

Emerson Pugh was quoted in Lyall Watson, *Lifetide* (New York: Simon and Schuster, 1979), 137.

CHAPTER 14:

IMMORTALITY

The 1998 survey of users of alternative health appeared in John A. Astin, 'Why Patients Use Alternative Medicine: Results of a National Survey,' *Journal of the American Medical Association* 279, no. 19 (1998): 1548–53. For other studies and reports concerning the relationship of spirituality and alternative medicine, see D. B. Larson and M. A. G. Milano, 'Are Religion and Spirituality Clinically Relevant in Health Care?' *Mind/Body Medicine* 1, no. 3 (1995): 147–57; Harold G. Koenig, Michael E. McCullough, and David B. Larson, *Handbook of Religion and Health: A Century of Research Reviewed*.

For an in-depth look at how Americans view the afterlife, see pollster George Gallup's *Adventures in Immortality*. A fascinating cross-cultural comparison of beliefs and images of the afterlife can be found in Sukie Miller, *After Death: How People around the World Map the Journey after Life*, 1997.

David Whyte's opinions on the Balkanization of language appeared in 'Interview with David Whyte,' *Salt* 2000 2, no. 2: 6–12.

Emerson was quoted in Carlos Baker, *Emerson among the Eccentrics* (New York: Penguin, 1996), 397.

The Bertrand Russell quotation appeared in Paul Edwards, *Immortality*, v.

The account of Sufi poet Rabia Basri is in Debra Denker, *Sisters on the Bridge of Fire*, 318.

Dennis Stillings's thoughts on our life on Earth were expressed in a conversation with the author in May 1999 in Kamuela, Hawaii.

The anonymous Day of the Dead poem was translated by Angel Maria Garibay and Michakle Leon Portilla and appears on page 149 of Sukie Miller's *After Death*.

The leading biologist's wish to suppress the possibility of immortality was reported in William James, *The Will to Believe* (Cambridge, Mass: Harvard University Press, 1979), 19, quoted by David Griffin in *Parapsychology, Philosophy, and Spirituality*, 29.

The views of the distinguished scientist who wouldn't believe in any extended form of consciousness 'even if it existed' was reported in an editorial (no author given) in 'Scanning the Issue,' *Proceedings of the IEEE* 64, no. 3 (March 1976): 291, cited in Russell Targ and Harold Puthoff, *Mind-Reach*, 169.

For the IEEE report on Puthoff and Targ's findings on remote viewing, see Hal Puthoff and Russell Targ, 'A Perceptual Channel for Information Transfer over Kilometer Distances: Historical Perspective and Recent Research,' *Proceedings of the IEEE* 64, no. 3 (1976): 229–54.

Dante, Emily Dickinson, and Baba Ram Das were quoted from the following sources, respectively: Brian Inglis, *Natural and Supernatural: A History of the Paranormal*, 13; Emily Dickinson, *The Complete Poems of Emily Dickinson*, no. 1129; Nick Herbert, *Elemental Mind*, 209.

Colin McGinn and Arthur Koestler were quoted in Paul Edwards, *Immortality*, pages 294 and 40, respectively.

The accounts of A. J. Ayer's NDE were published in A. J. Ayer, 'What I Saw When I Was Dead,' *Sunday Telegraph* (London), August 28, 1988; 'A. J. Ayer's Intimations of Immortality: What Happens When the World's Most Eminent Atheist Dies,' *National Review*, October 14, 1988; A. J. Ayer, 'What I Saw When I Was Dead,' in *Immortality*, ed. Paul Edwards, 269–75; A. J. Ayer, 'Postscript to a Postmortem,' *Spectator* (London), October 15, 1988.

Susan J. Blackmore's paper 'Near-Death Experiences in India: They Have Tunnels Too' was published in *Journal of Near-Death Experiences* 11, no. 4 (1993): 205–17.

Richard S. Blacher's commentary and rebuttal regarding NDEs appeared in R. S. Blacher, 'Commentary: "To Sleep, Perchance to Dream . . . ,"' *Journal of the American Medical Association* 242 (1979): 2291; R. S. Blacher, 'Near-Death Experiences' (letter), *Journal of the American Medical Association* 244 (1980): 30. Michael Sabom's response to Richard Blacher's disparagement can be found in Michael Sabom, *Recollections of Death*, 153.

Erwin Schrödinger was quoted in Jyoti Ananthu and T. S. Ananthu, eds., *Gandhi and World Peace* (New Delhi: Gandhi Peace Foundation, 1987), 11.

Emerson was quoted in Carlos Baker, *Emerson among the Eccentrics* (New York: Penguin, 1996.

Frank Tipler was quoted in a press release for *Physics of Immortality* and in an interview in *D* magazine (September 1994): 5, 28.

The comments of Paul Davies on time appeared in Paul Davies, *Space and Time in the Modern Universe*, 203.

C. G. Jung's letter in response to Fritz Pfäfflin was quoted in Jenny Yates, ed., *Jung on Death and Immortality* (Princeton, N.J.: Princeton University Press, 1999), 68–70.

The scientific developments that O. Costa de Beauregard believes are cordial to an infinite, 'all-pervading "collective unconscious"' and to parapsychological phenomena were presented in an address to the third annual meeting of the Society for Scientific Exploration, October 11–13, 1996, in Freiburg, Germany. The developments are: 'time extendedness of matter in Euler's variational calculus and in the relativistic spacetime concept; cause-effect reversibility in Bayesian conditional and Boltzmannian transition probabilities; negentropy-information reversibility; quantum non-separability and CPT invariance.' Analyzing these concepts is beyond the scope of this essay. The point is that many respected scientists see in modern science room for a form of consciousness that lies outside of space and time, which is a cordial move in the direction of immortality.

The C. D. Broad quotation is from C. D. Broad, *Lectures on Psychical Research* (London: Routledge and Kegan Paul, 1962), 6.

The dream in which Jung's patient was teaching a class was recounted in C. G. Jung, *Memories, Dreams, Reflections*, 305–6.

Jung's description of his NDE appeared in C. G. Jung, 'Psychological Commentary on *The Tibetan Book of the Dead*,' quoted in Jenny Yates, ed., *Jung on Death and Immortality* (Princeton, N.J.: Princeton University Press, 1999), 6.

David Griffin's list of benefits of belief in an afterlife is taken from David Griffin, *Parapsychology, Philosophy, and Spirituality*, 290–91.

For differing views on the relationship of spirituality and health, see R. P. Sloan, E. Bagiella, and T. Powell, 'Religion, Spirituality, and Medicine,' *Lancet* 353, no. 9153 (1999): 664–67; Larry Dossey, 'Do Religion and Spirituality Matter in Health? A Response to the Recent Article in *The Lancet*,' *Alternative Therapies in Health and Medicine* 5, no. 3 (1999): 16–18.

The reports on the number of medical schools offering courses on religion and spiritual issues in 1997 and currently appeared in J. S. Levin, D. B. Larson, and C. M. Puchalski, 'Religion and Spirituality in Medicine: Research and Education,' *Journal of the American Medical Association* 278, no. 9 (1997): 792–93; 'Better Times for Spirituality and Healing in Medicine,' *Research News* 1, no. 6 (February 2001): 12.

BIBLIOGRAPHY

Adamoli, Vida. *The Dog That Drove Home, the Snake-Eating Mouse, and Other Exotic Tales from the Animal Kingdom*. New York: St Martin's Press, 1991.

Athenaeus. *The Deipnosophists*. Leob Classical Library, 204. 1969.

Bächtold-Stäubli, Hanns, and E. Hoffman-Krayer. *Handwörterbuch des Deutschen Aberglaubens*. Vol. 2. Berlin and Leipzig: Walter de Gruyter, 1929/1930.

Bainton, Roland H. *Christian Attitudes toward War and Peace: A Historical Survey and Critical Re-evaluation*. Nashville, Tenn.: Abingdon, 1960.

Barzini, Luigi. *The Italians*. New York: Athenaeum, 1977.

Benor, Daniel. *Healing Research*. Vol. 1. Munich: Helix Verlag, 1993.

Berman, Morris. *The Reenchantment of the World*. Ithaca, N.Y.: Cornell University Press, 1981.

Bloom, Howard. *The Lucifer Principle: A Scientific Exploration into the Forces of History*. New York: Atlantic Monthly Press, 1995.

Bohm, David, *Wholeness and the Implicate Order*. London: Routledge, 1973.

Bonham, Tal D. *Humor: God's Gift*. Nashville, Tenn.: Broadman Press, 1988.

Briggs, John. *Fire in the Crucible*. Los Angeles: Jeremy P. Tarcher, 1990.

Broughton, Richard S. *Parapsychology: The Controversial Science*. New York: Ballantine, 1991.

Brunton, Paul. *The Quest of the Overself*. York Beach, Maine: Samuel Weiser, 1984.

Calvin, William H. *How Brains Think: Evolving Intelligence, Then and Now*. New York: Basic Books, 1996.

Chalmers, David J. *The Conscious Mind*. New York: Oxford University Press, 1996.

Constant, Wairy Louis. *Mémoires de Constant*. Paris: Garnier, 1894. Quoted in Louis Leo Snyder, 'Napoleon's Retreat from Moscow, 1812.'

Corliss, William. *The Catalog of Anomalies*. Vol. 1, *Tornados, Dark Days, Anomalous Precipitation, and Related Weather Phenomena*. Glen Arm, Md.: Sourcebook Project, 1983.

Cousins, Norman. *Anatomy of an Illness As Perceived by the Patient*. New York: W. W. Norton, 1979.

———. *Head First: The Biology of Hope*. New York: E. P. Dutton, 1989.

Creveld, Martin van. *The Transformation of War*. New York: Free Press, 1991.

Critchley, Macdonald. 'Musicogenic Epilepsy.' In *Music and the Brain*, edited by Macdonald Critchley and R. A. Henson. London: William Heinemann, 1977.

Crockett, Mike. Preface to *Flywater*, by Grant McClintock and Mike Crockett. New York: Lyons and Burford, 1994.

David, Marc. *Nourishing Wisdom*. New York: Bell Tower, 1991.

Davies, Paul. *Space and Time in the Modern Universe*. New York: Cambridge University Press, 1977.

Denker, Debra. *Sisters on the Bridge of Fire*. Mission Hills, Calif.: Burning Gate Press, 1993.

Dentan, Robert Knox. *Semai: A Nonviolent People of Malaya*. New York: Holt Rinehart, 1968.

Dickinson, Emily. *The Complete Poems of Emily Dickinson*. Edited by Thomas H. Johnson. Boston: Little, Brown, 1960.

Dossey, Larry. *Be Careful What You Pray For . . . You Just Might Get It*. San Francisco: HarperSanFrancisco, 1997.

———. *Healing Words: The Power of Prayer and the Practice of Medicine*. San Francisco: HarperSanFrancisco, 1993.

———. *Meaning & Medicine*. New York: Bantam, 1991.

———. *Prayer Is Good Medicine*. San Francisco: HarperSanFrancisco, 1996.

———. *Recovering the Soul*. New York: Bantam, 1989.

———. *Reinventing Medicine*. San Francisco, Calif.: HarperSanFrancisco, 1999.

———. *Space, Time & Medicine*. Boston: Shambhala Publications, 1982.

Dreher, Henry. *The Immune Power Personality*. New York: Dutton, 1995.

Eccles, Sir John. *The Wonder of Being Human*. Boston: Shambhala Publications, 1985.

Eckstein, Gustav. *Everyday Miracles*. New York: Harper and Brothers, 1940.

Edwards, Paul, ed. *Immortality*. Amherst, N.Y.: Prometheus Books, 1997.

Ehrenreich, Barbara. *Blood Rites: Origins and History of the Passions of War*. New York: Henry Holt, Metropolitan, 1997.

Ehrenwald, Jan. *Telepathy and Medical Psychology*. New York: W. W. Norton, 1948.

Epel, Naomi. *Writers Dreaming*. New York: Carol Southern Books, 1993.

Estés, Clarissa Pinkola. *Women Who Run with the Wolves*. New York: Ballantine, 1992.

Evans, Donald. *Spirituality and Human Nature*. Albany, N.Y.: SUNY Press, 1993.

Fenwick, Peter, and Elizabeth Fenwick. *The Truth in the Light*. New York: Berkley Books, 1997.

Fields, Rick. *The Code of the Warrior*. New York: HarperPerennial, 1991.

Findlay, Alexander. *A Hundred Years of Chemistry*. London: Pelican Books, 1953.

Friedmann, L. *The Law of War*. New York: Random House, 1972.

Fromm, Erich. *Creativity and Its Cultivation*. New York: Harper and Row, 1959.

Fry, William, and Waleed Salameh, eds. *Handbook of Humor and Psychotherapy*. Sarasota, Fla.: Professional Resource Exchange, 1986.

Fuhrman, Joel. *Fasting and Eating for Health*. New York: St Martin's Press, 1998.

Gallup, George. *Adventures in Immortality*. New York: McGraw-Hill, 1982.

Gardner, Howard. *Multiple Intelligences: The Theory in Practice*. New York: Basic Books, 1993.

Garrison, Fielding H. *An Introduction to the History of Medicine*. 4th ed. Philadelphia: W. B. Saunders, 1929.

Gheslin, Brewster. *The Creative Process*. New York: New American Library, 1952.

Gill, Sam D., and Irene F. Sullivan. *Dictionary of Native American Mythology*. New York: Oxford University Press, 1992.

Glieck, James. *Genius: The Life and Science of Richard Feynman*. New York: Vintage, 1993.

Goleman, Daniel. *Emotional Intelligence*. New York: Bantam, 1997.

Goswami, Amit. *The Self-Aware Universe: How Consciousness Creates the Material World*. New York: Tarcher/Putnam, 1993.

Griffin, David Ray. *Parapsychology, Philosophy, and Spirituality: A Postmodern Exploration*. Albany, N.Y.: SUNY Press, 1997.

Grof, Stanislav. *The Holotropic Mind: The Three Levels of Human Consciousness and How They Shape Our Lives*. San Francisco: HarperCollins, 1992.

Hadamard, Jacques. *The Psychology of Invention in the Mathematical Field*. Princeton, N.J.: Princeton University Press, 1949.

Hannah, Barbara. *Jung, His Life and Work: A Biographical Memoir*. New York: G. P. Putnam's Sons, 1976.

Hardy, Alister, Robert Harvie, and Arthur Koestler. *The Challenge of Chance*. New York: Random House, 1973.

Herbert, Nick. *Elemental Mind*. New York: Dutton, 1993.

———. *Quantum Reality*. New York: Dutton, 1986.

Horgan, Paul. *Great River: The Rio Grande in North American History*. Lincoln: University of Nebraska Press, 1991.

Huang, C. A., and Jerry Lynch. *Thinking Body, Dancing Mind*. New York: Bantam, 1992.

Hunt, Morton. *The Compassionate Beast: What Science Is Discovering about the Human Side of Humankind*. New York: William Morrow, 1987.

Inglis, Brian. *Natural and Supernatural: A History of the Paranormal*. Bridport, Dorset, England: Prism Press, 1992.

Jaffé, Aniela. *The Myth of Meaning: Jung and the Expansion of Consciousness*. Translated by R. F. C. Hull. New York: Penguin, 1975.

Jahn, Robert G., and Brenda J. Dunne. *Margins of Reality: The Role of Consciousness in the Physical World*. New York: Harcourt Brace Jovanovich, 1987.

James, William. *The Varieties of Religious Experience*. New York: Macmillan, 1961.

Jamison, Kay R. *Touched with Fire: Manic-Depressive Illness and the Artistic Temperament*. New York: Free Press, 1993.

Jeans, Sir James. *Physics and Philosophy*. New York: Dover, 1981.

Jennings, Paul. 'Report on Resistentialism.' In *Parodies: An Anthology from Chaucer to Beerbohm – and After*, edited by Dwight MacDonald. New York: Modern Library, 1965.

Jung, C. G. *Analytical Psychology: Its Theory and Practice*. New York: Random House, Vintage Books, 1968.

———. *Letters*. Vol. 1. Edited by Gerhard Adler and Aniela Jaffé. Princeton, N.J.: Princeton University Press, 1973.

———. *Memories, Dreams, Reflections*. Edited by Aniela Jaffé, translated by Richard Winston and Clara Winston. New York: Vintage Books, 1965.

———. 'On the Psychology of the Trickster-Figure.' In *The Archetypes and the Collective Unconscious*. 2nd ed. Princeton, N.J.: Princeton University Press, 1968.

———. *The Structure and Dynamics of the Psyche*. Vol. 8 of *Collected Works*. Translated by R. F. C. Hull. Bollingen Series –. Princeton, N.J.: Princeton University Press, 1973.

Jung, C. G., and Wolfgang Pauli. *The Interpretation and Nature of the Psyche*. Translated by R. F. C. Hull and P. Silz. Bollingen Series LI. New York: Pantheon, 1955.

Keegan, John. *The Face of Battle*. New York: Dorset Press, 1976.

Kesten, Deborah. *Feeding the Body, Nourishing the Soul*. Berkeley, Calif.: Conari Press, 1997.

Kierkegaard, Soren. *Fear and Trembling*. New York: Penguin, 1985.

Koenig, Harold G., Michael E. McCullough, and David B. Larson, *Handbook of Religion and Health*. New York: Oxford University Press, 2001.

Koestler, Arthur. *The Act of Creation: A Study of the Conscious and Unconscious in Science and Art*. New York: Dell, 1964.

——. *Janus: A Summing Up*. New York: Random House, 1978.

LaPlante, Eve. *Seized: Temporal Lobe Epilepsy as a Medical, Historical, and Artistic Phenomenon*. New York: HarperCollins, 1993.

Laszlo, Ervin. *The Interconnected Universe: Conceptual Foundations of Transdisciplinary Unified Theory*. River Edge, N.J.: World Scientific, 1995.

Latzko, Adolf Andreas. *Men in War*. Translated by Adele S. Seltzer. 1918. Reprint, North Stratford, N.H.: Ayer Company, 1971.

Lawrence, Tony. 'Bringing in the Sheep: A Meta-analysis of Sheep/Goat Experiments.' In *Proceedings of Presented Papers: Thirty-sixth Annual Parapsychological Association Convention*, edited by M. J. Schlitz. Fairhaven, Mass.: Parapsychological Association, 1993.

LeShan, Lawrence. *The Dilemma of Psychology*. New York: Dutton, 1990.

——. *The Medium, the Mystic, and the Physicist*. New York: Viking, 1974.

Levenstein, Harry. *Revolution at the Table: The Transformation of the American Diet*. New York: Oxford University Press, 1988.

Levin, Jeffrey S. *God, Faith, and Health*. New York: John Wiley and Sons, 2001.

Levy, Barry S., and Victor W. Sidel, eds. *War and Public Health*. New York: Oxford University Press, 1996.

Ludwig, Arnold. *The Price of Greatness: Resolving the Creativity and Madness Controversy*. New York: Guilford Press, 1995.

Lynch, James J. *The Broken Heart: The Medical Consequences of Loneliness*. New York: Basic Books, 1979.

Mansbridge, Jane J. *Why We Lost the ERA*. Chicago: University of Chicago Press, 1986.

Maurer, Herrymon, commentator and trans. *The Way of the Ways*. Princeton, N.J.: Fellowship in Prayer, 1982.

May, Rollo. *The Courage to Create*. New York: Norton, 1975.

Miller, Sukie (with Suzanne Lipsett). *After Death: How People around the World Map the Journey after Life*. New York: Simon and Schuster, Touchstone, 1997.

Milton, Julie. 'Ordinary State ESP Meta-Analysis.' In *Proceedings of Presented Papers: Thirty-sixth Annual Parapsychological Association Convention*, edited by M. J. Schlitz. Fairhaven, Mass.: Parapsychological Association, 1993.

Monod, Jacques. *Chance and Necessity*. New York: Random House, 1972.

Moody, Raymond. *Laugh after Laugh: The Healing Power of Humor*. Jacksonville, Fla.: Headwaters Press, 1978.

——. *Life after Life: The Investigation of a Phenomenon – Survival of Bodily Death*. New York: Bantam, 1975.

Moss, Robert. *Conscious Dreaming*. New York: Crown, 1996.

Newberg, Andrew, and Eugene d'Aquili (with Vince Rause). *Why God Won't Go Away: Brain Science and the Biology of Belief*. New York: Ballantine, 2001.

Nichols, John. *On the Mesa*. Santa Fe, N.Mex.: Ancient City Press, 1995.

Ornish, Dean. *Dr Dean Ornish's Program for Reversing Heart Disease*. New York: Ivy Books, 1996.

——. *Love and Survival*. New York: HarperCollins, 1998.

Oteri, Laura, ed. *Quantum Physics and Parapsychology*. New York: Parapsychology Foundation, 1975.

Pearce, Joseph Chilton. *Evolution's End: Claiming the Potential of Our Intelligence*. San Francisco: HarperCollins, 1992.

Peat, F. David. *Synchronicity: The Bridge between Matter and Mind*. New York: Bantam, 1987.

Pickover, Clifford A. *Strange Brains and Genius*. New York: Plenum, 1998.

Piper, John. *A Hunger for God: Desiring God through Fasting and Prayer*. New York: Good News Publishers, 1997.

Polidara, Jim. 'Mind-Body Wellness at Work.' In *Mind-Body Wellness*. Duluth, Minn.: Whole Person Associates, 1996.

Purce, Jill. *The Mystic Spiral: Journey of the Soul*. New York: Thames and Hudson, 1974. Puylkkänen, Paavo, ed. *The Search for Meaning*. Wellingborough, England: Crucible, 1989.

Quinnett, Paul. *Pavlov's Trout*. Sandpoint, Idaho: Keokee Publishing, 1994.

Radin, Dean. *The Conscious Universe: The Scientific Truth of Psychic Phenomena*. San Francisco: HarperSanFrancisco, 1997.

Raines, Howell. *Fly Fishing through the Midlife Crisis*. New York: William Morrow, 1993.

Rappley. W. C. *Medical Education: Final Report of the Commission on Medical Education*. New York: Association of American Medical Colleges Commission on Medical Education, 1932.

Rilke, Rainer Maria. *Letters to a Young Poet*. Translated by M. D. Herter Norton. New York: W.W. Norton, 1954.

Ring, Kenneth, and Evelyn E. Valarino. *Lessons from the Light: What We Can Learn from the Near-Death Experience*. New York: Plenum Press, Insight Books, 1998.

Robins, Don. *The Secret Language of Stone*. London: Rider, 1988.

Roll, W. G., ed. *Research in Parapsychology 1979*. Metuchen, N.J.: Scarecrow Press; 1980.

Roll, W. G., et al., eds. *Research in Parapsychology 1980*. Metuchen, N.J.: Scarecrow Press, 1981.

Roll, W. G., R. L. Morris, and J. D. Morris, eds. *Research in Parapsychology 1972*. Metuchen, N.J.: Scarecrow Press, 1973.

Rush, J. H. 'New Directions in Parapsychology Research.' In *Parapsychological Monographs*, no. 4. New York: Parapsychology Foundation, 1964.

Sabom, Michael B. *Recollections of Death: A Medical Investigation*. New York: Harper and Row, 1982.

Sade, Marquis de. *La Philosophie dans le boudoir*. Paris: 1793. Quoted in Thomson, *A History of Sin*.

Sagan, Carl. *The Demon-Haunted World*. New York: Random House, 1995.

Schrödinger, Erwin. *What Is Life? and Mind and Matter*. London: Cambridge University Press, 1969.

Seaward, Brian Luke. 'Humor Therapy: Comic Relief.' In *Managing Stress: Principles and Strategies for Health and Well-Being*. Boston: Jones and Bartlett, 1994.

Seifert, Ruth. 'War and Rape.' In *Mass Rape*, edited by Alexandra Stiglmayer. Lincoln: University of Nebraska, 1994.

Sheldrake, Rupert. *A New Science of Life*. Los Angeles, Calif.: Tarcher, 1981.

———. *The Presence of the Past: Morphic Resonance and the Habits of Nature*. New York: Time/Life, 1988.

———. *Seven Experiments That Could Change the World*. New York: Riverhead Books, 1995.

Smith, Morton. *Jesus the Magician*. New York: Barnes and Noble, 1993.

Snyder, Louis Leo. 'Napoleon's Retreat from Moscow, 1812.' In *Great Turning Points in History*. New York: Barnes and Noble, 1996.

Sontag, Susan. *Illness as Metaphor*. New York: Farrar, Straus and Giroux, 1977.

Stevenson, Ian. *Telepathic Impressions: A Review and Report of Thirty-five New Cases*. Charlottesville: University Press of Virginia, 1970.

Stoeber, Michael, and Hugo Meynell, eds. *Critical Reflections on the Paranormal*. Albany, N.Y.: SUNY Press, 1996.

Sulloway, Frank J. *Born to Rebel: Birth Order, Family Dynamics, and Creative Lives*. New York: Pantheon, 1996.

Tanagras, Angelos. *Psychological Elements in Parapsychological Traditions*, abridged. New York: Parapsychology Foundation, 1967.

Targ, Russell, and Hal E. Puthoff. *Mind-Reach: Scientists Look at Psychic Ability*. New York: Delta, 1977.

Targ, Russell, and Jane Katra. *Miracles of Mind: Exploring Nonlocal Mind and Spiritual Healing*. Novato, Calif.: New World Library, 1998.

Tenner, Edward. *Why Things Bite Back: Technology and the Revenge of Unintended Consequences*. New York: Knopf, 1996.

Thomas, Lewis. *The Medusa and the Snail*. New York: Bantam, 1983.

Thomson, Oliver. *A History of Sin*. New York: Barnes and Noble, 1995.

Tipler, Frank J. *The Physics of Immortality*. New York: Bantam, 1994.

Tocqueville, Alexis de. *Democracy in America*. Edited by Richard Heffner. New York: Mentor Books, 1966.

Toelken, Barry. 'From Entertainment to Realization in Navajo Fieldwork.' In *The World Observed: Reflections on the Fieldwork Process*. Edited by Bruce Jackson and Edward D. Ives. Champaign: University of Illinois Press, 1996.

Tolstoy, Leo. *War and Peace*. New York: Oxford University Press, 1998.

Treffert, Darold. *Extraordinary People: Understanding Savant Syndrome*. New York: Harper and Row, 1989.

Underhill, Evelyn. *Mysticism*. New York: Dutton, 1961.

Van de Castle, Robert L. *Our Dreaming Mind*. New York: Ballantine, 1994.

Walter, Jakob. *The Diary of a Napoleonic Footsoldier*. Edited and with an introduction by Marc Raeff. New York: Penguin, 1991.

Walzer, Michael. *Just and Unjust Wars*. New York: Scribners, 1977.

Watson, Lyall. *Dark Nature: A Natural History of Evil*. New York: HarperCollins, 1995.

———. *The Dreams of Dragons*. Rochester, Vt.: Destiny Books, 1992.

———. *The Nature of Things: The Secret Life of Inanimate Objects*. Rochester, Vt.: Destiny Books, 1990.

Weber, Renée. *Dialogue with Scientists and Sages: The Search for Unity*. London: Arkana, 1990.

Weizsäcker, Carl Friedrich von. Introduction to *The Biological Basis of Religion and Genius*, by Gopi Krishna. New York: Harper and Row, 1972.

Wilber, Ken. 'Human Potentials and the Boundaries of the Soul.' In *Beyond*

Health and Normality, edited by Roger Walsh and Deane H. Shapiro. New York: Van Nostrand Reinhold, 1983.

——, ed. *Quantum Questions: Mystical Writings of the World's Great Physicists*. Boston: Shambhala Publications, 1984.

Wilmer, Harry A. 'War Nightmares.' In *Vietnam in Remission*, edited by Harry A. Wilmer and James F. Veninga. College Station: Texas A&M University Press, 1985.

Wolinsky, Kim. *Letting Go with All Your Might*. Denver: ReDecisions Institute, 1995.

Woodhouse, Mark B. *Paradigm Wars*. Berkeley, Calif.: Frog, 1996.

Wooten, Patty. *Compassionate Laughter: Jest for Your Health*. Salt Lake City: Commune-a-Key Publishing, 1996.

Work in America: Report of a Special Task Force to the Secretary of Health, Education, and Welfare. Cambridge: MIT Press, 1973.

Worrall, Ambrose A., and Olga N. Worrall. *Explore Your Psychic World*. Memorial edition. Columbus, Ohio: Ariel Press, 1989.

Wrangham, Richard, and Dale Peterson. *Demonic Males: Apes and the Origins of Human Violence*. New York: Houghton Mifflin, 1996.

Zuboff, Shoshana. *In the Age of the Smart Machine: The Future of Work and Power*. New York: Basic Books, 1988.

CREDITS

Excerpt from *Physicians of the Twenty-first Century: Report of the Panel on the General Professional Education of the Physician and College Preparation for Medicine*, by the Association of American Medical Colleges, copyright 1984 by the Association of American Medical Colleges.

Excerpts from *The Medusa and the Snail* by Lewis Thomas copyright © 1974, 1976, 1976, 1977, 1979 by Lewis Thomas. Used by permission of Viking Penguin, a division of Penguin Putnam, Inc.

'We Are Transmitters' excerpted from *Complete Poems* by D. H. Lawrence, edited by Vivian De Sola Pinto and Warren Roberts. Copyright 1994 by Penguin Books USA. Used with permission from Penguin Books USA.

Excerpt from 'Two Tramps in Mudtime' reprinted from *The Poetry of Robert Frost*, edited by Edward Connery Lathem, copyright 1969 by Henry Holt and Co., copyright 1936 by Robert Frost, copyright 1964 by Lesley Frost Ballantine. Reprint by permission of Henry Holt and Company, LLC.

The quotation by Dennis Gersten in 'Whatever Happened to Healers' used with permission from Dennis J. Gersten, M.D., Solana Beach, California, 2001.

Blood Rites: Origins and History of the Passions of War, by Barbara Ehrenreich. Copyright 1997 by Barbara Ehrenreich. Reprinted by permission of Henry Holt and Company, LLC.

Excerpts from *Letters To a Young Poet* by Rainer Maria Rilke, translated by M. D. Herter Norton, copyright 1934, 1954 by W. W. Norton & Company, Inc., renewed © 1962, 1982 by M. D. Herter Norton. Used by permission of W. W. Norton & Company, Inc.

Excerpts from *Memories, Dreams, Reflections* by C. G. Jung copyright 1965 by Vintage Books/Random House. Used with permission from Vintage Books.

The Reenchantment of the World by Morris Berman. Copyright 1981 by Cornell University Press. Used with permission from Cornell University Press.

Excerpts from *Writers Dreaming* by Naomi Epel copyright 1993 by Carol Southern Books/Crown Publishing Group. Used by permission of Carol Southern Books.

'The Day of the Dead, a Mexican Tradition' translated from an unknown poet by Ángel María Garibay and Miguel León-Portilla. Appears in *After Death: How People around the World Map the Journey After Life* by Sukie Miller, Ph.D., with Suzanne Lipsett (New York: Simon & Schuster, 1997).

INDEX